Eclipse Plug-in Development Beginner's Guide

Second Edition

Develop skills to build powerful plug-ins with Eclipse IDE through examples

Dr Alex Blewitt

[PACKT] open source*

PUBLISHING

community experience distilled

BIRMINGHAM - MUMBAI

Eclipse Plug-in Development Beginner's Guide
Second Edition

First edition: June 2013

Second published: July 2016

Production reference: 1280716

Published by Packt Publishing Ltd.
Livery Place
35 Livery Street
Birmingham B3 2PB, UK.

ISBN 978-1-78398-069-7

www.packtpub.com

Time for action – enabling and disabling menus items   115
Time for action – contributing commands to pop-up menus   117
Jobs and progress   121
Time for action – running operations in the background   121
Time for action – reporting progress   123
Time for action – dealing with cancellation   124
Time for action – using subtasks and sub-progress monitors   125
Time for action – using null progress monitors and sub monitors   127
Time for action – setting job properties   129
Reporting errors   132
Time for action – showing errors   133
Summary   136

Chapter 5: Working with Preferences   137
Implementing additional FieldEditors Eclipse
preferences   137
Time for action – persisting a value   138
Time for action – injecting preferences   139
Time for action – injecting individual preferences   140
Time for action – responding to preference changes   141
Preference pages   142
Time for action – creating a preference page   142
Time for action – creating warning and error messages   144
Time for action: choosing from a list   145
Time for action – aligning field editors with a grid   146
Time for action – placing the preferences page   147
Time for action: using other field editors   149
Time for action – searching for preferences   151
Summary   152

Chapter 6: Working with Resources   153
Using the workspace and resources   153
Time for action – creating an editor   154
Time for action – writing the markup parser   157
Time for action – building the builder   158
Time for action – iterating through resources   161
Time for action – creating resources   164
Time for action – implementing incremental builds   165
Time for action: handling deletion   166
Using natures   169
Time for action – creating a nature   169

Using markers	173
Time for action – error markers if file is empty	173
Time for action – registering a marker type	175
Summary	177

Chapter 7: Creating Eclipse 4 Applications	**179**
Time for action – installing E4 tooling	180
Time for action – creating an E4 application	182
Time for action – creating a part	186
Using services and contexts	191
Time for action – adding logging	191
Time for action – getting the window	193
Time for action – obtaining the selection	194
Time for action – dealing with events	197
Time for action – calculating values on demand	200
Time for action – interacting with the UI	202
Using commands, handlers, and menu items	204
Time for action – wiring a menu to a command with a handler	204
Time for action: passing command parameters	208
Time for action – creating a direct menu and keybindings	211
Time for action – creating a pop-up menu and a view menu	213
Creating custom injectable classes	216
Time for action – creating a simple service	216
Time for action – injecting subtypes	218
Summary	220

Chapter 8: Migrating to Eclipse 4.x	**221**
Why Eclipse 4.x?	221
Time for action – creating a migration component	222
Time for action – updating to e4view	224
Time for action – upgrading the actions	226
Time for action – creating toolbars	228
Time for action – adding the view menu	231
Time for action – adding the pop-up	233
Migrating to Eclipse 4.x patterns	235
Time for action – creating a model fragment	235
Time for action – migrating the commands and handlers	238
Time for action – creating the view menu	242
Time for action – defining the pop-up view in the fragment	243
Summary	246

Chapter 9: Styling Eclipse 4 Applications — 247

Styling Eclipse with CSS — 247
Time for action – styling the UI with CSS — 248
Time for action – using custom CSS classes — 254
Using the Eclipse spies — 255
Time for action – using the CSS Spy — 255
Time for action – integrating the spy into a product — 258
Styling a custom widget — 259
Time for action – adding the clock — 259
Time for action – using a CSS property — 261
    Themes — 265
Time for action – going to the dark side — 266
Time for action – adding themes — 267
Time for action – switching between themes — 269
Summary — 271

Chapter 10: Creating Features, Update Sites, Applications, and Products — 273

Grouping plug-ins with features — 273
Time for action – creating a feature — 274
Time for action – exporting a feature — 276
Time for action – installing a feature — 278
Time for action – categorizing the update site — 280
Time for action – depending on other features — 284
Time for action – branding features — 286
Building applications and products — 289
Time for action – creating a headless application — 289
Time for action – creating a product — 293
Target platforms — 297
Time for action – creating a target definition — 297
Time for action – switching to a specific version — 300
Summary — 302

Chapter 11: Automated Testing of Plug-ins — 303

Using JUnit for automated testing — 303
Time for action – adding dependencies to the target platform — 304
Time for action – writing a simple JUnit 4 test case — 305
Time for action – writing a plug-in test — 306
Using SWTBot for user interface testing — 307
Time for action – writing an SWTBot test — 308
Time for action – working with menus — 310
Working with SWTBot — 313

Time for action – hiding the welcome screen   313
Time for action – avoiding SWTBot runtime errors   314
Working with views   314
Time for action: showing views   315
Time for action – interrogating views   316
Interacting with the UI   317
Time for action – getting values from the UI   317
Time for action – waiting for a condition   318
Summary   321

Chapter 12: Automated Builds with Tycho   **323**
Using Maven to build Eclipse plug-ins with Tycho   323
Time for action – installing Maven   324
Time for action – building with Tycho   326
Building features and update sites with Tycho   329
Time for action – creating a parent project   329
Time for action – building a feature   332
Time for action – building an update site   333
Time for action – building a product   335
Time for action – using the target platform   340
Testing and releasing   344
Time for action – running automated tests   344
Time for action – changing the version numbers   348
Signing update sites   350
Time for action – creating a self-signed certificate   350
Time for action – signing the plug-ins   351
Time for action – serving an update site   354
Summary   355

Chapter 13: Contributing to Eclipse   **357**
Open source contributions   357
Importing the source   358
Time for action – installing the sources   358
Time for action – debugging the platform   360
Time for action – modifying the platform   362
Checking out from git   363
Time for action – checking out from EGit and Git   364
Time for action – configuring the SWT project   367
Contributing to Eclipse   369
Creating bugs on Bugzilla   369
Time for action – creating an account at Eclipse   370

Time for action – creating a bug   **371**
   Submitting fixes   372
Time for action – setting up a Gerrit profile   **372**
Time for action – committing and pushing a patch   **374**
Summary   **379**

Appendix A: Using OSGi Services to Dynamically Wire Applications   381

Services overview   **381**
Registering a service programmatically   **382**
   Creating an activator   382
   Registering a service   384
   Priority of services   386
   Using the services   387
   Lazy activation of bundles   388
   Comparison of services and extension points   389
Registering a service declaratively   **390**
   Declarative Services   391
     Properties and Declarative Services   392
     Service references in Declarative Services   393
     Multiple components and debugging Declarative Services   395
   Dynamic Service annotations   395
     Processing annotations at Maven build time   396
Dynamic services   **398**
   Resolving services each time   398
   Using a ServiceTracker   399
     Filtering services   400
     Obtaining a BundleContext without using an activator   401
   Dependent Services   401
Dynamic service configuration   **402**
   Installing Felix FileInstall   402
   Installing ConfigAdmin   403
   Configuring Declarative Services   403
   Service factories   404
     Creating the EchoService   405
     Creating an EchoServiceFactory   406
     Configuring the EchoServices   408
Summary   **410**

Appendix B: Pop Quiz Answers   411

Index   423

Preface

This book provides a general introduction to developing plug-ins for the Eclipse platform. No prior experience, other than Java, is necessary to be able to follow the examples presented in this book. By the end of the book, you should be able to create an Eclipse plug-in from scratch, as well as be able to create an automated build of those plug-ins.

What this book covers

Chapter 1, Creating Your First Plug-in, provides an overview of how to download Eclipse, set it up for plug-in development, create a sample plug-in, launch and debug it.

Chapter 2, Creating Views with SWT, provides an overview of how to build views with SWT, along with other custom SWT components such as system trays and resource management.

Chapter 3, Creating JFace Viewers, will show how to create views with JFace using TreeViewers and TableViewers, along with integration with the properties view and user interaction.

Chapter 4, Interacting with the User, interacts with the user, as well as the Jobs and Progress APIs, using commands, handlers, and menus.

Chapter 5, Storing Preferences and Settings, shows how to store preference information persistently, as well as displaying information via the Preferences pages.

Chapter 6, Working with Resources, tells how to load and create Resources in the workbench, as well as how to create a builder and nature for automated processing.

Chapter 7, Creating Eclipse 4 Applications, discusses the key differences between the Eclipse 3.x and Eclipse 4.x models, along with commands, handlers and menu items.

Chapter 8, Migrating to Eclipse 4.x, teaches how to efficiently migrate views created for Eclipse 3.x to the new Eclipse 4.x model.

Chapter 9, Styling Eclipse 4 Applications, discusses how to style the UI with CSS, and create widgets that can adjust to CSS styles.

Chapter 10, Creating Features, Update Sites, Applications, and Products, takes the plug-ins created so far in this book, aggregates them into features, publishes to update sites, and teaches you how applications and products are used to create standalone entities.

Chapter 11, Automated Testing of Plug-ins, teaches how to write automated tests that exercise Eclipse plug-ins, including both UI and non-UI components.

Chapter 12, Automated Builds with Tycho, shows how to build Eclipse plug-ins, features, update sites, applications, and products automatically with Maven Tycho.

Chapter 13, Contributing to Eclipse, discusses how to use Git to check out Eclipse code bases, how to report bugs with Bugzilla, and how to upload patches into Gerrit.

Appendix A, Using OSGi Services to Dynamically Wire Applications, looks at OSGi services as an alternative means of providing dependent services in an Eclipse or OSGi application.

Appendix B, Pop Quiz Answers, covers all the answers enlisted in the pop quiz sections in the book.

What you need for this book

To run the exercises for this book, you will need a computer with an up-to-date operating system running Windows, Linux, or Mac OS X. Java also needs to be installed; JDK 1.8 is the current released version although the instructions should work for a newer version of Java.

This book has been tested with the Eclipse SDK (Classic/Standard) for Mars (4.5) and Neon (4.6). Newer versions of Eclipse may also work. Care should be taken to not install the Eclipse for RCP and RAP developers, as this will cause the applications created in *Chapter 7, Understanding the Eclipse 4 Model and RCP Applications* and *Chapter 8, Migrating Views to the Eclipse 4 Model*.

The first chapter explains how to get started with Eclipse, including how to obtain and install both Eclipse and Java.

Who this book is for

This book is aimed at Java developers who are interested in learning how to create plug-ins, products and applications for the Eclipse platform.

This book will also be useful to those who already have some experience in building Eclipse plug-ins and want to know how to create automated builds using Maven Tycho, which has become the de facto standard for building Eclipse plug-ins.

Time for action – running on the UI thread   40
Time for action – creating a reusable widget   41
Time for action – using layouts   44
Managing resources   47
Time for action – getting colorful   48
Time for action – finding the leak   49
Time for action – plugging the leak   52
Interacting with the user   54
Time for action – getting in focus   54
Time for action – responding to input   56
Using other SWT widgets   58
Time for action – adding items to the tray   58
Time for action – responding to the user   60
Time for action – modal and other effects   62
Time for action – groups and tab folders   64
Summary   70

Chapter 3: Creating JFace Viewers   71
Why JFace?   71
Creating TreeViewers   72
Time for action – creating a tree viewer   72
Time for action – using Images in JFace   77
Time for action – styling label providers   82
Sorting and filtering   85
Time for action – sorting items in a viewer   85
Time for action – filtering items in a viewer   87
Interaction   89
Time for action – adding a double-click listener   90
Tabular data   93
Time for action – viewing time zones in tables   93
Selection   98
Time for action – propagating selection   98
Time for action – responding to selection changes   99
Summary   102

Chapter 4: Interacting with the User   103
Creating menus, commands, and handlers   103
Time for action – installing the E4 tools   104
Time for action – creating commands and handlers   106
Time for action – binding commands to keys   111
Time for action – changing contexts   114

Table of Contents

Preface   ix

Chapter 1: Creating Your First Plug-in   1
  Getting started   1
  Time for action – setting up the Eclipse environment   2
    Creating your first plug-in   5
  Time for action – creating a plug-in   5
    Running plug-ins   10
  Time for action – launching Eclipse from within Eclipse   10
  Debugging a plug-in   14
  Time for action – debugging a plug-in   14
  Time for action – updating code in the debugger   18
    Debugging with step filters   19
  Time for action – setting up step filtering   19
    Using different breakpoint types   21
  Time for action – breaking at method entry and exit   21
    Using conditional breakpoints   22
  Time for action – setting a conditional breakpoint   22
    Using exceptional breakpoints   24
  Time for action – catching exceptions   24
  Time for action – inspecting and watching variables   26
  Summary   30

Chapter 2: Creating Views with SWT   31
  Creating views and widgets   31
  Time for action – creating a view   32
  Time for action – drawing a custom view   35
  Time for action – drawing a seconds hand   37
  Time for action – animating the second hand   39

This book is dedicated in memory of Anne Tongs
(née Blewitt)

www.PacktPub.com

eBooks, discount offers, and more

Did you know that Packt offers eBook versions of every book published, with PDF and ePub files available? You can upgrade to the eBook version at www.PacktPub.com and as a print book customer, you are entitled to a discount on the eBook copy. Get in touch with us at customercare@packtpub.com for more details.

At www.PacktPub.com, you can also read a collection of free technical articles, sign up for a range of free newsletters and receive exclusive discounts and offers on Packt books and eBooks.

https://www2.packtpub.com/books/subscription/packtlib

Do you need instant solutions to your IT questions? PacktLib is Packt's online digital book library. Here, you can search, access, and read Packt's entire library of books.

Why subscribe?

- ◆ Fully searchable across every book published by Packt
- ◆ Copy and paste, print, and bookmark content
- ◆ On demand and accessible via a web browser

About the Reviewers

Carla Guillen, PhD, works at the Leibniz Supercomputing Centre of the Bavarian Academy of Sciences in the field of performance and energy optimization of supercomputers. As part of the annual courses offered at the Leibniz Supercomputing Centre, she has been teaching a course on the use of the Eclipse IDE with the CDT and Photran plug-in for 4 years. Additionally, she reviewed a book on advanced Eclipse plug-in development in 2014.

Tom Seidel works as an independent software engineer with focus on projects using Eclipse technology. He has worked for over a decade with the Eclipse technology stack in many projects and nearly every industry. Furthermore, he is an Eclipse committer and an active member of the Eclipse community.

Acknowledgments

I'd like to thank my wife Amy who has been behind me for over fifteen years, supporting me during the development of this and other books. Behind every man is a great woman, and I wouldn't be where I am today if it were not for her.

I'd also like to thank my parents, Derek and Ann, for introducing me to technology at an early age with a ZX81 and setting me on a path and a career that would take me across the globe, even if my first company's name could have been better chosen.

Special thanks are due to Ann Ford, Carla Guillen, Jeff Maury and Peter Rice who provided detailed feedback about every chapter and the exercises therein for the first edition, and to Tom Seidel and Roberto Lo Giacco for the second edition. Without their diligence and attention, this book would contain many more errors than I would like. Thanks are also due to the Packt editing team, Kajal Thapar, Preeti Singh and Mohita Vyas for making this possible.

During the latter stages of the first edition of the book I was also fortunate enough to receive some good feedback and advice from Lars Vogel and Ian Bull, both of whom are heavily involved in the Eclipse platform. I am especially grateful for Lars' website at www.vogella.com which has been an invaluable resource.

Thanks to Scott James, David Jones and Charles Humble for all the help you have given me over the years. Thanks also to my Docklands.LJC co-founder Robert Barr who tweets from @DocklandsLJC.

Finally, congratulations to both Sam and Holly on all your achievements in music, maths and school. Keep up the good work!

About the Author

Dr Alex Blewitt has been developing Java applications since version 1.0 was released in 1996, and has been using the Eclipse platform since its first release as part of the IBM WebSphere Studio product suite. He got involved in the open source community as a tester when Eclipse 2.1 was being released for macOS, and then subsequently as an editor for EclipseZone, including being a finalist for Eclipse Ambassador in 2007. More recently, Alex has been writing for InfoQ, covering Java and specifically Eclipse and OSGi subjects.

He is co-founder of the Docklands.LJC, a regional branch of the London Java Community in the Docklands, and a regular speaker at conferences.

Alex currently works for an investment bank in London, and is a Director of Bandlem Limited. Alex blogs at `https://alblue.bandlem.com` and tweets as `@alblue` on Twitter, and is the author of both *Mastering Eclipse 4 Plug-in Development*, and *Swift Essentials*, both by *Packt Publishing*.

Alex Blewitt has been actively involved in the Eclipse community for many years. His knowledge of both the Eclipse platform and plug-in development is second to none. He has written an in-depth and fun-to-read introduction to plug-in development that I am sure will help many to build, test, deploy, and update their Eclipse-based products or applications. I am sure that you will find it to be an excellent addition to your Eclipse library.

Mike Milinkovich
Executive Director of the Eclipse Foundation

Foreword

The Eclipse platform is one of the world's most successful open source software projects. Millions of developers use Eclipse every day as their development tools. Millions of people use applications built on top of the Eclipse Rich Client Platform every day. The Eclipse community has hundreds of dedicated committers and thousands of contributors. Speaking on their behalf, I thank you for your interest in Eclipse, and wish you great success building your project with our free software platform. This book will provide you with an excellent introduction to the key aspects of the Eclipse platform, including the plug-in model, SWT, JFace, user interactions, and resources.

The success of the Eclipse platform has been based to a very large extent on its extensibility. Originally conceived as a platform for building integrated development environments, Eclipse quickly evolved into a platform for building portable desktop applications as well. For over a decade, the Eclipse Rich Client Platform has been one of the leading technologies for creating compelling user interfaces for business applications. The major refresh of the Eclipse application platform that came in 2012 with the launch of Eclipse 4 has seen even further adoption. The chapters on Eclipse 4 and styling your user interface do an excellent job of portraying those new features.

Eclipse projects are driven by great developers, and the Eclipse 4 project has had many important contributors. I would like to recognize the contributions of just a few: the present Eclipse platform leader Mike Wilson (IBM), and project leaders Dani Megert (IBM) and Lars Vogel (vogella), and past leaders John Arthorne (formerly IBM, now Shopify), and Boris Bokowski (formerly IBM, now Google). I would also like to recognize the special contributions to Eclipse 4 of Brian de Alwis, Oleg Besedin, Danail Branekov, Eric Moffatt, Bogdan Gheorghe, Paul Webster, Thomas Schindl, Remy Suen, Kai Tödter, and Lars Vogel.

As an open source product, Eclipse owes its success to the contributions of many people. I highly encourage everyone to follow the chapter on contributing to the Eclipse platform. The Eclipse community is a worldwide phenomenon, and we would love to welcome your contributions.

Credits

Author

Dr Alex Blewitt

Reviewers

Carla Guillen

Tom Seidel

Commissioning Editor

Kartikey Pandey

Acquisition Editor

Denim Pinto

Content Development Editor

Deepti Thore

Technical Editor

Vivek Arora

Copy Editor

Vikrant Phadke

Project Coordinator

Shweta H Birwatkar

Proofreader

Safis Editing

Indexer

Hemangini Bari

Graphics

Disha Haria

Production Coordinator

Aparna Bhagat

Cover Work

Aparna Bhagat

Finally, those Eclipse developers who are familiar with the Eclipse 3.x model but are interested in learning about the changes that the Eclipse 4.x model brings will find the information presented in Chapter 8 a useful summary of what opportunities the new model provides.

Sections

In this book, you will find several headings that appear frequently (Time for action, What just happened?, Pop quiz, and Have a go hero).

To give clear instructions on how to complete a procedure or task, we use these sections as follows:

Time for action – heading

1. Action 1
2. Action 2
3. Action 3

Instructions often need some extra explanation to ensure they make sense, so they are followed with these sections:

What just happened?

This section explains the working of the tasks or instructions that you have just completed.

You will also find some other learning aids in the book, for example:

Pop quiz – heading

These are short multiple-choice questions intended to help you test your own understanding.

Have a go hero – heading

These are practical challenges that give you ideas to experiment with what you have learned.

Conventions

You will also find a number of text styles that distinguish between different kinds of information. Here are some examples of these styles and an explanation of their meaning.

Code words in text, database table names, folder names, filenames, file extensions, pathnames, dummy URLs, user input, and Twitter handles are shown as follows: "Running `java -version` should give output like this."

A block of code is set as follows:

```
public class Utility {
  public static boolean breakpoint() {
    System.out.println("Breakpoint");
    return false;
  }
}
```

Any command-line input or output is written as follows:

```
java version "1.8.0_92"
Java(TM) SE Runtime Environment (build 1.8.0_92-b14)
Java HotSpot(TM) 64-Bit Server VM (build 25.92-b14, mixed mode)
```

New terms and **important words** are shown in bold. Words that you see on the screen, in menus or dialog boxes for example, appear in the text like this: "Choose a workspace, which is the location in which projects are to be stored, and click on **OK**:"

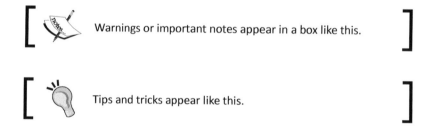

> Warnings or important notes appear in a box like this.

> Tips and tricks appear like this.

Reader feedback

Feedback from our readers is always welcome. Let us know what you think about this book—what you liked or disliked. Reader feedback is important for us as it helps us develop titles that you will really get the most out of.

To send us general feedback, simply e-mail feedback@packtpub.com, and mention the book's title in the subject of your message.

If there is a topic that you have expertise in and you are interested in either writing or contributing to a book, see our author guide at www.packtpub.com/authors.

Customer support

Now that you are the proud owner of a Packt book, we have a number of things to help you to get the most from your purchase.

Downloading the example code

You can download the example code files for this book from your account at `http://www.packtpub.com`. If you purchased this book elsewhere, you can visit `http://www.packtpub.com/support` and register to have the files e-mailed directly to you.

You can download the code files by following these steps:

1. Log in or register to our website using your e-mail address and password.
2. Hover the mouse pointer on the **SUPPORT** tab at the top.
3. Click on **Code Downloads & Errata**.
4. Enter the name of the book in the **Search** box.
5. Select the book for which you're looking to download the code files.
6. Choose from the drop-down menu where you purchased this book from.
7. Click on **Code Download**.

You can also download the code files by clicking on the **Code Files** button on the book's webpage at the Packt Publishing website. This page can be accessed by entering the book's name in the **Search** box. Please note that you need to be logged in to your Packt account.

Once the file is downloaded, please make sure that you unzip or extract the folder using the latest version of:

♦ WinRAR / 7-Zip for Windows
♦ Zipeg / iZip / UnRarX for Mac
♦ 7-Zip / PeaZip for Linux

The code bundle for the book is also hosted on GitHub at `https://github.com/alblue/com.packtpub.e4`. We also have other code bundles from our rich catalog of books and videos available at `https://github.com/PacktPublishing/`. Check them out!

Downloading the color images of this book

We also provide you with a PDF file that has color images of the screenshots/diagrams used in this book. The color images will help you better understand the changes in the output. You can download this file from `http://www.packtpub.com/sites/default/files/downloads/EclipsePluginDevelopmentBeginnersGuideSecondEdition_ColorImages.pdf`.

Errata

Although we have taken every care to ensure the accuracy of our content, mistakes do happen. If you find a mistake in one of our books—maybe a mistake in the text or the code—we would be grateful if you could report this to us. By doing so, you can save other readers from frustration and help us improve subsequent versions of this book. If you find any errata, please report them by visiting `http://www.packtpub.com/submit-errata`, selecting your book, clicking on the **Errata Submission Form** link, and entering the details of your errata. Once your errata are verified, your submission will be accepted and the errata will be uploaded to our website or added to any list of existing errata under the Errata section of that title.

To view the previously submitted errata, go to `https://www.packtpub.com/books/content/support` and enter the name of the book in the search field. The required information will appear under the **Errata** section.

Piracy

Piracy of copyrighted material on the Internet is an ongoing problem across all media. At Packt, we take the protection of our copyright and licenses very seriously. If you come across any illegal copies of our works in any form on the Internet, please provide us with the location address or website name immediately so that we can pursue a remedy.

Please contact us at `copyright@packtpub.com` with a link to the suspected pirated material.

We appreciate your help in protecting our authors and our ability to bring you valuable content.

Questions

If you have a problem with any aspect of this book, you can contact us at `questions@packtpub.com`, and we will do our best to address the problem.

1

Creating Your First Plug-in

Eclipse – an IDE for everything and nothing in particular.

Eclipse is a highly modular application consisting of hundreds of plug-ins, and can be extended by installing additional plug-ins. Plug-ins are developed and debugged with the Plug-in Development Environment (PDE).

In this chapter we will:

- Set up an Eclipse environment for doing plug-in development
- Create a plug-in with the new plug-in wizard
- Launch a new Eclipse instance with the plug-in enabled
- Debug the Eclipse plug-in

Getting started

Developing plug-ins requires an Eclipse development environment. This book has been developed and tested on Eclipse Mars 4.5 and Eclipse Neon 4.6, which was released in June 2016. Use the most recent version available.

Eclipse plug-ins are generally written in Java. Although it's possible to use other JVM-based languages (such as Groovy or Scala), this book will use the Java language.

There are several different packages of Eclipse available from the downloads page, each of which contains a different combination of plug-ins. This book has been tested with:

◆   Eclipse SDK from http://download.eclipse.org/eclipse/downloads/

◆   Eclipse IDE for Eclipse Committers from http://www.eclipse.org/downloads/

These contain the necessary **Plug-in Development Environment** (**PDE**) feature as well as source code, help documentation, and other useful features. The RCP and RAP package should not be used as it will cause problems with exercises in *Chapter 7, Understanding the Eclipse 4 Model and RCP Applications*.

It is also possible to install the Eclipse PDE feature in an existing Eclipse instance. To do this, go to the **Help** menu and select **Install New Software**, followed by choosing the **General Purpose Tools** category from the selected update site. The Eclipse PDE feature contains everything needed to create a new plug-in.

Time for action – setting up the Eclipse environment

Eclipse is a Java-based application; it needs Java installed. Eclipse is distributed as a compressed archive and doesn't require an explicit installation step.

1.   To obtain Java, go to http://java.com and follow the instructions to download and install Java.

> Note that Java comes in two flavors: a 32-bit installation and a 64-bit installation. If the running OS is 32-bit, then install the 32-bit JDK; alternatively, if the running OS is 64-bit, then install the 64-bit JDK.

2.   Running java -version should give output like this:

```
java version "1.8.0_92"

Java(TM) SE Runtime Environment (build 1.8.0_92-b14)

Java HotSpot(TM) 64-Bit Server VM (build 25.92-b14, mixed mode)
```

3.   Go to http://www.eclipse.org/downloads/ and select the Eclipse IDE for Eclipse Committers distribution.

4.   Download the one that matches the installed JDK. Running java -version should report either of these:

   ❏   If it's a 32-bit JDK:

   ```
   Java HotSpot(TM) Client VM
   ```

   ❏   If it's a 64-bit JDK:

   ```
   Java HotSpot(TM) 64-Bit Server VM
   ```

On Linux, Eclipse requires GTK+ 2 or 3 to be installed. Most Linux distributions have a window manager based on GNOME, which provides GTK+ 2 or 3.

5. To install Eclipse, download and extract the contents to a suitable location. Eclipse is shipped as an archive, and needs no administrator privileges to install. Do not run it from a networked drive as this will cause performance problems.

6. Note that Eclipse needs to write to the folder where it is extracted, so it's normal that the contents are writable afterwards. Generally, installing in /Applications or C:\Program Files as an administrator account is not recommended.

7. Run Eclipse by double-clicking on the Eclipse icon, or by running eclipse.exe (Windows), eclipse (Linux), or Eclipse.app (macOS).

8. On startup, the splash screen will be shown:

9. Choose a workspace, which is the location in which projects are to be stored, and click on **OK**:

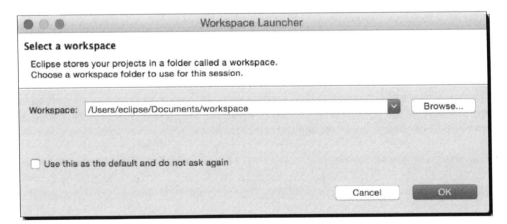

10. Close the welcome screen by clicking on the cross in the tab next to the welcome text. The welcome screen can be reopened by navigating to **Help | Welcome**:

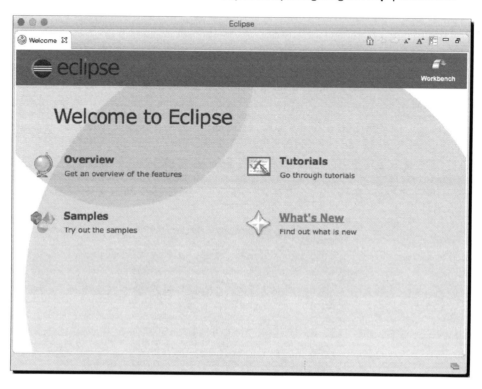

What just happened?

Eclipse needs Java to run, and so the first step involved in installing Eclipse is ensuring that an up-to-date Java installation is available. By default, Eclipse will find a copy of Java installed on the path or from one of the standard locations. It is also possible to specify a different Java by using the -vm command-line argument.

If the splash screen doesn't show, then the Eclipse version may be incompatible with the JDK (for example, a 64-bit JDK with a 32-bit Eclipse, or vice versa). Common error messages shown at the launcher may include **Unable to find companion launcher** or a cryptic message about being unable to find an SWT library.

On Windows, there is an additional eclipsec.exe launcher that allows log messages to be displayed on the console. This is sometimes useful if Eclipse fails to load and no other message is displayed. Other operating systems can use the eclipse command; and both support the -consolelog argument, which can display more diagnostic information about problems with launching Eclipse.

The Eclipse workspace is a directory used for two purposes: as the default project location, and to hold the `.metadata` directory containing Eclipse settings, preferences, and other runtime information. The Eclipse runtime log is stored in the `.metadata/.log` file.

The workspace chooser dialog has an option to set a default workspace. It can be changed within Eclipse by navigating to **File | Switch Workspace**. It can also be overridden by specifying a different workspace location with the `-data` command-line argument.

Finally, the welcome screen is useful for first-time users, but it is worth closing (rather than minimizing) once Eclipse has started.

Creating your first plug-in

In this task, Eclipse's plug-in wizard will be used to create a plug-in.

Time for action – creating a plug-in

In PDE, every plug-in has its own individual project. A plug-in project is typically created with the new project wizard, although it is also possible to upgrade an existing Java project to a plug-in project by adding the PDE nature and the required files by navigating to **Configure | Convert to plug-in project**.

1. To create a Hello World plug-in, navigate to **File | New | Project...**

2. The project types shown may be different from this list but should include **Plug-in Project** with Eclipse IDE for Eclipse Committers or Eclipse SDK. If nothing is shown when you navigate to **File | New**, then navigate to **Window | Open Perspective | Other | Plug-in Development** first; the entries should then be seen under the **New** menu.

3. Choose **Plug-in Project** and click on **Next**. Fill in the dialog as follows:

1. **Project name** should be `com.packtpub.e4.hello.ui`.

2. Ensure that **Use default location** is selected.

3. Ensure that **Create a Java project** is selected. The Eclipse version should be targeted to 3.5 or greater:

4. Click on **Next** again, and fill in the plug-in properties:

1. **ID** is set to `com.packtpub.e4.hello.ui`.

2. **Version** is set to `1.0.0.qualifier`.

3. **Name** is set to `Hello`.

4. **Vendor** is set to `PacktPub`.

5. For **Execution Environment**, use the default (for example, **JavaSE-1.8**).

6. Ensure that **Generate an Activator** is selected.

7. Set **Activator** to `com.packtpub.e4.hello.ui.Activator`.

8. Ensure that **This plug-in will make contributions to the UI** is selected.

9. **Rich client application** should be **No**:

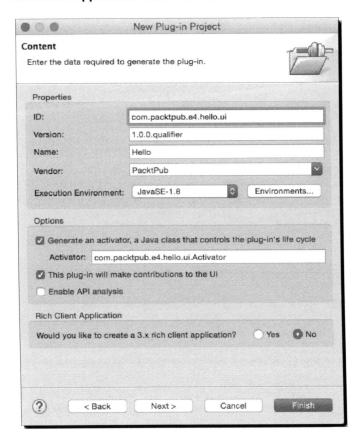

5. Click on **Next** and a set of templates will be provided:

    1. Ensure that **Create a plug-in using one of the templates** is selected.

    2. Choose the **Hello, World Command** template:

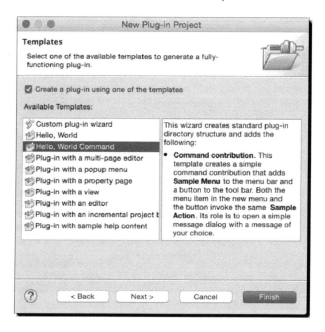

6. Click on **Next** to customize the sample, including:

    1. **Java Package Name**, which defaults to the project's name followed by `.handlers`

    2. **Handler Class Name**, which is the code that gets invoked for the action

    3. **Message Box Text**, which is the message to be displayed:

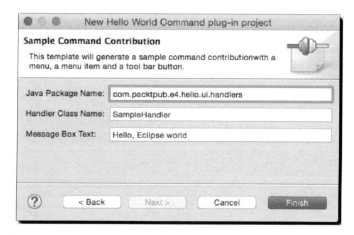

7. Finally, click on **Finish** and the project will be generated.

8. If an **Open Associated Perspective?** dialog asks, click on **Yes** to show the **Plug-in Development perspective**.

What just happened?

Creating a plug-in project is the first step towards creating a plug-in for Eclipse. The new plug-in project wizard was used with one of the sample templates to create a project.

Plug-ins are typically named in **reverse domain name** format, so these examples will be prefixed with `com.packtpub.e4`. This helps to distinguish between many plug-ins; the stock Eclipse IDE for Eclipse Committers comes with more than 450 individual plug-ins; the Eclipse-developed ones start with `org.eclipse`.

 Conventionally, plug-ins that create additions to (or require) the use of the UI have `.ui.` in their name. This helps to distinguish those that don't, which can often be used headlessly. Of the more than 450 plug-ins that make up the Eclipse IDE for Eclipse Committers, approximately 120 are UI-related and the rest are headless.

The project contains a number of files that are automatically generated based on the content filled in the wizard. The key files in an Eclipse plug-in are:

◆ `META-INF/MANIFEST.MF`: The `MANIFEST.MF` file, also known as the OSGi manifest, describes the plug-in's name, version, and dependencies. Double-clicking on it will open a custom editor, which shows the information entered in the wizards; or it can be opened in a standard text editor. The manifest follows standard Java conventions; line continuations are represented by a newline followed by a single space character, and the file must end with a newline.

◆ `plugin.xml`: The `plugin.xml` file declares what extensions the plug-in provides to the Eclipse runtime. Not all plug-ins need a `plugin.xml` file; headless (non-UI) plug-ins often don't need to have one. Extension points will be covered in more detail later; but the sample project creates an extension for the commands, handlers, bindings, and menus' extension points. Text labels for the commands/actions/menus are represented declaratively in the `plugin.xml` file, rather than programmatically; this allows Eclipse to show the menu before needing to load or execute any code.

This is one of the reasons Eclipse starts so quickly; by not needing to load or execute classes, it can scale by showing what's needed at the time, and then load the class on demand when the user invokes the action. Java Swing's Action class provides labels and tooltips programmatically, which can result in slower initialization of Swing-based user interfaces.

◆ build.properties: The build.properties file is used by PDE at development time and at build time. Generally it can be ignored, but if resources are added that need to be made available to the plug-in (such as images, properties files, HTML content and more), then an entry must be added here as otherwise it won't be found. Generally the easiest way to do this is by going to the **Build** tab of the build.properties file, which will gives a tree-like view of the project's contents. This file is an archaic hangover from the days of Ant builds, and is generally useless when using more up-to-date builds such as Maven Tycho, which will be covered in *Chapter 12, Automated Builds with Tycho.*

Pop quiz – Eclipse workspaces and plug-ins

Q1. What is an Eclipse workspace?

Q2. What is the naming convention for Eclipse plug-in projects?

Q3. What are the names of the three key files in an Eclipse plug-in?

Running plug-ins

To test an Eclipse plug-in, Eclipse is used to run or debug a new Eclipse instance with the plug-in installed.

Time for action – launching Eclipse from within Eclipse

Eclipse can launch a new Eclipse application by clicking on the run icon, or via the **Run** menu.

1. Select the plug-in project in the workspace.

2. Click on the run icon ◉ to launch the project. The first time this happens, a dialog will be shown; subsequent launches will remember the chosen type:

3. Choose the **Eclipse Application** type and click on **OK**. A new Eclipse instance will be launched.

4. Close the **Welcome** page in the launched application, if shown.

5. Click on the hello world icon in the menu bar, or navigate to **Sample Menu | Sample Command** from the menu, and the dialog box created via the wizard will be shown:

6. Quit the target Eclipse instance by closing the window, or via the usual keyboard shortcuts or menus (*Cmd + Q* on macOS or *Alt + F4* on Windows).

What just happened?

Upon clicking on run ◉ in the toolbar (or via **Run | Run As | Eclipse Application**) a launch configuration is created, which includes any plug-ins open in the workspace. A second copy of Eclipse—with its own temporary workspace—will enable the plug-in to be tested and verify that it works as expected.

The run operation is intelligent, in that it launches an application based on what is selected in the workspace. If a plug-in is selected, it will offer the opportunity to run as an **Eclipse Application**; if a Java project with a class with a `main` method, it will run it as a standard **Java Application**; and if it has tests, then it will offer to run the test launcher instead.

However, the run operation can also be counter-intuitive; if clicked a second time, and in a different project context, then something other than the expected launched might be run.

A list of the available launch configurations can be seen by going to the **Run** menu, or by going to the dropdown to the right of the run icon. The **Run | Run Configurations** menu shows all the available types, including any previously run:

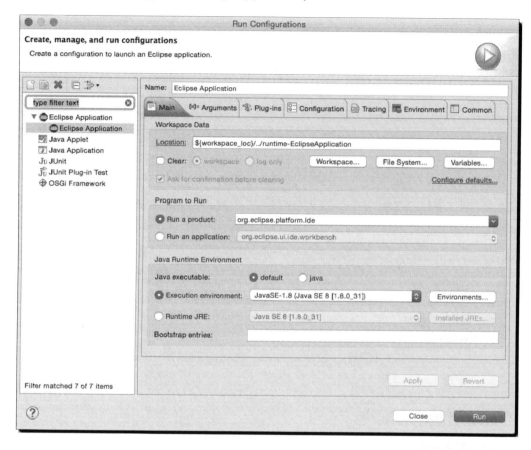

By default, the runtime workspace is kept between runs. The launch configuration for an Eclipse application has options that can be customized; in the preceding screenshot, the **Workspace Data** section in the **Main** tab shows where the runtime workspace is stored, and an option is shown that allows the workspace to be cleared (with or without confirmation) between runs.

Launch configurations can be deleted by clicking on the red delete icon on the top left, and new launch configurations can be created by clicking on the new icon. Each launch configuration has a type:

- **Eclipse Application**
- **Java Applet**
- **Java Application**
- **JUnit**
- **JUnit Plug-in Test**
- **OSGi Framework**

The launch configuration can be thought of as a pre-canned script that can launch different types of programs. Additional tabs are used to customize the launch, such as the environment variables, system properties, or command-line arguments. The type of the launch configuration specifies what parameters are required and how the launch is executed.

When a program is launched with the run icon, changes to the project's source code while it is running have no effect. However, as we'll see in the next section, if launched with the debug icon, changes can take effect.

If the target Eclipse is hanging or otherwise unresponsive, in the host Eclipse instance, the **Console** view (shown by navigating to **Window | View | Show View | Other | General | Console** menu) can be used to stop the target Eclipse instance.

Pop quiz: launching Eclipse

Q1. What are the two ways of terminating a launched Eclipse instance?

Q2. What are launch configurations?

Q3. How are launch configurations created and deleted?

Have a go hero – modifying the plug-in

Now that the Eclipse plug-in is running, try the following:

- Change the message of the label and title of the dialog box to something else
- Invoke the action by using the keyboard shortcut (defined in `plugin.xml`)
- Change the tooltip of the action to a different message
- Switch the action icon to a different graphic (if a different filename is used, remember to update it in `plugin.xml` and `build.properties`)

Debugging a plug-in

Since it's rare that everything works first time, it's often necessary to develop iteratively, adding progressively more functionality each time. Secondly, it's sometimes necessary to find out what's going on under the cover when trying to fix a bug, particularly if it's a hard-to-track-down exception such as `NullPointerException`.

Fortunately, Eclipse comes with excellent debugging support, which can be used to debug both standalone Java applications as well as Eclipse plug-ins.

Time for action – debugging a plug-in

Debugging an Eclipse plug-in is much the same as running an Eclipse plug-in, except that breakpoints can be used, the state of the program can be updated, and variables and minor changes to the code can be made. Rather than debugging plug-ins individually, the entire Eclipse launch configuration is started in debug mode. That way, all the plug-ins can be debugged at the same time.

Although run mode is slightly faster, the added flexibility of being able to make changes makes debug mode much more attractive to use as a default.

Start the target Eclipse instance by navigating to **Debug | Debug As | Eclipse Application**, or by clicking on debug in the toolbar.

1. Click on the hello world icon in the target Eclipse to display the dialog, as before, and click on **OK** to dismiss it.

2. In the host Eclipse, open the `SampleHandler` class and go to the first line of the `execute` method.

3. Add a breakpoint by double-clicking in the vertical ruler (the grey/blue bar on the left of the editor), or by pressing *Ctrl + Shift + B* (or *Cmd + Shift + B* on macOS). A blue dot representing the breakpoint will appear in the ruler:

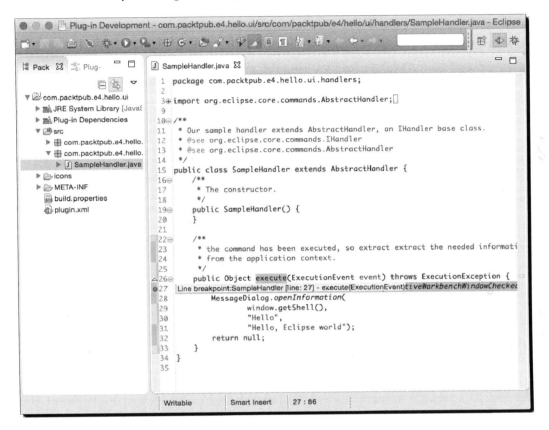

4. Click on the hello world icon in the target Eclipse to display the dialog, and the debugger will pause the thread at the breakpoint in the host Eclipse:

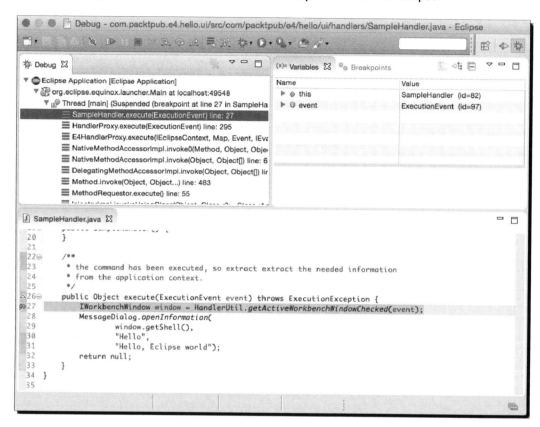

 The debugger perspective will open whenever a breakpoint is triggered and the program will be paused. While it is paused, the target Eclipse is unresponsive. Any clicks on the target Eclipse application will be ignored, and it will show a busy cursor.

5. In the top right, variables that are active in the line of code are shown. In this case, it's just the implicit variables (via `this`), any local variables (none yet), as well as the parameter (in this case, `event`).

6. Click on Step Over or press *F6*, and window will be added to the list of available variables:

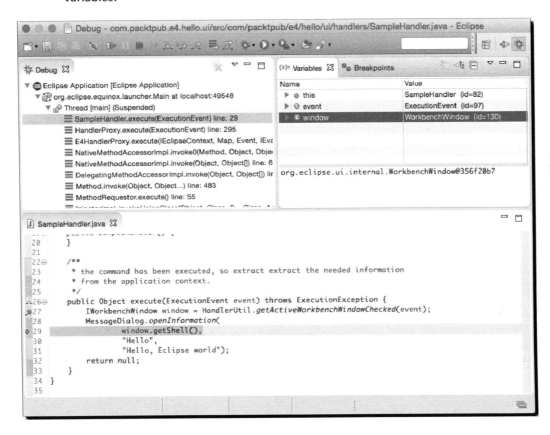

7. When ready to continue, click on resume 🔲▷ or press *F8* to keep running.

What just happened?

The built-in Eclipse debugger was used to launch Eclipse in debug mode. By triggering an action that led to a breakpoint, the debugger was revealed, allowing the local variables to be inspected.

When in the debugger, there are several ways to step through the code:

- ◆ **Step Over**: This allows stepping over line by line in the method
- ◆ **Step Into**: This follows the method calls recursively as execution unfolds

There is also a **Run | Step into Selection** menu item; it does not have a toolbar icon. It can be invoked with *Ctrl + F5* (*Alt + F5* on macOS) and is used to step into a specific expression.

◆ **Step Return**: This jumps to the end of a method

◆ **Drop to Frame**: This returns to a stack frame in the thread to re-run an operation

Time for action – updating code in the debugger

When an Eclipse instance is launched in run mode, changes made to the source code aren't reflected in the running instance. However, debug mode allows changes made to the source to be reflected in the running target Eclipse instance.

1. Launch the target Eclipse in debug mode by clicking on the debug icon.

2. Click on the hello world icon in the target Eclipse to display the dialog, as before, and click on **OK** to dismiss it. It may be necessary to remove or resume the breakpoint in the host Eclipse instance to allow execution to continue.

3. In the host Eclipse, open the `SampleHandler` class and go to the `execute` method.

4. Change the title of the dialog to `Hello again, Eclipse world` and save the file. Provided the **Build Automatically** option in **Project** menu is enabled, the change will be automatically recompiled.

5. Click on the hello world icon in the target Eclipse instance again. The new message should be shown.

What just happened?

By default, Eclipse ships with the **Build Automatically** option in **Project** menu enabled. Whenever changes are made to Java files, they are recompiled along with their dependencies if necessary.

When a Java program is launched in run mode, it will load classes on demand and then keep using that definition until the JVM shuts down. Even if the classes are changed, the JVM won't notice that they have been updated, and so no differences will be seen in the running application.

However, when a Java program is launched in debug mode, whenever changes to classes are made, Eclipse will update the running JVM with the new code if possible. The limits to what can be replaced are controlled by the JVM through the **Java Virtual Machine Tools Interface (JVMTI)**. Generally, updating an existing method and adding a new method or field will work, but changes to interfaces and superclasses may not be.

The Hotspot JVM cannot replace classes if methods are added or interfaces are updated. Some JVMs have additional capabilities that can substitute more code on demand. Other JVMs, such as IBM's, can deal with a wider range of replacements.

Note that there are some types of changes that won't be picked up, for example, new extensions added to the `plugin.xml` file. In order to see these changes, it is possible to start and stop the plug-in through the command-line OSGi console, or restart Eclipse inside or outside of the host Eclipse to see the change.

Debugging with step filters

When debugging using **Step Into**, the code will frequently go into Java internals, such as the implementation of Java collections classes or other internal JVM classes. These don't usually add value, so fortunately Eclipse has a way of ignoring uninteresting classes.

Time for action – setting up step filtering

Step filters allow for uninteresting packages and classes to be ignored during step debugging.

1. Run the target Eclipse instance in debug mode.

2. Ensure that a breakpoint is set at the start of the `execute` method of the `SampleHandler` class.

3. Click on the hello world icon, and the debugger should open at the first line, as before.

4. Click on **Step Into** five or six times. At each point, the code will jump to the next method in the expression, first through various methods in `HandlerUtil` and then into `ExecutionEvent`.

5. Click on resume ⏸▶ to continue.

6. Open **Preferences** and then navigate to **Java | Debug | Step Filtering**. Select the **Use Step Filters** option.

7. Click on **Add Package** and enter `org.eclipse.ui`, followed by a click on **OK**:

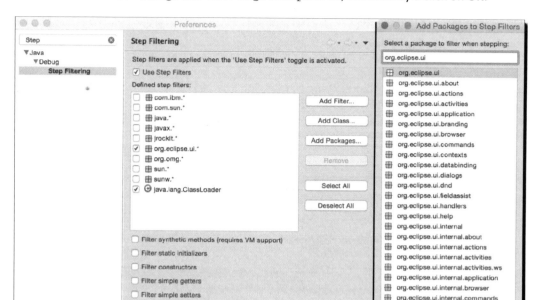

8. Click on the hello world icon again.

9. Click on **Step Into** as before. This time, the debugger goes straight to the `getApplicationContext` method in the `ExecutionEvent` class.

10. Click on resume ▯▷ to continue.

11. To make debugging more efficient by skipping accessors, go back to the **Step Filters** preference and select **Filter Simple Getters** from the **Step Filters** preferences page.

12. Click on the hello world icon again.

13. Click on **Step Into** as before.

14. Instead of going into the `getApplicationContext` method, the execution will drop through to the `getVariable` method of the `ExpressionContext` class instead.

What just happened?

Step Filters allows uninteresting packages to be skipped, at least from the point of debugging. Typically, JVM internal classes (such as those beginning with `sun` or `sunw`) are not helpful when debugging and can easily be ignored. This also avoids debugging through the `ClassLoader` as it loads classes on demand.

Typically it makes sense to enable all the default packages in the **Step Filters** dialog, as it's pretty rare to need to debug any of the JVM libraries (internal or public interfaces). This means that when stepping through code, if a common method such as `toString` is called, debugging won't step through the internal implementation.

It also makes sense to filter out simple setters and getters (those that just set a variable or those that just return a variable). If the method is more complex (like the `getVariable` method previously), then it will still stop in the debugger.

Constructors and static initializers can also be filtered specifically.

Using different breakpoint types

Although it's possible to place a breakpoint anywhere in a method, a special breakpoint type exists that can fire on method entry, exit, or both. Breakpoints can also be customized to only fire in certain situations or when certain conditions are met.

Time for action – breaking at method entry and exit

Method breakpoints allow the user to see when a method is entered or exited.

1. Open the `SampleHandler` class, and go to the `execute` method.

2. Double-click in the vertical ruler at the method signature, or select **Toggle Method Breakpoint** from the method in one of the **Outline**, **Package Explorer** or **Members** views.

3. The breakpoint should be shown on the line:

   ```
   public Object execute(...) throws ExecutionException {
   ```

4. Open the breakpoint properties by right-clicking on the breakpoint or via the **Breakpoints** view, which is shown in the **Debug** perspective. Set the breakpoint to trigger at method entry and method exit.

5. Click on the hello world icon again.

6. When the debugger stops at method entry, click on resume ▯▶.

7. When the debugger stops at method exit, click on resume ▯▶.

What just happened?

The breakpoint triggers at the time the method enters and subsequently when the method's `return` is reached. Note that the exit is only triggered if the method returns normally; if an uncaught exception is raised, it is not treated as a normal method exit, and so the breakpoint won't fire.

Other than the breakpoint type, there's no significant difference between creating a breakpoint on method entry and creating one on the first statement of the method. Both give the ability to inspect the parameters and do further debugging before any statements in the method itself are called.

The method exit breakpoint will only trigger once the `return` statement is about to leave the method. Thus any expression in the method's `return` value will have been evaluated prior to the exit breakpoint firing. Compare and contrast this with the line breakpoint, which will wait to evaluate the argument of the return statement.

Note that Eclipse's **Step Return** has the same effect; this will run until the method's return statement is about to be executed. However, to find when a method returns, using a method exit breakpoint is far faster than stopping at a specific line and then doing **Step Return**.

Using conditional breakpoints

Breakpoints are useful since they can be invoked on every occasion when a line of code is triggered. However, they sometimes need to break for specific actions only—such as when a particular option is set, or when a value has been incorrectly initialized. Fortunately, this can be done with conditional breakpoints.

Time for action – setting a conditional breakpoint

Normally breakpoints fire on each invocation. It is possible to configure breakpoints such that they fire when certain conditions are met; these are known as conditional breakpoints.

1. Go to the `execute` method of the `SampleHandler` class.

2. Clear any existing breakpoints, by double-clicking on them or using **Remove All Breakpoints** from the **Breakpoints** view.

3. Add a breakpoint to the first line of the `execute` method body.

4. Right-click on the breakpoint, and select the **Breakpoint Properties** menu (it can also be shown by *Ctrl* + double-clicking—or *Cmd* + double-clicking on macOS—on the breakpoint icon itself):

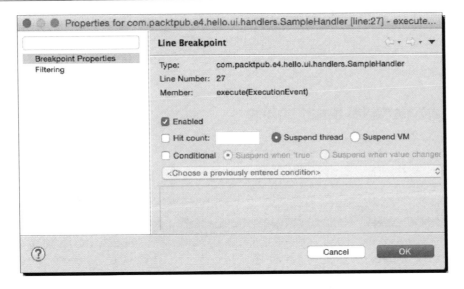

5. Set **Hit Count** to 3, and click on **OK**.

6. Click on the hello world icon button three times. On the third click, the debugger will open up at that line of code.

7. Open the breakpoint properties, deselect **Hit Count**, and select the **Enabled** and **Conditional** options. Put the following line into the conditional trigger field:

   ```
   ((org.eclipse.swt.widgets.Event)event.trigger).stateMask==65536
   ```

8. Click on the hello world icon, and the breakpoint will not fire.

9. Hold down *Alt* + click on the hello world icon, and the debugger will open (65536 is the value of SWT.MOD3, which is the *Alt* key).

What just happened?

When a breakpoint is created, it is enabled by default. A breakpoint can be temporarily disabled, which has the effect of removing it from the flow of execution. Disabled breakpoints can be easily re-enabled on a per breakpoint basis, or from the **Breakpoints** view. Quite often it's useful to have a set of breakpoints defined in the code base, but not necessarily have them all enabled at once.

It is also possible to temporarily disable all breakpoints using the **Skip All Breakpoints** setting, which can be changed from the corresponding item in the **Run** menu (when the **Debug** perspective is shown) or the corresponding icon in the **Breakpoints** view. When this is enabled, no breakpoints will be fired.

Conditional breakpoints must return a value. If the breakpoint is set to break whether or not the condition is true, it must be a Boolean expression. If the breakpoint is set to stop whenever the value changes, then it can be any Java expression. Multiple statements can be used provided that there is a `return` keyword with a value expression.

Using exceptional breakpoints

Sometimes when debugging a program, an exception occurs. Typically this isn't known about until it happens, when an exception message is printed or displayed to the user via some kind of dialog box.

Time for action – catching exceptions

Although it's easy to put a breakpoint in the `catch` block, this is merely the location where the failure was ultimately caught, not where it was caused. The place where it was caught can often be in a completely different plug-in from where it was raised, and depending on the amount of information encoded within the exception (particularly if it has been transliterated into a different exception type) may hide the original source of the problem. Fortunately, Eclipse can handle such cases with a Java Exception Breakpoint.

1. Introduce a bug into the execute method of the `SampleHandler` class, by adding the following just before the `MessageDialog.openInformation()` call:

   ```
   window = null;
   ```

2. Click on the hello world icon.

3. Nothing will appear to happen in the target Eclipse, but in the **Console** view of the host Eclipse instance, the error message should be seen:

   ```
   Caused by: java.lang.NullPointerException
       at com.packtpub.e4.hello.ui.handlers.SampleHandler.execute
       at org.eclipse.ui.internal.handlers.HandlerProxy.execute
       at org.eclipse.ui.internal.handlers.E4HandlerProxy.execute
   ```

4. Create a **Java Exception Breakpoint** in the **Breakpoints** view of the **Debug** perspective. The **Add Java Exception Breakpoint** dialog will be shown:

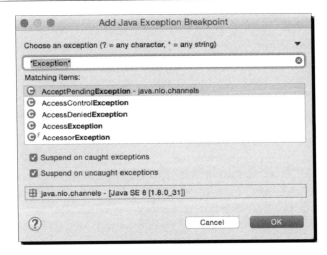

5. Enter `NullPointerException` in the search dialog, and click on **OK**.

6. Click on the hello world icon, and the debugger will stop at the line where the exception is thrown, instead of where it is caught:

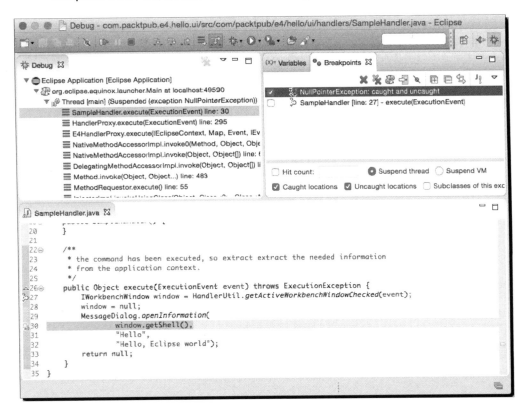

What just happened?

The **Java Exception Breakpoint** stops when an exception is thrown, not when it is caught. The dialog asks for a single exception class to catch, and by default, the wizard has been pre-filled with any class whose name includes `*Exception*`. However, any name (or filter) can be typed into the search box, including abbreviations such as `FNFE` for `FileNotFoundException`. Wildcard patterns can also be used, which allows searching for `Nu*Ex` or `*Unknown*`.

By default, the exception breakpoint corresponds to instances of that specific class. This is useful (and quick) for exceptions such as `NullPointerException`, but not so useful for ones with an extensive class hierarchy, such as `IOException`. In this case, there is a checkbox visible on the breakpoint properties and at the bottom of the breakpoints view, which allows the capture of all **Subclasses of this exception**, not just of the specific class.

There are also two other checkboxes that say whether the debugger should stop when the exception is **Caught** or **Uncaught**. Both of these are selected by default; if both are deselected, then the breakpoint effectively becomes disabled. **Caught** means that the exception is thrown in a corresponding `try/catch` block, and **Uncaught** means that the exception is thrown without a `try/catch` block (this bubbles up to the method's caller).

Time for action – inspecting and watching variables

Finally, it's worth seeing what the **Variables** view can do.

1. Create a breakpoint at the start of the `execute` method.
2. Click on the hello world icon again.
3. Highlight the `openInformation` call and navigate to **Run | Step Into Selection**.
4. Select the `title` variable in the the **Variables** view.

5. Modify where it says **Hello** in the bottom half of the variables view and change it to **Goodbye**:

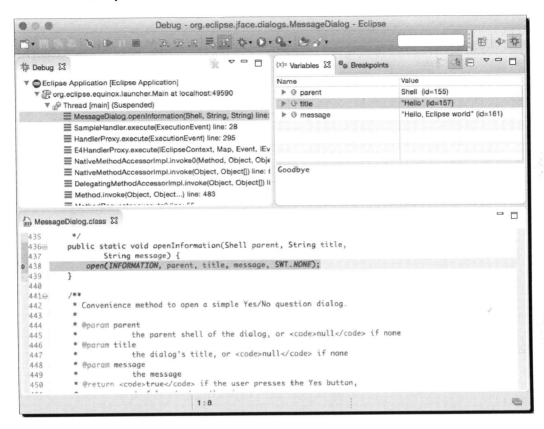

6. Save the value with *Ctrl + S* (or *Cmd + S* on macOS).

7. Click on resume, and the newly updated title can be seen in the dialog.

8. Click on the hello world icon again.

9. With the debugger stopped in the `execute` method, highlight the event in the **Variables** view.

10. Right-click on the value and choose **Inspect** (by navigating to *Ctrl + Shift + I* or *Cmd + Shift + I* on macOS) and the value is opened in the **Expressions** view:

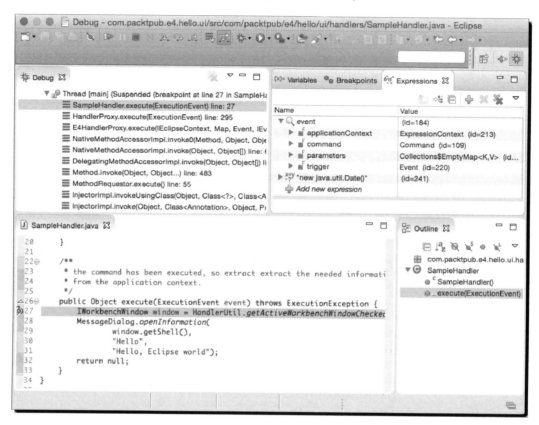

11. Click on **Add new expression** at the bottom of the **Expressions** view.

12. Add `new java.util.Date()` and the right-hand side will show the current time.

13. Right-click on the `new java.util.Date()` and choose **Re-evaluate Watch Expression**. The right-hand-side pane shows the new value.

14. Step through the code line by line, and notice that the watch expression is re-evaluated after each step.

15. Disable the watch expression by right-clicking on it and choosing **Disable**.

16. Step through the code line by line, and the watch expression will not be updated.

What just happened?

The Eclipse debugger has many powerful features, and the ability to inspect (and change) the state of the program is one of the more important ones.

Watch expressions, when combined with conditional breakpoints, can be used to find out when data becomes corrupted or used to show the state of a particular object's value.

Expressions can also be evaluated based on objects in the variables view, and code completion is available to select methods, with the result being shown with **Display**.

Pop quiz: debugging

Q1. How can an Eclipse plug-in be launched in debug mode?

Q2. How can certain packages be avoided when debugging?

Q3. What are the different types of breakpoints that can be set?

Q4. How can a loop that only exhibits a bug after 256 iterations be debugged?

Q5. How can a breakpoint be set on a method when its argument is null?

Q6. What does inspecting an object do?

Q7. How can the value of an expression be calculated?

Q8. How can multiple statements be executed in breakpoint conditions?

Have a go hero – working with breakpoints

Using a conditional breakpoint to stop at a certain method is fine if the data is simple, but sometimes there needs to be more than one expression. Although it is possible to use multiple statements in the breakpoint condition definition, the code is not very reusable. To implement additional reusable functionality, the breakpoint can be delegated to a breakpoint utility class.

1. Create a `Utility` class in the `com.packtpub.e4.hello.ui.handlers` package with a `static` method `breakpoint` that returns a `true` value if the breakpoint should stop, and `false` otherwise:

```
public class Utility {
  public static boolean breakpoint() {
    System.out.println("Breakpoint");
    return false;
  }
}
```

2. Create a conditional breakpoint in the `execute` method that calls `Utility.breakpoint()`.

3. Click on the hello world icon again, and the message will be printed to the host Eclipse's **Console** view. The breakpoint will not stop.

4. Modify the `breakpoint` method to return `true` instead of `false`. Run the action again. The debugger will stop.

5. Modify the `breakpoint` method to take the message as an argument, along with a Boolean value that is returned to say whether the breakpoint should stop.

6. Set up a conditional breakpoint with the expression:

```
Utility.breakpoint(
  ((org.eclipse.swt.widgets.Event)event.trigger).stateMask != 0,
  "Breakpoint")
```

7. Modify the breakpoint method to take a variable `Object` array, and use that in conjunction with the message to use `String.format()` for the resulting message:

```
Utility.breakpoint(
  ((org.eclipse.swt.widgets.Event)event.trigger).stateMask != 0,
  "Breakpoint %s %h",
  event,
  java.time.Instant.now())
```

Summary

In this chapter, we covered how to get started with Eclipse plug-in development. From downloading the right Eclipse package to getting started with a wizard-generated plug-in, you should now have the tools to follow through with the remainder of the chapters of this book.

Specifically, we learned these things:

♦ The Eclipse SDK and the Eclipse IDE for Eclipse Committers have the necessary plug-in development environment to get you started

♦ The plug-in creation wizard can be used to create a plug-in project, optionally using one of the example templates

♦ Testing an Eclipse plug-in launches a second copy of Eclipse with the plug-in installed and available for use

♦ Launching Eclipse in debug mode allows you to update code and stop execution at breakpoints defined via the editor

Now that we've learned how to get started with Eclipse plug-ins, we're ready to look at creating plug-ins that contribute to the IDE, starting with SWT and Views—which is the topic of the next chapter.

2
Creating Views with SWT

SWT – the Standard Widget Toolkit

SWT is the widget toolkit used by Eclipse that gives performant access to the platform's native tools in a portable manner. Unlike Swing, which is rendered with Java native drawing operations, SWT delegates the drawing to the underlying operating system.

In this chapter we will:

- Create an Eclipse view with SWT widgets
- Create a custom SWT widget
- Work with SWT resources and learn how to detect and fix resource leaks
- Handle focus operations
- Group components and resize them automatically
- Create system tray items
- Display nonrectangular windows
- Provide scrolling and tabbed navigation

Creating views and widgets

This section introduces views and widgets by creating clocks that can be used to display time zones in Eclipse.

Time for action – creating a view

The Eclipse UI consists of multiple views, which are the rectangular areas that display content, such as the **Outline**, **Console**, or **Package Explorer**. In Eclipse 3.x, views are created by adding an extension point to an existing plug-in, or using a template. A `clock.ui` plug-in will be created to host the clock widgets and views.

1. Open the plug-in wizard by navigating to **File | New | Other | Plug-in Project**. Enter the details as follows:

   1. Set **Project name** to `com.packtpub.e4.clock.ui`.
   2. Ensure that **Use default location** is selected.
   3. Ensure that **Create a Java project** is selected.
   4. The **Eclipse Version** should be targeted to 3.5 or greater.

2. Click on **Next** again, and fill in the plug-in properties:

   1. Set **ID** to `com.packtpub.e4.clock.ui`.
   2. Set **Version** to `1.0.0.qualifier`.
   3. Set **Name** to **Clock**.
   4. Set **Vendor** to **PacktPub**.
   5. Ensure that **Generate an Activator** is selected.
   6. Set the **Activator** to `com.packtpub.e4.clock.ui.Activator`.
   7. Ensure that **This plug-in will make contributions to the UI** is selected.
   8. **Rich client application** should be **No**.

3. Click on **Next** to choose from a set of templates:

   1. Ensure that **Create a plug-in using one of the templates** is selected.
   2. Choose the **Plug-in with a view** template.

4. Click on **Next** to customize the aspects of the sample; set:

   1. **Java package name** to `com.packtpub.e4.clock.ui.views`.
   2. **View class name** to `ClockView`.
   3. **View name** to **Clock View**.
   4. **View category ID** to `com.packtpub.e4.clock.ui`.
   5. **View category name** to `Timekeeping`.
   6. **Viewer type** to **Table Viewer**.

5. Deselect the **Add** checkboxes as these are not required.

6. Click on **Finish** to create the project.

7. Run the target Eclipse application via the run toolbar icon.

8. Navigate to **Window | Show View | Other | Timekeeping | Clock View** to show the **Clock View**, which has a simple list view with **One**, **Two**, and **Three** listed:

What just happened?

Functionality in Eclipse will typically be implemented in multiple plug-ins. Since the clock functionality developed in this chapter is unrelated to that of the `hello` plug-in, a new plug-in was created to host the code. Plug-ins typically will have more than just one view or extension, grouped logically.

The plug-in wizard created an empty plug-in project as well as two key files: MANIFEST.MF and `plugin.xml`.

Manifest.mf

The manifest contains references to dependent plug-ins and interfaces, and includes the following:

```
Bundle-SymbolicName: com.packtpub.e4.clock.ui;singleton:=true
Bundle-Version: 1.0.0.qualifier
Bundle-Activator: com.packtpub.e4.clock.ui.Activator
Require-Bundle: org.eclipse.ui,
 org.eclipse.core.runtime
```

Plug-ins that contribute to the user interface need to do two things:

◆   Depend on `org.eclipse.ui`

◆   Have `;singleton:=true` after the bundle's symbolic name

The dependency on the `org.eclipse.ui` bundle gives access to the Standard Widget Toolkit and other key parts of the Eclipse framework.

> The clause `;singleton:=true` is an OSGi directive, which means that only one version of this plug-in can be installed in Eclipse at a time. For plug-ins that add dependencies to the UI, there is a restriction that they must be singletons (this constraint is one of the main reasons why installing a new plug-requires the IDE to restart).

The manifest sets up the project's class path. Any additional plug-in dependencies need to be to the manifest.

plugin.xml

The `plugin.xml` file defines a list of extensions that this plug-in provides. Extension points are how Eclipse advertises the plug-in extensions, much like a USB hub provides a generic connector that allows many other types of device to be plugged in.

The Eclipse extension points are documented in the help system, and each has a point identifier, with optional children that are point-specific. In this case, the extension is defined using the `org.eclipse.ui.views` point, which expects a combination of `category` and `view` elements. In this case, it will look like the following:

```
<plugin>
    <extension point="org.eclipse.ui.views">
        <category name="Timekeeping"
           id="com.packtpub.e4.clock.ui"/>
        <view name="Clock View"
           icon="icons/sample.gif"
           category="com.packtpub.e4.clock.ui"
           class="com.packtpub.e4.clock.ui.views.ClockView"
           id="com.packtpub.e4.clock.ui.views.ClockView"/>
    </extension>
</plugin>
```

The class in this case extends the `ViewPart` abstract class, which is used for all views in the Eclipse 3.x model.

> The **Eclipse 4 (E4)** model defines views in a different way, which is covered in more detail in *Chapter 7, Creating Eclipse 4 Applications*. The Eclipse 4.x SDK includes a 3.x compatibility layer, so these examples will work in Eclipse 4.x SDKs.

The viewer component is a default table view, which will be replaced in the next section.

Time for action – drawing a custom view

An SWT Canvas can be used to provide custom rendering for a view. As a starting point for drawing a clock, the Canvas will use drawArc to create a circle.

1. Remove the content of the ClockView, leaving behind an empty implementation of the setFocus and createPartControl methods.

2. Run the target Eclipse instance and you will see that the ClockView is now empty.

3. Create a new method called drawClock that takes a PaintEvent, and use the graphics context gc from the event to draw the circle.

4. In the createPartControl method, do the following:

    1. Create a new Canvas, which is a drawable widget.

    2. Add a PaintListener to the Canvas that uses a method reference to the drawClock method.

5. The code will look like this:

```
package com.packtpub.e4.clock.ui.views;
import org.eclipse.swt.*;
import org.eclipse.swt.events.*;
import org.eclipse.swt.widgets.*;
import org.eclipse.ui.part.ViewPart;
public class ClockView extends ViewPart {
  public void createPartControl(Composite parent) {
    final Canvas clock = new Canvas(parent, SWT.NONE);
    clock.addPaintListener(this::drawClock);
  }
  private void drawClock(PaintEvent e) {
    e.gc.drawArc(e.x, e.y, e.width-1, e.height-1, 0, 360);
  }
  public void setFocus() {
  }
}
```

6. Run the target Eclipse instance, and show the ClockView.

7. Resize the view, and the clock should change size with it:

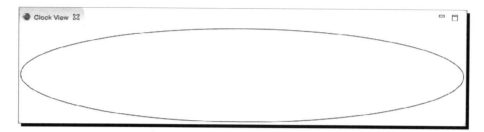

What just happened?

In SWT, the widget used for custom drawing is `Canvas`. The `View` is constructed with a call to `createPartControl`, which is invoked once when the view is shown for the first time. If the view is minimized and then maximized, it will not be invoked again; however, if the view is closed and a new view is opened, then a call will be made to a new instance of the `ClockView` to initialize it.

Unlike other Java GUI frameworks, a widget is not added to or removed from a containing parent after creation; instead, the widget's parent is specified at construction time. The constructor also takes a `style` flag. This is used by widgets in different ways; for example, the `Button` widget takes various flags to indicate whether it should be rendered as a push button, radio button, checkbox, toggle, or arrow. For consistency, in SWT all widgets have an `int style` flag, which enables up to 32 bits of different options to be configured.

> These are defined as constants in the SWT class; for example, the checkbox button style is represented as `SWT.CHECKBOX`. Options can be combined. To specify a flat button, the `SWT.PUSH` and `SWT.FLAT` options can be combined together with `new Button(parent, SWT.PUSH | SWT.FLAT)`. Generally, the value `SWT.NONE` is used to represent default options.

The code adds an empty `Canvas` to the view, but how can graphics be drawn? SWT does not expose a paint method on any of its widgets. Instead, a `PaintListener` is called whenever the canvas needs to be repainted.

All in the name of performance

You may wonder why all these little things are different between the way SWT handles its widgets compared to how AWT or Swing handles them. The answer is in the name of speed and delegation to native rendering and controls if at all possible. This mattered back in the early days of Java (Eclipse 1.0 was released when Java 1.3 was the most advanced runtime available), when neither the JITs nor CPUs were as powerful as today.

Secondly, the goal of SWT was to offload as much of the processing onto native components (such as AWT) as possible and let the OS do the heavy work instead of Java. By doing that, the time spent in the JVM could be minimized, while allowing the OS to render the graphics in the most appropriate (and performant) way. The `PaintListener` is one such example of avoiding performing unnecessary drawing-related calls unless a component actually needs it.

The `drawClock` method is called with a `PaintEvent` argument, which contains references to all of the data needed to draw the component. To minimize method calls, the fields are publicly readable. It also contains a reference to the **graphics context (gc)** which can be used to invoke drawing commands.

Finally, the event also records the region in which the paint event is to be fired. The `x` and `y` fields show the position of the top left to start from, and the width and height fields of the event show the drawing bounds.

In this case, the graphics context is set up with the necessary foreground color, and `drawArc` is called between the bounds specified. Note that the arc is specified in degrees (from 0 with a 360 span) rather than radians.

Time for action – drawing a seconds hand

A clock with no hands and no numbers is just a circle. To change this, a second hand will be drawn using a filled arc.

Since arcs are drawn anticlockwise from 0 (on the right, or 3 o'clock) through 90 degrees (12 o'clock), then 180 degrees (9 o'clock), then 270 degrees (6 o'clock), and finally back to 360 degrees (3 o'clock), it is possible to calculate the arc's position for the second hand using the expression *(15 – seconds) * 6 % 360*.

1. Go to the `drawClock` method of the `ClockView` class.
2. Add a variable called `seconds` that is initialized to `LocalTime.now().getSecond()`.
3. Get the `SWT.COLOR_BLUE` via the display, and store it in a local variable, `blue`.

4. Set the background color of the graphics context to `blue`.

5. Draw an arc using the formula mentioned earlier to draw the second hand.

6. The code should look like this:

```
public void paintControl(PaintEvent e) {
    e.gc.drawArc(e.x, e.y, e.width-1, e.height-1, 0, 360);
    int seconds = LocalTime.now().getSecond();
    int arc = (15 - seconds) * 6 % 360;
    Color blue = e.display.getSystemColor(SWT.COLOR_BLUE);
    e.gc.setBackground(blue);
    e.gc.fillArc(e.x, e.y, e.width-1, e.height-1, arc-1, 2);
}
```

> Make sure that `org.eclipse.swt.graphics.Color` is used rather than the same-named classes from `java.awt`.

7. Start Eclipse and show the **Clock View**. The second hand will be shown once but won't change.

8. Resize the view. Then the second hand will be drawn in the new location:

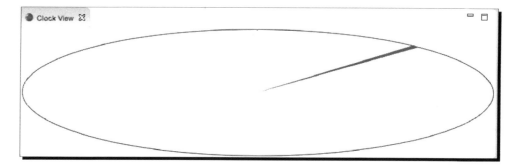

What just happened?

The code calculates the position on the arc at which the second hand will need to be drawn. Since the arc degrees go anticlockwise, the seconds have to be negative. The offset of 15 represents the fact that an arc of 0 is at the 3 o'clock position, which is 15 seconds. This is then multiplied by 6 (60 seconds = 360 degrees) and finally the result is calculated modulus 360, to ensure that it's up to 360 degrees (the value can be negative; the arc calculation works in this way as well).

Although `drawArc` colors in the foreground color, the `fillArc` colors in the background color. The GC maintains two colors; a foreground color and a background color. Normally an SWT `Color` object needs to have a `dispose` after use, but to simplify this example, the `Display` class's `getSystemColor` method is used, whose result does not need to be disposed.

Finally, the arc is drawn 2 degrees wide. To center it, the arc starts from `pos-1`, so it is drawn from `pos-1` to `pos+1`.

When the view is resized, a redraw is issued on the canvas, and so the second hand is drawn in the correct position. However, to be useful as a clock, this should be done automatically do this while the view is visible.

Time for action – animating the second hand

The second hand is drawn with a `redraw` on the `Canvas`, but this will need to be run periodically. If it is redrawn once per second, it can emulate a clock ticking.

Eclipse has a `jobs` plug-in, which would be just right for this task, but this will be covered in *Chapter 4, Interacting with the User*. So to begin with, a simple `Thread` will be used to issue the redraw.

1. Open the `ClockView` class.
2. Add the following at the bottom of the `createPartControl` method:

```
Runnable redraw = () -> {
  while (!clock.isDisposed()) {
    clock.redraw();
    try {
      Thread.sleep(1000);
    } catch (InterruptedException e) {
      return;
    }
  }
};
new Thread(redraw, "TickTock").start();
```

3. Relaunch the test Eclipse instance, and open the **Clock View**.
4. Open the host Eclipse instance and look in the **Console View** for the errors.

What just happened?

When the `ClockView` is shown, a `Thread` is created and started, which redraws the clock once per second. When it is shown, an exception is generated, which can be seen in the host Eclipse instance's **Console View**:

```
Exception in thread "TickTock"
org.eclipse.swt.SWTException: Invalid thread access
    at org.eclipse.swt.SWT.error(SWT.java:4477)
    at org.eclipse.swt.SWT.error(SWT.java:4392)
    at org.eclipse.swt.SWT.error(SWT.java:4363)
    at org.eclipse.swt.widgets.Widget.error(Widget.java:783)
    at org.eclipse.swt.widgets.Widget.checkWidget(Widget.java:574)
    at org.eclipse.swt.widgets.Control.redraw(Control.java:2279)
    at com.packtpub.e4.clock.ui.views.ClockView$2.run(ClockView.java:29)
```

This is expected behavior in this case, but it's worth taking a dive into the SWT internals to understand why.

Many windowing systems have a **UI thread**, which is responsible for coordinating the user interface updates with the program code. If long-running operations execute on the UI thread, then the program can appear to hang and become unresponsive. Many windowing systems will have an automated process that changes the cursor into an hourglass or spinning beach ball if the UI thread for an application is blocked for more than a short period of time.

SWT mirrors this by providing a UI thread for interacting with the user interface, and ensures that updates to SWT components are performed on this thread. Redraws occur on the SWT thread, as do calls to methods such as `createPartControl`.

In the clock update example, updates are being fired on a different thread (in this case, the `TickTock` thread), and this results in the exception shown earlier. So how are these updates run on the correct thread?

Time for action – running on the UI thread

To execute code on the UI thread, `Runnable` instances must be posted to the `Display` via one of two methods, `syncExec` or `asyncExec`. The `syncExec` method runs the code synchronously (the caller blocks until the code has been run) while the `asyncExec` method runs the code asynchronously (the caller continues while the code is run in the background).

The `Display` class is SWT's handle to a monitor (so a runtime may have more than one `Display` object, and each may have its own resolution). To get hold of an instance, call either `Display.getCurrent()` or `Display.getDefault()`. However, it's much better to get a `Display` from an associated view or widget. In this case, the `Canvas` has an associated `Display`.

1. Go to the `TickTock` thread inside the `createPartControl` method of the `ClockView` class.

2. Inside the `redraw` lambda, replace the call to `clock.redraw()` with this:

```
// clock.redraw();
clock.getDisplay().asyncExec(() -> clock.redraw());
```

3. Run the target Eclipse instance and show the **Clock View**. The second hand should now update automatically.

What just happened?

This time, the event will execute as expected. One thread (`TickTock`) is running in the background, and every second it posts a `Runnable` to the UI thread, which then runs asynchronously. This example could have used `syncExec` and the difference would not have been noticeable—but in general, using `asyncExec` should be preferred unless there is a specific reason to need the synchronous blocking behavior.

The thread is in a `while` loop and is guarded with a call to `clock.isDisposed()`. Each SWT widget can be disposed with a call to `dispose`. Once a widget is disposed, any native operating system resources are returned and any further operations will throw an exception. In this example, the `Canvas` is disposed when the view is closed, which in turn disposes any components contained. As a result, when the view is closed, the `Thread` automatically ceases its loop (the thread can also be aborted by interrupting it during its 1-second sleep pauses).

Time for action – creating a reusable widget

Although the `ClockView` shows a single animated clock, creating an independent widget will allow the clock to be reused in other places.

1. Create a new class in the `com.packtpub.e4.clock.ui` package, called `ClockWidget`, that extends `Canvas`.

2. Create a constructor that takes a `Composite` parent and an `int style` bits parameter, and pass them to the superclass:

```
public ClockWidget(Composite parent, int style) {
  super(parent, style);
}
```

3. Move the implementation of the `drawClock` method from the `ClockView` to the `ClockWidget`. Remove the `PaintListener` references from the `ClockView` class.

4. In the `ClockWidget` constructor, register a `PaintListener` that delegates the call to the `drawClock` method:

```
addPaintListener(this::drawClock);
```

5. Move the `TickTock` thread from the `ClockView` to the `ClockWidget` constructor; this will allow the `ClockWidget` to operate independently. Change any references for `clock` to this:

```
Runnable redraw = () -> {
  while (!this.isDisposed()) {
    this.getDisplay().asyncExec(() -> this.redraw());
    try {
      Thread.sleep(1000);
    } catch (InterruptedException e) {
      return;
    }
  }
}
new Thread(redraw, "TickTock").start();
```

6. Add a `computeSize` method to allow the clock to have a square appearance that is the minimum of the width and height. Note that `SWT.DEFAULT` may be passed in, which has the value `-1`, so this needs to be handled explicitly:

```
public Point computeSize(int w, int h, boolean changed) {
  int size;
  if (w == SWT.DEFAULT) {
    size = h;
  } else if (h == SWT.DEFAULT) {
    size = w;
  } else {
    size = Math.min(w, h);
  }
  if (size == SWT.DEFAULT) {
    size = 50;
  }
  return new Point(size, size);
}
```

7. Finally, change the `ClockView` to instantiate the `ClockWidget` instead of the `Canvas` in the `createPartControl` method:

```
new ClockWidget(parent, SWT.NONE);
```

8. Run the target Eclipse instance and the clock should be shown as earlier.

What just happened?

The drawing logic was moved into its own widget, and registered a `PaintListener` to a method in the `ClockWidget` to render itself. This allows the `Clock` to be used as a standalone in any Eclipse or SWT application.

In a real application, the clocks would not have their own thread; it would either be the case that a single `Thread` would control updates to all `Clock` instances, or they would be set up with repeating `Job` instances using the Eclipse jobs framework, which will be covered in *Chapter 4, Interacting with the User*.

The technique of using a method reference (or anonymous class) to bind a specific listener type to the instance of the class is a common pattern in SWT. When using inner classes, the convention is to use the same method name in the enclosing class; this helps to disambiguate the use.

 Remember to set the listener at startup, as otherwise it can be confusing as to why it's not getting called.

It's also possible for the `ClockWidget` to implement `PaintListener` directly; in this case, `addPaintListener(this)` would be called in the constructor. Modern JITs will optimize the calls to equivalent code paths in any case; it comes down to a style decision as to whether the `ClockWidget` class should implement the `PaintListener` interface or not.

Finally, the size can be computed based on the hints. This is called by the layout manager to determine what size the widget should be. For widgets with a fixed size (say, a text string or an image), the size can vary depending on the layout. In this case, it returns a square, based on the minimum size of the supplied width and height hints, or 50, whichever is bigger. The `SWT.DEFAULT` value is `-1`, which has to be dealt with specifically.

Time for action – using layouts

Now that the `ClockWidget` has been created, multiple instances can be added into the `ClockView`.

1. Modify the `createPartControl` method in the `ClockView` class to create three `ClockWidget` instances, and assign them to local variables:

```
final ClockWidget clock1 = new ClockWidget(parent, SWT.NONE);
final ClockWidget clock2 = new ClockWidget(parent, SWT.NONE);
final ClockWidget clock3 = new ClockWidget(parent, SWT.NONE);
```

2. Run the target Eclipse instance, and show the **Clock View**. Three clocks will be shown, counting in seconds:

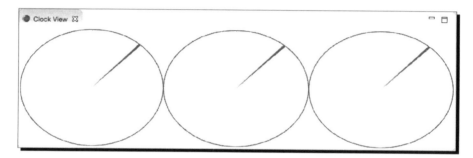

3. At the start of the `ClockView` class's `createPartControl` method, create a new `RowLayout` with `SWT.HORIZONTAL`, and then set it as the layout on the parent `Composite`:

```
public void createPartControl(Composite parent) {
   RowLayout layout = new RowLayout(SWT.HORIZONTAL);
   parent.setLayout(layout);
```

4. Run the code again now, and the clocks will be in a horizontal row:

5. Resize the view; the clocks will flow into different rows:

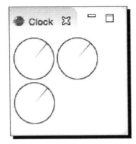

> The RowLayout has a number of fields that can affect how widgets are laid out:
>
>
>
> ◆ center: If components are centered (vertically or horizontally)
> ◆ fill: If the entire size of the parent should be taken up
> ◆ justify: If the components should be spaced so that they reach the end
> ◆ pack: If components should get their preferred size or be expanded to fill space
> ◆ wrap: If the components should wrap at the end of the line
>
> There are also options to control any pixel spacing between elements (spacing) and any margins at the edge (marginHeight and marginWidth, or ones that can be specified individually such as marginTop, marginBottom, marginLeft, and marginRight).

6. Every SWT widget has an optional layout data object, which is specific to the kind of layout being used by its containing parent. In the ClockView method createPartControl, add a RowData object to the clocks with a different size:

```
clock1.setLayoutData(new RowData(20,20));
clock2.setLayoutData(new RowData(50,50));
clock3.setLayoutData(new RowData(100,100));
```

7. Open the **Clock View**, and the clocks will be shown in increasing size:

What just happened?

A `Composite` is capable of handling multiple widgets, and the job of deciding where to put these components is performed by the associated `LayoutManager`. The standard layout managers include `FillLayout`, `RowLayout`, `GridLayout`, `FormLayout`, and `CellLayout`. The default for Eclipse views is to use a `FillLayout`, though a manually created `Composite` has no associated layout by default.

Both `FillLayout` and `RowLayout` create a horizontal or vertical set of widgets with controlled sizes. The `FillLayout` is the default for views and expands the size of the widgets to the space available. `RowLayout` will set the component's sizes to their default as calculated by `computeSize(0,0)`.

Layout managers have different properties, such as `SWT.HORIZONTAL` and `SWT.VERTICAL`, and to change how elements are wrapped if the row gets full. The documentation for each layout manager has information as to what it supports.

Layout data objects are used to specify different values for objects within the `Composite`. The preceding example looked at the `RowData` options.

The corresponding `FillData` class for the `FillLayout` has no public fields. Other layout managers such as `GridLayout` have more extensive customization options in the `GridData` class. Remember that when changing a `LayoutManager`, the associated layout data objects will need to be modified accordingly.

Pop quiz: understanding views

Q1. What is the parent class of any view in the Eclipse 3.x model?

Q2. How do you register views with the Eclipse workbench?

Q3. Which two arguments are passed into every SWT widget and what are they for?

Q4. What does it mean for a widget to be disposed?

Q5. How do you draw a circle on a `Canvas`?

Q6. What listener do you have to register to execute drawing operations?

Q7. What happens if you try and update an SWT object from outside a UI thread?

Q8. How do you update SWT components from a different thread?

Q9. What value is `SWT.DEFAULT` used for?

Q10. How do you specify a specific size for a widget in a `RowLayout`?

Have a go hero – drawing hour and minute hands

Now that the clock view is animating a second hand, do the same calculation for the hour and minute hands. Minutes will be calculated the same way as seconds; for hours, multiply the hours by 5 to map onto the same path.

Draw lines for every five minutes using the drawLine method. Some simple math will be required to calculate the start and end points of the line.

Finally, draw the text lettering for the numbers in the right locations. The drawText method can be used to place a string at a particular place. Use this to print out the current time in the center of the clock, or print out the date.

Managing resources

One of the challenges in adopting SWT is that native resources must be disposed when they are no longer needed. Unlike AWT or Swing, which perform these operations automatically when an object is garbage-collected, SWT needs manual resource management.

Why does SWT need manual resource management?

A common question asked is why SWT has this rule when Java has had perfectly acceptable garbage collection for many years. In part, it's because SWT pre-dates acceptable garbage collection, but it's also to try and return native resources as soon as they are no longer needed.

From a performance perspective, adding a finalize method to an object also causes the garbage collector to work harder; much of the speed in today's garbage collectors is because they don't need to call methods as they are invariably missing. It also hurts in SWT's case because the object must post its dispose request onto the UI thread, which delays its garbage collection until the object becomes reachable again.

Not all objects need to be disposed; in fact, there is an abstract class called Resource which is the parent of all resources that need disposal. It is this class that implements the dispose method, as well as the isDisposed call. Once a resource is disposed, subsequent calls to its methods will throw an exception with a **Widget is disposed** or **Graphic is disposed** message.

Further confusing matters, some Resource instances should not be disposed by the caller. Generally, instances owned by other classes in accessors should not be disposed; for example, the Color instance returned by the Display method getSystemColor is owned by the Display class, so it shouldn't be disposed by the caller. Resource objects that are instantiated by the caller must be disposed of explicitly.

Time for action – getting colorful

To add an option for the `ClockWidget` to have a different color, an instance must be obtained instead of the hardcoded `BLUE` reference. Since `Color` objects are `Resource` objects, they must be disposed correctly when the widget is disposed.

To avoid passing in a `Color` directly, the constructor will be changed to take an `RGB` value (which is three `int` values), and use that to instantiate a `Color` object to store for later. The lifetime of the `Color` instance can be tied to the lifetime of the `ClockWidget`.

1. Add a private final `Color` field called `color` to the `ClockWidget`:

```
private final Color color;
```

2. Modify the constructor of the `ClockWidget` to take an `RGB` instance, and use it to instantiate a `Color` object. Note that the color is leaked at this point, and will be fixed later:

```
public ClockWidget(Composite parent, int style, RGB rgb) {
    super(parent, style);
    // FIXME color is leaked!
    this.color = new Color(parent.getDisplay(), rgb);
    ...
```

3. Modify the `drawClock` method to use this custom color:

```
protected void drawClock(PaintEvent e) {
    ...
    e.gc.setBackground(color);
    e.gc.fillArc(e.x, e.y, e.width-1, e.height-1, arc-1, 2);
```

4. Finally, change the `ClockView` to instantiate the three clocks with different colors:

```
public void createPartControl(Composite parent) {
    ...
    final ClockWidget clock =
      new ClockWidget(parent, SWT.NONE, new RGB(255,0,0));
    final ClockWidget clock2 =
      new ClockWidget(parent, SWT.NONE, new RGB(0,255,0));
    final ClockWidget clock3 =
      new ClockWidget(parent, SWT.NONE, new RGB(0,0,255));
```

5. Now run the application and see the new colors in use:

What just happened?

The `Color` was created based on the red, green, blue value passed into the `ClockWidget` constructor. Since the `RGB` is just a value object (it isn't a `Resource`), it doesn't need to be disposed afterwards.

Once the `Color` is created, it is assigned to the instance field. When the clocks are drawn, the second hands are in the appropriate colors.

 One problem with this approach is that the `Color` instance is leaked. When the view is disposed, the associated `Color` instance is garbage-collected, but the resources associated with the native handle are not.

Time for action – finding the leak

It is necessary to know how many resources are allocated in order to know whether the leak has been plugged or not. Fortunately, SWT provides a mechanism to do this via the `Display` and the `DeviceData` class. Normally, this is done by a separate plug-in, but in this example, the `ClockView` will be modified to show this behavior.

1. At the start of the `ClockView` class's `createPartControl` method, add a call to obtain the number of allocated objects, via the `DeviceData` of the `Display` class:

```
public void createPartControl(Composite parent) {
    Object[] objects = parent.getDisplay().getDeviceData().objects;
```

2. Iterate through the allocated `objects`, counting how many are instances of `Color`:

```
int count = 0;
for (int i = 0; i < objects.length; i++) {
  if (objects[i] instanceof Color) {
    count++;
  }
}
```

3. Print the `count` to the standard error stream:

```
System.err.println("There are " + count + " Color instances");
```

4. Now run the code in debug mode and show the **Clock View**. The following lines will be displayed in the host Eclipse **Console View**:

```
There are 0 Color instances
There are 0 Color instances
There are 0 Color instances
```

> For efficiency, SWT doesn't log all the allocated resources all the time. Instead, it's an option that is enabled at startup through an `options` file, which is a text properties file with `name=value` pairs. This can be passed to an Eclipse instance at launch via the `-debug` flag. Fortunately, it is easy to set within Eclipse from the launch configuration's tracing tab.

5. Close the target Eclipse application, if it is running.

6. Go to the launch configuration via the **Debug | Debug Configurations** menu.

7. Select the **Eclipse Application** (if it's not selected already) and go to the **Tracing** tab. Enable the tracing option, and select the `org.eclipse.ui` plug-in. Select both the debug (at the top) and the trace/graphics options:

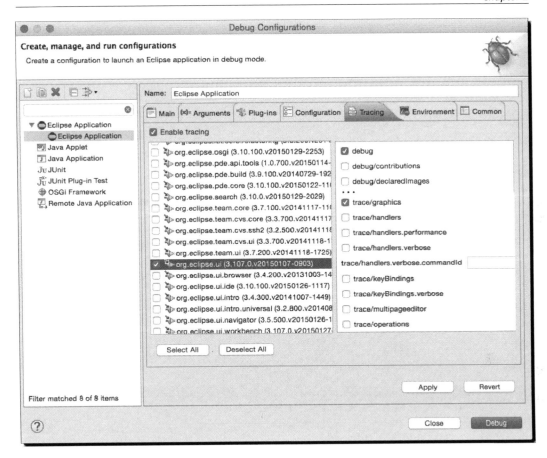

8. Now launch the application by hitting **Debug**, and open and close the `ClockView` a few times:

```
There are 87 Color instances
There are 92 Color instances
There are 95 Color instances
There are 98 Color instances
```

What just happened?

Clearly, something is leaking three `Color` instances each time the **Clock View** is opened. Not surprisingly, three instances of the `Color` are allocated in the three instances of `ClockWidget`. This suggests that there is a resource leak in the `ClockView` or `ClockWidget`.

When SWT is running in trace mode, it will keep a list of previously allocated resources in a global list, which is accessible through the `DeviceData` object. When the resource is disposed, it will be removed from the allocated list. This allows monitoring of the state of resources at play in the Eclipse workbench and discovering leaks, typically through repeated actions, noting an increase each time in the resource count.

Other object types are also stored in this list (for example, `Font` and `Image` instances), so it's important to filter by type when looking for a resource set. It's also important to note that Eclipse has its own runtime resources which are used, and so during tracing, these are included in the list as well.

By learning how to enable tracing and how to programmatically detect what objects are allocated, it will be possible to discover such leaks or check whether they have been fixed afterwards.

Time for action – plugging the leak

Now that the leak has been discovered, it needs to be fixed. The solution is to call `dispose` on the `Color` once the view itself is removed.

A quick investigation of the `ClockWidget` suggests that overriding `dispose` might work, though this is not the correct solution; see later for why.

1. Create a dispose method in `ClockWidget` with the following code:

    ```
    @Override
    public void dispose() {
      if (color != null && !color.isDisposed())
        color.dispose();
      super.dispose();
    }
    ```

2. Run the target Eclipse application in debug mode (with the tracing enabled, as before) and open and close the view. The output will show something like this:

    ```
    There are 87 Color instances
    There are 91 Color instances
    There are 94 Color instances
    There are 98 Color instances
    ```

3. Remove the `dispose` method (since it doesn't work as intended) and modify the constructor of the `ClockWidget` to add an anonymous `DisposeListener` that disposes of the associated `Color`:

    ```
    public ClockWidget(Composite parent, int style, RGB rgb) {
      super(parent, style);
    ```

```
        this.color = new Color(parent.getDisplay(), rgb);
        addDisposeListener(e -> color.dispose());
    }
```

4. Now run the code and see what happens when the view is opened and closed a few times:

```
There are 87 Color instances
There are 88 Color instances
There are 88 Color instances
There are 88 Color instances
```

5. The leak has been plugged.

What just happened?

Once the source of the leak has been identified, the correct course of action is to `dispose` the `Color` when no longer needed. However, although it is tempting to think that overriding the `dispose` method of the `ClockWidget` would be all that is needed, it doesn't work. The only time `dispose` is called is at the top level `Shell` (or `View`), and if there are no registered listeners, then the `dispose` method is not called on any components beneath. Since this can be quite counter-intuitive, it is of value to step through the code to verify that that is the behavior so that it can be avoided in the future.

Detecting and resolving resource leaks can be a time-consuming process. There are SWT Tools plug-ins developed by the SWT team that can perform a snapshot of resources and check whether there are any leaks using a similar technique. The plug-ins are located at the SWT tools update site (which are listed at `http://www.eclipse.org/swt/updatesite.php`) and can be installed to avoid having to modify code (for the purpose of monitoring allocated resources).

Don't forget when performing tests that the first one or two runs may give different results by virtue of the fact that other resources may be getting initialized at the time. Take a couple of readings first before relying on any data, and bear in mind that other plug-ins (which may be executing in the background) could be doing resource allocation at the same time.

Finally, when working with any SWT widget, it is good practice to check whether the resource is already disposed. The JavaDoc for the `dispose` method says that this is not strictly necessary, and that resources that are already disposed will treat this as a no-op method.

Pop quiz – understanding resources

Q1. Where do resource leaks come from?

Q2. What are the different types of `Resource` classes?

Q3. How can you enable SWT resource tracking?

Q4. Once enabled, how do you find out what objects are tracked?

Q5. What's the right way, and wrong way, to free resources after use?

Have a go hero

Now that the `ClockWidget` is running, try the following:

♦ Write a Sleak-like view that periodically counts allocated objects by type

♦ Modify any text written by acquiring a `Font` object, with disposal

♦ Create a generic dispose listener that takes an instance of `Resource`

♦ Provide a `setColor` method that allows you to change the color

Interacting with the user

The whole point of a user interface is to interact with the user. Having a view that displays information may be useful, but it is often necessary to ask the user for data or respond to user actions.

Time for action – getting in focus

To allow the time zone of the clock widgets to be changed, a drop-down box (known as `Combo`) as well as a `Button` will be added to the view. The `Combo` will be created from a set of `ZoneId` instances.

1. Create a `timeZones` field in the `ClockView` class:

```
private Combo timeZones;
```

2. At the end of the `createPartControl` method, add this snippet to create the drop-down list:

```
public void createPartControl(Composite parent) {
  ...
  timeZones = new Combo(parent, SWT.DROP_DOWN);
  timeZones.setVisibleItemCount(5);
```

```
for (String zone : ZoneId.getAvailableZoneIds()) {
    timeZones.add(zone);
}
}
```

3. Run the target Eclipse and open the **Clock View** again; a list of time zone names will be shown in a drop-down:

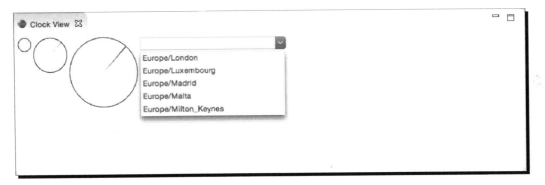

4. It's conventional to set the focus on a particular widget when a view is opened. Implement the appropriate call in the `ClockView` method `setFocus`:

```
public void setFocus() {
    timeZones.setFocus();
}
```

5. Run Eclipse and show the **Clock View**; the time zone drop-down widget will be focused automatically.

What just happened?

Every SWT `Control` has a `setFocus` method, which is used to switch focus for the application to that particular widget. When the view is focused (which happens both when it's opened and also when the user switches to it after being in a different view), its `setFocus` method is called.

 As will be discussed in *Chapter 7, Creating Eclipse 4 Applications*, in E4 the method may be called anything and annotated with the @Focus annotation. Conventionally, and to save sanity, it helps to call this method `setFocus`.

Time for action – responding to input

To show the effect of changing the `TimeZone`, it is necessary to add an hour hand to the clock. When the `TimeZone` is changed in the drop-down, the hour hand will be updated.

1. Add a `zone` field to the `ClockWidget` along with a setter:

```
private ZoneId zone = ZoneId.systemDefault();
public void setZone(ZoneId zone) {
  this.zone = zone;
}
```

2. Getters and setters can be generated automatically. Once the field is added, navigate to **Source | Generate Getters and Setters**. It can be used to generate all missing getters and/or setters; in addition, a single getter/setter can be generated by typing `set` in the class body, followed by *Ctrl* + Space (*Cmd* + Space on macOS).

3. Add an hour hand in the `drawClock` method using the following:

```
e.gc.setBackground(e.display.getSystemColor(SWT.COLOR_BLACK));
ZonedDateTime now = ZonedDateTime.now(zone);
int hours = now.getHour();
arc = (3 - hours) * 30 % 360;
e.gc.fillArc(e.x, e.y, e.width-1, e.height-1, arc - 5, 10);
```

4. To update the clock when the time zone is selected, register a `SelectionListener` on the `Combo` in the `createPartControl` method of the `ClockView` class:

```
timeZones.addSelectionListener(new SelectionListener() {
  public void widgetSelected(SelectionEvent e) {
    String id = timeZones.getText();
    clock3.setZone(ZoneId.of(id));
    clock3.redraw();
  }
  public void widgetDefaultSelected(SelectionEvent e) {
    clock3.setZone(ZoneId.systemDefault());
    clock3.redraw();
  }
});
```

5. Run the target Eclipse instance, and change the time zone. The updates should be drawn on the last clock instance:

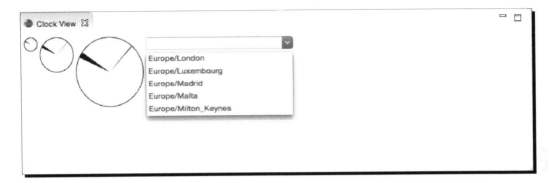

What just happened?

The `Combo` method `addSelectionListener` notifies any changes in the drop-down list. When a notification is received, the text from the `Combo` box is used to look up the corresponding time zone from the `ZoneId` class.

If the selection is not found or the default selection is chosen (in this case, the one with no value), then the offset is reset to the system time zone.

The clock's hour hand doesn't quite behave properly; typically, the hour hand is shorter than the second hand, and the hour hand jumps between hours instead of smoothly moving around as time progresses. Fixing this is left as an exercise for the reader.

To render the changes immediately, the clock is asked to redraw itself. This could be done inside the `ClockView` method `setZone`; but it would have to verify that it was done from the SWT thread, or arrange for it to be posted on the thread asynchronously. Instead, for convenience `clock3.redraw()` is done immediately after setting the offset while still inside the SWT thread.

Pop quiz: understanding widgets

Q1. How do you mark the default widget of a view?

Q2. How do you update a widget after modifying it?

Q3. What listener can you register with a `Combo`?

Q4. What's the purpose of the `widgetDefaultSelected` method?

Have a go hero – updating the clock widget

Now that the ClockWidget can handle time zones, do the following:

◆ Update the hour hand so that the position is calculated based on fractional hours

◆ Display the time zone underneath the clock face in the ClockWidget

◆ Show whether the time displayed is in summer or not

Using other SWT widgets

SWT contains many widgets other than Canvas, and this section covers some of them.
JFace will be covered in the next chapter, which provides a model-view-controller view for
designing GUIs, but it's helpful to know the base SWT classes upon which they are built.

Time for action – adding items to the tray

Most operating systems have a concept of tray, as a set of icons visible from the main
window that can provide quick access components. On macOS, these are represented as
icons across the top menu bar, and on Windows, as icons on the bottom-right near the
clock. Linux systems have various approaches that do similar things, and some operating
systems have none. Since there is only one tray, it is necessary to add the item only once.
The Activator class can be used to ensure that the TrayItem is created at startup and
removed at shutdown.

1. Open the Activator class, and add two private fields:

```
private TrayItem trayItem;
private Image image;
```

2. Add the following to the start method:

```
final Display display = Display.getDefault();
display.asyncExec(() -> {
  image = new Image(display,
  Activator.class.getResourceAsStream("/icons/sample.gif"));
  Tray tray = display.getSystemTray();
  if (tray != null && image != null) {
    trayItem = new TrayItem(tray, SWT.NONE);
    trayItem.setToolTipText("Hello World");
    trayItem.setVisible(true);
    trayItem.setText("Hello World");
    trayItem.setImage(image);
  }
});
```

3. Run the target Eclipse instance, and show the **Clock View**. The small `sample.gif` icon should appear in the task area (top right in macOS, bottom right in Windows).

4. To test the effect of stopping and restarting the bundle, open the **Console View** in the target Eclipse instance. Click on the drop-down on the top right of the view to create a **Host OSGi Console**:

```
WARNING: This console is connected to the current running instance
of Eclipse!
osgi>
"Framework is launched."
```

5. Type `ss clock` at the **osgi>** prompt and it will show a bundle ID, which can be used to start/stop:

```
osgi> ss clock

id  State       Bundle
4   RESOLVED    com.packtpub.e4.clock.ui_1.0.0.qualifier
```

6. Start and stop the bundle by typing `start` and `stop` into the console with the `ID` given the preceding output:

```
osgi> stop 4
osgi> start 4
osgi> stop 4
osgi> start 4
```

7. Notice that a new `TrayItem` appears in the `Tray` each time it is started. The clean routine needs to be added in the `Activator` method `stop`:

```
public void stop(BundleContext context) throws Exception {
  if (trayItem != null) {
    Display.getDefault().asyncExec(trayItem::dispose);
  }
  if (image != null) {
    Display.getDefault().asyncExec(image::dispose);
  }
}
```

8. Re-run the application and start and stop the bundle—the SWT tray icon should go and come back each time the bundle is stopped and started.

What just happened?

An SWT `TrayItem` is added to the system's `Tray` when the bundle is started and removed when the bundle is stopped. The icon that came with the sample project was used. To use a different one, don't forget to update the `build.properties` file.

Since the tray is a graphical component, if there's no image, then the item isn't shown. The tooltips are optional. Note also that not every system has the concept of a tray, so `null` is a legitimate return value for `display.getSystemTray()`.

A bundle is started automatically when it is loaded, and the loading is triggered by showing a view or selecting a menu item. If a view is opened, the bundle that class is loaded from is automatically started. Bundles can also be started and stopped programmatically, or through the **Host OSGi Console**, which is useful to test whether the `Activator` class's `start` and `stop` methods are working correctly.

Time for action – responding to the user

When the user clicks on the icon, nothing happens. That's because there is no registered listener on the `TrayItem` itself. There are two listeners that can be registered; a `SelectionListener`, called when the icon is clicked, and a `MenuDetectListener`, which can respond to a context-sensitive menu. The former will be used to present a clock in its own window, which in SWT terms is called a `Shell`.

1. Open the `Activator` class.

2. Go to the lambda inside the `asyncExec` in the `Activator` class's `start` method.

3. After the creation of the `TrayItem`, call `addSelectionListener` with a new anonymous inner subclass of `SelectionListener`. In the `widgetSelected` method, a new `Shell` should be created with a `ClockView` and then shown:

```
trayItem.addSelectionListener(new SelectionAdapter() {
  public void widgetSelected(SelectionEvent e) {
    Shell shell = new Shell(display);
    shell.setLayout(new FillLayout());
    new ClockWidget(shell, SWT.NONE, new RGB(255, 0, 255));
    shell.pack();
    shell.open();
  }
});
```

4. Run the target Eclipse instance, open the **Clock View**, and click on the tray icon. A windowed clock will be shown:

5. Run the target Eclipse instance, click on the `TrayItem`, and use the **Host OSGi Console** to stop and start the bundle.

What just happened?

When the `TrayItem` is installed into the system's `Tray`, event listeners can be registered to respond to user input. The listener that gets called when the icon is clicked on is the `SelectionListener`, and this gives the opportunity to display the window (or Shell in SWT terminology).

The `Display` associated with the `TrayItem` is used when instantiating the `Shell`. Although either `Display.getDefault()` or `Display.getCurrent()` could be used, neither of these would be the right option. When developers are running in multi-monitor mode, or with a virtual display (which spans multiple desktops), it's important to ensure that the `Shell` is shown on the same display as the corresponding `Tray`.

Without a `LayoutManager`, the clock won't show up. A `FillLayout` is used here to ensure that the clock is made as large as the window (and resizes accordingly to the window itself). Once the window is created, the `pack` method is called, which sets the size of the window to the preferred size of its children; in this case, it's the `ClockView`.

Finally, the window is shown with the `open` call. When the window is closed, it is automatically disposed.

Time for action – modal and other effects

There are a number of style bits that are applicable to windows, and some useful methods to affect how the window appears. For example, it might be desirable to make the clock appear semi-transparent, which allows the clock to float above other windows. SWT's `Shell` has a number of these options that can be set.

1. Modify the instantiation of the `Shell` inside the `widgetSelected` method in the `Activator` inner class to add `SWT.NO_TRIM` (no close/minimise/maximise widgets) and `SWT.ON_TOP` (floating on top of other windows):

```
shell = new Shell(trayItem.getDisplay(),
  SWT.NO_TRIM | SWT.ON_TOP);
```

2. Set the `alpha` value as `128`, which is semi-transparent:

```
shell.setAlpha(128);
```

3. Run the target Eclipse instance, and click on the `tray` item to see what kind of window is created.

4. To create a modal window (and thus, prevent interaction on the main window), change the flag to use `SWT.APPLICATION_MODAL`:

```
shell = new Shell(trayItem.getDisplay(), SWT.APPLICATION_MODAL);
```

5. To make the application full-screen, call either `setFullScreen` or the `setMaximized` depending on the platform:

```
shell.setFullScreen(true);
shell.setMaximized(true);
```

 Note that without trims, it may be necessary to add controls such as detecting selection events to close the window.

6. Run the target Eclipse application and see the effect these flags have on the window.

7. Change the `Shell` back to use `SWT.NO_TRIM` and `SWT.ON_TOP`.

8. To calculate a circular shape for the floating clock window, add the circle method to the `Activator` class, which has been taken from SWT's `Snippet134.java`, from `http://www.eclipse.org/swt/snippets/`:

```
private static int[] circle(int r, int offsetX, int offsetY) {
  int[] polygon = new int[8 * r + 4];
  // x^2 + y^2 = r^2
  for (int i = 0; i < 2 * r + 1; i++) {
    int x = i - r;
```

```
        int y = (int)Math.sqrt(r*r - x*x);
        polygon[2*i] = offsetX + x;
        polygon[2*i+1] = offsetY + y;
        polygon[8*r - 2*i - 2] = offsetX + x;
        polygon[8*r - 2*i - 1] = offsetY - y;
    }
    return polygon;
}
```

9. Finally, change the shape of the window to be circular by setting the `Region` of the `Shell`. This will have the effect of making it look as if the clock itself is floating. Add the following code after the `Shell` is created in the `widgetSelected` method:

```
final Region region = new Region();
region.add(circle(25, 25, 25));
shell.setRegion(region);
```

10. When run, the clock will look something like this:

11. For completeness, register a `dispose` listener on the shell to ensure that the `Region` is cleaned up:

```
shell.addDisposeListener(event -> region.dispose());
```

What just happened?

Changing the flags affects how that window is displayed and interacts with the user. Other calls on the shell can programmatically drive transitions to full-screen and maximized or minimized status, which can be useful in specific circumstances. Some windowing systems do not differentiate maximized and full-screen; others have distinct properties.

The `SWT.NO_TRIM` flag is used to display a window without the normal window furniture. This can be combined with setting a region via `setRegion`, which allows creation of a non-rectangular shape.

Often, windows without trim are floating—that is, they stay on top of the application window even when it hasn't got the focus. To achieve this, set the `SWT.ON_TOP` flag as well, and adjust the alpha (transparency) value with `setAlpha`. The `alpha` value is between `0` (fully transparent) and `255` (fully opaque).

A `Region` can be defined from a set of connected points, or set on a pixel-by-pixel basis. It's important to note that a `Region` is also a `Resource`, and thus it must be `disposed` after use (which is typically when the `Shell` is closed). The cleanup operation is similar to that of the others previously mentioned, via the `addDisposeListener` on the `Shell`.

Time for action – groups and tab folders

A new `TimeZoneView` will show a list of clocks in time zones around the world. This time, instead of using the plug-in wizard, the extension will be added manually.

> The way views are defined for E4 is covered in *Chapter 7, Creating Eclipse 4 Applications*. This chapter discusses how to do it in Eclipse 3.x and the Eclipse 3.x compatibility model of Eclipse 4.x.

1. Right-click on the project and navigate to **Plug-in Tools | Open Manifest**, or find the `plugin.xml` file in the navigator and double-click on it.

2. Go to the manifest editor's **Extensions** tab. The extensions will list `org.eclipse.ui.views`. Expand this, and underneath the **Timekeeping (category)** the **Clock View (view)** will be displayed, added via the plug-in wizard.

3. Right-click on **org.eclipse.ui.views** and navigate to **New | view** from the menu. A placeholder entry **name (view)** will be added to the list, and the right side lists properties such as the **id**, **name**, **class**, and **category**. Fill in the following:

    1. **ID:** `com.packtpub.e4.clock.ui.views.TimeZoneView`
    2. **Name:** `Time Zone View`
    3. **Class:** `com.packtpub.e4.clock.ui.views.TimeZoneView`
    4. **Category:** `com.packtpub.e4.clock.ui`
    5. **Icon:** `icons/sample.gif`

4. Save the file. This code will be added into the `plugin.xml` file:

```
<view
  category="com.packtpub.e4.clock.ui"
  class="com.packtpub.e4.clock.ui.views.TimeZoneView"
  icon="icons/sample.gif"
  id="com.packtpub.e4.clock.ui.views.TimeZoneView"
  name="Time Zone View"
  restorable="true">
</view>
```

5. Create the `TimeZoneView` class. The easiest way is to go to the **Extensions** tab of the `plugin.xml` file, select the **Time Zone View**, and click on the hyperlinked **class*** label next to the class name. Alternatively, navigate to **File | New | Class** wizard to create the `TimeZoneView` as a subclass of `ViewPart`, in the `com.packtpub.e4.clock.ui.views` package.

6. Create a class called `TimeZoneComparator`, which implements `Comparator`, in a new package `com.packtpub.e4.clock.ui.internal`. It is conventional to provide utility classes in an internal package to ensure that the implementation is not visible to others. The `compare` method should use the `Id` property of the `ZoneId` and use the String's `compareTo` method:

```
public class TimeZoneComparator implements Comparator<ZoneId> {
  public int compare(ZoneId o1, ZoneId o2) {
      return o1.getId().compareTo(o2.getId());
  }
}
```

7. Add a `public static` method to the `TimeZoneComparator` called `getTimeZones`, which will return a `Map` of `Set` instances containing `ZoneId` instances. The `Map` will be indexed by the region of the `ZoneId` (a `ZoneId` is something like `Europe/Milton_Keynes` or `America/New_York`). This will group all the European `ZoneId` instances together and all `ZoneId` instances in America together:

```
public static Map<String, Set<ZoneId>> getTimeZones(){
  Supplier<Set<ZoneId>> sortedZones = () ->
   new TreeSet<>(new TimeZoneComparator());
  return ZoneId.getAvailableZoneIds().stream() // stream
    .filter(s -> s.contains("/")) // with / in them
    .map(ZoneId::of) // convert String to ZoneId
    .collect(Collectors.groupingBy( // and group by
      z -> z.getId().split("/")[0],
      TreeMap::new, Collectors.toCollection(sortedZones)
    ));
}
```

8. In the `TimeZoneView` class's `createPartControl` method, create a `CTabFolder` and then iterate through the time zones, creating a `CTabItem` for each one:

```
public void createPartControl(Composite parent) {
  Map<String, Set<ZoneId>> timeZones =
   TimeZoneComparator.getTimeZones();
  CTabFolder tabs = new CTabFolder(parent, SWT.BOTTOM);
  timeZones.forEach((region, zones) -> {
    CTabItem item = new CTabItem(tabs, SWT.NONE);
```

```
            item.setText(region);
        }
        tabs.setSelection(0);
    }
```

9. Run this example, and show the **Time Zone View**; there should be a populated list of tabs along the bottom:

10. Inside the `while` loop, add a `Composite` to hold multiple `ClockWidget` instances for each `ZoneId` group:

```
item.setText(region); // from before
Composite clocks = new Composite(tabs, SWT.NONE);
clocks.setLayout(new RowLayout());
item.setControl(clocks);
```

11. Now iterate through the `ZoneId` instances, adding a `ClockWidget` for each:

```
RGB rgb = new RGB(128, 128, 128);
zones.forEach(zone -> {
    ClockWidget clock = new ClockWidget(clocks, SWT.NONE, rgb);
    clock.setZone(zone);
}
```

12. Run the target Eclipse instance and open the **Time Zone View** to see all the clocks:

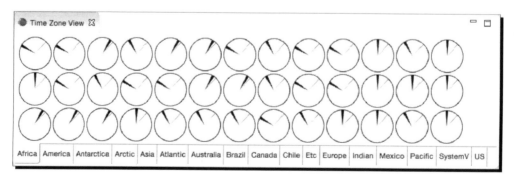

13. To make the clocks more identifiable, each will be put into a `Group` with an associated text label so that the view hierarchy goes from `CTabItem – Composite – ClockWidget` to `CTabItem – Composite – Group – ClockWidget`. Replace the call to create the the `ClockWidget` with this:

```
// ClockWidget clock = new ClockWidget(clocks, SWT.NONE, rgb);
Group group = new Group(clocks, SWT.SHADOW_ETCHED_IN);
group.setText(zone.getId().split("/")[1]);
ClockWidget clock = new ClockWidget(group, SWT.NONE, rgb);
```

14. Run it again, and a series of blank elements will be shown:

15. Since the default layout manager for `Composite` is `null`, `Group` instances don't have a layout manager—and so the clocks are not getting sized appropriately. This can be fixed by setting a layout manager explicitly:

```
group.setLayout(new FillLayout());
```

16. Run it again, and now it looks a little bit more sensible:

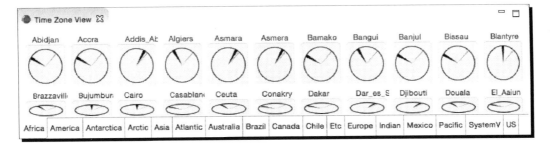

17. The clocks at the bottom are squashed and the view can't be scrolled even though there are clearly more time zones available. To add scrolling to a widget, the ScrolledComposite class can be used. This provides automatic scroll bars and interaction with the user to permit a much larger virtual area to be scrolled. The view hierarchy will change from CTabItem − Composite − Group − ClockWidget to CTabItem − ScrolledComposite − Composite − Group − ClockWidget instead:

```
// Composite clocks = new Composite(tabs, SWT.NONE);
// item.setControl(clocks);
ScrolledComposite scrolled = new
  ScrolledComposite(tabs, SWT.H_SCROLL | SWT.V_SCROLL);
Composite clocks = new Composite(scrolled, SWT.NONE);
item.setControl(scrolled);
scrolled.setContent(clocks);
clocks.setLayout(new RowLayout());
```

18. Run it again, but unfortunately this will be seen:

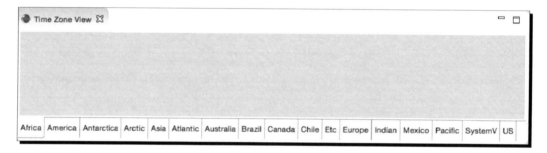

19. The problem is that ScrolledComposite has no minimum size. This can be calculated from the clocks container by adding this to the bottom of the while loop, after the contents of the ScrolledComposite have been created:

```
Point size = clocks.computeSize(SWT.DEFAULT, SWT.DEFAULT);
scrolled.setMinSize(size);
scrolled.setExpandHorizontal(true);
scrolled.setExpandVertical(true);
```

20. Run it again, and the clocks now show up as expected:

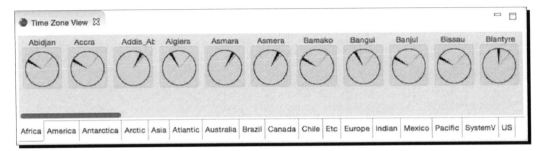

21. The `ScrolledComposite` has a different background. To change it, add this line after constructing the clock's `Composite`:

```
clocks.setBackground(clocks.getDisplay()
  .getSystemColor(SWT.COLOR_LIST_BACKGROUND));
```

22. Now the **Time Zone View** is complete:

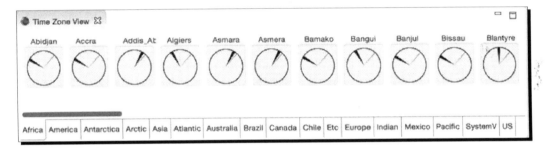

What just happened?

A combination of `Composite` types created a tabbed interface using `CTabFolder` and `CTabItem` instances. Inside each `CTabItem`, a `ScrolledComposite` contained a `Composite` of `Group` instances, each of which had a single `ClockWidget`. Adding the `ScrolledComposite` provided the scrolling for free, and the `Group` allowed us to place text above the `ClockWidget` to display its time zone.

Some of the components used here are in the `org.eclipse.swt.custom` package instead of the `org.eclipse.swt.widgets` package. Several of these begin with C as a custom designator to distinguish similarly named widgets. The `CTabFolder/Item` is an SWT-implemented class that provides the tab functionality; the corresponding OS widget, `TabFolder/Item`, uses a native rendered tab switcher.

Pop quiz: using SWT

Q1. How do you add an icon to the system menu?

Q2. What does the SWT.NO_TRIM style do for a Shell?

Q3. How do you make a Shell transparent?

Q4. What do you need to set to create a non-rectangular Shell?

Q5. What Composite allows you to attach a label to a set of related items?

Q6. What is the default layout manager for a Group?

Q7. How do you add scrolling to an existing widget?

Have a go hero: enhancing the time zones

A set of times are displayed in different time zones, but there is scope for enhancements:

◆ Switch to the tab with the user's default time zone when the view is created

◆ Sort the clocks by time zone offset rather than by the name of the region

◆ Create a favorites tab and allow it to be populated by drag-and-drop

◆ Improve the speed of updates by sharing a single Thread to update all clocks

◆ Improve the sizing of the ScrollableComposite so that more than one row is displayed

Summary

In this chapter, we covered how to create views with SWT widgets. We looked at both standard widget types as well as creating our own, and how those widgets can be assembled into groups with Composite and Layout classes. We also looked at how resources are managed within SWT, including following through the debug procedure for detecting and eliminating leaks.

In the next chapter, we will look at how to use a higher level of abstraction, JFace.

3
Creating JFace Viewers

JFace – the Eclipse model/view/controller architecture

In the last chapter, we looked at the basic building blocks of SWT, which provide a glue layer between the native operating system's widgets and Java. We will now look at JFace, which builds upon SWT to provide an MVC architecture as well as many of the common widgets used by Eclipse.

In this chapter, we shall:

- ◆ Create a view for showing hierarchical data
- ◆ Use image, font, and color resources
- ◆ Generate styled text
- ◆ Sort and filter entries in viewers
- ◆ Add double-click actions
- ◆ Create a view for showing tabular data
- ◆ Synchronize selections between views

Why JFace?

While SWT provides generic implementations for basic widgets (such as trees, buttons, labels, and so on), these often work at a level that deals with strings and responds to selection by integer index. To make it easier to display structured content, JFace provides several viewers that provide combinations of SWT widgets and event managers to provide a UI for structured content.

There are many types of viewer—which are all subclasses of `Viewer`—but the most common ones are `ContentViewer` subclasses such as `TreeViewer` and `TableViewer`. There are also text-based viewers such as `TextViewer` and `SourceViewer`, as well as operational views such as `DetailedProgressViewer` for the `Progress` view. In this chapter, we will create views based on `TreeViewer` and `TableViewer`. Since JFace is based on SWT (described in *Chapter 2, Creating Views with SWT*), knowing how SWT works is essential to understand how JFace is used.

Creating TreeViewers

Many views in Eclipse use a tree-like view, from a file navigator to the contents of source files. The JFace framework provides a `TreeViewer`, which provides the basic tree navigation functionality. This will be used to implement a `TimeZoneTreeView`.

Time for action – creating a tree viewer

As with the previous chapter, a new `TimeZoneTreeView` class will be created using the `plugin.xml` editor, as an E4 view. This will show time zones, organized hierarchically by region.

1. Right-click on the `com.packtpub.e4.clock.ui` project and navigate to **Plug-in Tools | Open Manifest** if it's not open already.

2. Open the **Extensions** tab and go to the `org.eclipse.ui.views` entry. Right-click on this, navigate to **New | e4view**, and fill in the following:

    1. **ID**: com.packtpub.e4.clock.ui.views.TimeZoneTreeView
    2. **Name**: Time Zone Tree View
    3. **Class**: com.packtpub.e4.clock.ui.views.TimeZoneTreeView
    4. **Category**: com.packtpub.e4.clock.ui
    5. **Icon**: icons/sample.gif

3. An entry is created in the `plugin.xml` file that looks like:

```
<e4view
   category="com.packtpub.e4.clock.ui"
   class="com.packtpub.e4.clock.ui.views.TimeZoneTreeView"
   icon="icons/sample.gif"
   id="com.packtpub.e4.clock.ui.views.TimeZoneTreeView"
   name="Time Zone Tree View"
   restorable="true">
</e4view>
```

4. On the **Dependencies** tab, click on **Add** in the **Imported Packages** section, and add the `org.eclipse.e4.ui.di` package, which adds the `@Focus` annotation used by E4 views. The `@Inject` and `@PostConstruct` annotations are re-exported from the `org.eclipse.ui` bundle.

5. Create a class called `TimeZoneTreeView` in the `com.packtpub.e4.clock.ui.views` package.

6. Add a `create` method taking a `Composite` parent and annotate it with `@PostConstruct`. Inside the method, create an instance of a `TreeViewer`, with the `H_SCROLL`, `V_SCROLL`, and `MULTI` flags set, and store it in a field `treeViewer`:

```
package com.packtpub.e4.clock.ui.views;
import javax.annotation.PostConstruct;
public class TimeZoneTreeView {
  private TreeViewer treeViewer;
  @PostConstruct
  public void create(Composite parent) {
    treeViewer = new TreeViewer(parent,
      SWT.H_SCROLL | SWT.V_SCROLL | SWT.MULTI );
  }
}
```

7. Run the Eclipse application, and show the view by navigating to **Window | Show View | Timekeeping | Time Zone Tree View**:

8. Unlike Swing, which expects data to be presented in a specific interface, the JFace viewers don't expect any specific data class. Instead, they expect an object value to display (the input), an interface that can read that data (the content provider), and an interface for displaying that data (the label provider).

9. Create a new class called `TimeZoneLabelProvider`, which extends `LabelProvider` (from the `org.eclipse.jface.viewers` package). This has a method called `getText`, which is passed an object and translates that into a textual representation. Instead of a `toString` call here, return an appropriate value for a `Map.Entry` or a `ZoneId`:

```
public class TimeZoneLabelProvider extends LabelProvider {
  @SuppressWarnings("rawtypes")
  public String getText(Object element) {
    if (element instanceof Map) {
      return "Time Zones";
    } else if (element instanceof Map.Entry) {
      return ((Map.Entry) element).getKey().toString();
    } else if (element instanceof ZoneId) {
      return ((ZoneId) element).getId().split("/")[1];
    } else {
      return "Unknown type: " + element.getClass();
    }
  }
}
```

10. Since a `TreeViewer` can have multiple roots, the `instanceof Map` test is used to represent the top of the tree, called **Time Zones**.

 It's usually a good idea to have a default value—even if it's only an empty string—so that when an unexpected value type is seen in the list, it can be recognized and debugged.

11. Create a new class `TimeZoneContentProvider`, which implements the `ITreeContentProvider` interface. This requires the implementation of three of the six methods as follows, leaving the other three empty:

- `hasChildren`: Returns true if the node has children
- `getChildren`: Provides the children of a given node
- `getElements`: Provides the top-level roots

12. The `hasChildren` method will return `true` if passed a non-empty `Map` or `Collection`; otherwise, recurse into the `Map.Entry` value:

```
@SuppressWarnings("rawtypes")
public boolean hasChildren(Object element) {
  if (element instanceof Map) {
    return !((Map) element).isEmpty();
  } else if (element instanceof Map.Entry) {
    return hasChildren(((Map.Entry)element).getValue());
```

```
    } else if (element instanceof Collection) {
      return !((Collection) element).isEmpty();
    } else {
      return false;
    }
  }
```

13. The `getChildren` implementation recurses into a `Map`, `Map.Entry`, or
`Collection` following the same pattern. Since the return of this function is an
`Object[]`, the `entrySet` method in the `Map` class can be used to convert the
contents to an array:

```
@SuppressWarnings("rawtypes")
public Object[] getChildren(Object parentElement) {
  if (parentElement instanceof Map) {
    return ((Map) parentElement).entrySet().toArray();
  } else if (parentElement instanceof Map.Entry) {
      return
      getChildren(((Map.Entry)parentElement).getValue());
  } else if (parentElement instanceof Collection) {
      return ((Collection) parentElement).toArray();
  } else {
    return new Object[0];
  }
}
```

> The key to implementing an `ITreeContentProvider` is to
> remember to keep the implementation of the `getChildren`
> and `hasChildren` methods in sync. One way of doing this is
> to implement the `hasChildren` method as testing whether
> `getChildren` returns an empty array, but this may not be
> performant if `getChildren` is an expensive operation.

14. Since a `TreeViewer` can have multiple roots, there is a method to get the array of
roots from the input element object. A bug in the JFace framework prevents the
`getElements` argument containing its own value; it is therefore conventional to
pass in an array (containing a single element) and return it:

```
public Object[] getElements(Object inputElement) {
  if (inputElement instanceof Object[]) {
    return (Object[]) inputElement;
  } else {
    return new Object[0];
  }
}
```

15. Now that the provider methods are implemented, connect the providers to the viewer and set the input data object in the `create` method of the `TimeZoneTreeView` class:

```
treeViewer.setLabelProvider(new TimeZoneLabelProvider());
treeViewer.setContentProvider(new TimeZoneContentProvider());
treeViewer.setInput(new Object[]
   {TimeZoneComparator.getTimeZones()});
```

16. Run the Eclipse instance, open the view by navigating to **Window | Show View | Timekeeping | Time Zone Tree View**, and see the results:

17. Optionally, create a `focus` method with a `@Focus` annotation, which sets the focus on the viewer's `control`. The `@Focus` annotation needs to be imported from the `org.eclipse.e4.ui.di` package:

```
import org.eclipse.e4.ui.di.Focus;
...
@Focus
public void focus() {
   treeViewer.getControl().setFocus();
}
```

18. Run the Eclipse instance again, and now when the view is opened, the tree viewer will have the focus.

What just happened?

The data for `TreeViewer` was provided by the `setInput` method, which is almost always an array of objects containing a single element.

To traverse the data structure, the `ITreeContentProvider` interface provides two key methods: `hasChildren` and `getChildren`. These methods allow the data structure to be interrogated on demand as the user opens and closes nodes in the tree. The rationale for having two separate methods is that the calculation for `getChildren` may be expensive; so the `hasChildren` call is used to display the expandable icon on the node, but the `getChildren` call is deferred until the user opens that specific node in the tree.

 For data structures that support it, implement the `getParent` method as well; this makes accessing (or revealing) the object possible. When this method is implemented, `viewer.reveal(Object)` will expand the nodes in the hierarchy to reveal that particular object.

To render the labels in the tree, a `LabelProvider` is used. This provides a label (and optional image) for each element. It is possible to present a different icon for each type of object; this is used by the **Package View** in the **Java** perspective to present a class icon for the classes, a package icon for the packages, and so on.

The `LabelProvider` can render the text in different ways; for example, it could append the `timezone` offset or only show the difference between that and GMT.

Time for action – using Images in JFace

The `TimeZoneLabelProvider` can return an SWT `Image`. Although they can be loaded dynamically as in the previous chapter, JFace provides a number of resource registries that can be used to manage a set of resources for the application. Standard registries include the `ImageRegistry`, `FontRegistry`, and `ColorRegistry` classes. The purpose of a resource registry is to maintain a list of `Resource` instances and ensure that they are correctly disposed when they are no longer needed.

JFace has a set of these global registries; but there are specific ones, for example, those used by the IDE to maintain folder and file type icons. These use resource descriptors as a lightweight handle for the resource, and a means to acquire an instance of the resource based on that descriptor. The returned resource is owned by the registry, and as such, should not be disposed by clients that acquire or use them.

Standard images can be acquired by injecting an `ISharedImages` instance from the `org.eclipse.ui` package.

1. In the `TimeZoneTreeView` class, add an injected field of type `ISharedImages`:

```
@Inject
private ISharedImages images;
```

2. Update the call in the `create` method where the `TimeZoneLabelProvider` is instantiated to pass the shared images as an argument:

```
treeViewer.setLabelProvider(new TimeZoneLabelProvider(images));
```

3. In the `TimeZoneLabelProvider` class, create a constructor that takes the `ISharedImages` instance and save it as a `private final` field:

```
private final ISharedImages images;
public TimeZoneLabelProvider(ISharedImages images) {
  this.images = images;
}
```

4. Add a method called `getImage` that uses the `images` to provide the folder icon:

```
public Image getImage(Object element) {
  if (element instanceof Map.Entry) {
    return images.getImage(ISharedImages.IMG_OBJ_FOLDER);
  } else {
    return super.getImage(element);
  }
}
```

5. Run the Eclipse instance, and open the **Time Zone Tree View**. A folder icon will be shown for each of the time zones in the view. The `Image` doesn't need to be disposed because it's owned by the provider of the `ISharedImages` instance (the images are disposed when the `PlatformUI` shuts down):

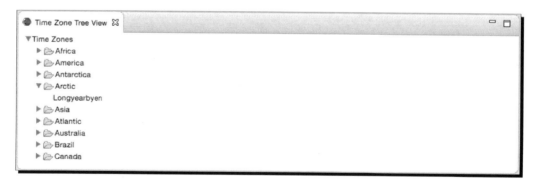

6. To use a different image, either the global `ImageRegistry` from `JFaceRegistry` can be used, or one can be created. Although using the global one will work, it means that effectively the `Image` never gets disposed, since the `JFaceRegistry` will last for the lifetime of the Eclipse instance.

Instead, create a `LocalResourceManager` instance based on the `JFaceResources` resource manager, which is tied to the lifetime of the parent. When the `parent` control is disposed, the images will be disposed automatically. These should be added to the `create` method of `TimeZoneTreeView`:

```
public void create(Composite parent) {
   ResourceManager rm = JFaceResources.getResources();
   LocalResourceManager lrm = new LocalResourceManager(rm, parent);
```

7. Using the `LocalResourceManger`, create an `ImageRegistry` and add an `ImageDescriptor` from a URL using the `createFromURL` method:

```
ImageRegistry ir = new ImageRegistry(lrm);
URL sample = getClass().getResource("/icons/sample.gif");
ir.put("sample", ImageDescriptor.createFromURL(sample));
```

8. Now that the `ImageRegistry` is populated, it must be connected up to the `LabelProvider` so that it can show the right image on demand. Pass the image registry into the constructor of the `TimeZoneLabelProvider`:

```
treeViewer.setLabelProvider(new TimeZoneLabelProvider(images,
ir));
```

9. Modify the constructor in the `TimeZoneLabelProvider` to store the `ImageRegistry`, and use it to acquire the image in the `getImage` call:

```
private final ImageRegistry images:
private final ImageRegistry ir;
public TimeZoneLabelProvider(ISharedImages images, ImageRegistry
ir) {
   this.ir = ir;
}
public Image getImage(Object element) {
   if (element instanceof Map.Entry) {
     return images.getImage(ISharedImages.IMG_OBJ_FOLDER);
   } else if (element instanceof ZoneId) {
     return ir.get("sample");
   } else {
     return super.getImage(element);
   }
}
```

10. Now, when opening the view, the sample `gif` is used as a zone icon:

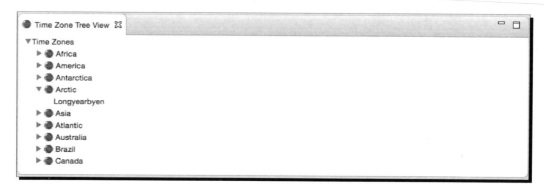

What just happened?

To start with, standard images (injected from the `PlatformUI` plug-in) were used, with pre-defined descriptors from `ISharedImages`. The names of the descriptors begin with `IMG`, and then follow a pre-defined pattern:

- ◆ `etool`: Enabled toolbar icons
- ◆ `dtool`: Disabled toolbar icons
- ◆ `elcl`: Enabled local toolbar icons
- ◆ `dlcl`: Disabled local toolbar icons
- ◆ `dec`: Decorator
- ◆ `obj` and `objs`: Objects such as file and folder icons

The `ISharedImages` instance was injected into the part since the `@Inject` annotation was present on the field. When E4 instantiates the view, it ensures that all the `@Inject` dependencies are satisfied.

What is injection?

JSR 330 standardized dependency injection annotations in the `javax.inject` package, the most common of which is `@Inject`. Dependency injection systems provide a *Don't call us, we'll call you* approach to wiring together dependent components, and this separates the component's implementation from knowing how to satisfy its own dependencies.

By annotating a field or method with `@Inject`, when the class is instantiated by the dependency injection framework (E4 in this case), it will try and satisfy all the required dependencies (since this is achieved with introspection, the fields don't have to be exposed with setters or getters). It is the job of the dependency injection framework to know how to acquire or create the required dependencies; all the client code is concerned with is that there is a dependency injected into the code.

The net effect in this case is that when the `TimeZoneTreeViewer` is instantiated, the dependency injection mechanism will automatically insert an appropriate `ISharedImages` instance that has been acquired from elsewhere.

To use custom images instead, an `ImageRegistry` was created, backed by a `LocalResourceManager`. When a `Control` is passed into the constructor, it registers itself as a `DisposeListener`—so that when the control is disposed, so are the associated images. This also makes the code cleaner, because the `ImageRegistry` can be passed into the `TimeZoneContentProvider`.

Finally, the `ImageRegistry` was initialized with a set of `ImageDescriptor` objects—in this case, the `icons/sample.gif` that came from the new plug-in project wizard. The same key is used when both initializing and accessing the image. Some Eclipse projects follow a convention of having an `ISharedImages` interface with a set of constants. Other plug-ins have a similar set of images, such as JDT UI, which adds icons for packages, classes, methods, and fields.

Time for action – styling label providers

The `IStyledLabelProvider` is used to style the representation of the tree viewer, as used by the Java outline viewer to display the return type of the method, and by the team's decorator when showing when changes have occurred.

1. Add the `IStyledLabelProvider` interface to the `TimeZoneLabelProvider` class, and create the `getStyledText` method. If the selected element is a `Map.Entry` that contains a `ZoneId`, add the offset afterwards in brackets:

```
public class TimeZoneLabelProvider extends LabelProvider
  implements IStyledLabelProvider {
    public StyledString getStyledText(Object element) {
      String text = getText(element);
      StyledString styledString = new StyledString(text);
      if (element instanceof ZoneId) {
        ZoneId zone = (ZoneId)element;
        ZoneOffset offset = ZonedDateTime.now(zone).getOffset();
        styledString.append(" (" + offset + ")",
          StyledString.DECORATIONS_STYLER);
      }
      return styledString;
    }
}
```

2. In order to use the styled label provider, it has to be wrapped within a `DelegatingStyledCellLabelProvider`. Modify the constructor, called from the create method of `TimeZoneTreeView`, as follows:

```
treeViewer.setLabelProvider(
  new DelegatingStyledCellLabelProvider(
    new TimeZoneLabelProvider(ir)));
```

3. Run the Eclipse instance, open the **Time Zone Tree View**, and the offset should be shown, displayed in a different color:

4. To change the `Font` used by the view, the `TimeZoneLabelProvider` needs to implement the `IFontProvider` interface. JFace's `FontRegistry` can be used to return an italicized version of the default font. Add a `FontRegistry` parameter to the `TimeZoneLabelProvider` constructor, and implement the `getFont` method as follows:

```
public class TimeZoneLabelProvider extends LabelProvider
  implements IStyledLabelProvider, IFontProvider {
    private final ImageRegistry ir;
    private final FontRegistry fr;
    public TimeZoneLabelProvider(ImageRegistry ir, FontRegistry fr){
       this.ir = ir;
       this.fr = fr;
    }
    public Font getFont(Object element) {
       Font italic = fr.getItalic(JFaceResources.DEFAULT_FONT);
       return italic;
    }
    // as before
}
```

5. Modify the `TimeZoneTreeView` to instantiate and pass in the global `FontRegistry` from the `JFaceResources` class:

```
// treeViewer.setLabelProvider(
//   new DelegatingStyledCellLabelProvider(
//    new TimeZoneLabelProvider(ir)));
FontRegistry fr = JFaceResources.getFontRegistry();
treeViewer.setLabelProvider(
 new DelegatingStyledCellLabelProvider(
  new TimeZoneLabelProvider(ir, fr)));
```

6. Run the Eclipse instance again, and now the time zones should be shown in an italic font.

What just happened?

By implementing the `IStyledLabelProvider` interface and wrapping it with a `DelegatingStyledCellLabelProvider` class, the style of the individual elements in the tree can be controlled, including any additions or style/colors of the item. The `StyledText` can render the string in different styles.

Although `DecorationsStyler` was used here, additional styles can be defined with the `createColorRegistryStyler` method of the `StyledString` class where the two arguments are keys in the global JFace `ColorRegistry`.

While colors can be changed on a character-by-character basis, the `Font` is shared for the entire string. That's because when the label is calculated, its size is calculated based on the assumption that the string is displayed in a single `Font`.

It's generally good programming practice to have the content or label providers use resource managers that are passed in at construction time. That way, the code can be tested using automated tests or other mock resources. Whether using the Eclipse 3.x or the Eclipse 4.x programming model, decoupling where the resources come from is key to testing.

Pop quiz – understanding JFace

Q1. What methods are present on `LabelProvider`?

Q2. What is the difference between the `hasChildren` and `getChildren` methods on the `ContentProvider` class?

Q3. What is an `ImageRegistry` used for?

Q4. How do you style entries in a `TreeView`?

Have a go hero – adding images for regions

Now that the basics have been covered, try extending the example as follows:

- Update the plug-in with a number of flag icons, and then create entries for the image registry. (The name of the time zone can be used for the key, which will make accessing it easier.)
- Display the name of the region in italics, but the time zones themselves in bold font.

Sorting and filtering

One of the features of JFace is that ordering of the data can be processed by the view, rather than having the data pre-processed. This makes it easy to present sorted or filtered views, where the user either searches for a particular term, or performs a sort in a different manner. These filters are used heavily in the Eclipse IDE, where options such as **Hide libraries from external** and **Hide closed projects** can be found in many of the drop-down actions for the view.

Time for action – sorting items in a viewer

The `TreeViewer` already shows data in a sorted list, but this is not a view-imposed sort. Because the data is stored in a `TreeMap`, the sort ordering is created by the `TreeMap` itself, which in turn is sorting on the value of the `toString` method. To use a different ordering (say, based on the timezone offset) the choices are either to modify the `TreeMap` to add a `Comparator` and sort the data at creation time, or add a sorter to the `TreeViewer`. The first choice is applicable if the data is only used by a single view, or if the data is coming from a large external data store which can perform the sorting more efficiently (such as a relational database). For smaller data sets, the sorting can be done in the viewer itself.

1. JFace structured viewers allow view-specific sorting with the `ViewerComparator`. Create a new subclass called `TimeZoneViewerComparator` in the `com.packtpub.e4.clock.ui.internal` package, and implement the `compare` method as follows:

```
public class TimeZoneViewerComparator extends ViewerComparator {
  public int compare(Viewer viewer, Object z1, Object z2) {
    int compare;
    if (z1 instanceof ZoneId && z2 instanceof ZoneId) {
      Instant now = Instant.now();
      ZonedDateTime zdt1 = ZonedDateTime.ofInstant(now,(ZoneId)z1);
      ZonedDateTime zdt2 = ZonedDateTime.ofInstant(now,(ZoneId)z2);
      compare = zdt1.compareTo(zdt2);
    } else {
      compare = o1.toString().compareTo(o2.toString());
    }
    return compare;
  }
}
```

2. Set the comparator on the `treeViewer` in the `TimeZoneTreeView` as follows:

```
treeViewer.setComparator(new TimeZoneViewerComparator());
```

3. Run the Eclipse instance, open the **Time Zone Tree View**, and the time zones should be sorted first by offset, then alphabetically:

4. To add a viewer-specific sort, modify the compare method of the `TimeZoneViewerComparator` class to get a REVERSE key from the viewer's data. Use it to invert the results of the sort:

```
// return compare;
boolean reverse = Boolean.parseBoolean(
  String.valueOf(viewer.getData("REVERSE")));
  return reverse ? -compare : compare;
```

5. To see the effect of this sort, set the REVERSE key just before the `setComparator()` call at the end of the create method of `TimeZoneTreeView`:

```
treeViewer.setData("REVERSE", Boolean.TRUE);
treeViewer.setComparator(new TimeZoneViewerComparator());
```

6. Re-launch the Eclipse instance, and the view should be in the reverse order.

What just happened?

By adding the `TimeZoneViewerComparator` to the `TimeZoneTreeViewer`, data can be sorted in an appropriate manner for the viewer in question. Typically this will be done in conjunction with selecting an option in the view—for example, an option may be present to reverse the ordering, or to sort by name or offset.

 When implementing a specific `Comparator`, check that the method can handle multiple object types (including ones that may not be expected). The data in the viewer may change, or be different at run-time than expected. Use `instanceof` to check that the items are of the expected type.

To store properties that are specific to a viewer, use the `setData` and `getData` calls on the viewer itself. This allows a generic comparator to be used across views while still respecting per view filtration/sorting operations.

The preceding example hard-codes the sort data, which requires an Eclipse re-launch to see the effect. Typically after modifying properties that may affect the view's sorting or filtering, refresh is invoked on the viewer to bring the display in line with the new settings.

Time for action – filtering items in a viewer

Another common feature of viewers is filtering. This is used both when performing a manual search, as well as for filtering specific aspects from a view. Quite often, the filtering is connected to the view's menu, which is the drop-down triangle on the top right of the view, using a common name such as **Filters**. The `ViewerFilter` class provides a filtering method, confusingly called `select` (there are some filter methods, but these are used to filter the entire array; the **select** is used to determine if a specific element is shown or not).

1. Create a class `TimeZoneViewerFilter` in the `com.packtpub.e4.clock.ui.internal` package, which extends `ViewerFilter`. It should take a `String` pattern in the constructor, and return `true` if the element is a `TimeZone` with that pattern in its display name:

```
public class TimeZoneViewerFilter extends ViewerFilter {
  private String pattern;
  public TimeZoneViewerFilter(String pattern) {
    this.pattern = pattern;
  }
  public boolean select(Viewer v, Object parent, Object element) {
    if (element instanceof ZoneId) {
      ZoneId zone = (ZoneId) element;
      String displayName = zone.getDisplayName(
       TextStyle.FULL,
       Locale.getDefault());
      return displayName.contains(pattern);
    } else {
      return true;
    }
  }
}
```

2. Since views can have multiple filters, the `TimeZoneViewerFilter` is set as a single element array on the corresponding viewer. The pattern to filter is passed in to the constructor in this case, but would normally be taken from the user. Modify the `TimeZoneTreeView` class at the bottom of the `create` method:

```
treeViewer.setFilters(new ViewerFilter[] {
    new TimeZoneViewerFilter("GMT")});
```

3. To remove the triangular expand icon next to the tree items with no children, the `TreeViewer` can be configured to expand nodes automatically:

```
treeViewer.setExpandPreCheckFilters(true);
```

4. Now run the Eclipse instance and open the **Time Zone Tree View**. Only time zones in the **Etc** region are listed:

What just happened?

The filter class was created as a subclass of `ViewerFilter` and set on the `TreeViewer`. When displaying and filtering the data, the filter is called for every element in the tree including the root node.

By default, if the `hasChildren` method returns `true`, the expandable icon is shown. When clicked, it will iterate through the children, applying the filter to them. If all the elements are filtered, the expandable marker will be removed and display no children.

By calling `setExpandPreCheckFilters(true)` on the viewer, it will verify that at least one child is left after filtration. This has no negative effect when there aren't any filters set. If there are filters set and there are large data sets, it may take some time to perform the calculation of whether they should be filtered or not.

To show all the tree's elements by default, or collapse it down to a single tree, use the `expandAll` and `collapseAll` methods on the viewer. This is typically bound to a local view command with a [+] and [-] icon (for example the **Synchronize** or the **Package Explorer** views).

If the data is a tree structure which only needs to show up to a specific level by default, there are `expandToLevel` and `collapseToLevel` methods, which take an integer and an object (use the `getRoot` of the tree if not specified) and mark everything as expanded or collapsed to that level. The `expandAll` method is a short-hand for `expandToLevel(getRoot(),` `ALL_LEVELS)`.

When responding to a selection event which contains a hidden object, it is conventional to perform a `reveal()` on the object to make it visible in the tree. Note that `reveal()` only works when the `getParent()` is correctly implemented, which isn't in this example.

Pop quiz – understanding sorting and filters

Q1. How can elements of a tree be sorted in an order which isn't its default?

Q2. What method is used to filter elements?

Q3. How can multiple filters be combined?

Have a go hero – expanding and filtering

Now that views can be sorted and filtered, try the following:

- Add a second filter which removes all `ZoneId` objects that have a negative offset.
- When the view is opened, perform an `expandAll` of the elements.
- Provide a sort that sorts the regions in reverse order but the time zones in ascending order.
- Provide a dialog which can be used to update the filter, and use the empty string which can be used to reset the filter.

Interaction

Being able to display data is one thing, but invariably views need to be interactive. Whether that's hooking up the sort or filter functionality from the previous chapter, or seeing information about the selected item, views must be interactive not only for exploring data, but also for working with data.

Time for action – adding a double-click listener

Typically, a tree view is used to show content in a hierarchical manner. However, a tree on its own is not enough to be able to show all the details associated with an object. When the user double-clicks on an element, more details can be shown.

1. At the end of the create method in `TimeZoneTreeView`, register a lambda block that implements the `IDoubleClickListener` interface with the `addDoubleClickListener` method on the `treeViewer`. As with the example in *Chapter 1, Creating Your First Plug-in*, this will open a message dialog to verify that it works as expected:

```
treeViewer.addDoubleClickListener(event -> {
    Viewer viewer = event.getViewer();
    Shell shell = viewer.getControl().getShell();
    MessageDialog.openInformation(shell, "Double click",
      "Double click detected");
});
```

2. Run the target Eclipse instance, and open the **Time Zone Tree View**. Double-click on the tree, and a shell will be displayed with the message **Double click detected**. The dialog is modal and prevents other components in the user interface from being selected until it is dismissed.

3. To find the selected objects, a viewer returns an `ISelection` interface (which only provides an `isEmpty` method) and an `IStructuredSelection` (which provides an iterator and other accessor methods). There are also a couple of specialized subtypes, such as `ITreeSelection`, which can be interrogated for the path that led to the selection in the tree. In the `create` method of the `TimeZoneTreeView` class, where the `doubleClick` method of the `DoubleClickListener` lambda is present, replace the `MessageDialog` as follows:

```
// MessageDialog.openInformation(shell, "Double click",
//   "Double click detected");
ISelection sel = viewer.getSelection();
Object selectedValue;
if (!(sel instanceof IStructuredSelection) || sel.isEmpty()) {
  selectedValue = null;
} else {
  selectedValue = ((IStructuredSelection)sel).getFirstElement();
}
if (selectedValue instanceof ZoneId) {
  ZoneId timeZone = (ZoneId)selectedValue;
  MessageDialog.openInformation(shell, timeZone.getId(),
    timeZone.toString());
}
```

4. Run the Eclipse instance, and open the **Time Zone Tree View**. Double-click on the tree, and a shell will be displayed with the `ZoneId` string representation.

5. To display more information about the `ZoneId` in the displayed window, create a subclass of `MessageDialog` called `TimeZoneDialog` in the `com.packtpub.e4.clock.ui.internal` package:

```
public class TimeZoneDialog extends MessageDialog {
  private ZoneId timeZone;
  public TimeZoneDialog(Shell parentShell, ZoneId timeZone) {
    super(parentShell, timeZone.getId(), null, "Time Zone "
    + timeZone.getId(), INFORMATION,
    new String[] { IDialogConstants.OK_LABEL }, 0);
    this.timeZone = timeZone;
  }
}
```

6. The `TimeZoneDialog` content is created in the `createCustomArea` method, which can be implemented as follows:

```
protected Control createCustomArea(Composite parent) {
  ClockWidget clock =
   new ClockWidget(parent,SWT.NONE, new RGB(128,255,0));
  return parent;
}
```

7. Finally, change the `TimeZoneTreeView` call to `MessageDialog.open()` to use the `TimeZoneDialog` instead:

```
if (selectedValue instanceof ZoneId) {
  ZoneId timeZone = (ZoneId) selectedValue;
  // MessageDialog.openInformation(shell, timeZone.getID(),
  // timeZone.toString());
  new TimeZoneDialog(shell, timeZone).open();
}
```

8. Run the Eclipse instance, double-click on a time zone, and the dialog should appear:

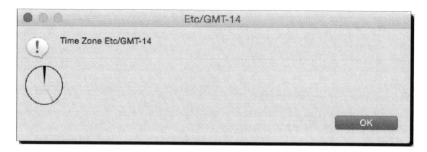

What just happened?

A double-click listener was added to the viewer by registering it with
addDoubleClickListener. Initially, a standard information dialog was displayed; but
then a custom subclass of MessageDialog was used which included a ClockWidget.
In order to get the appropriate ZoneId, it was accessed via the currently selected object
from the TreeViewer.

Selection handled by viewers is managed through an ISelection interface. The viewer's
getSelection method should always return a non-null value, although it may be isEmpty.
There are two relevant sub-interfaces: IStructuredSelection and ITreeSelection.

The ITreeSelection interface is a subtype of IStructuredSelection, which adds
methods specific to trees. This includes the ability to find out what the selected object(s) and
their parents are in the tree.

The IStructuredSelection interface is the most commonly used interface when dealing
with selection types for viewers. If the selection is not empty, it is almost always an instance
of an IStructuredSelection. As a result, the following snippet of code appears regularly:

```
ISelection sel = viewer.getSelection();
Object selectedValue;
if (!(sel instanceof IStructuredSelection) || sel.isEmpty()) {
  selectedValue = null;
} else {
  selectedValue = ((IStructuredSelection)sel).getFirstElement();
}
```

This snippet gets the selection from the viewer, and if it's not an IStructuredSelection,
or it's empty, assigns null to selectedValue. If it's not empty, it casts it to
IStructuredSelection and calls getFirstElement to get the single selected value.

Note that the selection may have more than one selected value, in which case the `getFirstElement` only returns the first selected element. `IStructuredSelection` provides an iterator to step through all selected objects.

Pop quiz – understanding interaction

Q1. How can `TreeViewer` instances be made to respond to a click?

Q2. Why are `Dialog` subclasses created?

Tabular data

The tree viewer is used in many situations in Eclipse, but sometimes being able to display more information for a single element is required. JFace provides a `TableViewer` which is similar to the `TreeViewer`, except that instead of a single label there are multiple columns available. There is also a combined `TableTreeViewer`, which combines functionality from the two classes.

Time for action – viewing time zones in tables

To display the time zones in tabular form, a new view will be created called **Time Zone Table View**.

1. Right-click on the `com.packtpub.e4.clock.ui` project and navigate to **Plug-in Tools | Open Manifest**. Open the **Extensions** tab and right-click on the `org.eclipse.ui.views`, followed by navigating to **New | e4view** and filling in the following:

    1. **ID**: `com.packtpub.e4.clock.ui.views.TimeZoneTableView`

    2. **Name**: `Time Zone Table View`

    3. **Class**: `com.packtpub.e4.clock.ui.views.TimeZoneTableView`

    4. **Category**: `com.packtpub.e4.clock.ui`

    5. **Icon**: `icons/sample.gif`

2. The `plugin.xml` should now contain:

```
<e4view
  category="com.packtpub.e4.clock.ui"
  class="com.packtpub.e4.clock.ui.views.TimeZoneTableView"
  icon="icons/sample.gif"
  id="com.packtpub.e4.clock.ui.views.TimeZoneTableView"
  name="Time Zone Table View"
  restorable="true">
</e4view>
```

3. Create the class using the editor's short-cuts to create a new class
`TimeZoneTableView` in the `com.packtpub.e4.clock.ui.views` package, or
with the new class wizard. Once the view is created, add an empty `TableViewer`,
and use an `ArrayContentProvider` with the set of available `ZoneIds`:

```
package com.packtpub.e4.clock.ui.views;
import javax.annotation.PostConstruct;
import org.eclipse.e4.ui.di.Focus;
public class TimeZoneTableView {
  private TableViewer tableViewer;
  @PostConstruct
  public void create(Composite parent) {
    tableViewer = new TableViewer(parent, SWT.H_SCROLL |
    SWT.V_SCROLL);
    tableViewer.getTable().setHeaderVisible(true);
    tableViewer.setContentProvider(
     ArrayContentProvider.getInstance());
    tableViewer.setInput(ZoneId.getAvailableZoneIds());
  }
  @Focus
  public void focus() {
    tableViewer.getControl().setFocus();
  }
}
```

4. Run the Eclipse instance, and a one-dimensional list of time zones will be shown in
the **Time Zone Table View**:

5. Convert the array of `String` instances to an array of `ZoneId` instances and set that
as the input:

```
// tableViewer.setInput(ZoneId.getAvailableZoneIds());
tableViewer.setInput(ZoneId.getAvailableZoneIds() // get ids
  .stream().map(ZoneId::of).toArray());
```

6. The table shows a list of the `ZoneId` objects. That's because there is no `LabelProvider`, so they're just being rendered with their `toString()` representation. Because a table has multiple columns, a `TableViewer` has multiple `TableViewerColumn` instances. Each one represents a column in the `Table`, and each has its own size, title, and label provider. Creating a new column often involves setting up standard features (such as the width) as well as hooking in the required fields to display. To make it easy to reuse, create an `abstract` subclass of `ColumnLabelProvider` called `TimeZoneColumn` (in the `com.packtpub.e4.clock.ui.internal` package) with abstract `getText` and `getTitle` methods, and concrete `getWidth` and `getAlignment` methods:

```
public abstract class TimeZoneColumn extends ColumnLabelProvider {
  public abstract String getText(Object element);
  public abstract String getTitle();
  public int getWidth() {
    return 250;
  }
  public int getAlignment() {
    return SWT.LEFT;
  }
}
```

7. Add a helper method `addColumnTo` to the `TimeZoneColumn` class, which makes it easier to add it to a viewer:

```
public TableViewerColumn addColumnTo(TableViewer viewer) {
  TableViewerColumn tableViewerColumn =
   new TableViewerColumn(viewer, SWT.NONE);
  TableColumn column = tableViewerColumn.getColumn();
  column.setMoveable(true);
  column.setResizable(true);
  column.setText(getTitle());
  column.setWidth(getWidth());
  column.setAlignment(getAlignment());
  tableViewerColumn.setLabelProvider(this);
  return tableViewerColumn;
}
```

8. Now create a custom subclass `TimeZoneIDColumn` in the same package that returns the `ID` column for a `TimeZone`:

```
public class TimeZoneIDColumn extends TimeZoneColumn {
  public String getText(Object element) {
    if (element instanceof ZoneId) {
      return ((ZoneId) element).getId();
    } else {
```

```
        return "";
      }
    }
  }
  public String getTitle() {
   return "ID";
  }
}
```

9. Modify the `TimeZoneTableView` class, and at the end of the `create` method, instantiate the column and call the `addColumnTo` method, above the call to the `setInput` method:

```
new TimeZoneIDColumn().addColumnTo(tableViewer);
tableViewer.setInput(ZoneId.getAvailableZoneIds()...);
```

 Note that the columns need to be created before the `setInput()` call, as otherwise they won't display properly.

10. Run the Eclipse instance, and show the **Time Zone Table View**. The `ID` column should be displayed on its own.

11. To add more columns, copy the `TimeZoneIDColumn` class, modifying the title returned and the returned property of the associated time zone. For example, create a copy of the `TimeZoneIDColumn` called `TimeZoneDisplayNameColumn`, and modify the get method and title:

```
// return ((ZoneId) element).getId();
return ((ZoneId) element).getDisplayName(TextStyle.FULL, Locale.
getDefault());
// return "ID";
return "Display Name";
```

12. Optionally, do the same with the other properties of `TimeZone`, such as the offset (with `getOffset()`), and whether it's in daylight savings time or not (with `useDaylightTime()`). The columns can then be added to the table:

```
new TimeZoneDisplayNameColumn().addColumnTo(tableViewer);
new TimeZoneOffsetColumn().addColumnTo(tableViewer);
new TimeZoneSummerTimeColumn().addColumnTo(tableViewer);
```

13. Run the Eclipse instance, go to the **Time Zone Table View**, and the additional column(s) should be seen:

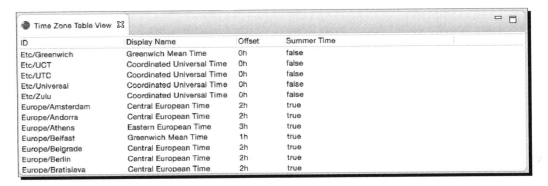

What just happened?

A `TableViewer` was created and multiple `ColumnLabelProvider` instances were added to it for displaying individual fields of an object. Subclassing `ColumnLabelProvider` avoids the need to use anonymous inner classes, and it gives a helper function which can be used to create and wire in the column (with specified title and width) while delegating those properties to the concrete subclasses of `TimeZoneColumn`. This avoids the need for tracking columns by `ID`.

For specific customizations of the columns, the underlying SWT `Column` is used to set functionality required by the application, including allowing the column to be movable with `setMovable(true)` and resizable with `setResizable(true)`. Similarly, table-wide operations (such as showing the header) are done by manipulating the underlying SWT `Table` and invoking `setHeaderVisible(true)`.

It's important to note that the columns of the tree viewer are calculated when the `setInput` method is called, so columns that are added after this line may not show properly. Generally the `setInput` should be left until the end of the table's construction.

Pop quiz: understanding tables

Q1. How are a column's headers enabled in a `TableViewer`?

Q2. What is a `TableViewerColumn` for?

Q3. What standard content provider can be used with a `TableViewer`?

Q4. What's the difference between a `TableViewerColumn` and a `TableColumn`?

Selection

Selection in Eclipse is handled using two distinct implementations. The original Eclipse workbench implementation, along with JFace, uses interfaces such as `ISelection` and `IStructuredSelection` to represent a selected object. The Eclipse 3.x Platform UI provided an `ISelectionService` to keep track of a global selected object in the current window.

Since both JFace and the Eclipse Platform UI depend upon SWT, the traditional selection service was tied to a specific implementation of the graphics library, which limited its use outside of SWT. As a result, the `ESelectionService` was created to provide closer ties with the E4 platform, without the SWT/JFace dependencies. Both of these selection mechanisms are seen in modern Eclipse applications.

Time for action – propagating selection

When the user selects an item in a viewer component, any registered selection listeners will be notified. In order to forward changes to the E4 selection service, a listener needs to be created to forward the selection to the `ESelectionService`.

1. Add the required packages to the bundle's package imports, by right-clicking on the `com.packtpub.e4.clock.ui` project and navigating to **Plug-in Tools | Open Manifest** to open the bundle's manifest. On the **Dependencies** tab, click on **Add** under the **Imported Packages** section and enter `org.eclipse.e4.ui.workbench.modeling` as well as `org.eclipse.e4.core.di.annotations`.

2. In order to forward selection changes to the E4 selection service, it must be injected into the view. Add a field `ESelectionService selectionService` annotated with `@Inject` and `@Optional`. When the part is created, the field will be filled with a selection service instance or `null` as appropriate:

```
@Inject
@Optional
private ESelectionService selectionService;
```

3. The selection changed event needs to trigger finding the selected object, then forwarding that on to the selection service. Add an `ISelectionChangeListener` to the `treeViewer` with the following:

```
treeViewer.addSelectionChangedListener(event -> {
  // forward selection
  Object selection =
  ((IStructuredSelection)event.getSelection()).
   getFirstElement();
  if (selection != null && selectionService != null) {
    selectionService.setSelection(selection);
  }
});
```

4. Test the application by putting a breakpoint in the `stSelection` method, and launch the Eclipse application in `Debug` mode. Once it is running, open the **Time Zone Tree View** and select a time zone, after which the debugger should be presented. Verify that the selected time zone and the `selectionService` have been injected correctly.

What just happened?

To receive selection events from the tree viewer, a listener must be registered to pick up changes. In order to forward this to the E4 selection service, it must be obtained using injection. By marking the field with `@Inject`, the selection service will be automatically injected when the part is created.

By marking the field as `@Optional`, if the selection service is not available, then a null value will be injected instead. If the field is not marked as `@Optional` and the service is not available, the part would fail to be created. Since the selection updates aren't a core part of the view's functionality, it is better to fail safely and work with reduced functionality rather than fail completely.

Finally, when the selection change event occurs, the selected object is extracted from the viewer and then forwarded onto the selection service, but only if both the selection and the selection service are not `null`.

Although the selection mechanism in Eclipse 3.x uses `ISelection` interfaces (almost always `IStructuredSelection`), the E4 selection service permits objects to be set directly. This also allows the type of the object to be selectively filtered when received. In Eclipse 3.x, the viewer would set the `selectionProvider` on the `viewPart`, which would handle the selection changes automatically.

Time for action – responding to selection changes

When the selection is changed in the E4 selection service, parts can be notified that a new selection is available through injection. Although an `@Inject` field could be used, there would be no trigger that could be used to update the view. Instead, a method with an injected parameter will be used to trigger the update.

1. Add the required packages to the bundle's package imports, by right-clicking on the `com.packtpub.e4.clock.ui` project and navigating to **Plug-in Tools | Open Manifest** to open the bundle's manifest. On the **Dependencies** tab, click on **Add** under the **Imported Packages** section and enter `org.eclipse.e4.ui.services`.

2. In the `TimeZoneTableView` class, create a method called `setTimeZone`. The method name isn't specifically important, but the method needs to be annotated with `@Inject` and `@Optional`, and the argument needs to be annotated with `@Named(IServiceConstants.ACTIVE_SELECTION)`. It should look like:

```
@Inject
@Optional
public void setTimeZone(
  @Named(IServiceConstants.ACTIVE_SELECTION) ZoneId timeZone) {
}
```

3. In the method, if the selection is not `null`, set the value on the `tableViewer` using the `setSelection` method. Since this takes an `ISelection` type, wrap the selected `TimeZone` within a `StructuredSelection` instance as follows:

```
if (timeZone != null) {
  // NOTE may generate a NullPointerException
  tableViewer.setSelection(new StructuredSelection(timeZone));
  tableViewer.reveal(timeZone);
}
```

4. If the application is run, a `NullPointerException` will be thrown from inside the `setSelection` call, which indicates that the `tableViewer` variable is `null`. The reason is because the call to set the time zone occurs before the `@PostConstruct` annotated method is called, so the `tableViewer` has not been instantiated yet. The solution is to ignore selection events when the viewer has not been constructed, by adding a guard to the surrounding `if` block that checks to see that the `tableViewer` is not `null`:

```
if (timeZone != null && tableViewer != null) {
  tableViewer.setSelection(new StructuredSelection(timeZone));
  tableViewer.reveal(timeZone);
}
```

5. Now when the application is run, and a time zone is selected in the **Time Zone Tree View**, the corresponding object should be selected in the **Time Zone Table View**.

What just happened?

The selected object is stored in the E4 scope, with the key specified in the `IServiceConstants.ACTIVE_SELECTION` constant. When the selection changes, the `setTimeZone` method is automatically called. To prevent problems with propagating empty selections, if the selected value is `null` then it is not forwarded on.

Since the selection can change and be set at any time, including before the part is fully constructed, it is necessary to guard the code to ignore selections if the viewer is `null`.

The `treeViewer` expects a value of type `ISelection`, so the time zone is wrapped in a `StructuredSelection` instance, and then passed to the `treeViewer`. The reveal step is optional, and will focus the viewer on the selected object if it is available.

Have a go hero – adding selection support to the table view

Now that the selection works from the tree viewer to the table viewer, try the following:

- Add a `setTimeZone` method to the `TimeZoneTreeViewer` to allow the selection to display items in the tree viewer.
- Add a `SelectionChangeListener` to the `TimeZoneTableViewer` so that a selection in the table view will trigger a change in other views.
- In the `setTimeZone` methods, check that the `tableViewer` hasn't been disposed as well as the null check.
- To prevent calls to the `setTimeZone` method from taking effect before the viewer has been constructed, assign the viewer to a local variable in the corresponding @`PostContstruct` method first, and then at the end of the method assign the local variable to the field.
- Create a standard `StructuredChangeListener` class that can forward selection events to a generic JFace viewer which can be re-used.
- Convert the optional `ESelectionService` with a non-optional `Provider<ESelectionService>`, and use the `get` method to acquire the selection service on demand or pass it into the generic class created in the previous step.

Pop quiz – understanding selection

Q1. How do viewers work with selected objects?

Q2. What event listener is used to receive notifications of a viewer's selection updates?

Q3. What service is used in E4 to maintain the selected object in the current window?

Q4. How does the selected object in E4 get propagated to parts?

Summary

This chapter covered how to use JFace to build viewers for structured data: both tree-based views (with a `TreeViewer`) and table based views (with a `TableViewer`). It also covered some JFace built-in features for managing fonts and images.

To synchronize data between views in Eclipse, services such as the `ISelectionService` are used (or in E4, the `ESelectionService`). Having views generate and consume selection events provides a visual consistency even though the views may be exposed by different plug-ins. The next chapter will look at how to interact with the user, with menus, commands and handlers.

4

Interacting with the User

In the last chapter, we looked at some of the basic JFace viewers that provide a representation of data. However, we need to interact with the user and we can do this in multiple ways, from responding to mouse clicks to processing data-intensive operations in the background.

In this chapter we will:

- Create a menu in response to a user popup
- Add a command and a handler in a menu
- Use progress managers to report work
- Add commands to the progress manager
- Show errors and deal with failure

Creating menus, commands, and handlers

In Eclipse, menus can be used to trigger user actions. These menus can be displayed at the top of the application window (or top of the screen on macOS). Menus can also be associated with a view through a contextual popup using the right mouse button.

A **menu** can be associated with a **command**, which represents a generic operation. The command is then dynamically associated with a **handler**, which is the code that executes the operation. This allows a generic operation (such as copy) to be executed by different handlers depending on the context.

Time for action – installing the E4 tools

A model fragment needs to be created to add commands and handlers into an E4 plug-in or application. This can be created with the E4 tools that are part of the default Eclipse repository for Eclipse Mars and Eclipse Neon, or can be installed from the E4 page for Luna and below versions.

1. Go to the **Help | Install New Software...** menu. For Eclipse Mars, Eclipse Neon and later, choose the `http://download.eclipse.org/releases/neon/` site, substituting the platform name if necessary. For Eclipse Luna and below, choose the corresponding update site from the `http://download.eclipse.org/e4/downloads/` page instead.

2. Type `e4 tools` into the search box and select the **Eclipse e4 Tools** feature:

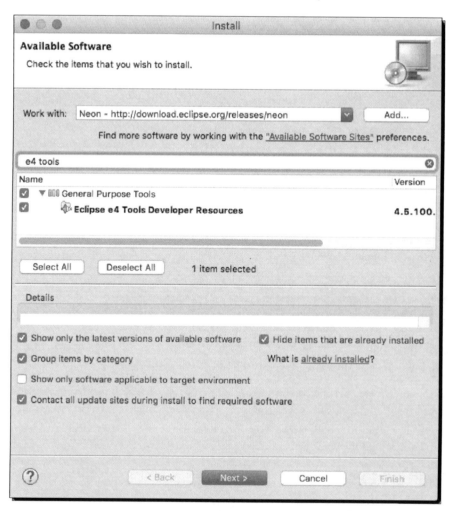

3. Click on **Finish** to continue installing the tools and restart Eclipse when prompted.

4. To verify that the tools have been installed correctly, select the
`com.packtpub.e4.clock.ui` project, go to the **File | New** menu, and
search for `new model fragment`. This should show an entry under
Eclipse 4 **| Model | New Model Fragment**:

5. Click on **Next** and choose the `com.packtpub.e4.clock.ui` as the container with
`fragment.e4xmi` as the filename.

6. The `plugin.xml` should have a new fragment entry:

```
<extension
  id="com.packtpub.e4.clock.ui.fragment"
  point="org.eclipse.e4.workbench.model">
   <fragment uri="fragment.e4xmi"/>
</extension>
```

What just happened?

The Eclipse E4 tools are used to create application fragments that allow E4 content to be created and hosted in a plug-in. The E4 tools have been present in the default update site since Eclipse Mars.

An E4 application fragment is stored in another XML file, linked to from the `plugin.xml` file. Although it is possible to have multiple fragments in a single plug-in, it's more common to have only a single fragment per plug-in. The default fragment name is `fragment.e4xmi`, but other names with the `e4xmi` extension can be used instead, provided that the reference from the `plugin.xml` points to the file.

Time for action – creating commands and handlers

Commands and handlers are common to both Eclipse 3.x and the Eclipse 4 model. In Eclipse 3.x, they are represented as extension points in the `plugin.xml` file under `org.eclipse.ui.commands`. In Eclipse 4, they are stored in the E4 fragment file.

A **command** will be created to represent saying "hello world," and a **handler** will be created to display the message. These will then be used to add a **menu** item to execute the operation.

1. Open the fragment for the project, or double-click on the `fragment.e4xmi` file.

> This should open a model editor; if it opens plain XML content, then verify that the E4 tools have been installed correctly.

2. Select the **Model Fragment Definition** element and click on **Add** to create a new fragment. Fill in the fields as follows:

    1. **Extended Element ID**: `org.eclipse.e4.legacy.ide.application` (this can be found under the **Container-Type: Application** from the search field)

    2. **Feature Name**: `commands`

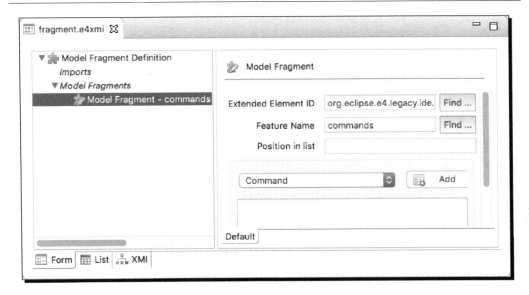

3. Select the newly created **Model Fragment** if it is not already selected.

4. Choose **Command** from the dropdown and click on **Add**. Fill in the fields as follows:

1. **ID**: com.packtpub.e4.clock.ui.command.hello

2. **Name:** Hello

3. **Description**: Says Hello World

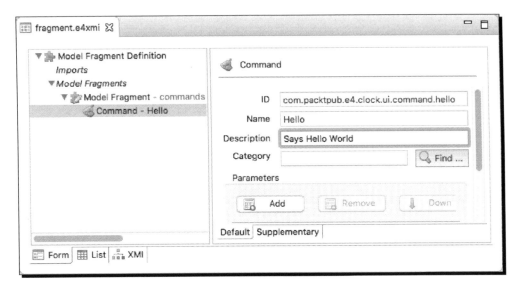

5. This creates a command that is just an identifier and a name. To specify what it does, it must be connected to a handler, which is done by adding another model fragment. Right-click on the **Model Fragments** and add a **Model Fragment** child, using the **Extended Element ID** `org.eclipse.e4.legacy.ide.application`, but this time with the **Feature Name** `handlers`.

6. Choose **Handler** from the dropdown and click on **Add**. Fill in the fields as follows, using the **Find...** buttons next to the fields to find the elements:

    1. **ID**: `com.packtpub.e4.clock.ui.handler.HelloHandler`

    2. **Command**: `Hello - com.packtpub.e4.clock.ui.command.hello`

    3. **Class URI**: `bundleclass://com.packtpub.e4.clock.ui/com.packtub.e4.clock.ui.handlers.HleloHandler`

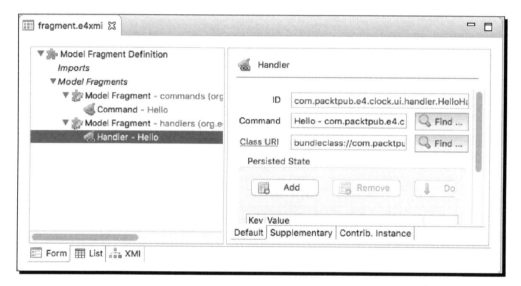

7. To create a new class, click on **Class URI** and fill in the fields as follows:

    1. **Source folder**: `com.packtpub.e4.clock.ui/src`

    2. **Package**: `com.packtpub.e4.clock.ui.handlers`

    3. **Name**: `HelloHandler`

    4. **Execute Method**: `execute`

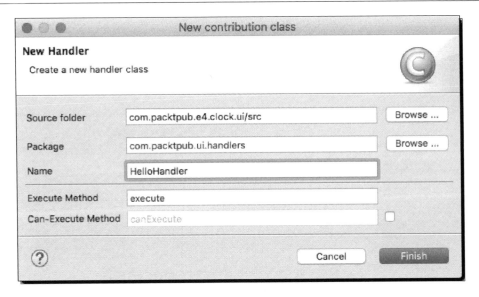

8. The handler joins the processing of the command. In Eclipse 3.x, this was a class that implemented `IHandler` (typically `AbstractHandler`); but in Eclipse 4, this interface is no longer necessary. Implement the class `HelloHandler` as follows:

```
package com.packtpub.e4.clock.ui.handlers;
import org.eclipse.e4.core.di.annotations.Execute;
public class HelloHandler {
  public void execute() {
    MessageDialog.openInformation(null, "Hello", "World");
  }
}
```

9. The command's ID `com.packtpub.e4.clock.ui.command.hello` is used to refer to it from menus or other locations. To place the contribution in an existing menu structure, it needs to be added as a `menuContribution`. Create a new **Model Fragment** using the **Extended Element ID** `org.eclipse.e4.legacy.ide.application` and **Feature Name** handlers.

10. Select the newly created **Model Fragment**, choose **Menu Contribution** from the dropdown, and click on **Add**. Ensure that the **Parent-ID** is set to **help**.

11. Select the newly created **Menu Contribution**, select **Handled Menu Item** from the dropdown, and click on **Add**. Fill in the fields as follows:

1. **ID:** `com.packtpub.e4.clock.ui.handledmenuitem.Hello`

2. **Label:** `Hello`

3. **Command:** `Hello - com.packtpub.e4.clock.ui.command.hello`

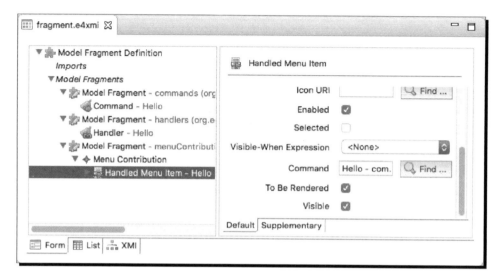

12. Run the target Eclipse instance, and there will be a **Hello** menu item under the **Help** menu. When selected, it will pop up the **Hello World** message.

 If the menu isn't shown, go to the **Run | Run Configurations...** menu and ensure that the **Clear** button is selected, to reset the Eclipse instance in order to merge the E4 fragment. Typically this fixes problems where changes to the E4 model aren't seen.

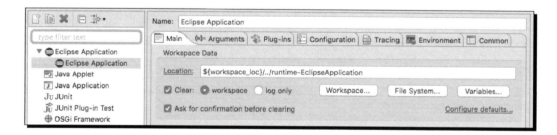

What just happened?

Eclipse 3.x introduced the concept of commands and handlers as a means of separating their interface from their implementation. This allows a generic command (such as **Copy**) to be overridden by specific views. Unlike the traditional command design pattern, which provides implementation as subclasses, the Command in Eclipse uses a retargetable handler to perform the actual execution. In Eclipse 4, the concepts of commands and handlers are used extensively to provide the components of the user interface. The key difference is in their definition; for Eclipse 3.x, this typically occurs in the plugin.xml, whereas in Eclipse 4, it is part of the application model.

In the example, a specific handler was defined for the command, which is valid in all contexts. The handler's class is the implementation; the command ID is the reference.

The menuContributions fragment entry allows menus to be added anywhere in the user interface. The parent defines where the menu item can be created. The syntax for the parent is as follows:

- identifier: This can be a known short name (such as file, window, or help), the global menu (org.eclipse.ui.main.menu), the global toolbar (org.eclipse.ui.main.toolbar), a view identifier (org.eclipse.ui.views.ContentOutline), or an ID explicitly defined in a popup menu's registerContextMenu call
- ?after|before=key: This is a placement instruction to put this after or before other items; typically additions is used as an extensible location for others to contribute to

This allows plug-ins to contribute to other menus, regardless of where they are ultimately located.

Time for action – binding commands to keys

Hooking up the command to a keystroke requires a **KeyBinding**. This allows a key (or series of keys) to be used to invoke the command instead of only via the menu. KeyBindings are set up inside a Binding Table and associated with a Binding Context.

1. Open the fragment.e4xmi in the clock.ui project.

2. In the **imports**, select the **Binding Context** from the dropdown and click on **Add**. In the **Reference-ID**, click on **Find...** and a dialog will be shown with the contexts. Choose the `org.eclipse.ui.contexts.dialogAndWindow` context:

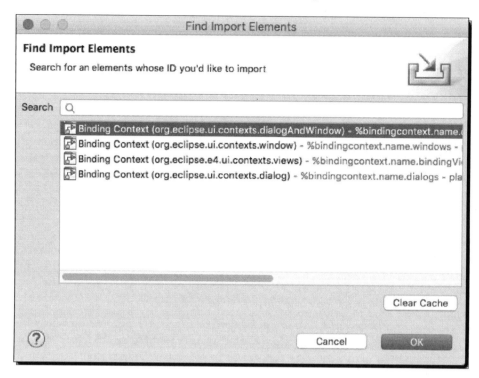

3. Once the binding context has been imported, it can be used within a binding table. Click on **Model Fragments** and select **Add** to create a new fragment. Fill in the details as follows:

1. **Extended Element ID**: `org.eclipse.e4.legacy.ide.application`
2. **Feature Name**: `bindingTables`

4. In the **BindingTable** element, choose the `org.eclipse.ui.contexts.dialogAndWindow` context. This will ensure that the key binding is available in all windows and dialogs:

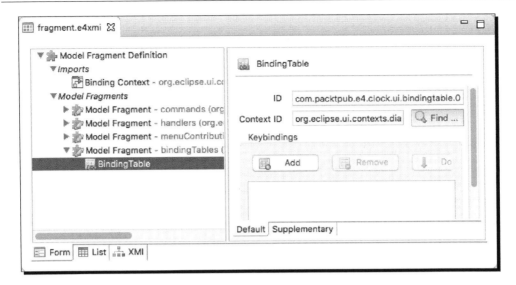

5. Click on **Add** and a **KeyBinding** window will be shown. In the **Sequence**, enter M1+9. Next to the **Command**, click on **Find...** and choose the **Hello** command:

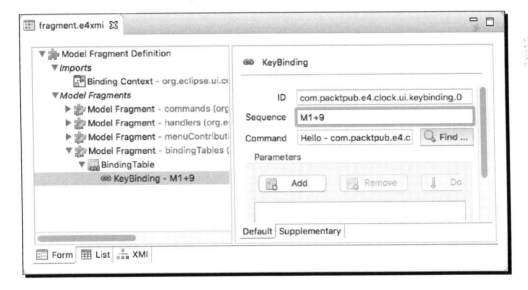

6. Run the target Eclipse instance, and press *Cmd + 9* (for macOS) or *Ctrl + 9* (for Windows/Linux). The same **Hello** dialog should be displayed, as if it were shown from the menu. The same keystroke should be displayed in the **Help** menu.

What just happened?

The **M1** key is the primary meta key, which is *Cmd* on macOS and *Ctrl* on Windows/Linux. This is typically used for the main operations; for example, M1+C is copy and M1+V is paste on all systems. The sequence notation M1+9 is used to indicate pressing both keys at the same time.

The command that gets invoked is referenced by its commandId. This may be defined in the same plug-in, but it does not have to be; it is possible for one application to provide a set of commands and another plug-in to provide keystrokes that bind them.

It is also possible to set up a sequence of key presses; for example, M1+9 8 7 would require pressing *Cmd* (or *Ctrl*) with 9 followed by 8 and then 7 before the command is executed. This allows a set of keystrokes to be used to invoke a command; for example, it's possible to emulate an Emacs quit operation with the KeyBinding *Ctrl + X Ctrl + C* to the quit command.

Other modifier keys include M2 (*Shift*), M3 (*Alt* or *Option*), and M4 (*Ctrl* on macOS). It is possible to use CTRL, SHIFT or ALT as long names but the meta names are preferred, since M1 tends to be bound to different keys on different operating systems.

The non-modifier keys themselves can either be single characters (A-Z), numbers (0-9), or one of a set of longer name key-codes such as F12, ARROW_UP, TAB, and PAGE_UP. Certain common variations are allowed, for example, ESC/ESCAPE and ENTER/RETURN.

Time for action – changing contexts

The context is the location in which this binding is valid. For commands that are visible everywhere—typically the kind of options in the default menu—they can be associated with the org.eclipse.ui.contexts.dialogAndWindow context. If the command should only be invoked from dialogs, then the org.eclipse.ui.contexts.dialog context would be used instead.

1. Open the fragment.e4xmi of the com.packtpub.e4.clock.ui project.

2. To enable the command only for dialogs, go to the **Binding Context**, and modify the **Reference-ID** to point to org.eclipse.ui.contexts.dialog.

3. Run the Eclipse instance, and try the command with *Cmd + 9* or *Ctrl + 9* depending on platform. The command should not work unless a dialog is being shown. Open a dialog by navigating to the **File | New | Other** menu and then try *Cmd + 9* or *Ctrl + 9* again.

If there is no change in the behavior, try cleaning the workspace of the target instance at launch, by going to the **Run | Run...** menu and choosing **Clear** on the workspace. This is sometimes necessary when making changes to the fragment.e4xmi file, as some extensions are cached and may lead to strange behavior.

What just happened?

Context scopes allow bindings to be valid for certain situations, such as when a dialog is open. This allows the same KeyBinding to be used for different situations, such as a **Format** operation—which may have a different effect in a Java editor than an XML editor for instance.

Since scopes are hierarchical, they can be specifically targeted for the contexts in which they may be used. The Java editor context is a sub-context of the general text editor, which in turn is a sub-context of the window context, which in turn is a sub-context of the windowAndDialog context.

Time for action – enabling and disabling menus items

The previous section showed how to hide or show a specific KeyBinding depending on the open editor type. However, it doesn't stop the command from being called via the menu, or from it showing up in the menu itself. Instead of just hiding the KeyBinding, the menu can be hidden as well by adding a visibleWhen block to the command.

The expressions framework provides a number of variables, including activeContexts, which contains a list of the active contexts at the time. Since many contexts can be active simultaneously, the active contexts is a list (for example, [dialogAndWindow, window, textEditor, javaEditor])—so to find an entry (in effect, a contains operation), an iterate with equals expression is used. Although it's possible to copy and paste expressions between places where they are used, it is preferable to reuse an identical expression.

1. Open the plugin.xml file, and add declare an expression using the expressions extension point as follows:

```
<extension point="org.eclipse.core.expressions.definitions">
  <definition id="when.hello.is.active">
    <with variable="activeContexts">
      <iterate operator="or">
        <equals value="org.eclipse.ui.contexts.dialog"/>
      </iterate>
    </with>
  </definition>
</extension>
```

2. Add a **Visible-When** expression to the **Handled Menu Item – Hello** element by choosing **CoreExpression** from the dropdown:

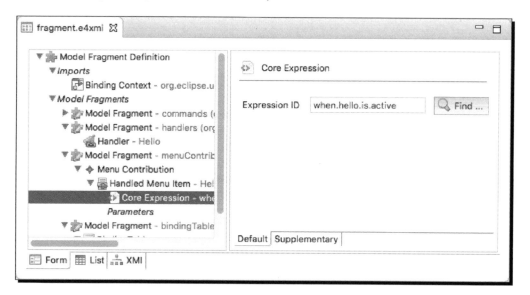

3. Run the target Eclipse instance, and verify that the menu is hidden until a dialog is opened. If this behavior is not seen, run the Eclipse application with the `-clean` argument to clear the workspace. After clearing, it will be necessary to open a dialog to verify that the menu visibility is correct.

What just happened?

Menus have a `visibleWhen` guard that is evaluated when the menu is shown. If it is false, then the menu is hidden.

The expressions syntax is based on nested XML elements with certain conditions. For example, an `<and>` block is true if all of its children are true, whereas an `<or>` block is true if at least one of its children is true. Variables can also be used with a property test using a combination of a `<with>` block (which binds the specified variable to the stack) and an `<equals>` block or other comparison.

In the case of variables that have lists, an `<iterate>` can be used to step through elements using either `operator="or"` or `operator="and"` to dynamically calculate enablement.

There are a number of variables that can be used in tests; these are listed in the Eclipse help documentation under the **Workbench Core Expressions** chapter, and include:

- `activeContexts`: This is a list of context IDs that are active at the time
- `activeShell`: This is the active shell (dialog or window)

- ◆ `activeWorkbenchWindow`: This is the active window
- ◆ `activeEditor`: This is the current or last active editor
- ◆ `activePart`: This is the active part (editor or view)
- ◆ `selection`: This is the current selection
- ◆ `org.eclipse.core.runtime.Platform`: This is the `Platform` object

The `Platform` object is useful for performing dynamic tests using `test`, such as:

```
<test value="ACTIVE"
  property="org.eclipse.core.runtime.bundleState"
  args="org.eclipse.core.expressions"/>
<test
  property="org.eclipse.core.runtime.isBundleInstalled"
  args="org.eclipse.core.expressions"/>
```

Knowing if a bundle is installed is often useful; it's better to only enable functionality if a bundle is started (or in OSGi terminology, `ACTIVE`). As a result, uses of `isBundleInstalled` have been replaced by `bundleState=ACTIVE` tests.

The `org.eclipse.core.expressions` extension point defined a virtual condition that is re-evaluated when the user's context changes, so that both the menu and the handler can be made visible and enabled at the same time.

Since references can be used anywhere, expressions can also be defined in terms of other expressions. As long as the expressions aren't recursive, they can be built up in any manner.

Time for action – contributing commands to pop-up menus

It's useful to be able to add contributions to pop-up menus so that they can be used by different places. Fortunately this can be done fairly easily with the `menuContribution` fragment and a combination of enablement tests. However, to implement this in E4, the view must be moved into the `fragment.e4xmi` file in order to attach a **PopupMenu**.

1. Add the `org.eclipse.ui.services` package as a dependency to the `plugin.xml` in the **Dependencies** tab, if it's not already added.

2. Open the `TimeZoneTableView` class and add the following to the end of the `createPartControl` method:

```
private void createPartControl(Composite parent, EMenuService
menuService) {
  menuService.registerContextMenu(tableViewer.getControl(),
  "com.packtpub.e4.clock.ui.popup");
  tableViewer.addSelectionChangedListener(event -> {
```

```
      // forward selection
      Object selection = ((IStructuredSelection)
      event.getSelection()).getFirstElement();
      if (selection != null && selectionService != null) {
        selectionService.setSelection(selection);
      }
    });
```

3. Running the Eclipse instance and showing the menu results in nothing being displayed, because no menu items have been added to it yet.

4. Create a command and a handler fragment called **Show the Time** by adding them to the `fragment.e4xmi` file as before.

5. Create a class called `ShowTheTime` in the `com.packtpub.e4.clock. ui.handlers` package to show the time in a specific time zone:

```
public class ShowTheTime {
@Execute
public void execute(ESelectionService selectionService) {
  Object selection = selectionService.getSelection();
  if (selection instanceof ZoneId) {
    DateTimeFormatter formatter =
    DateTimeFormatter.ISO_DATE_TIME;
    String theTime = ZonedDateTime.now((ZoneId)
    selection).format(formatter);
    MessageDialog.openInformation(null, "The time is",
      theTime);
  }
}
}
```

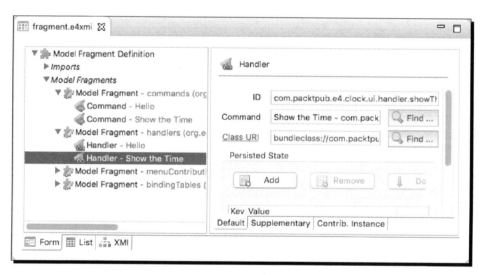

6. To add a popup menu, the **Time Zone Table View** first needs to be converted into an E4 **PartDescriptor**. Comment out the `e4view` in the `plugin.xml`, and in the `fragment.e4xmi` file, add a new **Model Fragment** with the following information:

   1. **Extended Element ID**: `org.eclipse.e4.legacy.ide.application`

   2. **Feature Name**: `descriptors`

7. Select the **PartDescriptor** from the drop-down list and click on **Add**. Fill in the fields as follows:

   1. **ID**: `com.packtpub.e4.clock.ui.partdescriptor.timeZoneTableView`

   2. **Label**: `Time Zone Table View`

   3. **Icon URI**: `platform:/plugin/com.packtpub.e4.clock.ui/icons/sample.gif`

   4. **Class URI**: `bundleclass://com.packtpub.e4.clock.ui/com.packtpub.e4.clock.ui.views.TimeZoneTableView`

   5. **Category**: `Timekeeping`

8. Under the **Menus** node, select **Popup Menu** from the drop-down list and click on **Add**. Give it the **ID** `com.packtpub.e4.clock.ui.popup`, which corresponds to the argument used in the `menuService.registerContextMenu` call previously.

9. Under the **Popup Menu** node, select **Handled Menu Item** from the drop-down list and click on **Add**. Fill in the fields as follows:

   1. **ID**: `com.packtpub.e4.clock.ui.handledmenuitem.showTheTime`

   2. **Label**: `Show the Time`

   3. **Command**: `Show the Time - com.packtpub.e4.clock.ui.command.show`

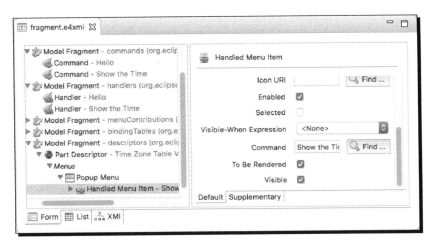

10. Run the target Eclipse instance, and open the `TimeZoneTableView`. Right-click on a time zone in the table, and the command **Show the Time** will be displayed in a pop-up menu. Select the menu item and a dialog should show the time.

What just happened?

The E4 fragment can be used to add views, commands, and handlers, and wire them together. This approach to registering commands is powerful, because any time a time zone is exposed as a selection in the future will now have a **Show the Time** menu added to it automatically.

The commands define a generic operation, and handlers bind those commands to implementations. The context-sensitive menu is provided by the pop-up menu extension point using the LocationURI `popup:org.eclipse.ui.popup.any`. This allows the menu to be added to any pop-up menu that uses the `EMenuService` and when the selection contains a `ZoneId`. The `EMenuService` is responsible for listening to the mouse gestures to show a menu, and filling it with details when it is shown.

In the example, the command was enabled when the object was an instance of a `ZoneId`, and also if it could be adapted to a `ZoneId`. This would allow another object type (say, a contact card) to have an adapter to convert it to a `ZoneId`, and thus show the time in that contact's location. This could be used to provide compatibility with older Java runtimes, using a `TimeZone` for example.

Have a go hero – using view menus and toolbars

The way to add a view menu is similar to adding a pop-up menu; the location URI used is the view's ID rather than the menu item itself. Add a **Show the Time** menu to the **Time Zone View** as a view menu.

Another way of adding the menu is to add it as a toolbar, which is an icon in the main Eclipse window. Add the **Show the Time** icon by adding it to the global toolbar instead.

Pop quiz – understanding menus

Q1. How can a `Command` be connected to a menu?

Q2. What is the `M1` key?

Q3. How are keystrokes bound to `Command` instances?

Q4. What is a menu `locationURI`?

Q5. How is a pop-up menu created?

Jobs and progress

Since the user interface is single-threaded, if a command takes a long amount of time, it will block the user interface from being redrawn or processed. As a result, it is necessary to run long-running operations in a background thread to prevent the UI from hanging.

Although the core Java library contains `java.util.Timer`, the Eclipse Jobs API provides a mechanism to both run jobs and report progress. It also allows jobs to be grouped together and paused or joined as a whole.

Time for action – running operations in the background

If the command takes a long time to execute, the user interface will be blocked. This happens because there is only one user interface thread, and because the command is launched from the UI, it will run in the UI thread. Instead, long-running operations should run in a background thread, and then once finished, be able to display the results. Clearly creating a new `Thread` (like the clock updates initially) or other techniques such as a `Timer` would work. However, the Eclipse system has a mechanism to provide a `Job` to do the work instead, or `UIJob` to run in the context of the UI thread.

1. Open the `HelloHandler` and go to the `execute` method. Replace its contents with the following:

```
public void execute() {
  Job job = new Job("About to say hello") {
    protected IStatus run(IProgressMonitor monitor) {
      try {
        Thread.sleep(5000);
      } catch (InterruptedException e) {
      }
      MessageDialog.openInformation(null, "Hello", "World");
      return Status.OK_STATUS;
    }
  };
  job.schedule();
  return;
}
```

2. Run the Eclipse instance, and click on the **Help** | **Hello** menu item (in order to enable the menu item again, modify the `activeContexts` in the `plugin.xml` to allow the command to be shown in the `org.eclipse.ui.contexts.dialogAndWindow` context). Open the **Progress** view, and a `Job` will be listed with **About to say hello** running. Unfortunately, an error dialog will then be shown:

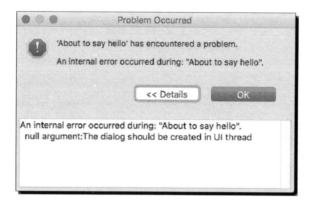

3. This occurs because the `Job` runs on a non-UI background thread, so when the `MessageDialog` is shown, an exception occurs. To fix this, instead of showing the `MessageDialog` directly, a second `Job` or `Runnable` can be created to run specifically on the UI thread. Replace the call to the `MessageDialog` with:

```
public void execute(final UISynchronize display) {
...
// MessageDialog.openInformation(null, "Hello", "World");
display.asyncExec(() -> {
    MessageDialog.openInformation(null, "Hello", "World");
});
```

   This example uses the `asyncExec` method to run a `Runnable` on the UI thread (similar to `SwingUtilities.invokeLater` method in Swing).

4. Run the target Eclipse instance, select the **Hello** menu, and after a 5-second pause, the dialog should be shown.

What just happened?

Every modification to the Eclipse UI must run on the UI thread; so if the command takes a significant time to run and is running on the UI thread, it will give the impression that the user interface is blocked. The way to avoid this is to drop out of the UI thread before doing any long-term work. Any updates that need to be done involving the UI should be rescheduled back on the UI thread.

The example used both the `Job` API (a mechanism for scheduling named processes that can be monitored via the progress view) as well as the `UISynchronize` method `asyncExec` to launch the resulting message dialog.

Have a go hero – using a UIJob

Instead of scheduling the UI notification piece as a `display.asyncExec`, create it as a `UIJob`. This works in exactly the same way as a `Job` does, but it is necessary to override the `runInUIThread` method instead of the `run` method. This may be useful when there is more UI interaction required, such as asking the user for more information.

Time for action – reporting progress

Normally when a `Job` is running, it is necessary to periodically update the user to let them know the state of the progress. By default, if a `Job` provides no information, a generic *busy* indicator is shown. When a `Job` is executed, it is passed an `IProgressMonitor`, which can be used to notify the user of the progress (and provide a way to cancel the operation). A progress monitor has a number of tasks, each of which has a total unit of work that it can do. For jobs that don't have a known amount of work, UNKNOWN can be specified and it will display in a generic busy indicator.

1. Open the `HelloHandler` and go to the `execute` method. In the inner `run` method, add a `beginTask` at the beginning, and a `worked` in the loop after each second's sleep, for five iterations. The code will look like:

```
protected IStatus run(IProgressMonitor monitor) {
  try {
    monitor.beginTask("Preparing", 5000);
    for (int i = 0; i < 5; i++) {
      Thread.sleep(1000);
      monitor.worked(1000);
    }
  } catch (InterruptedException e) {
  } finally {
    monitor.done();
  }
  display.asyncExec(() -> {
    MessageDialog.openInformation(null, "Hello", "World");
  });
  return Status.OK_STATUS;
}
```

2. Run the target Eclipse instance, and open the **Progress** view by navigating to **Window | Show View | Other | General | Progress**. Now invoke the **Help | Hello** menu; the **Progress** view should show the progress as the sleep occurs.

3. To make the reporting more accurate, report the status more frequently:

```
for (int i = 0; i < 50; i++) {
  Thread.sleep(100);
  monitor.worked(100);
}
```

4. Run the target Eclipse instance again. Now when the job is run via the **Help | Hello** menu, the status will be updated in the **Progress** view more frequently.

What just happened?

When running a Job, the progress monitor can be used to indicate how much work has been done. It must start with a beginTask—this gives both the total number of work units as well as a textual name that can be used to identify what's happening.

If the amount of work is unknown, use IProgressMonitor.UNKNOWN.

The unit scale doesn't really matter; it could have been 50 or 50,000. As long as the total number of work units adds up and they're appropriately used, it will still give the user a good idea of the operation.

Don't just report based on the number of lines (or tasks). If there are four work items but the fifth one takes as long as the previous four, then the amount of work reported needs be balanced; for example, provide a total of 8 units, with 1 unit for each of the first four and then the remaining 4 for the fifth item.

Finally, done was called on the progress monitor. This signifies that the Job has been completed, and can be removed from any views that are reporting the status. This is wrapped inside a finally block to ensure that the monitor is completed even if the job finishes abnormally (for example, if an exception occurs).

Time for action – dealing with cancellation

Sometimes the user will change their mind; they may have selected the wrong option, or something more important may have come up. The progress monitor allows for two-way communication; the user can signify when they want to cancel as well. There is a method, isCancelled, which returns true if the user has signified in some way that they want the job to finish early.

Periodically checking this during the operation of the `Job` allows the user to cancel a long-running job before it reaches the end.

1. Modify the `for` loop in the `HelloHandler` to check on each iteration whether the monitor is cancelled:

    ```
    for (int i = 0; i < 50 && !monitor.isCanceled(); i++) {
      ...
    }
    if (!monitor.isCancelled()) {
       display.asyncExec(() -> {...});
    }
    ```

2. Run the Eclipse instance and click on the **Hello** command. This time, go into the **Progress** view and click on the red stop square next to the job; the job should cancel and the dialog showing the message shouldn't be shown:

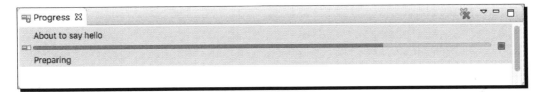

What just happened?

Being responsive to the user is a key point in implementing plug-ins. If there are long-running operations, make sure to check whether the user has cancelled the operation—there's no point in tying up the CPU if the user doesn't want it to continue.

The `monitor.isCancelled` call is generally implemented with a single field access, so calling it frequently often has no negative performance implications. Calling the `isCancelled` method too much is never noticed by users; however, not calling it enough certainly is noticed.

Time for action – using subtasks and sub-progress monitors

When performing a set of operations, subtasks can give the user additional details about the state of the operation. A subtask is merely a named message that is displayed along with the task name in the **Progress** view.

1. Add a `monitor.subTask` during the operation to give feedback:

    ```
    for (int i=0; i<50 && !monitor.isCanceled(); i++) {
       if (i == 10) {
          monitor.subTask("Doing something");
       } else if (i == 25) {
    ```

```
      monitor.subTask("Doing something else");
    } else if (i == 40) {
      monitor.subTask("Nearly there");
    }
    Thread.sleep(100);
    monitor.worked(100);
  }
```

2. Run the Eclipse instance, and look at the **Progress** view. The subtask should be shown underneath the status bar:

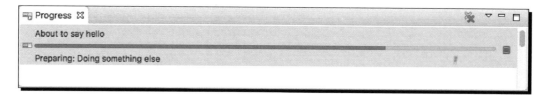

3. When calling another method with a progress monitor, if the monitor is passed as is, it can have undesirable effects. Add a new method, checkDozen, to the anonymous Job class inside the HelloHandler class, and add a condition in the for loop that breaks out on reaching 12:

```
protected IStatus run(IProgressMonitor monitor) {
  ...
    } else if (i == 12) {
      checkDozen(monitor);
    }
  ...
}
private void checkDozen(IProgressMonitor monitor) {
  try {
    monitor.beginTask("Checking a dozen", 12);
    for (int i = 0; i < 12; i++) {
      Thread.sleep(10);
      monitor.worked(1);
    }
  } catch (InterruptedException e) {
  } finally {
    monitor.done();
  }
}
```

4. Run the target Eclipse instance, select the **Hello** menu, and open the **Progress** view. The progress status completely disappears after it reaches that point:

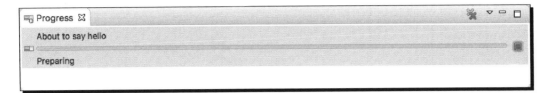

5. To solve this problem, create another IProgressMonitor instance and pass that into the method call using a SubProgressMonitor:

```
} else if (i == 12) {
    // NB SubProgressMonitor is deprecated
    // Will be replaced with SubMonitor next
    checkDozen(new SubProgressMonitor(monitor, 100));
    continue;
}
```

6. Now run the action, and the progress will update as expected. Note that the continue is used here to avoid calling monitor.worked(100) below.

What just happened?

The checkDozen method took an IProgressMonitor argument, and simulated a set of different tasks (with different units of work). Passing the same monitor instance causes problems as the work gets missed between the two.

To fix this behavior, a SubProgressMonitor was used. Because the SubProgressMonitor got 100 units of work from its parent, when the done method was called on the SubProgressMonitor the parent saw the completion of the 100 units of work.

Importantly, this also allows the child to use a completely different scale of work units and be completely decoupled from the parent's use of work units.

Time for action – using null progress monitors and sub monitors

When a method uses progress monitors extensively, it is inelegant to keep checking whether the monitor is null or not. Instead, the progress monitor can be replaced with a NullProgressMonitor, which acts as a no-op for all monitor calls.

1. Update the checkDozen to use a NullProgressMonitor if null is passed:

```
private void checkDozen(IProgressMonitor monitor) {
    if (monitor == null)
        monitor = new NullProgressMonitor();
```

This allows the remainder of the method to run without modification and saves any `NullPointerException` errors that may result.

2. A similar result to both the `NullProgressMonitor` and a `SubProgressMonitor` with a wrapper/factory class called `SubMonitor`. This provides factory methods to wrap the monitor and create child progress monitors:

```
protected IStatus run(IProgressMonitor monitor) {
  try {
    SubMonitor subMonitor =
      SubMonitor.convert(monitor,"Preparing", 5000);
    for (int i = 0; i < 50 && !subMonitor.isCanceled(); i++) {
      if (i == 10) {
        subMonitor.subTask("Doing something");
      } else if (i == 12) {
        checkDozen(subMonitor.newChild(100));
        continue;
      } else if (i == 25) {
        subMonitor.subTask("Doing something else");
      } else if (i == 40) {
        subMonitor.subTask("Nearly there");
      }
      Thread.sleep(100);
      subMonitor.worked(100);
    }
  } catch (InterruptedException e) {
  } finally {
    monitor.done();
  }
}
```

3. Running the code has the same effect as the previous one, but is more efficient. Note that the `subMonitor` is used everywhere in the method until the end, where `monitor` is used to invoke `done`.

What just happened?

The `NullProgressMonitor` and `SubProgressMonitor` were replaced by a `SubMonitor`. To convert an arbitrary `IProgessMonitor` into a `SubMonitor`, use the `convert` factory method. This has the advantage of testing for `null` (and using an embedded `NullProgressMonitor` if necessary) as well as facilitating the construction of `SubProgressMonitor` instances with the `newChild` call.

Note that the contract of SubMonitor requires the caller to invoke done on the underlying progress monitor at the end of the method, so it is an error to do an assignment like monitor = SubMonitor. convert(monitor) in code.

Since the isCancelled check will ultimately call the parent monitor, it doesn't strictly matter whether it is called on the sub monitor or the parent monitor. However, if the parent monitor is null, invoking it on the parent will result in a NullPointerException, whereas the SubProgressMonitor will never be null.

In situations where there will be lots of recursive tasks, the SubProgessMonitor will handle nesting better than instantiating a SubProgressMonitor each time. That's because the implementation of the newChild doesn't necessarily need to create a new SubMonitor instance each time; it can keep track of how many times it has been called recursively.

The SubMonitor also has a setWorkRemaining call, which can be used to reset the amount of work for the outstanding progress monitor. This can be useful if the job doesn't know at the start how much work is there to be done, but it does become known later in the process.

Time for action – setting job properties

It is possible to associate arbitrary properties with a Job, which can be used to present its progress in different ways. For example, by specifying a command, it's possible to click on a running job and then execute something in the user interface, such as a detailed job description. Job properties are set with setProperty and can include any key/value combination. The keys use a QualifiedName, which is like a pair of strings for namespace/ value. In the case of the progress view, there is an IProgressConstants2 interface that defines what values can be set, including COMMAND_PROPERTY, which can be used to associate a command with a Job.

1. Open the HelloHandler and go to the execute method. Just before the Job is scheduled, acquire the Command from the ICommandService and then stamp it on the job as a property. This will require adding an argument into the method signature and adding org.eclipse.core.commands as a dependent bundle:

```
public void execute(final UISynchronize display,
final ICommandService commandService) {
  ...
  Command command = commandService.getCommand(
    "com.packtpub.e4.clock.ui.command.hello");
  if (command != null) {
    job.setProperty(IProgressConstants2.COMMAND_PROPERTY,
      command);
  }
  job.schedule()
  return;
```

2. Run the target Eclipse instance, open the **Hello** command, and go to the **Progress** view. Nothing will be shown, because the `Job` expects a `ParameterizedCommand` instead. Use the `ParameterizedCommand` method `generateCommand` to wrap a non-parameterized command:

```
if (command != null) {
  // job.setProperty(IProgressConstants2.COMMAND_PROPERTY,
command);
   job.setProperty(IProgressConstants2.COMMAND_PROPERTY,
    ParameterizedCommand.generateCommand(command, null));
}
```

3. Now run the target Eclipse instance, go to the **Progress** view, and click on the **Hello** command. Underneath the **Progress** view, a hyperlink will be provided to allow firing off of another **Hello** command:

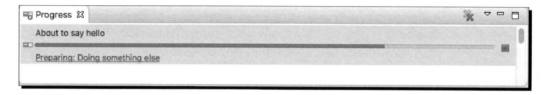

4. If the command is handled, clicking on the link will run the command, which in this case runs the `HelloHandler` and launches another job instance. Each click will spawn off a new job:

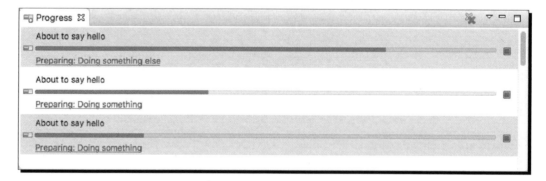

5. It's possible to change the icon shown in the view, by specifying an
    `ImageDescriptor` as a `Job` property with the key `ICON_PROPERTY`. The image
    descriptor can be loaded from the `ImageDescriptor` method `createFromURL`
    and set as a property:

    ```
    job.setProperty(IProgressConstants2.ICON_PROPERTY,
       ImageDescriptor.createFromURL(
          HelloHandler.class.getResource("/icons/sample.gif")));
    ```

6. Run the Eclipse instance, go to the **Progress** view, and then click on the **Hello** menu.
    The icon should be shown against the `Job`:

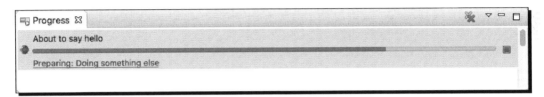

What just happened?

Setting properties on the running `Job` allows viewers to extract information and present it in
different ways. Properties are specified with a `QualifiedName` key, and the value is passed
in as an object, which is property-specific.

The purpose of the `QualifiedName` is to act as a string identifier, but partitioned into
different namespaces. For example, the properties used by the `IProgressConstants` use
`org.eclipse.ui.workbench.progress` as the namespace qualifier and shorter strings
such as `command` and `icon` for individual properties. The benefit of this (instead of using, for
example, `org.eclipse.ui.workbench.properties.command`) is that the long prefix
string is stored only once in memory.

Valid values for the `Job` in the progress view can be found in the `IProgressConstants`
and `IProgressContstants2` interfaces. Note that this is not a fixed set; additional
`Job` properties can be added for use both elsewhere in the Eclipse platform and by
independent extensions.

The `Command` can be acquired from the `ICommandService`, which is acquired through
injection in E4.

To associate a command with a `Job`, set a property that contains a
`ParameterizedCommand`, if necessary using the factory method `generateCommand` to
convert a `Command` into a `ParameterizedCommand`.

Have a go hero – displaying in the taskbar

The `IProgressConstants2` interface also defines a property named `SHOW_IN_TASKBAR_ICON_PROPERTY`, which shows whether the progress of the job is exposed to those operating systems that support it. On macOS, a bar will be shown over the Eclipse application icon. Set the property to the value `Boolean.TRUE` and see the effect it has on the `Job`.

The `Job` can also indicate whether it is running in the foreground or the background, and can query its state via the `Job` property `PROPERTY_IN_DIALOG`. This is not intended to be set by clients, but can be read and displayed (or different actions taken).

Pop quiz – understanding Jobs

Q1. What is the difference between `UISynchronize.syncExec` and `UISynchronize.asyncExec`?

Q2. What is `UISynchronize` used for?

Q3. What is the difference between `Job` and `UIJob`?

Q4. What is the singleton `Status` object that indicates everything is OK?

Q5. How is the `CommandService` obtained in Eclipse?

Q6. How is an icon associated with a `Job` in the **Progress** view?

Q7. When should a `SubMonitor` be used instead of a `SubProgressMonitor`?

Q8. How frequently should the job cancellation status be checked?

Reporting errors

As long as everything works as expected, the IDE won't need to tell the user that something has gone wrong. Unfortunately, even the most optimistic programmer won't believe that the code will work in every situation. Bad data, threading issues, simple bugs, and environmental issues can result in operations failing, and when they fail, the user needs to be notified.

Eclipse has built-in mechanisms to report problems, and these should be used in response to a user interaction that has failed.

Time for action – showing errors

So far, the code has been using an information dialog as the demonstration of the handler. There's an equivalent method that can be used to create an Error message instead. Instead of calling `MessageDialog.openInformation()`, there's an `openError()` that presents the same kind of dialog, but with an error message.

Using dialogs to report errors may be useful for certain environments, but unless the user has just invoked something (and the UI is blocked whilst doing it), reporting errors via a dialog is not a very useful thing to do. Instead, Eclipse offers a standard way to encapsulate both success and failure, in the `Status` object and the interface `IStatus` that it implements. When a `Job` completes, it returns an `IStatus` object to denote success or failure of executing the `Job`.

1. Introduce an error into the `HelloHandler` method `run` that will generate a `NullPointerException`. Add a `catch` to the existing `try` block and use that to return an error status. Since the `OK_STATUS` is a singleton instance of `Status`, it is necessary to instantiate a new `Status` object with the error information enclosed:

```
protected IStatus run(IProgressMonitor monitor) {
  try {
    SubMonitor subMonitor =
     SubMonitor.convert(monitor,"Preparing", 5000);
    subMonitor = null; // the bug
    ...
  } catch (RuntimeException e) {
    return new Status(IStatus.ERROR,
     Activator.PLUGIN_ID, "Programming bug?", e);
  } finally {
```

2. Run the Eclipse instance, and invoke the `Hello` command. An exception will be generated, and the status object containing the information needed will be passed to Eclipse. If the job is running in the foreground, the job scheduler will present the status message if it is an error:

3. Open the **Window** | **Show View** | **Other** | **General** | **Error Log** in the target Eclipse instance to see the error, which has also been written into the `workspace/.metadata/.log` file:

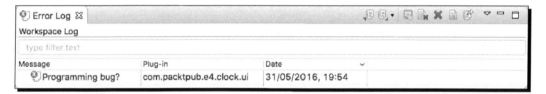

4. Double-click on the entry in the error log to bring up specific details:

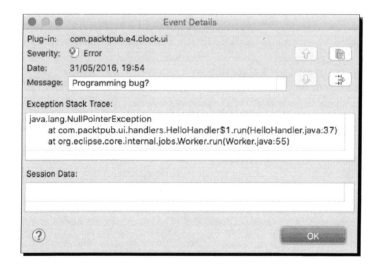

5. Instead of returning an error status, it's also possible to log the error message programmatically, using `StatusReporter`. This requires that the package `org.eclipse.e4.core.services` be imported in the `Manifest`. The `StatusReporter` is a service that can be injected. To just log the information but keep going, don't return the `status` object:

```
public void execute(final UISynchronize display,
  final ICommandService commandService,
  final StatusReporter statusReporter) {
...
} catch (NullPointerException e) {
  // return new Status(IStatus.ERROR,
  //   Activator.PLUGIN_ID, "Programming bug?", e);
  Status status = new Status(IStatus.ERROR,
    Activator.PLUGIN_ID, "Programming bug?", e);
  statusReporter.report(status,
    StatusReporter.LOG);
} ...
```

6. Run the target Eclipse instance, invoke the `Hello` command, and see the error being logged without displaying a dialog.

7. Modify the status flags to add SHOW as well:

```
statusReporter.handle(status,
    StatusReporter.LOG | StatusReporter.SHOW );
```

8. Re-run the Eclipse instance, invoke the `Hello` command, and the error will be shown as well as logged.

9. Finally, remove the bug from the `HelloHandler` so that it doesn't cause errors:

```
// subMonitor = null; // the bug
```

What just happened?

First, `openError` was used to show an error, which is useful for specific cases, such as when the user is interacting with the UI and has just done an operation that is problematic.

The next step looked at status reporting and handling in Eclipse, including how exceptions are captured and associated with a specific plugin. A `Status` was used to indicate a single issue—though there's a `MultiStatus` that can be used to add more `Status` instances if required. Generally, the status should be logged but not shown as dialogs popping up in the user's screen (especially from a background job) are a UX anti-pattern.

These flags can be combined; so LOG indicates that the status message should be logged but not otherwise displayed to the user, while SHOW indicates that the message should be shown in the standard dialog. Both of these happen asynchronously; the code will continue executing after invoking these calls, regardless of how the messages are shown to the user. There is a BLOCK flag as well, which prevents continued execution of the thread, but this should not be used as it may lead to inadvertent deadlocks.

Pop quiz – understanding errors

Q1. How is an info/warning/error dialog shown?

Q2. What is a StatusReporter?

Q3. Are status reports asynchronous or synchronous by default?

Q4. How can more than one problem be reported at the same time?

Summary

This chapter covered how user interfaces respond to user input, by defining menus associated with abstract commands that are associated with handlers to execute code. It also covered how to run code in the background with jobs, and report the errors via the standard error reporting mechanism.

The next chapter will look at how to store preferences so that configuration items can be kept between restarts of the Eclipse platform.

5
Working with Preferences

Preferences – customizing the runtime

An IDE is powerful if it provides a number of different utility windows to help the developer as they do their job. It becomes more powerful when they can customize it to their tastes, whether it is something as simple as colors or more targeted as filters. The preference store in Eclipse allows users to customize it in the way they want.

In this chapter, we will:

◆ Read and write preferences from a `PreferenceStore`

◆ Create a `PreferencePage` using `FieldEditors`

Eclipse Preferences

A user preference is a stored configuration option that persists between different Eclipse runtimes. Preferences are simple values (such as `int`, `String`, and `boolean`) and are identified with a `String` key, typically associated with the plug-in's identifier. `Preferences` can also be edited via a standard preference panel, contributed through an extension point.

They can also be imported and exported from an Eclipse workbench by navigating to **File | Import/Export | Preferences**, and saved with an `epf` extension (short for Eclipse Preference File).

Time for action – persisting a value

To save and load preferences, an instance of `Preferences` (from the `org.osgi.service.prefs` package) is typically obtained from an instance of `InstanceScope` (from the `org.eclipse.core.runtime.preferences` package). The `INSTANCE` singleton returns an instance of `Preferences` that has a `getNode` method. This returns a store that can be used to persist key/value pairs.

1. Open the `Activator` of the `com.packtpub.e4.clock.ui` plug-in.

2. Add the following to the `start` method to count the number of times the plug-in has been launched:

```
// import org.osgi.service.prefs.Preferences;
// import org.eclipse.core.runtime.preferences.InstanceScope;
// ^ add these if necessary to top of the class
Preferences preferences =
  InstanceScope.INSTANCE.getNode("com.packtpub.e4.clock.ui");
int launchCount = preferences.getInt("launchCount", 0)+1;
System.out.println("I have been launched "+launchCount+" times");
preferences.putInt("launchCount", launchCount);
preferences.sync();
```

3. Run the target Eclipse instance, and open **Time Zone Tree View**.

4. In the host Eclipse, open the **Console** view. It should say:

```
I have been launched 0 times
```

5. Close the target Eclipse instance, and rerun it (but do not clear the workspace). Open **Time Zone Tree View** again.

6. In the host Eclipse, open the **Console** view. It should now say:

```
I have been launched 1 times
```

What just happened?

The `Preferences` interface is a standard OSGi service, and in Eclipse, it's usually loaded via the `InstanceScope` constructor through the `getNode` method. This API provides getter and setter methods for `String` data (with `get`) and primitive types (such as the `getInt`, `getBoolean`, and `getDouble` methods), along with the corresponding `setValue` methods for the same types. Changes to preferences can be flushed to disk with the `sync` method.

The bundle's ID (`Bundle-SymbolicName` in the manifest) is typically used as the node's ID to allow bundles to coexist without conflicting preference values.

When this code is run, the number of times the plug-in has been launched will be stored as a value in the preferences store. If run from Eclipse, the message **I have been launched 0 times** is shown the first time the application is run; the second time, it's **I have been launched 1 times**, and each restart will update the counter.

> Note that the preferences API generally shouldn't be used to store plug-in-specific state; there's a method called `getDataFile` on the `BundleContext` (passed into the `Activator`) that returns a `File` that can be used to store such transient state.

If the message **I have been launched 0 times** is displayed repeatedly, the **Clear workspace before launching** option may be selected in the launch configurations menu. To disable this, navigate to **Run | Run Configurations...** for **Eclipse Application**, and in the **Main** tab, ensure that the **Clear** checkbox is deselected.

Time for action – injecting preferences

The top-level preferences store can be injected into the object by using standard dependency injection techniques, using the `IEclipsePreferences` interface. The underlying nodes can also be injected by using an `@Preferences` annotation, specifying the node path of interest.

1. Add the `org.eclipse.e4.core.di.extensions` package to the manifest of the `com.packtpub.e4.clock.ui` project, which contains the `@Preferences` annotation.

2. In the `TimeZoneTreeView` class, add a new field of type `IEclipsePreferences` called `preferences`. Annotate it with `@Inject` and `@Preferences(nodePath = "com.packtpub.e4.clock.ui")`:

    ```
    @Preference(nodePath = "com.packtpub.e4.clock.ui")
    @Inject
    IEclipsePreferences preferences;
    ```

> The `IEclipsePreferences` interface is a subtype of the `Preferences` interface used in the previous section. However, the `@Preference` annotation requires that the `IEclipsePreferences` type be used here; otherwise a runtime exception will occur.

3. In the `create` method, print a message that reads the `launchCount` from the preferences as an `int`, defaulting to `0` if it is not found:

```
@PostConstruct
public void create(Composite parent) {
    ...
    System.out.println("Launch count is: "
        + preferences.getInt("launchCount", 0));
```

4. Run the target Eclipse instance, and open the **Time Zone Tree View**. In the **Console** view, there should be an additional **Launch count is:** message with the same value as before.

What just happened?

The preferences are accessed through an `IEclipsePreferences` interface, which is a subtype of the `Preferences` interface. E4 injection is used to find the preferences object for the specific bundle, using the `@Preferences` annotation to find the preferences associated with a specific `nodePath`.

The convention is to use the bundle's symbolic name as the node path, which is the same as using the `InstanceScope` method `getNode` in the previous example. The preferences node can also be used to save or change values.

Time for action – injecting individual preferences

Although it is possible to inject an entire preference node, sometimes it is more convenient to inject just a single preference value. This can reduce the amount of code needed to extract and use a preference value. In addition, this can remove the runtime dependency on `IEclipsePreferences`, which can make the code more portable.

1. Replace the injected `IEclipsePreferences` node with an `int launchCount` field, and append `value = "launchCount"` to the `@Preferences` annotation:

```
@Preference(nodePath = "com.packtpub.e4.clock.ui",
 value = "launchCount")
@Inject
// IEclipsePreferences preferences;
int launchCount;
```

2. Update the print message to use the `launchCount` value directly:

```
System.out.println("Launch count is: " + launchCount);
```

3. Run the target Eclipse instance, and open the **Time Zone Tree View**. In the **Console** view, there should be a **Launch count is:** message with the same value as before.

What just happened?

Instead of injecting the entire preferences node, the single preference value is injected. If the preference value doesn't exist, then it will be assigned a default value (0 for numeric values, `false` for boolean, and `null` for object values). By removing the `IEclipsePreferences` and `Preferences` interfaces, the code is less tied to the Eclipse framework (the runtime visible annotation `@Preference` is still present, but this isn't required at runtime by the application outside of an Eclipse environment).

 Note that the preference is injected once—when the view is created. If the preference value is updated, then it will not be re-injected into the application.

Time for action – responding to preference changes

In order to react when preferences are changed, it is necessary to inject the preference value as part of a method call. When the preference value is changed, the method will be invoked again with the new value.

1. Remove the annotations associated with the `launchCount` instance field.

2. Create a `setLaunchCount` method that takes an `int` argument and assigns it to the `launchCount` instance field.

 Type `setL` and press *Ctrl + space* to suggest creating this method automatically.

3. Add the `@Inject` annotation to the `setLaunchCount` method.

4. Add the `@Preference(nodePath = "com.packtpub.e4.clock.ui", value = "launchCount")` annotation to the method argument. The resulting method will look like this:

```
int launchCount;

@Inject
public void setLaunchCount(
  @Preference(nodePath = "com.packtpub.e4.clock.ui",
    value = "launchCount") int launchCount) {
  this.launchCount = launchCount;
}
```

5. Run the target Eclipse instance, and open the **Time Zone Tree View**. In the **Console** view, there should be a **Launch count is:** message with the same value as before.

What just happened?

Instead of the value being injected when the view is created, the value is set by calling the method. This has the same effect as before, but this time, if the preference value subsequently changes, the value will be re-injected by calling the method again. If the preference affects the way the component is shown, the method can trigger the user interface to be updated.

Preference pages

Preference pages are a type of user interface used in the Eclipse workbench that allow the user to search and change preferences. These are contributed as extensions of the `org.eclipse.ui.preferencePages` point, and can present preferences with a number of standard editors or with custom content.

Time for action – creating a preference page

Although preferences can be stored programmatically, users will typically change them through the user interface. The canonical way of presenting preferences is through a preference page in Eclipse, which can be accessed through the **Preferences** menu. A preference page implements the `IPreferencePage` interface, but the easiest way is to use the `FieldEditorPreferencePage` as a superclass, which provides most of the standard plug-in behavior needed, along with the `IWorkbenchPreferencePage` interface.

1. Open the `plugin.xml` of the `com.packtpub.e4.clock.ui` plug-in. To declare a new preference page, use the `org.eclipse.ui.preferencePages` extension point. Add the following:

```
<extension point="org.eclipse.ui.preferencePages">
  <page name="Clock"
        class="com.packtpub.e4.clock.ui.ClockPreferencePage"
        id="com.packtpub.e4.clock.ui.preference.page"/>
</extension>
```

 The same effect can be achieved by editing `plugin.xml` in the editor, clicking on **Add** in the **Extensions** tab, and selecting the `preferencePages` extension point.

2. Create a class called `ClockPreferencePage` that extends `FieldEditorPreferencePage` and implements `IWorkbenchPreferencePage` in the `com.packtpub.e4.clock.ui` package, as follows:

```
public class ClockPreferencePage extends FieldEditorPreferencePage
  implements IWorkbenchPreferencePage {
```

```
    protected void createFieldEditors() {
    }
    public void init(IWorkbench workbench) {
    }
}
```

3. Run the target Eclipse application, and go to the preferences window by navigating to **Eclipse | Preferences** on macOS or **Window | Preferences** on Windows/Linux. In the preferences list, a **Clock** preference page should be displayed, although at present there will be no content.

4. Add a new `IntegerFieldEditor` for storing the launch count, by adding it to the `createFieldEditors` method:

```
protected void createFieldEditors() {
    addField(new IntegerFieldEditor("launchCount",
    "Number of times it has been launched",
     getFieldEditorParent()));
}
```

5. Run the target Eclipse application, go to **Preferences**, and look at the **Clock** preference page. To get it to display the correct value, `FieldEditorPreferencePage` needs to be connected to the plug-in's `PreferenceStore`:

```
public void init(IWorkbench workbench) {
    setPreferenceStore(new ScopedPreferenceStore(
     InstanceScope.INSTANCE, "com.packtpub.e4.clock.ui"));
}
```

6. Now run the target Eclipse application, go to **Preferences**, and look at the **Clock** preference page. The number will update based on the number of times the Eclipse application has launched:

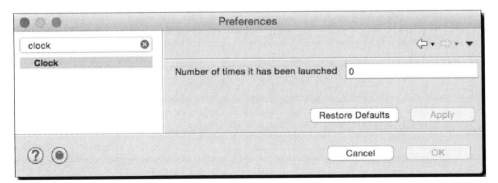

What just happened?

The Preferences page was created and connected to the preferences window and the correct preference store. Instances of `FieldEditor` were added to display properties on a per property basis.

The implementation of `getFieldEditorParent` is something that needs to be called each time a field editor is created. It might be tempting to refactor this into a common variable, but the JavaDoc says that the value cannot be cached; if the `FLAT` style is used, then it will create a new instance of the parent each time it is called.

Time for action – creating warning and error messages

In free-form text fields, it's sometimes possible to enter a value that isn't valid. For example, when asking for an e-mail address, it might be necessary to validate it against some kind of regular expression such as `.+@.+` to provide a simple check.

1. To test the default validation, run the target Eclipse instance and go to the **Clock** preference page. Type some text in the numeric field. A warning message, **Value must be an integer**, will be displayed:

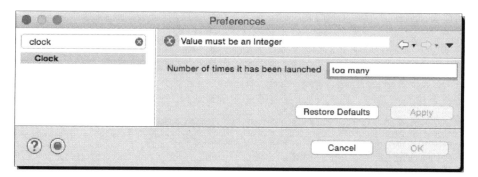

2. To add validation, create a new field called `offset` that allows values between `-14` and `+12` (by default, `IntegerFieldEditor` validates against the `0..MAX_INT` range). Add the following to the `createFieldEditors` method:

```
IntegerFieldEditor offset = new IntegerFieldEditor("offset",
  "Current offset from GMT", getFieldEditorParent());
offset.setValidRange(-14, +12);
addField(offset);
```

3. Run the target Eclipse instance, go to the **Clock** preference page, and type in an invalid value:

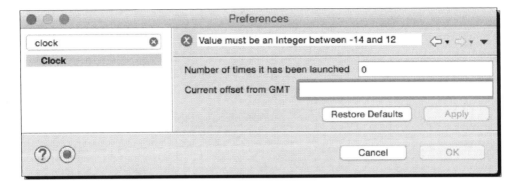

What just happened?

Each field editor can determine what is (or is not) valid, and the validity of the page as a whole is a conjunction of all of the individual field editors' validity. It's also possible to create custom validation rules by creating a subclass of the appropriate `FieldEditor`, overriding the `isValid` method appropriately.

The error message will show a message like **Value must be an Integer between -14 and 12** at the top of the preference page.

Time for action: choosing from a list

Although free text may be appropriate for some types of preference, choosing from a set of values may be more appropriate for other types. A `ComboFieldEditor` instance can be used to present the user with a selection of time zones, from which the user can set their favorite `ZoneId`. The combo drop-down is built from an array of pairs of strings; the first string in each pair is the display label, while the second value in each pair is the string identifier that will be persisted in the preferences store.

1. In the `ClockPreferencePage` method `createFieldEditors`, add the following code to populate a `ComboFieldEditor` with the list of `ZoneId` elements:

```
protected void createFieldEditors() {
  // ...
  String[][] data = ZoneId.getAvailableZoneIds() //
    .stream().sorted().map(s -> new String[] { s, s }) //
    .collect(Collectors.toList()).toArray(new String[][] {});
  addField(new ComboFieldEditor("favorite",
    "Favorite time zone", data, getFieldEditorParent()));
}
```

2. Run the target Eclipse instance, and go to the **Clock** preference page. A new drop-down will allow the user to select their favorite `ZoneId`. Choose a value, and then close and reopen the target Eclipse instance; the previous value should be stored:

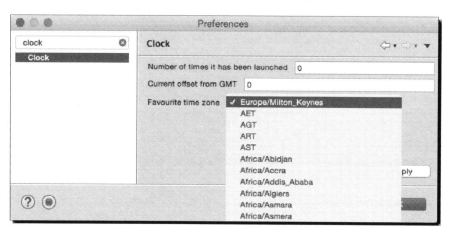

What just happened?

Field editors can be used to customize stored data. Since preference values are saved as a string, the `ComboFieldEditor` takes a set of pairs of strings, one for the display label and one for the persisted value.

The combo field editor was initialized with a `ZoneId` list, using the ID for both the display label and the persisted value. The display could present more information, such as the display name, the offset from GMT, or other metadata. However, the string value that is persisted to the preferences should be unique and not subject to parsing or loading errors. In this case, using the ID means that a later iteration of the preferences plug-in could render the display text in a different form while still persisting the same ID in the preference store.

Time for action – aligning field editors with a grid

The preference values weren't lined up as might be expected. This is because the default preference field editor uses a `FLAT` style of rendering, which simply lays out the fields similar to a vertical `RowLayout`.

1. Change it to be a more natural look by specifying a `GRID` style of rendering:

```
public ClockPreferencePage() {
  super(GRID);
}
```

2. Now, when the preference page is displayed, it will look more natural:

What just happened?

The default `FLAT` style does not render well. It was added in 2007 before the popularity of the grid layout increased and typically needs to be overridden to provide a decent user interface experience. Switching to `GRID` does this, by working out the label length and field lengths and setting up the split accordingly. Furthermore, the view is resizable, with the fields taking up additional stretch space.

If the layout needs further customization or the widget set needs to be extended, then it is possible to create a plain subclass of `PreferencePage` and create the contents by overriding the `createContents` method, applying any changes in the `performOk` or `performApply` methods.

Time for action – placing the preferences page

When the preference page is created, if it does not specify a location (known as a `category` in the `plugin.xml` file and manifest editor), it is inserted into the top level. This is appropriate for some kinds of project (for example, Mylyn, Java, and Plug-in Development); but many plug-ins should contribute into an existing location in the preference page tree.

1. Preference pages can be nested by specifying the parent preference page's ID. To move the **Clock** preference page underneath the **General** preference page, specify `org.eclipse.ui.preferencePages.Workbench` as the category:

```
<extension point="org.eclipse.ui.preferencePages">
  <page name="Clock"
    id="com.packtpub.e4.clock.ui.preference.page"
    category="org.eclipse.ui.preferencePages.Workbench"
    class="com.packtpub.e4.clock.ui.ClockPreferencePage"/>
</extension>
```

2. Run the target Eclipse instance and look at the `Preferences`. The **Clock** preference page should now be under the **General** tree node instead:

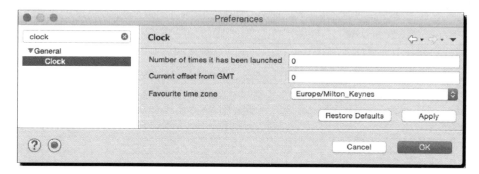

What just happened?

The preference page can be placed anywhere in the hierarchy by specifying the parent page's ID in the category attribute. The parent pages can be listed by navigating to **Window | Show View | Other | Console** and opening a **Host OSGI Console**, followed by running the following command:

```
osgi> pt -v org.eclipse.ui.preferencePages
Extension point: org.eclipse.ui.preferencePages [from org.eclipse.ui]


Extension(s):
------------------
null [from org.eclipse.ant.ui]
    <page>
        name = Ant
        class = org.eclipse.ant.internal.ui.preferences.AntPreferencePage
        id = org.eclipse.ant.ui.AntPreferencePage
    </page>
...
```

Another way of listing the IDs is to use the **Browse** button via the `plugin.xml` editor. From the extension point defining the **Clock** preference page, the **Browse** button next to the category field will bring up a dialog containing all the valid IDs, including a search filter to reduce the number of matches:

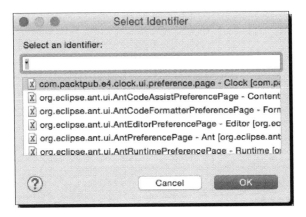

Time for action: using other field editors

The `FieldEditorPreferencePage` supports other types of field editors.
These different types include `BooleanFieldEditor`, `ColorFieldEditor`,
`ScaleFieldEditor`, `FileFieldEditor`, `DirectoryFieldEditor`, `PathEditor`, and
`RadioGroupFieldEditor`. Add a sample of each of these types to the **Clock** preference
page to find out what they can store.

1. Open the `createFieldEditors` method of `ClockPreferencePage` and add the
following at the bottom of the method:

```
addField(new BooleanFieldEditor("tick", "Boolean value",
  getFieldEditorParent()));
addField(new ColorFieldEditor("color", "Favorite color",
  getFieldEditorParent()));
addField(new ScaleFieldEditor("scale", "Scale",
  getFieldEditorParent(), 0, 360, 10, 90));
addField(new FileFieldEditor("file", "Pick a file",
  getFieldEditorParent()));
addField(new DirectoryFieldEditor("dir", "Pick a directory",
  getFieldEditorParent()));
addField(new PathEditor("path", "Path",
  "Directory", getFieldEditorParent()));
addField(new RadioGroupFieldEditor("group", "Radio choices", 3,
  data, getFieldEditorParent(), true));
```

2. Run the target Eclipse instance, and go to the **Clock** preference page. It will look like this:

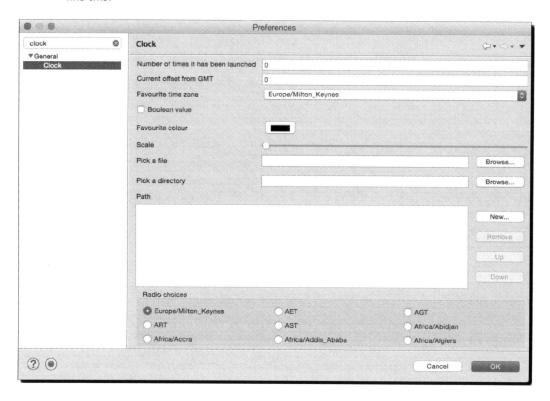

What just happened?

This change added different types of standard field editors provided by the JFace package, to give a flavor of the types of data entry elements that can be shown.

Some of the editors are specific to the kinds of entry points that are used in Eclipse itself, such as file, directory, or path editors. Others are more general, such as color, scale, boolean, or radio choices.

The values are persisted in the preferences format as text values, appropriate to the data type. To see what the values are written to, go to the `runtime-EclipseApplication/.metadata/.plugins/org.eclipse.core.runtime/.settings/com.packtpub.e4.clock.ui.prefs` file. The contents look like this:

```
color=49,241,180
eclipse.preferences.version=1
favorite=Europe/Milton_Keynes
group=Europe/Milton_Keynes
```

```
launchCount=28
scale=78
tick=true
```

The persisted color value is stored as a red/green/blue triple, while the boolean value is stored as a `true` or `false` value.

Time for action – searching for preferences

Eclipse has a search field in the preferences list. This is defined not from the UI but from a separate `keyword` extension instead. The `keyword` has an `id` and a `label`. The `label` is a space-separated list of words that can be used in the filtering dialog.

1. To add the `offset` and `timezone` keywords to `ClockPreferencePage`, create a new extension point in `plugin.xml` for `org.eclipse.ui.keywords`:

    ```
    <extension point="org.eclipse.ui.keywords">
       <keyword id="com.packtpub.e4.clock.ui.keywords"
         label="offset timezone"/>
    </extension>
    ```

2. Now associate these keywords with the preference page itself:

    ```
    <extension point="org.eclipse.ui.preferencePages">
       <page name="Clock" ... >
          <keywordReference id="com.packtpub.e4.clock.ui.keywords"/>
       </page>
    </extension>
    ```

3. Run the target Eclipse instance, go to the **Preferences** page, and type `timezone` or `offset` in the search box. The **Clock** preference page should be shown in both cases:

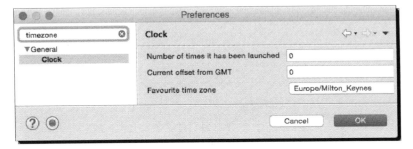

What just happened?

By providing a list of keywords and associating them with the preferences page, the user can search for the item in the preferences tree. The same keyword support is used to search for items in other places, such as the New dialog wizards and the properties page.

Furthermore, these keywords are translatable. By specifying a key with a percent symbol (%), Eclipse can load the keywords from an externalized file called `plugin.properties`. If `%clock.keywords` was used as the label and the `plugin.properties` had an entry `clock.keywords=timezone` offset, then other translations could be provided; for example, a French translation of the keywords can be provided in a `plugin_fr.properties` file.

Have a go hero – translating into different languages

Eclipse's internationalization support is provided by a `plugin.properties` file. In `plugin.xml`, instead of using strings for the values, use `%keys`. The `%` instructs the engine to look for a corresponding entry in `plugin.properties` to display the value.

To support different languages, use different language codes, such as `plugin_fr.properties` and `plugin_de.properties` for French and German respectively (remember to add these files to `build.properties` or else they won't be found). The keys are still the same, but the values can be localized appropriately. The search keywords are an example of something that can be searched as well, so use an online translation service or make up a translation to test out the effect of running Eclipse in a different language. Eclipse can be launched in different languages with `eclipse -nl de` on the command line.

Pop quiz – understanding preferences

Q1. What is the default style used for `FieldEditorPreferencePage` and how can it be changed to something more aesthetically pleasing?

Q2. What kinds of primitive values can be edited with a `FieldEditorPreferencePage`?

Q3. How can a preference value be searched for in the preference page?

Q4. How can preference values be injected into an E4 part?

Q5. How can a part respond to changes in a preference value?

Summary

We covered the mechanisms that Eclipse uses to store metadata values. A preference store is the key/value pair mechanism used by preference pages as well as interacted with programmatically from headless plug-ins.

In the next chapter, we will see how to work with `Resource` objects inside Eclipse.

6

Working with Resources

Resources – files, folders, and builders

As an IDE, Eclipse is used to work with files and folders. Eclipse creates the concept of a workspace (a group of related projects), a number of projects, and then files and folders underneath each. These resources are then used by builders to be able to create derived resources upon change, which is how Eclipse compiles Java source files into .class files.

In this chapter, we will:

- ◆ Create a custom editor
- ◆ Read the contents of a file
- ◆ Create a resource file
- ◆ Use a builder to automatically process changes
- ◆ Integrate the builder with a nature
- ◆ Highlight problems in the editor with markers

Using the workspace and resources

Everything in the Eclipse IDE is based on the concept of a **workspace**, which contains a number of **projects**, which in turn contain **files** and **folders**. Generically, these are all **resources** and are represented with a **path** and then either a set of contents or a set of children.

Time for action – creating an editor

The example will be based on a (made-up) markup language called `minimark`—which is essentially a plain text file with blank delimited paragraphs that can be translated into an HTML file. This will involve creating an editor for text-based content for `minimark` files.

1. Create a new plug-in project called `com.packtpub.e4.minimark.ui` by going to **File | New | Project | Plug-in project** and fill in:

    1. **Project name**: `com.packtpub.e4.minimark.ui`

2. Click on **Next** and fill in:

    1. **ID**: `com.packtpub.e4.minimark.ui`

    2. **Version**: `1.0.0.qualifier`

    3. **Name**: `Minimark`

    4. **Vendor**: `PACKTPUB`

    5. Ensure that the **Create an Activator** option is selected

    6. Ensure that this plug-in will make contributions to the UI option is selected

    7. Ensure that the **Create a Rich Client Application** option is not selected

3. Click on **Finish** and a new plug-in will be created.

4. The next step is to create an editor for the `minimark` files. Open the plug-in's manifest, by right-clicking on the project and selecting **Plug-in Tools | Open Manifest**, or by double-clicking on the `MANIFEST.MF` or `plugin.xml` files.

5. Go to the extensions tab and click on **Add**. The extension points dialog will show; search for `editors` and it should show up in the list (if it doesn't, uncheck the **Show only extension points from the required plug-ins** option and it will prompt to add `org.eclipse.ui.editors` to the required dependencies).

 If you see a warning saying **Plug-ins declaring extension points must set the singleton directive to true**, then go into the `MANIFEST.MF` file and add `;singleton:=true` at the end of the line containing the `Bundle-SymbolicName` header. A quick fix is provided and can be chosen by clicking on the lightbulb in the margin or by pressing *Ctrl + 1* when the cursor is on that line.

6. Once the extension point has been added, select the **name (editor)** child of the `org.eclipse.ui.editors` extension point (if this is not added automatically, right-click on the extension point and select **New | Editor** from the menu to add a template extension point). Fill it in as follows:

1. **id**: com.packtpub.e4.minimark.ui.minimarkeditor
2. **name**: Minimark
3. **extensions**: minimark
4. **class**: com.packtpub.e4.minimark.ui.MinimarkEditor

7. The resulting plugin.xml will look like:

```
<extension point="org.eclipse.ui.editors">
  <editor name="Minimark" extensions="minimark" default="false"
    class="com.packtpub.e4.minimark.ui.MinimarkEditor"
    id="com.packtpub.e4.minimark.ui.minimarkeditor"/>
</extension>
```

8. Now add the required bundle dependencies in the **Dependencies** tab:

1. org.eclipse.jface.text: This provides text-processing libraries
2. org.eclipse.ui.editors: This provides general editor support
3. org.eclipse.ui.workbench.texteditor: This provides general text editor

9. Use the **File | New | Class** wizard to create a MinimarkEditor class in the com.packtpub.e4.minimark.ui package as a subclass of AbstractTextEditor:

```
public class MinimarkEditor extends AbstractTextEditor {
```

10. Run the target Eclipse instance, and create a project with **File | New | Project | General Project** called EditorTest. Then use the **File | New | File** to create a file called test.minimark. Double-click on this file, and an error will be seen:

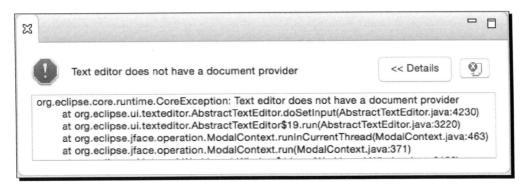

11. This happens because an editor needs to be hooked up to a document provider, which synchronizes the content of the document with any other open editors (this allows Eclipse to open multiple editors on the same file and show changes in both editors). To resolve the error, add a constructor that sets the editor's document provider to a general TextFileDocumentProvider:

```
import org.eclipse.ui.editors.text.TextFileDocumentProvider;
public class MinimarkEditor extends AbstractTextEditor {
  public MinimarkEditor() {
    setDocumentProvider(new TextFileDocumentProvider());
  }
}
```

12. Run the Eclipse instance again, double-click on the test.minimark file, and an empty text editor will be opened.

What just happened?

A basic text editor was created and associated with files ending in .minimark.

To add an editor type, the following bundles are needed:

◆ org.eclipse.core.runtime

◆ org.eclipse.jface.text

◆ org.eclipse.ui

◆ org.eclipse.ui.editors

◆ org.eclipse.ui.workbench.texteditor

The editor needs to be a subtype of an EditorPart. In this case, AbstractTextEditor provides the basic functionality for editing text-based files. It also needs to be registered with the org.eclipse.ui.editors extension point.

Note that building editors and the document providers that underpin them is a book in its own right; the implementation of the editor here is to support the resource processing examples. More information on writing custom editors is available in the online help.

Time for action – writing the markup parser

First, the format of the markup language needs to be explained. The first line will be a title, and then subsequent paragraphs are blank-line separated. This can be translated into an HTML file as follows.

Minimark source	Translated HTML
This is the title	`<html><head><title>This is the title</title></head><body><h1>This is the title</h1>`

A paragraph with some text	`<p>`
	`A paragraph with some text`
	`</p>`

Another paragraph	`<p>`
	`Another paragraph`
	`</p></body></html>`

1. Create a class called `MinimarkTranslator` in the `com.packtpub.e4.minimark.ui` package as follows:

```
public class MinimarkTranslator {
  public static void convert(Reader reader, Writer writer)
    throws IOException {
    BufferedReader lines = new BufferedReader(reader);
    String line;
    String title = String.valueOf(lines.readLine());
    writer.write("<html><head><title>");
    writer.write(title);
    writer.write("</title></head><body><h1>");
    writer.write("</h1><p>");
    while (null != (line = lines.readLine())) {
      if ("".equals(line)) {
        writer.write("</p><p>");
      } else {
        writer.write(line);
        writer.write('\n');
      }
    }
    writer.write("</p></body></html>");
    writer.flush();
  }
}
```

2. Copy the example text from the start of this section and save it as a file `in.txt` in the `com.packtpub.e4.minimark.ui` project.

3. Add a `main` method to the `MinimarkTranslator` to read in the `in.txt` file and write it out as `out.txt`:

```
public static void main(String[] args) throws IOException {
  convert(
    new FileReader("in.txt"),
    new FileWriter("out.txt"));
}
```

4. Run this as a Java application, and refresh the project. The file `out.txt` should be shown, and opening it should show an HTML file like the one at the start of this section.

5. After testing that the `MinimarkConverter` works as expected, delete the `main` method.

What just happened?

The minimal markup language can take plain ASCII text and translate it into an HTML file. The purpose of this exercise is not to define a fully comprehensive markup processor, but rather to provide a simple translator that can be shown to generate HTML as rendered in a browser from a plain text file.

 Note that the translator has at least one bug; if the file is empty, then the title may well be `null`, which would result in a title of `null` in the HTML browser.

The reader is invited to replace the translator with a different implementation, such as one of the Markdown parsers available on GitHub or Maven Central.

Time for action – building the builder

Compilers (and every other kind of translator) in Eclipse are implemented with builders. These are notified when a file or a set of files are changed, and can take appropriate action. In the case of the Java builder, it translates `.java` source files into `.class` files.

1. Open the `.project` file in the `com.packtpub.e4.minimark.ui` project. This is visible in the **Navigator** view, but not in the **Package Explorer** or other views. Alternatively, use *Cmd + Shift + R* on macOS (or *Ctrl + Shift + R* on other platforms) to open the resource by name. Builders are associated to a project within the `.project` file. The builder ID is referenced via the `buildCommand`, for example:

```
<projectDescription>
  <name>com.packtpub.e4.minimark.ui</name>
  <buildSpec>
    <buildCommand>
      <name>org.eclipse.jdt.core.javabuilder</name>
    </buildCommand>
      . . .
```

2. To translate a `.minimark` file into HTML automatically, a builder is needed. A builder is a class that extends `IncrementalProjectBuilder` and implements a `build` method. This is called by the framework when files are saved, and either gives a list of changed files or requests that the full project is built. Since this is defined in the core resources bundle, open the `plugin.xml` file and add the `org.eclipse.core.resources` bundle to the dependency list.

3. Create a class in the `com.packtpub.e4.minimark.ui` package called `MinimarkBuilder`:

```
public class MinimarkBuilder extends IncrementalProjectBuilder {
  protected IProject[] build(int kind,
    Map<String, String> args,
    IProgressMonitor monitor) throws CoreException {
    return null;
  }
}
```

4. Builds are called with different kinds—a flag which indicates whether the entire project is being built, or whether a subset of the project is being built. For builds that aren't `FULL_BUILD`, there's also a resource delta, which contains the set of resources that have been changed. Calculating a resource delta is a costly operation, so it should only be accessed if needed. The `build` method is typically implemented as follows:

```
protected IProject[] build(int kind, Map<String, String> args,
  IProgressMonitor monitor) throws CoreException {
  if (kind == FULL_BUILD) {
    fullBuild(getProject(), monitor);
  } else {
    incrementalBuild(getProject(), monitor,
      getDelta(getProject()));
  }
  return null;
}
```

5. The `fullBuild` and `incrementalBuild` methods need to be defined. It is also necessary to handle the cases where the `getDelta` method returns a `null` value, and invoke the full builder accordingly:

```
private void incrementalBuild(IProject project,
IProgressMonitor
 monitor, IResourceDelta delta) throws CoreException {
   if (delta == null) {
     fullBuild(project, monitor);
   } else {
     System.out.println("Doing an incremental build");
   }
}
private void fullBuild(IProject project, IProgressMonitor
monitor)
  throws CoreException {
   System.out.println("Doing a full build");
}
```

6. Finally, to hook up a builder, declare its reference in an extension point `org.eclipse.core.resources.builders`. This defines a reference (via an ID) to a class that implements the `IncrementalProjectBuilder`. Add the following to the `plugin.xml` file:

```
<extension id="MinimarkBuilder"
 point="org.eclipse.core.resources.builders">
   <builder
    callOnEmptyDelta="false"
    hasNature="false"
    isConfigurable="false"
    supportsConfigurations="false">
     <run class="com.packtpub.e4.minimark.ui.MinimarkBuilder"/>
   </builder>
</extension>
```

Note that this extension point requires an ID to be given, since the name defined in the `.project` file will be the plug-in's ID concatenated with the extension ID. It is conventional, but not necessary, for the full ID to be the name of the class.

7. Run the target Eclipse instance. Create a new **General** project in the test workspace, and once created, open the `.project` file. Add the builder manually by adding in a `buildCommand` with the ID from the extension point:

```
<buildSpec>
  <buildCommand>
    <name>com.packtpub.e4.minimark.ui.MinimarkBuilder</name>
  </buildCommand>
</buildSpec>
```

8. Clean the project by going to the **Project | Clean** menu. The message **Doing a full build** can be seen in the host console when the builder is added, or if the project is cleaned. Edit and save a `.minimark` file, and the message **Doing an incremental build** should be displayed.

What just happened?

The builder is capable of being invoked when files in a project are changed. To associate the builder with the project, it was added as a build command to the project, which is contained in the `.project` file. The name used for the builder is the extension's unique ID, which is formed as a dot-separated concatenation of the plug-in's ID and the element in the `plugin.xml` file.

The incremental builder has a kind that allows an implementation to determine whether it is doing a full or incremental build. There is also a `clean` method (which wasn't implemented here) that is used to remove all resources that have been created by a builder.

Time for action – iterating through resources

A project (represented by the `IProject` interface) is a top-level unit in the workspace (which is represented by the `IWorkspaceRoot` interface). These can contain resources (represented by the `IResource` interface), which are either folders or files (represented by the `IFolder` or `IFile` interfaces). They can be iterated with the `members` method, but this will result in the creation of `IResource` objects for every element processed, even if they aren't relevant. Instead, defer to the platform's internal tree by passing it a visitor that will step through each element required.

1. Create a class `MinimarkVisitor` in the `com.packtpub.e4.minimark.ui` package that implements the `IResourceProxyVisitor` and `IResourceDeltaVisitor` interfaces.

2. Implement the `visit(IResourceProxy)` method to get the name of the resource, and display a message if it finds a file whose name ends with `.minimark`. It should return `true` to allow child resources to be processed:

```
public boolean visit(IResourceProxy proxy) throws CoreException {
  String name = proxy.getName();
  if(name != null && name.endsWith(".minimark")) {
    // found a source file
    System.out.println("Processing " + name);
  }
  return true;
}
```

3. Modify the `incrementalBuild` and `fullBuild` methods to connect the builder to the `MinimarkVisitor` class, and add `CoreException` to the `throws` list:

```
private void incrementalBuild(IProject project, IProgressMonitor
 monitor, IResourceDelta delta) throws CoreException {
  if (delta == null) {
    fullBuild(project, monitor);
  } else {
    delta.accept(new MinimarkVisitor());
  }
}
private void fullBuild(IProject project, IProgressMonitor monitor)
 throws CoreException {
  project.accept(new MinimarkVisitor(),IResource.NONE);
}
```

4. Run the Eclipse instance, select a project that has the `minimark` builder configured and a `.minimark` file, and navigate to the **Project | Clean** menu. The host Eclipse instance should display a message saying **Processing test.minimark** in the **Console** view.

5. Now create a method in the `MinimarkVisitor` class called `processResource`. This will get contents of the file and pass it to the translator. To start with, the translated file will be written to `System.out`:

```
private void processResource(IResource resource) throws
 CoreException {
  if (resource instanceof IFile) {
    try {
      IFile file = (IFile) resource;
      InputStream in = file.getContents();
      MinimarkTranslator.convert(new InputStreamReader(in),
        new OutputStreamWriter(System.out));
    } catch (IOException e) {
      throw new CoreException(new Status(Status.ERROR,
```

```
                Activator.PLUGIN_ID, "Failed to generate resource", e));
        }
    }
}
```

6. Now modify the `visit` method to invoke `processResource`:

```
public boolean visit(IResourceProxy proxy) throws CoreException {
    String name = proxy.getName();
    if (name != null && name.endsWith(".minimark")) {
        // System.out.println("Processing " + name);
        processResource(proxy.requestResource());
    }
    return true;
}
```

 The method is called `requestResource` instead of `getResource` to signify that it isn't just a simple accessor, but that objects are created in calling the method.

7. Run the target Eclipse instance, make a change to a `.minimark` file, and perform a clean build with **Project | Clean**. The host Eclipse instance should print the translated output in the **Console** view.

What just happened?

When notified of changes in the build, the files are processed with a visitor. This abstracts away the need to know how the resources are organized. Resources such as team-private files (`.git`, `.svn`, or CVS directories) are automatically excluded from the caller.

Using the `IResourceProxyVisitor` interface to obtain the content is faster than using an `IResourceVisitor` interface, since the former can be used to test for properties on the name. This provides a much faster way of getting resources that follow a naming pattern as it does not require the creation of an `IResource` object for every item, some of which may not be necessary.

The builder communicates errors through a `CoreException`, which is the standard exception for many of Eclipse's errors. This takes as its parameter a `Status` object (with an associated exception and plug-in ID).

Finally, when a full build is invoked (by performing a **Project | Clean** on the project) the output is seen in the **Console** view of the development Eclipse.

Time for action – creating resources

The next step is to create an `IFile` resource for the `.html` file (based on the name of the `.minimark` file). Eclipse uses an `IPath` object to represent the filename from the root of the workspace. An `IPath` with `/project/folder/file.txt` refers to the `file.txt` file in a folder called `folder` contained within the project `project`. The root path represents the `IWorkspaceRoot`.

1. In the `processResource` method of the `MinimarkVisitor` class, calculate the new filename, and use it to get an `IFile` object from the file's parent `IContainer` object:

```
try {
  IFile file = (IFile) resource;
  InputStream in = file.getContents();
  String htmlName = file.getName().replace(".minimark", ".html");
  IContainer container = file.getParent();
  IFile htmlFile = container.getFile(new Path(htmlName));
```

2. To create the contents of the file, an `InputStream` instance has to be passed to the `setContents` method. The easiest way to create this is to pass a `ByteArrayOutputStream` instance to the `convert` method, and then use a `ByteArrayInputStream` instance to set the contents of the file:

```
ByteArrayOutputStream baos = new ByteArrayOutputStream();
MinimarkTranslator.convert(new InputStreamReader(in),
  // new OutputStreamWriter(System.out));
  new OutputStreamWriter(baos));
ByteArrayInputStream contents =
  new ByteArrayInputStream(baos.toByteArray());
```

3. Now the contents need to be set on the file. If the file exists, the contents are set with the `setContents` method, but if it doesn't, the `create` method needs to be called instead:

```
if (htmlFile.exists()) {
  htmlFile.setContents(contents, true, false, null);
} else {
  htmlFile.create(contents, true, null);
}
```

The second argument `true` forces the change; that is, the contents will be written even if the resource has been updated elsewhere. The third argument `false` indicates that changes should not be recorded, and the final argument `null` for both methods is for passing an optional `ProgressMonitor`.

4. Finally the resource needs to be marked as derived, which tells Eclipse that this is an automatically generated file and not a user-edited one:

```
htmlFile.setDerived(true, null);
```

5. Run the target Eclipse instance, navigate to the **Project | Clean** menu, and the corresponding HTML file should be generated. Modify the `.minimark` file, do a clean again, and the HTML file should be regenerated.

What just happened?

The build was modified to invoke the `MinimarkTranslator` and create a resource in the filesystem. Since it uses a stream to set the contents, a `ByteArrayOutputStream` is used to build up the translated contents, and a `ByteArrayInputStream` is used to read it back for the purpose of setting the file's contents.

The `exists` check is necessary because setting the contents on a non-existent file throws a `CoreException`.

The files are represented as a generic `IPath` object, which is concretely implemented with the `Path` class. Paths are represented as slash (/) separated filenames, regardless of the operating system, but each path component needs to obey the local filesystem's constraints, such as not allowing colons on Windows.

Time for action – implementing incremental builds

The final part of the puzzle is to implement the incremental part of the builder. Most of the builds that Eclipse performs are incremental, which means that it only compiles the files that are needed at each point. An incremental build gives a resource delta, which contains which files have been modified, added, or removed. This is implemented in an `IResourceDelta` interface, which is handed to the `IResourceDeltaVisitor` method `visit`. A resource delta combines an `IResource` instance with a flag that says whether it was added or removed.

1. Open the `MinimarkVisitor` and go to the `visit(IResourceDelta)` method. This is used by the incremental build when individual files are changed. Since the delta already has a resource, it can be used to determine whether the file is relevant, and if so, pass it to the `processResource` method:

```
public boolean visit(IResourceDelta delta) throws CoreException {
    IResource resource = delta.getResource();
    if (resource.getName().endsWith(".minimark")) {
        processResource(resource);
    }
    return true;
}
```

2. Run the target Eclipse instance, and edit and save the `.minimark` file. The builder's incremental builder will be invoked, with the given resource, and the file will be updated. Eclipse's HTML editor won't automatically refresh the change, but if the `.html` file is opened with a text editor, a side-by-side view shows that the file is being updated with each save.

What just happened?

An incremental build and a full build are very similar; they both process a set of resources. In the former case, it's the set of files that were changed in a workspace update operation (such as a **Save** or **Save All**). In the latter case, it's all files in an individual project. Refactoring to a common `processResource` method allows the implementation to be written once and then called from either situation.

Time for action: handling deletion

The incremental builder does not handle deletion in its current implementation. To handle deletion, the `IResourceDelta` instance needs to be inspected to find out what kind of delta took place and handle deleted resources accordingly.

1. Run the target Eclipse instance, and delete a `.minimark` file. An exception is thrown and reported to the user:

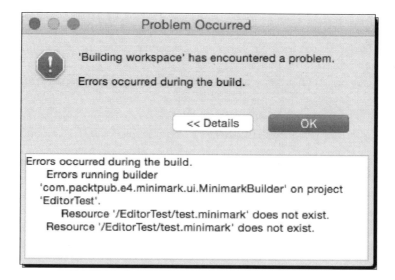

2. To fix this issue, modify the check in the `MinimarkVisitor` method `processResource` to see whether the resource exists or not:

```
private void processResource(IResource resource) throws
  CoreException {
    if (resource instanceof IFile && resource.exists()) {
```

3. This solves the `NullPointerException`, but the generated HTML file is left behind. If the `.minimark` file is deleted, and there is a corresponding `.html` file, that can be deleted as well. Modify the `visit(IResourceDelta)` method as follows:

```
public boolean visit(IResourceDelta delta) throws CoreException {
    boolean deleted = (IResourceDelta.REMOVED & delta.getKind())!=0;
    IResource resource = delta.getResource();
    String name = resource.getName();
    if (deleted) {
        String htmlName = name.replace(".minimark",".html");
        IFile htmlFile = resource.getParent().
          getFile(new Path(htmlName));
        if (htmlFile.exists()) {
            htmlFile.delete(true, null);
        }
    } else {
        processResource(resource);
    }
    return true;
}
```

4. Run the target Eclipse instance, and create a new `test.minimark` file. Save it, and a corresponding `test.html` file will be created. Delete the `test.minimark` file, and the `test.html` file should also be deleted.

5. Create the `test.minimark` file again, and the `test.html` file will be generated. Delete the `test.html` file, and it won't be regenerated automatically. To fix this, the `IResourceDelta` needs to track deletions of `.html` files as well and process the corresponding `.minimark` resource. Modify the `visit(IResourceDelta)` method as follows:

```
public boolean visit(IResourceDelta delta) throws CoreException {
    boolean deleted = (IResourceDelta.REMOVED & delta.getKind())!=0;
    IResource resource = delta.getResource();
    String name = resource.getName();
    if (name.endsWith(".minimark")) {
        if (deleted) {
            String htmlName = name.replace(".minimark",".html");
            IFile htmlFile = resource.getParent().getFile(
                new Path(htmlName));
```

```
        if (htmlFile.exists()) {
          htmlFile.delete(true, null);
        }
      } else {
        processResource(resource);
      }
    } else if (name.endsWith(".html")) {
      String minimarkName = name.replace(".html",".minimark");
      IFile minimarkFile = resource.getParent().getFile(
        new Path(minimarkName));
      if (minimarkFile.exists()) {
        processResource(minimarkFile);
      }
    }
  }
  return true;
}
```

6. Run the target Eclipse instance, and delete the generated `test.html` file. It should be automatically regenerated by the `MinimarkBuilder` and `MinimarkVisitor` classes. Now delete the `test.minimark` file, and the corresponding `test.html` file should be deleted as well.

What just happened?

When a `.minimark` file was deleted, a `NullPointerException` was seen. This was fixed by guarding the `visit` method with a check to see whether the resource existed or not.

For consistency, the deletion of associated resources was also handled. If the `.html` file is deleted, it is regenerated (but only if a corresponding `.minimark` file is present). When the `.minimark` file is deleted, the corresponding `.html` file is also deleted.

Have a go hero – builder upgrades

As well as reacting to changes and creating content, builders are also responsible for removing content when the project is cleaned. The `IncrementalProjectBuilder` interface defines a `clean` method, which is invoked when the user performs a **Project | Clean** on either that specific project or the workspace as a whole.

Implement a `clean` method in the `MinimarkBuilder` class which walks the project and, for each `.minimark` file, deletes any corresponding `.html` file. Note that not all `.html` files should be deleted as some may be legitimate source files in a project.

Using natures

Although builders can be configured on a project manually, they aren't usually added directly. Instead, a project may have natures which describe the type of project; and natures can be automatically associated with builders. For example, a Java project is identified with a Java nature, and others (such as the PDE project) are identified as both a Java project and an additional nature for PDE processing. Other languages have their own natures, such as C.

Time for action – creating a nature

A nature is created by implementing the `IProjectNature` interface. This will be used to create a `MinimarkNature` class, which will allow projects to be associated with the `MinimarkBuilder` class.

1. Create a class called `MinimarkNature` in the `com.packtpub.e4.minimark.ui` package as follows:

```
public class MinimarkNature implements IProjectNature {
  public static final String ID =
    "com.packtpub.e4.minimark.ui.MinimarkNature";
  private IProject project;
  public IProject getProject() {
    return project;
  }
  public void setProject(IProject project) {
    this.project = project;
  }
  public void configure() throws CoreException {
  }
  public void deconfigure() throws CoreException {
  }
}
```

2. The purpose of a nature is to assist by adding (or configuring) the builders, which are associated by an ID. To make cross-referencing possible, define a constant in the `MinimarkBuilder` class, which can be used to refer to it by the nature:

```
public class MinimarkBuilder extends IncrementalProjectBuilder {
  public static final String ID =
    "com.packtpub.e4.minimark.ui.MinimarkBuilder";
```

3. The way a builder is added to the project is by accessing the project descriptor and adding a build command. There is no easy way of adding or removing a builder, so acquire the set of commands, search to see whether it is present, and then add or remove it. Using the `Arrays` class takes away some of the pain. Implement the `configure` method in the `MinimarkNature` class as follows:

```java
public void configure() throws CoreException {
  IProjectDescription desc = project.getDescription();
  List<ICommand> commands = new ArrayList<ICommand>(
   Arrays.asList(desc.getBuildSpec()));
  Iterator<ICommand> iterator = commands.iterator();
  while (iterator.hasNext()) {
    ICommand command = iterator.next();
    if (MinimarkBuilder.ID.equals(command.getBuilderName())) {
      return;
    }
  }
  ICommand newCommand = desc.newCommand();
  newCommand.setBuilderName(MinimarkBuilder.ID);
  commands.add(newCommand);
  desc.setBuildSpec(commands.toArray(new ICommand[0]));
  project.setDescription(desc,null);
}
```

The project description's build spec is an array, and should be kept in the same order if it is updated. As a result, non-order-preserving data structures such as a `Set` or `Map` cannot be used here.

4. To de-configure a project, the reverse is done. Implement the `deconfigure` method as follows:

```java
public void deconfigure() throws CoreException {
  IProjectDescription desc = project.getDescription();
  List<ICommand> commands = new ArrayList<ICommand>(
   Arrays.asList(desc.getBuildSpec()));
  Iterator<ICommand> iterator = commands.iterator();
  while (iterator.hasNext()) {
    ICommand command = iterator.next();
    if (MinimarkBuilder.ID.equals(command.getBuilderName())) {
      iterator.remove();
    }
  }
  desc.setBuildSpec(commands.toArray(new ICommand[0]));
  project.setDescription(desc, null);
}
```

5. Having implemented the nature, it needs to be defined as an extension point within the `plugin.xml` file in the `com.packtpub.e4.minimark.ui` project:

```
<extension id="MinimarkNature"
 point="org.eclipse.core.resources.natures">
  <runtime>
    <run class="com.packtpub.e4.minimark.ui.MinimarkNature"/>
  </runtime>
</extension>
```

6. To associate the nature with a project, a menu needs to be added to the **Configure** menu associated with projects. Create an entry in the `plugin.xml` file for the Add Minimark Nature command, and put it in the `projectConfigure` menu:

```
<extension point="org.eclipse.ui.commands">
  <command name="Add Minimark Nature"
   defaultHandler="com.packtpub.e4.minimark
   .ui.AddMinimarkHandler"
   id="com.packtpub.e4.minimark.ui.AddMinimarkNature"/>
</extension>
<extension point="org.eclipse.ui.menus">
  <menuContribution allPopups="false" locationURI=
    "popup:org.eclipse.ui.projectConfigure?after=additions">
    <command label="Add Minimark Nature" style="push"
      commandId="com.packtpub.e4.minimark
      .ui.AddMinimarkNature"/>
  </menuContribution>
</extension>
```

7. Create a new class in the `com.packtpub.e4.minimark.ui` package called AddMinimarkNature as follows:

```
public class AddMinimarkHandler extends AbstractHandler {
  public Object execute(ExecutionEvent event)
    throws ExecutionException {
    ISelection sel = HandlerUtil.getCurrentSelection(event);
    if (sel instanceof IStructuredSelection) {
      Iterator<?> it = ((IStructuredSelection)sel).iterator();
      while (it.hasNext()) {
        Object object = (Object) it.next();
        if(object instanceof IProject) {
          try {
            addProjectNature((IProject)object,
              MinimarkNature.ID);
          } catch (CoreException e) {
            throw new ExecutionException("Failed to set nature
            on" + object,e);
```

```
                    }
                  }
                }
              }
            return null;
          }
        private void addProjectNature(IProject project, String
        nature)
          throws CoreException {
            IProjectDescription description = project.getDescription();
            List<String> natures = new ArrayList<String>(
              Arrays.asList(description.getNatureIds()));
            if(!natures.contains(nature)) {
              natures.add(nature);
              description.setNatureIds(natures.toArray(new String[0]));
              project.setDescription(description, null);
            }
          }
        }
      }
```

8. Run the Eclipse instance, create a new **General** project, and open the .project
   file using the **Navigator** view. Now right-click on the project, and select **Configure |
   Add Minimark Nature** to add the nature. When the nature is added, it will add the
   commands automatically, and the changes will be visible in the .project file.

What just happened?

The MinimarkNature class was created to inject a builder into the project description
when added. Changing the .project file manually does not add the builder, so an action to
programmatically add the nature was created and added to the standard **Configure** menu.

Both the nature and the builder are referred to via IDs; these are stored in the .project
and .classpath files. Since these may be checked into a version control system, the names
of these IDs should be consistent between releases.

The project descriptor contains the content from the .project file, and stores an array of
nature IDs and commands. To add a nature to a project, its identifier is appended to this
list—however, note that the change only takes effect when the updated project descriptor
is set on the project.

Since the nature's modifications only take effect when set programmatically, the Add Minimark Nature command was created to add the nature. The command was put into the popup:org.eclipse.ui.projectConfigure?after=additions menu, which is the standard location for adding and configuring natures. Conventionally, either a separate command to Add Minimark Nature and Remove Minimark Nature is used, or a Toggle Minimark Nature could be used for both menu items. The advantage of the separate add or remove menu items is that their visibility can be controlled based on whether the project already has the nature or not.

The handler class used HandlerUtil to extract the current selection, although this just extracts the object from the parameter map via the variable name selection.

To avoid spelling errors, it makes sense to define constants as static final variables. If they are related with class names, it can be better to use class.getName() as the identifier, so that if they are renamed then the identifiers are automatically updated as well. Alternatively, they can be created from a concatenation with the plug-in's ID (in this case, via Activator.ID).

Have a go hero – enable for selected object type

It is conventional to only show the **Configure** option if it is strictly necessary. In the case where projects already have a MinimarkNature, the command should not be shown. Use the visibleWhen property to target the selection and only enable it if the projectNature of the selected object is that of the MinimarkNature. Alternatively, implement another handler that performs the removal of the nature, and then use an expression to determine whether the handler should be shown based on whether the project already has the nature or not.

The handler here was implemented using Eclipse 3.x classes. Convert these to a handler using the E4 model, as shown in *Chapter 4, Interacting with the User*.

Using markers

The final section in this chapter is devoted to markers. These are the errors and warnings that the compiler shows when it detects problems in files. They can be created automatically, typically from a builder.

Time for action – error markers if file is empty

Errors and warning markers are used to indicate if there are problems in the source files. These are used by the Eclipse compiler to indicate Java compile errors, but they are also used for non-Java errors. For example, text editors also show warnings when words are misspelled. A warning can be shown if the .minimark file is empty and the title is missing.

There isn't a simple way of accessing the file's size in Eclipse, so one heuristic is that if the generated HTML file is less than about 100 bytes then there probably wasn't much to start with anyway.

1. Open the `MinimarkVisitor` class and go to the `processResource` method.

2. When the HTML file is generated, put in a test to determine if the size is less than 100 bytes:

```
ByteArrayOutputStream baos = new ByteArrayOutputStream();
MinimarkTranslator.convert(new InputStreamReader(in),
 new OutputStreamWriter(baos));
ByteArrayInputStream contents = new ByteArrayInputStream(
 baos.toByteArray());
if (baos.size() < 100) {
  System.out.println("Minimark file is empty");
}
```

3. The problem with printing out an error message is that it won't be seen by the user. Instead, it can represented with an `IMarker` object, created on the source resource, and with additional properties to set the type and location of the error:

```
// System.out.println("Minimark file is empty");
IMarker marker = resource.createMarker(IMarker.PROBLEM);
marker.setAttribute(IMarker.SEVERITY, IMarker.SEVERITY_ERROR);
marker.setAttribute(IMarker.MESSAGE, "Minimark file is empty");
marker.setAttribute(IMarker.LINE_NUMBER, 1);
marker.setAttribute(IMarker.CHAR_START, 0);
marker.setAttribute(IMarker.CHAR_END, 0);
```

4. Run the Eclipse instance and create a new empty `.minimark` file. When it is saved, an error will be reported in the **Problems** view. If it's not shown, it can be opened with **Window | Show View | Other | General | Problems**:

What just happened?

A heuristic that detected when the input file was likely to be empty was used to generate a marker in the build view. When creating an empty file, the builder runs and the problem is generated in the problems view.

The marker also allows additional fields to be set if the location of the problem is known. These are optional fields but can be used to give a user more information as to the source of the problem. In the cases of a misspelled word, the CHAR_START and CHAR_END constants can be used to pinpoint the exact word on a line; in the cases of more general errors, the LINE_NUMBER constant can be used to indicate the approximate location in the file.

Each time the file is changed; additional markers are created in the problems view. Even if content is added, the existing errors aren't removed. That will be fixed in the next section.

Time for action – registering a marker type

The current implementation has a flaw, in that it doesn't appear to fix the problems after they have been resolved. That's because the marker types are kept associated with a resource even if that resource is changed. The reason this isn't seen in Java files is that the builder wipes out all (Java) errors prior to the start of a build, and then adds new ones as applicable. To avoid wiping out other plug-ins' markers, each marker has an associated marker type. JDT uses this to distinguish between its markers and others contributed by different systems. This can be done for MinimarkMarker instances as well.

1. Open the plugin.xml file in the com.packtpub.e4.minimark.ui project. Add the following extension to define a MinimarkMarker:

```
<extension id="com.packtpub.e4.minimark.ui.MinimarkMarker"
  name="Minimark Marker"
  point="org.eclipse.core.resources.markers">
    <persistent value="false"/>
    <super type="org.eclipse.core.resources.problemmarker"/>
</extension>
```

2. To use this marker when the error is created, instead of using IMarker.PROBLEM, use its extension ID from the plugin.xml in the processResource method of the MinimarkVisitor class:

```
// IMarker marker = resource.createMarker(IMarker.PROBLEM);
IMarker marker = resource.createMarker(
    "com.packtpub.e4.minimark.ui.MinimarkMarker");
```

3. At the start of the `processResource` method, flush all the markers associated with the resource of this type:

```
resource.deleteMarkers(
    "com.packtpub.e4.minimark.ui.MinimarkMarker",
    true, IResource.DEPTH_INFINITE);
```

4. Run the Eclipse instance, and verify that as soon as some content is put in a `.minimark` file, the errors are cleared. Delete the content, save the file, and the errors should re-appear.

5. Finally, the editor doesn't show up warnings in the column. To make that happen, change the superclass of the `MinimarkEditor` class from `AbstractEditor` to `AbstractDecoratedTextEditor`. Run the target Eclipse instance again. Now errors will be reported in the editor as well:

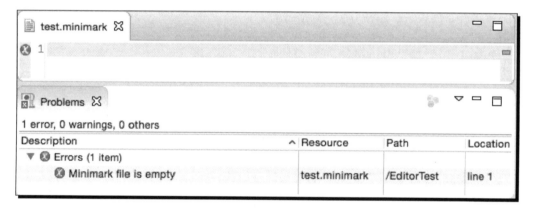

What just happened?

Now the custom markers for the resource are being deleted at the start of a build, and if there's a problem a marker will be automatically added. When the problem is resolved, the resource's markers are automatically deleted anyway.

In the deletion code, the `boolean` argument says whether to delete markers that are a subtype of that marker type or not. The second argument says what happens in the case that it's a folder or other container, and if deletion should recurse.

Generally builders delete and create a specific type of problem marker, so that they do not affect the other markers that may be associated with that resource. This allows other contributors (such as the spell checking editor) to raise warnings or informational dialogs that are not cleaned by a particular builder.

Have a go hero – work out when the file is really empty

Fix the file detection so that it works out when the source file is really empty. Do this by using EFS and the file's locationURI to get a FileInfo, which contains the file's size.

Pop quiz – understanding resources, builders, and markers

Q1. How is an error with a missing document provider fixed?

Q2. What is an IResourceProxy and why is it useful?

Q3. What is an IPath?

Q4. What is a nature and how is one set on a project?

Q5. How are markers created on a project?

Summary

In this chapter, we looked at how resources are accessed, created, and processed. We used an example of a markup language to associate a builder that translated markup items into HTML when the source files were saved. We then hooked up the builder with a nature so that a project can automatically be configured with content when needed.

The next chapter will look at the E4 model and how it differs from Eclipse 3.x in creating views and contributing to a Rich Client Platform.

7
Creating Eclipse 4 Applications

Eclipse 4 – the new Eclipse platform

The last major change to Eclipse was with the 3.0 release, when it migrated to OSGi. The Eclipse 4 model provides a significant departure from the Eclipse 3.x line, with the user interface being represented as a dynamic Eclipse Modeling Framework (EMF) model. In addition, both model and views can be represented as simple Plain Old Java Objects (POJOs) with services provided by dependency injection. There is also a separate rendering mechanism that allows an E4 application to be hosted by different UIs, although we'll look at the SWT renderer specifically. In this chapter, we'll take a look at the differences and how you can evolve Eclipse plug-ins forward.

In this chapter, we shall:

- ◆ Set up an Eclipse 4 instance for development
- ◆ Create an E4 application with parts
- ◆ Send and receive events
- ◆ Create commands, handlers, and menus
- ◆ Inject custom POJOs

Since Eclipse was first released in November 2001, its user interface has remained mostly static. Each window has a perspective, which contains zero or one editor area, and zero or more views. In early releases, every perspective had exactly one editor area, and it was not until the release of Eclipse RCP with Eclipse 3.0 in 2004 that it was possible to disable the editor, and have a custom application suitable for a non-IDE use. However, customizing the presentation of the perspective always proved difficult, such as changing the background color or arrangement of the windows or toolbars. The Eclipse 4 model provides a way to model an application at design time, and also interpret and modify it at runtime. An application has a top-level model, but may also have additional model fragments contributed by different bundles. Additionally, the separate rendering framework allows the UI to be represented with different frameworks such as JavaFX and HTML. In this book, the default SWT rendering framework will be used, since that closely matches the existing Eclipse 3.x UI.

The other significant change is that it is no longer necessary to create subclasses of specific classes to contribute to the Eclipse infrastructure. Instead, classes are created with dependency injection (similar to how Spring components are configured) and may consume platform-level services separately to the user interface. Instead of referring to global singletons through accessor methods, these are now available through injection. This allows components to be built as simple POJOs, which allows them to be tested headlessly and provides a looser binding to the services that they consume.

Time for action – installing E4 tooling

To work with Eclipse 4 application models, it is necessary to install the E4 tools to allow the application XML to be edited through an editor. These are not shipped with all the Eclipse packages, and must be installed separately.

1. Add the following update site by going to the **Preferences** menu (from the **Eclipse** menu on macOS or the **Window** menu on other operating systems), followed by navigating to **Install/Update | Available Software Sites**, then clicking on **Add...**, and entering `http://download.eclipse.org/e4/updates/0.17`.

> Some of the E4 tools are available in the Eclipse Mars update site, but not all of them. There may be updates available or additional releases of the E4 tools site; check out `http://download.eclipse.org/e4/updates/` and look at the directory contents to find a later release for later versions of Eclipse.

2. Click on **OK** on the **Add Site** dialog and **OK** on the **Preferences** page to add it. Once added, navigate to the **Help | Install New Software** menu and then select the newly added site in the list. Select the following features:

    1.   E4 CSS Spy

    2.   Eclipse e4 Tools

    3.   Eclipse 4 - Model Spy

These add the ability to create Eclipse 4 Applications and edit both `css` and `e4xmi` files, which are used to create and render the user interface in Eclipse 4:

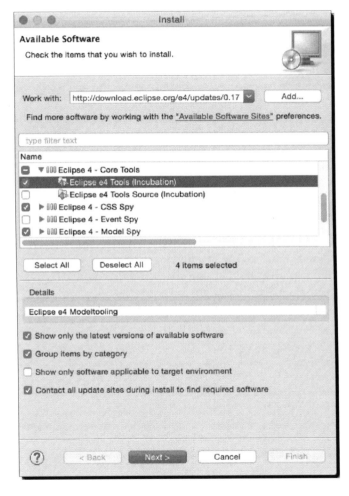

3. Restart Eclipse after the install has completed.

4. Go to the **File | New | Project** menu and verify that **Eclipse 4 | Eclipse 4 Application Project** is seen in the **New Project** wizard's choices.

What just happened?

Installing the Eclipse E4 tools and E4 CSS Spy provides a custom editor for `e4xmi` files as well as `css` files. In addition, the CSS Spy can be displayed by pressing *Alt + Shift + F5*, or with the **Quick Access** search bar.

To run the CSS spy in a launched application, add `org.eclipse.e4.tools.css.spy` to the required bundles in the launch configuration (don't add them to the product definition unless the product's end users need to be able to invoke the CSS spy).

There is also a live EMF editor that can be displayed by pressing *Alt + Shift + F9*. This is useful for exploring the Eclipse runtime, either in the IDE or in the launched application. To add the live EMF editor in a launched application, add `org.eclipse.e4.tools.emf.liveeditor` to the launch configuration.

Don't forget to click on **Validate plug-ins** and if necessary **Add required plug-ins** to ensure that the tools' dependencies are present in the launched product.

Time for action – creating an E4 application

Eclipse applications use an application ID to launch and start execution. For E4 applications, `org.eclipse.e4.ui.workbench.swt.E4Application` is used. A new E4 application will be created to demonstrate a standalone E4 application.

1. Go to the **File | New | Project...** menu and choose **Plug-in Project**.

2. Use the name `com.packtpub.e4.application`, and step through the wizard. Choose the default values for each field, ensuring that the activator checkbox is selected, the **This plug-in will make contributions to the UI** is selected, and **Would you like to create a rich client application?** is **Yes**:

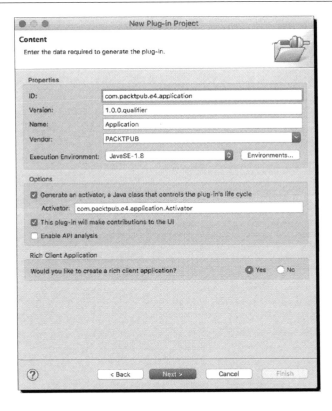

3. Click on **Next** and then choose the **Eclipse 4 RCP application** template. Click on **Next** again and ensure that **Create sample content** is selected:

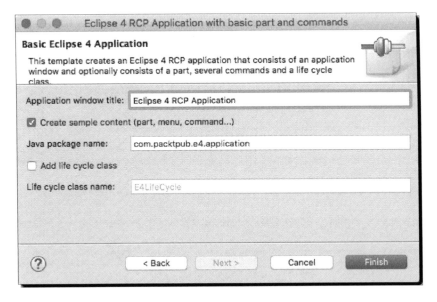

4. Click on **Finish** and the project will be created.

5. Right-click on the `com.packtpub.e4.application` project and choose **Run As |
Eclipse Application**. This launches a new version of the IDE, which is not intended.

To launch the project instead, double-click on the product file (called `com.
packtpub.e4.application.product`) and click on the run icon in the
top right:

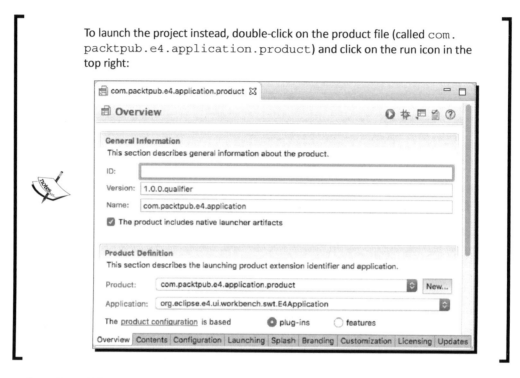

6. If a web-browser is launched when invoking the product, it may be that RAP is
installed. If this happens, the product can be launched by going to the **Run |
Run As...** and selecting the **Eclipse Application** type, followed by **Run a product:
com.packtpub.e4.application.product**. Alternatively, the **Overview** tab has a
Testing section, which includes a link to **Launch an Eclipse Application**. When the
application is run, the default window should be shown:

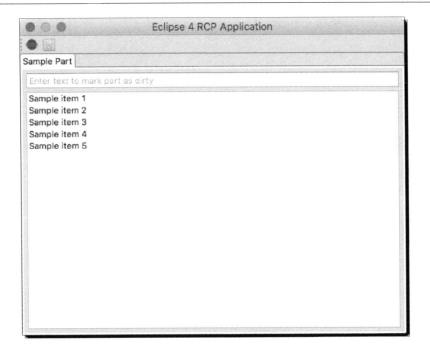

What just happened?

The new E4 wizard created a simple E4 rich client application, including creating
some sample content (menus, commands, and so on). After fixing issues with missing
dependencies, the application can be launched as a product. If the application fails to launch
with a message **No application id has been found**, it may be a missing dependency such
as `javax.xml`:

```
!MESSAGE Application error
!STACK 1
java.lang.RuntimeException: No application id has been found.
```

When running any kind of Eclipse application, it is good practice to prevent launching when there are missing dependencies. The launch configuration, visible from the **Run | Run Configurations...** menu, has an option on the plug-ins tab **Validate plug-ins automatically prior to launching**, which performs a check prior to launching:

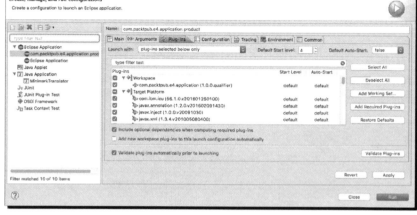

Now, when launching the product without adding the necessary plug-ins, a warning will be shown. The **Validate Plug-ins** button can be clicked to run this validation at any time.

Time for action – creating a part

Having created a sample application, the next step is to create a view, known as a **part** in E4. Parts are the generic name for views, editors, and other grouping components in an E4 application. Unlike views in Eclipse 3, the view class doesn't have to have any references to the Eclipse APIs. This makes it particularly easy to build and test in isolation.

1. Create a new class called `Hello` in the `com.packtpub.e4.application.parts` package.

2. Add a `private` field called `label` of type `Label`.

3. Add a `create` method annotated with `@PostConstruct` that instantiates the `Label` and sets its text to `"Hello"`.

4. Optionally, add an `onFocus` method annotated with `@Focus` that sets the focus on the `Label`.

5. The class will look like:

```
package com.packtpub.e4.application.parts;
import javax.annotation.PostConstruct;
import org.eclipse.e4.ui.di.Focus;
import org.eclipse.swt.SWT;
import org.eclipse.swt.widgets.Composite;
import org.eclipse.swt.widgets.Label;
public class Hello {
  private Label label;
  @PostConstruct
  public void create(Composite parent) {
    label = new Label(parent, SWT.NONE);
    label.setText("Hello");
  }
  @Focus
  public void onFocus() {
    label.setFocus();
  }
}
```

6. Double-click on the `Application.e4xmi` file and it should open up in the application editor (if it doesn't, ensure that the E4 Tools are installed from the update site as described earlier in this chapter).

7. Navigate to **Application | Windows and Dialogs | Trimmed Window | Controls | Perspective Stack | Perspective | Controls | Part Sash Container | Part Stack**.

8. Delete the **Sample Part**, if present, by right-clicking on it and choosing **Remove**.

9. Right-click on the **Part Stack**, and select **Add child** followed by **Part**. The part should be created as follows:

　　1. **ID:** `com.packtpub.e4.application.part.hello`

　　2. **Label:** `Hello`

　　3. **Class URI:** Click on **Find** and enter `Hello` as the class name, and it will add `bundleclass://com.packtpub.e4.application/com.packtpub.e4.application.parts.Hello`

　　4. Ensure that the **Closeable** checkbox is not selected

5. Ensure that the **To Be Rendered** checkbox is selected

6. Ensure that the **Visible** checkbox is selected

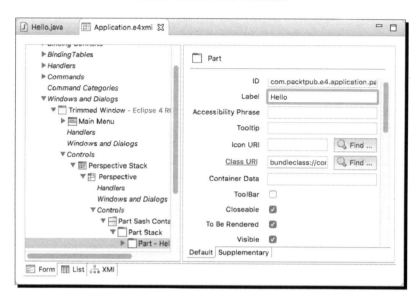

10. Finally, save the `e4xmi` file and then launch the product. If all has gone well, **Hello** should be displayed in the generated window:

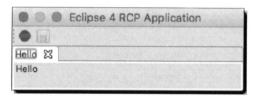

11. If nothing is shown, the first debug point is to delete the workspace of the run-time application. The launch configuration can be set to clear the contents of the workspace each time it launches, which is a good idea for E4 development as often the new files aren't copied over or stale files can be left behind.

12. Go to the **Run | Run Configurations...** menu, and select the `com.packtpub.` `e4.application` configuration. On the **Main** tab, there is an option to **Clear**:

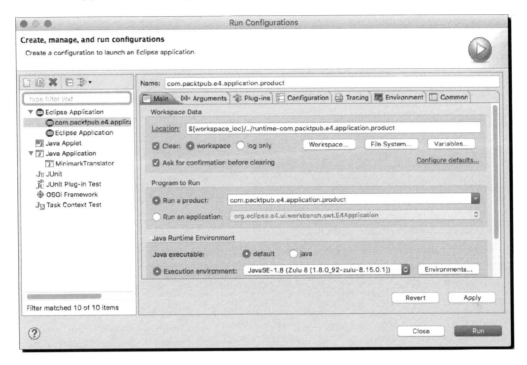

13. Leave the option to **Ask for confirmation before clearing** selected to be prompted with a dialog each time the product is run, or deselected to delete the contents of the run-time workspace each time.

14. If still not shown, put a breakpoint in the `@PostConstruct` method to verify that it is being called. If not, verify that the `@javax.annotation.PostConstruct` annotation is on the method, that the right class name is specified in the `e4xmi` file, and that everything is saved before launching. Another approach is to delete the launch configuration and launch a new one via the product launch as before.

What just happened?

Eclipse 4 applications are modeled with an `e4xmi` file, which defines both visual and non-visual contents. At runtime, an Eclipse 4 application is booted with `org.eclipse.` `e4.ui.workbench.swt.E4Application`, which reads the file specified in the product's `applicationXMI` property. The default name created by the wizard is `Application.` `e4xmi`, but this can be changed if necessary.

Parts in E4 are the equivalent of views/editors in Eclipse 3.x. The structure of viewable content in an E4 application is:

- Application, which contains
- (Trimmed) Windows, which contain
- Perspective stacks, which contain
- Perspectives, which contain
- Part Sash Container, which contain
- Part Stacks, which contain
- Parts

In addition, Trimmed Windows can also contain Menus and Menu Items, both of which are covered later in this chapter.

The default application uses a Trimmed Window, which means it can have toolbars such as the **Save** and **Open** tools (these are shown as a **Handled Tool Item** or **Direct** in the application editor). Each element can have a control which allows parts to be mixed and matched; for example, it's not mandatory for a Window to use any perspectives at all; they can just contain controls if desired.

The **Hello** Part was created and added into the application by adding it to the model. At runtime, the class is instantiated, followed by an invocation of the method annotated with @PostConstruct. Any required arguments are injected automatically, which are obtained from the runtime context, which is akin to a HashMap of services by class name. Finally, the @Focus call is invoked when the part gets the focus; it should delegate that call to the key widget within the part.

Note that since the hook between the application model and the code is the pointer in the **Class URI** reference to the fully qualified class name, when renaming Java class names or packages, it's important to select the option that allows the fully qualified name to be replaced in other files, as otherwise links between the application model and the parts may be broken.

During development, it may be necessary to clear the workspace when starting. This is because the application model is not only used for an initial starting point of the application; it's also used to model the runtime of the application. Any changes to the model (creating new views, resizing the parts) update the runtime model. When the application shuts down normally, the updated state of the model is saved and used for subsequent launches. As a result, a newly launched application with the same workspace will show the state of the workspace at the last time it shut down, not any new state that may have been added at development time. Workspaces can be cleaned by running Eclipse with the -clean and -clearPersistedState flags.

Using services and contexts

An IDE is more than a collection of its component parts, and the Eclipse 4 framework allows these to coordinate and communicate with each other.

In prior releases of Eclipse, the `Platform` (or `PlatformUI`) object would act as an oracle of all the known services in the runtime infrastructure, as well as providing hooks for accessing those services, for example:

```
IExtensionRegistry registry = Platform.getExtensionRegistry();
IWorkbench workbench = PlatformUI.getWorkbench();
```

Although this provides a programmatic way of making the services available, it has two key disadvantages:

- The provider of the interface is tightly coupled with the bundle containing the accessor, even if they are unrelated
- Introducing new services requires a code change to a core object, and has disadvantages in being introduced to existing systems

The goal of E4 is to decouple service providers and service consumers through the use of OSGi services. These are contributed to the runtime, and can be looked up via interface name using either standard OSGi mechanisms, or through E4 injection. Although that is the general trend, some platform services accessed by the `IServiceLocator` aren't backed by OSGi services.

Time for action – adding logging

The OSGi platform defines a `LogService` which allows messages to be logged to a central collector. In the E4 platform, an instance of `LogService` is available as part of the platform, routing error messages through to the console.

1. Open the `Hello` class and add a `private` field `LogService logService`.

2. Add an `@Inject` annotation to the `LogService` field.

3. In the `create` method, add a call to the log service.

4. The `Hello` class will look like:

```
import javax.inject.Inject;
import org.osgi.service.log.LogService;
public class Hello {
    @Inject
    private LogService logService;
    @PostConstruct
```

```
      public void create(Composite parent) {
        label = new Label(parent, SWT.NONE);
        label.setText("Hello");
        logService.log(LogService.LOG_ERROR, "Hello");
      }
      ...
    }
```

5. Run the application, and a log message will be printed out to the console of the host Eclipse:

```
!ENTRY org.eclipse.e4.ui.workbench 4 0 2016-06-02 13:36:42.381
!MESSAGE Hello
```

What just happened?

The E4 runtime infrastructure injected the reference into the class when it was constructed. The instance was obtained from the E4 context, which looks through a hierarchy of contexts until it can find an instance that matches the class type. At the root of the context tree, the list of OSGi services is consulted.

If `LogService` cannot be found in the context, the part will fail to be created with an error message:

```
!ENTRY org.eclipse.e4.ui.workbench 4 0 2016-06-02 13:36:42.381
!MESSAGE Unable to create class 'com.packtpub.e4.app.parts.Hello'
 from bundle '29'
!STACK 0
org.eclipse.e4.core.di.InjectionException: Unable to process
 "Hello.log": no actual value was found for the argument "LogService"
  at org.eclipse.e4.core.internal.di.InjectorImpl.
    reportUnresolvedArgument(InjectorImpl.java:394)
```

To mark that the service is optional (that is, it can be `null`), annotate it with `@Optional`:

```
    import org.eclipse.e4.core.di.annotations.Optional;
    public class Hello {
      @Inject @Optional
      private LogService log;
      @PostConstruct
      public void create(Composite parent) {
        if (logService != null) {
          logService.log(LogService.LOG_ERROR, "Hello");
        }
```

Remember that @Optional annotated fields or parameters have to be guarded against the possibility of being null.

If a service arrives after instantiation, the service will be injected into the part.

Time for action – getting the window

In an Eclipse 3.x application, the main window is typically accessed via a static accessor such as Display.getDisplay() or workbench.getWorkbenchWindows(). Both of these assume that there is a way of getting to this global list in the first place, often through tightly coupled code references. As well as OSGi services, E4 can also be used to inject references to GUI components. However, rather than accessing the GUI components directly, models are used instead. As a result, components in E4 tend to start with **M** (for **Model**)—such as MPart, MWindow, and MPerspective.

1. To obtain the reference to the window, add a private field MWindow window to the Hello class, along with an @Inject annotation.

2. Modify the create method so that the label of the text is taken from the window's title (label). The class will look like:

```
import org.eclipse.e4.ui.model.application.ui.basic.MWindow;
public class Hello {
  @Inject
  private MWindow window;
  @PostConstruct
  public void create(Composite parent) {
    Label label = new Label(parent, SWT.NONE);
    label.setText(window.getLabel());
  }
  ...
}
```

3. Run the application, and the name of the label should be the name of the window, which is initially com.packtpub.e4.application.

4. Open the Application.e4xmi file, and go to **Application | Windows and Dialogs | Trimmed Window** which is where the label is defined. Change the label to Hello E4 and save the file.

5. Run the application, and the name of the label and window should be Hello E4.

6. Go back to the Application.e4xmi file, select the **Trimmed Window** node and perform a copy with **Edit | Copy**. Select the **Windows and Dialogs** node and paste with **Edit | Paste**. This will create a duplicate node for the **Trimmed Window**. Change the label to Other E4 and save the file.

7. Run the application, and two windows should be displayed. The first will contain a label `Hello E4` while the other will contain `Other E4`.

8. Finally, modify the `Other E4` part to be invisible by unchecking the **Visible** checkbox on the **Trimmed Window**.

What just happened?

A reference to the enclosing `MWindow` was acquired, using the same mechanism as for the OSGi `LogService`. However, while the `LogService` is a global instance, the `MWindow` is local to the currently selected part.

The lookup strategy for objects follows a hierarchical set of contexts, which are hash-table-like structures that contain named objects. These are represented with the `MContext` interface, which is implemented by:

♦ `MApplication`

♦ `MWindow`

♦ `MPerspective`

♦ `MPart`

♦ `MPopupMenu`

The context search starts at the most specific element, and works its way up to the top level. If they aren't found in the `MApplication`, OSGi services are consulted.

Each of these are organized into a hierarchy with `IEclipseContext`, which maintains parent/child relationships between them. The lookup automatically follows the chain if an object cannot be located in the current context.

In the last example, having two separate windows means that two contexts are used, and so although the code is identical between the two, one has the **Hello E4** window model injected, while the other has the **Other E4** window model injected.

Time for action – obtaining the selection

The current selection can be obtained through the selection service with a listener, similar to Eclipse 3.x. However, the `ISelectionService` in Eclipse 3.x has been replaced with an almost identical `ESelectionService` in Eclipse 4.x (other than the minor lack of JavaDoc and change of package name, the only significant difference between the two is that there are no `add/removePostSelection` methods).

1. Create a class called `Rainbow` in the `com.packtpub.e4.application.parts` package. Add a `private static final` array of strings with colors of the rainbow.

2. Add a `create` method, along with a `@PostConstruct` annotation, that takes a `Composite` parent. Inside, create a `ListViewer` and set the input to the array of rainbow colors. The class will look like:

```
public class Rainbow {
  private static final Object[] rainbow = { "Red", "Orange",
    "Yellow", "Green", "Blue", "Indigo", "Violet" };
  @PostConstruct
  public void create(Composite parent) {
    ListViewer lv = new ListViewer(parent, SWT.NONE);
    lv.setContentProvider(new ArrayContentProvider());
    lv.setInput(rainbow);
  }
}
```

3. Open the `Application.e4xmi` and go to **Application | Windows and Dialogs | Trimmed Window | Controls | Perspective Stack | Perspective | Controls | Part Sash Container | Part Stack**. Right-click on the **Part Stack** and choose **Add child** followed by **Part**. Set the label as `Rainbow` and find the `Rainbow` class with the **Find** button, or by using the `bundleclass` URI `bundleclass://com.packtpub.` `e4.application/com.packtpub.e4.application.parts.Rainbow`.

4. Run the application, and two tabs should be shown. Next to the **Hello** tab, the **Rainbow** tab will be shown, containing the rainbow colors in a list.

5. To synchronize the selection between the two tabs, add a field of type `ESelectionService` called `selectionService`, along with an `@Inject` annotation. In the `create` method, add an anonymous `ISelectionChangedListener` to the `ListViewer`, such that if a selection event is received, the selection is reflected in the `selectionService`. The implementation will look like:

```
@Inject
private ESelectionService selectionService;
@PostConstruct
public void create(Composite parent) {
  ListViewer lv = new ListViewer(parent, SWT.NONE);
  lv.setContentProvider(new ArrayContentProvider());
  lv.addSelectionChangedListener(event -> {
      selectionService.setSelection(event.getSelection()));
  ...
}
```

6. When a selection is made on the `ListViewer`, it will send a selection event to the platform's selection service. To determine what objects are selected, the `Hello` part can register for changes in the selection, and use that to display the text in the label. Add a `setSelection` method to the `Hello` class as follows:

```
@Inject
@Optional
public void setSelection(
    @Named(IServiceConstants.ACTIVE_SELECTION)
    Object selection) {
    if (selection != null) {
        label.setText(selection.toString());
    }
}
```

7. Run the application, switch to the **Rainbow** part, and select the **Red** color from the list. Switch back to the **Hello** part and it should show **[Red]** in the label.

What just happened?

The list viewer is similar to the previous example. Here, a simple array of `String` values is being used, backed with an `ArrayContentProvider`. By creating a new part, it is possible to switch between the tabs to see the effect of changing the selection.

In order to hook up the viewer's selection with the platform's selection, the viewer's `selectionChanged` event needs to be delegated to the platform. To do that, the `ESelectionService` needs to be injected.

The E4 context contains a set of name/value pairs (like a `HashMap`), and one of these is used to track the current selection. When the selection changes, the new value is set into the context, and this triggers the method calls on the corresponding parts.

Because there may not be a selection when the part is created, it is necessary to annotate it with `@Optional`. If a method is marked with `@Optional` then it may not be called at all; if a parameter is marked as `@Optional` then the method will be called, but with a `null` parameter.

In general, for methods that receive events, mark them as `@Optional` so that they are not called at creation time.

E4 can automatically inject the active selection as it changes. The context contains an object with a key of `IServiceConstants.ACTIVE_SELECTION` (the value `org.eclipse.ui.selection`), which can be injected as a `@Named` parameter in a method call. Since there may not be a selection, the `@Optional` annotation must be used, as otherwise exceptions will be reported when the part is created.

Time for action – dealing with events

There's a more generic way of passing information between components in Eclipse 4, using the OSGi `EventAdmin` service. This is a message bus, like JMS, but operates in memory. There is also an Eclipse-specific `IEventBroker`, which provides a slightly simpler API to send messages.

1. Add the following bundles as dependencies to the `com.packtpub.e4.application` project, by double-clicking on the project's `META-INF/MANIFEST.MF` file and going to the **Dependencies** tab:

    1. `org.eclipse.osgi.services`

    2. `org.eclipse.e4.core.services`

    3. `org.eclipse.e4.core.di.extensions`

2. Open the `Rainbow` class and inject an instance of `IEventBroker` into a `private` field `broker`:

    ```
    @Inject
    private IEventBroker broker;
    ```

3. Modify the `selectionChanged` method, so that instead of setting a selection, it uses the `IEventBroker` to `post` the color asynchronously to the `rainbow/color` topic:

    ```
    public void selectionChanged(SelectionChangedEvent event) {
      // selectionService.setSelection(event.getSelection());
      IStructuredSelection sel = (IStructuredSelection)
       event.getSelection();
      Object color = sel.getFirstElement();
      broker.post("rainbow/color", color);
    }
    ```

4. Open the `Hello` class, and add a new method `receiveEvent`. It should be annotated with `@Inject` and `@Optional`. The parameter should be defined with an annotation `@EventTopic("rainbow/color")` to pick up the data from the event:

    ```
    @Inject
    @Optional
    public void receiveEvent(
      @EventTopic("rainbow/color") String data) {
        label.setText(data);
    }
    ```

5. Run the application, and switch to the **Rainbow** tab. Select an item in the list, and go back to the **Hello** tab. Nothing will be displayed. Open the **Console** view in the host Eclipse, and an error will be visible:

```
!MESSAGE Exception while dispatching event
    org.osgi.service.event.Event [topic=rainbow/colour]
    {org.eclipse.e4.data=Orange} to handler
    org.eclipse.e4.core.di.internal.extensions.
       EventObjectSupplier$DIEventHandler@4ad72dc9
!STACK 0
org.eclipse.e4.core.di.InjectionException:
    org.eclipse.swt.SWTException: Invalid thread access at
org.eclipse.e4.core.internal.di.MethodRequestor.
       execute(MethodRequestor.java:68)
```

6. This happens because the dispatched event runs on a non-UI thread by default. There are two ways of solving this problem: either re-dispatch the call to the UI thread, or use @UIEventTopic instead of @EventTopic. Modify the receiveEvent as follows:

```
public void receiveEvent(
  // @EventTopic("rainbow/color") String data) {
  @UIEventTopic("rainbow/color") String data) {
    label.setText(data);
}
```

7. Run the application, go to the **Rainbow** tab and select a color. Switch back to the **Hello** tab and the text of the label will be updated appropriately.

What just happened?

Events allow components to communicate in a highly decoupled mechanism. Using events to pass data means that the only shared context is the name of the topic.

The OSGi EventAdmin service is a key component and will always be available in current Eclipse 3.x and E4 applications, since most of the lower level implementations are based on events. Either the Eclipse IEventBroker wrapper or the EventAdmin can be used, depending on personal preferences. However, if the code is to be used in other OSGi systems, building directly on top of the EventAdmin will give the greatest portability.

The `Event` object is either created automatically using `IEventBroker` or can be created manually. Each `Event` has an associated topic, which is a `String` identifier that allows producers and consumers to co-ordinate with each other:

```
Map<String, Object> properties = new HashMap<String, Object>();
properties.put("message", "Hello World");
properties.put(IEventBroker.DATA, "E4 Data Object");
eventAdmin.postEvent(new Event("topic/name", properties));
```

> Note that if the object passed in is a `Map` or `Dictionary`, it gets passed to the `EventAdmin` as is. To pass a `Map` and receive it using the E4 tools, another `Map`, must be created and passed in with the `IEventBroker.DATA` key. Alternatively, the `EventAdmin` service can be used directly.

The `Event` can be posted synchronously (that is on the same thread as the delivery agent) or asynchronously (on a non-background thread):

- Synchronously, using the `sendEvent` or `send` methods
- Asynchronously, using the `postEvent` or `post` methods

Synchronous or asynchronous event delivery?

Generally using asynchronous delivery is recommended, since synchronous delivery will block the calling thread. When delivering events from the UI asynchronous delivery should always be used, since it is not possible to place any bounds on how long the event receivers may take to execute.

To receive an event, a listener needs to be registered with the topic. This can be done via the OSGi `EventAdmin` service, or with the `@EventTopic` and `@UIEventTopic` annotations on a method marked with `@Inject @Optional`.

If an `Event` needs to be processed on the UI thread, it should not be sent synchronously from the UI thread. Doing so invites delays and blocking the UI, since it is possible for other listeners to pick up on the event and do excessive computation on an unnecessary thread. Instead, send it from a non-UI thread, and in the event hander, delegate it to the UI thread or consume it via the `@UIEventTopic` annotation.

The topic name is specified in the annotation (or via the subscription in the `EventHandler` interface). Topic names can be any string, but are typically separated with / characters. This is because the OSGi specification allows for subscription to both topics by exact match and partial matches. The subscription `topic/*` will pick up both `topic/name` and `topic/another/example`. Note that it is not a regular expression; the topics are explicitly delimited by the / character, and /* means "and everything below." So `topic/n*e` won't match anything, and nor will `topic/*/example`.

To be more selective about the topics subscribed, use the `EventAdmin EVENT_FILTER` to specify an LDAP style query. Subscribe to the highest level that made sense (such as `topic/*`) and then use an LDAP filter to refine it further, using `event.filter` with `(event.topic=topic/n*e)`.

Currently, the annotations cannot be used to apply an LDAP filter, but it's possible to register an `EventHandler` interface which supplies this property.

Finally, it is conventional for the topic name to be constructed from the same kind of reverse domain names used for bundles, with `.` replaced with `/` (for example, `com/packtpub/e4/application/`).

Time for action – calculating values on demand

The Eclipse context can supply not only services but also dynamically calculated values. These are supplied via an interface `IContextFunction`. By registering a service with that class name and a key name with the `service.context.key`, it is possible to create a value upon request.

1. Create a class called `RandomFunction`, which extends `ContextFunction` and which returns a random value:

```
package com.packtpub.e4.application;
import org.eclipse.e4.core.contexts.ContextFunction;
import org.eclipse.e4.core.contexts.IEclipseContext;
public final class RandomFunction extends ContextFunction {
  @Override
  public Object compute(final IEclipseContext context) {
    return Math.random();
  }
}
```

2. To allow E4 to recognize the function, register an instance with the OSGi runtime. Although this could be done within the `Activator`, currently a service ordering bug prevents this from happening. Instead, register it using declarative services.

Create a file called `random.xml` in a folder called `OSGI-INF` with the following content:

```
<?xml version="1.0" encoding="UTF-8"?>
<scr:component xmlns:scr="http://www.osgi.org/xmlns/scr/v1.1.0"
 name="math.random">
  <implementation
  class="com.packtpub.e4.application.RandomFunction"/>
  <service>
    <provide
```

```
      interface="org.eclipse.e4.core
      .contexts.IContextFunction"/>
  </service>
  <property name="service.context.key" type="String"
   value="math.random"/>
</scr:component>
```

3. Add the `OSGI-INF` folder to the `build.properties`, to ensure that it gets added when the bundle is built:

```
bin.includes = OSGI-INF/,\
               META-INF/,\
```

4. To allow declarative services to load and create the component, add this header into `META-INF/MANIFEST.MF`:

```
Service-Component: OSGI-INF/*.xml
```

5. Finally, inject this value into the application. In the `Hello` part, add the following:

```
@Inject
@Named("math.random")
private Object random;
@PostConstruct
public void create(Composite parent) {
  label = new Label(parent, SWT.NONE);
  label.setText(window.getLabel() + " " + random);
}
```

6. Run the application, and this time, the **Hello** tab starts out with a random value appended to the window's title text. Each time the application is started, a different value is calculated.

What just happened?

The `IEclipseContext` can acquire calculated values as well as values inserted into the runtime. The calculation is done through a function, registered with the `IContextFunction` interface—though currently the only way to register it is with the declarative services model, as shown previously. Declarative services are discussed in more detail in *Appendix A, Using OSGi Service to Dynamically Wire Applications*.

The implementation class should extend `ContextFunction`, as the interface `IContextFunction` is marked as `@NoImplement`. This allows additional methods to be added; for example, in Eclipse 4.3, a new method was added to the interface `compute(IEclipseContext, String)` which was also added to the `ContextFunction` parent class. Java 8 adds default methods, which means this pattern is less likely to occur in future.

The OSGi declarative services API allows a service to be created and made available to clients that need to use it. To register a service with declarative services, a service document is created (in the example, this is `random.xml`), and it is referred to with the `Service-Component` header in the `MANIFEST.MF` file. When the plug-in is installed, the declarative services implementation notices this header, reads the service document and then creates the class. This class then becomes available through the E4 context for inclusion in injection of parts.

Note that the value of the function is cached upon first calculation. So even if the code is changed to inject the value as a method parameter, only the first value calculated will be seen. Although the `IEclipseContext` has a method to remove the value, it doesn't necessarily trigger the removal from all contexts. The recommendation is to use an OSGi service for data that must be calculated each time.

Time for action – interacting with the UI

Sometimes it is necessary to write code to run in the UI thread, but when called back via a handler it's not always clear if the method is in the UI thread or not. In Eclipse 3.x, there is a `Display.getDefault().syncExec()` for running `Runnable` instances inside the UI thread immediately, or `.asyncExec()` for running them on the UI thread later. Eclipse 4 introduces the `UISynchronize` class, which is an abstract mechanism for executing code on the UI thread (it's like an interface for `Display`, except that `Display` doesn't implement it and it's not an interface). The `syncExec` and `asyncExec` methods can be used to schedule `Runnable` events. If a long calculation needs to update the UI after concluding, using `UISynchronize` allows the UI update to be scheduled on the right thread.

1. Create a new `Button` as a field in the `Hello` part, and attach a selection listener such that when it is pressed, it invokes `setEnabled(false)` on itself. At the same time, schedule a `Job` to run after one second that invokes `setEnabled(true)` again:

```
private Button button;
@PostConstruct
public void create(Composite parent) {
  button = new Button(parent, SWT.PUSH);
  button.setText("Do not push");
  button.addSelectionListener(new SelectionListener() {
  @Override
  public void widgetSelected(SelectionEvent e) {
    button.setEnabled(false);
    new Job("Button Pusher") {
      @Override
```

```
        protected IStatus run(IProgressMonitor monitor) {
          button.setEnabled(true);
          return Status.OK_STATUS;
        }
      }.schedule(1000);
    }
    @Override
    public void widgetDefaultSelected(SelectionEvent e) {
    }
  });
  ...
}
```

2. Run the application, and when the button is pushed, the button will be disabled (grayed out) immediately. One second later, an exception will be logged to the console with an `Invalid thread access` message:

   ```
   !MESSAGE An internal error occurred during: "Button Pusher".
   !STACK 0
   org.eclipse.swt.SWTException: Invalid thread access
       at org.eclipse.swt.SWT.error(SWT.java:4491)
   ```

3. The error occurs because the `setEnabled` call must be made on the UI thread. Although `Display.getDefault().syncExec()` can be used to do this, E4 provides an annotation-based way of doing the same thing. Inject an instance of the `UISynchronize` into the `Hello` part:

   ```
   @Inject
   private UISynchronize ui;
   ```

4. Modify the `Job` implementation in the `create` method as follows:

   ```
   protected IStatus run(IProgressMonitor monitor) {
     ui.asyncExec(() -> button.setEnabled(true));
     return Status.OK_STATUS;
   }
   ```

5. Now run the application and press the button. It will be disabled for one second, and then re-enabled afterwards.

What just happened?

1. Using `UISynchronize` provides a way to interact with the UI thread safely. Another way of achieving this would be to use a `UIJob`.

2. One advantage of using `UISynchronize` is that it is not necessarily tied down to SWT. E4 provides the option of having different part renderers, which could allow for future runtimes based on HTML or Swing, or JavaFX such as e(fx)clipse.

> When building plug-ins that will be shared between E4 and Eclipse 3.x systems, continue to use `Display.getDefault()` or `Display.getCurrent()` in order to schedule UI updates, as the `UISynchronize` class is not present in earlier releases.

Using commands, handlers, and menu items

The command and handlers in Eclipse 4 work the same way as in Eclipse 3. A command represents a generic operation, and the handler is the code that implements the operation. However, the implementation for the handler takes advantage of E4's annotations, instead of a custom subclass.

Time for action – wiring a menu to a command with a handler

As with Eclipse 3.x, a command has an identifier and an associated handler class, which can be bound to menus. Unlike Eclipse 3.x, it is not specified in the `plugin.xml` file; instead, it is specified in the `Application.e4xmi` file.

1. Open the `Application.e4xmi` file in the `com.packtpub.e4.application` project.

2. Navigate to the **Application | Commands** node in the tree, and click on **Add child** to add a new **Command**:

    1. **ID:** `com.packtpub.e4.application.command.hello`

    2. **Name:** `helloCommand`

    3. **Description:** `Says Hello`

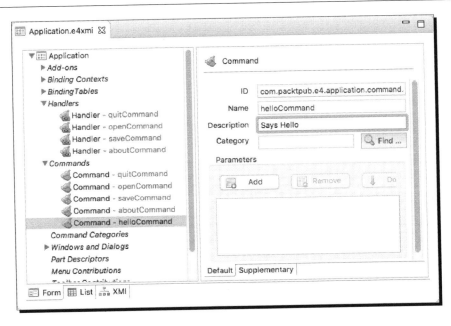

3. Create a class `HelloHandler` in the `com.packtpub.e4.application.handlers` package. It doesn't need to have any specific superclass or method implementation. Instead, create a method called `hello` which takes no arguments, and prints a message to `System.out`. The method needs the `@Execute` annotation:

```java
package com.packtpub.e4.application.handlers;
import org.eclipse.e4.core.di.annotations.Execute;
public class HelloHandler {
  @Execute
  public void hello() {
    System.out.println("Hello World");
  }
}
```

4. The handler needs to be defined in the `Application.e4xmi`. Navigate to the **Application | Handlers** node in the tree, and right-click and **Add child** to add a new handler. Fill in the details as follows:

1. **ID:** `com.packtpub.e4.application.handler.hello`

2. **Command:** `helloCommand - com.packtpub.e4.application.command.hello`

3. **Class URI:** `bundleclass://com.packtpub.e4.application/com.packtpub.e4.application.handlers.HelloHandler`

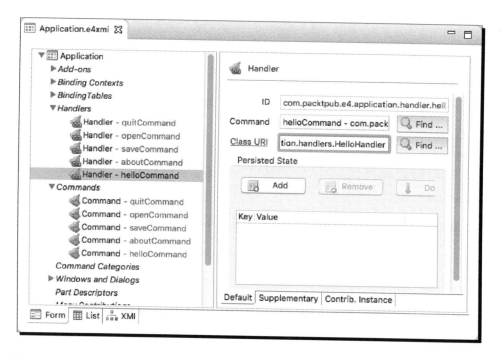

5. Finally, to associate the handler with a menu, go into the **Application | Windows and Dialogs | Trimmed Window | Main Menu | File** node and click on **Add child** to add a new **Handled Menu Item** (this can also be done by right-clicking on the **Menu | File** node and choosing **Add child | Handled Menu Item**). Add it as follows:

1. **ID:** `com.packtpub.e4.application.handledmenuitem.hello`

2. **Label:** `Hello`

3. **Tooltip:** `Says Hello World`

4. **Command:** `helloCommand - com.packtpub.e4.application.command.hello`

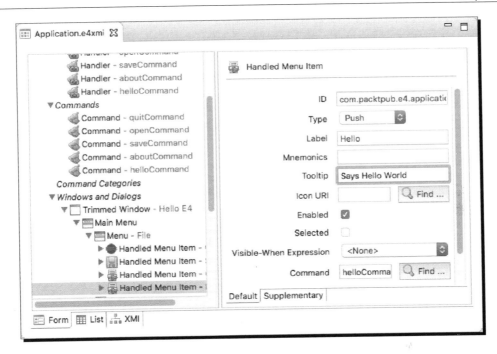

6. Save the `Application.e4xmi` and run the application. Go to the **File** menu, and clicking **Hello** from the menu item should display `Hello World` in the **Console** view of the host Eclipse.

What just happened?

The `HelloHandler` provides a simple message output and an entry point annotated with `@Execute`. The handler can also report whether it can be executed through a `boolean` returning method annotated with `@CanExecute`, but this defaults to `true` if a handler is always valid.

A command is a generic ID that can be associated with one or more handlers and with one or more UI elements, such as a `MenuItem`, `Button`, or programmatic execution. The `helloCommand` is associated by default to the `HelloHandler`.

Finally, the command is associated with the **File | Hello** menu item so that it can be invoked.

Time for action: passing command parameters

Displaying a message to `System.out` shows that the command works, but what if the command needed to pick up local state? Fortunately, the `@Named` and `@Inject` annotations allow objects to be injected into the method when it is called.

1. Modify the `hello` method so that instead of printing a message to `System.out`, it opens a dialog window, using the active shell:

```
public void hello(@Named(IServiceConstants.ACTIVE_SHELL) Shell s){
  MessageDialog.openInformation(s, "Hello World",
    "Welcome to Eclipse 4 technology");
}
```

2. Other arguments can be passed in from the context, managed by the `IEclipseContext` interface. For example, using the `math.random` function from earlier, a value could be injected into the handler:

```
public void hello(@Named(IServiceConstants.ACTIVE_SHELL) Shell s,
  @Named("math.random") double value) {
```

3. If the same handler is being used for different functions (for example, **Paste** and **Paste Special**), they can be disambiguated by passing in a hard-coded value in the command. Modify the `helloCommand` to add a parameter, by opening the `Application.e4xmi` and navigating to the **Application | Commands | helloCommand**; right-click and go to **Add child | Command Parameter** to add a command parameter:

1. **ID**: `com.packtpub.e4.application.commandparameter.hello.value`
2. **Name**: `hello.value`
3. Ensure that the **Optional** checkbox is selected:

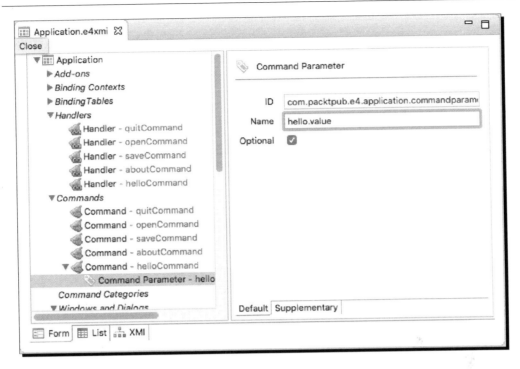

4. To pass a value into the command, open the `Application.e4xmi` and navigate to the **Application | Windows and Dialogs | Main Menu | Menu (File) | Handled Menu Item (Hello) | Parameters** node. Right-click on **Parameters** and choose **Add child | Parameter** to create a parameter:

   1. **ID**: `com.packtpub.e4.application.parameter.hello.value`

   2. **Name**: `com.packtpub.e4.application.commandparameter.hello.value`

   3. **Value**: `Hello World Parameter`

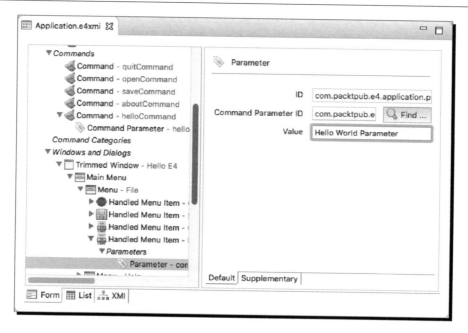

5. Finally, modify the command handler so that it receives the value encoded with the handler:

```
public void hello(@Named(IServiceConstants.ACTIVE_SHELL) Shell s,
  @Optional
  @Named("com.packtpub.e4.application.commandparameter.hello.
value")
    String hello,
  @Named("math.random") double value) {
    MessageDialog.openInformation(s, "Hello World", hello +
value);
}
```

6. Run the application, and go to the **File | Hello** menu. The parameter will be passed in to the handler.

What just happened?

Any values can be injected into the method when it is invoked, provided that they are available in the context when the handler is called. These can be taken from standard constants (such as those in IServiceConstants) or be custom values injected at runtime. Other values include:

♦ ACTIVE_WINDOW: The currently displayed window

♦ ACTIVE_PART: The currently selected part

♦ ACTIVE_SELECTION: The current selection

If the values are one of a set of values, they can be encoded in the menu or other command invocation. They can also be set via code which calls `IEclipseContext.set()` with an appropriate value.

Time for action – creating a direct menu and keybindings

Although using commands and handlers provides a generic way for reusing content, it is possible to provide a shorter route to implementing menus with a **Direct Menu Item**. The difference between this and a **Handled Menu Item** is that **Direct Menu Item** contains a direct reference to the `@Executable` class, instead of indirect through a handler.

1. To add a new direct menu item, open the `Application.e4xmi` file and navigate to the **Application | Windows and Dialogs | Trimmed Window | Main Menu | Menu (File)**. Right-click on the menu and choose **Add child | Direct Menu Item**. In the dialog shown, fill in the following details, including the class URI link to the `HelloHandler`, defined previously:

    1. **ID:** `com.packtpub.e4.application.directmenuitem.hello`

    2. **Label:** `Direct Hello`

    3. **Class URI:** `bundleclass://com.packtpub.e4.application/ com.packtpub.e4.application.handlers.HelloHandler`

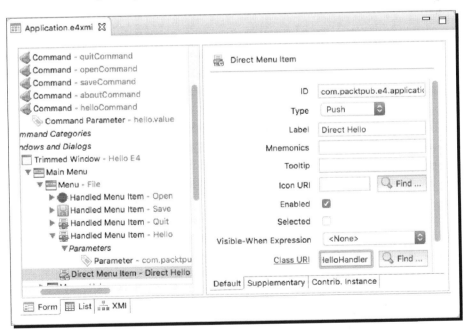

2. Run the application, and navigate to the **File | Direct Hello** menu, which shows the same message as previously.

 Keys can be bound to commands in an application, and can be enabled in one of several UI contexts. By default, these include **In Dialogs and Windows**, **In Dialogs**, and **In Windows**; additional contexts can also be created.

3. To set a keybinding to the menu, open the `Application.e4xmi` and navigate to the **Application | BindingTables | BindingTable – In Dialog and Windows** node. Right-click on the binding table and choose **Add child | KeyBinding**. Fill in the fields as follows:

1. **ID:** `com.packtpub.e4.application.keybinding.m1l`

2. **Sequence:** `M1+L`

3. **Command:** `helloCommand - com.packtpub.e4.application.command.hello`

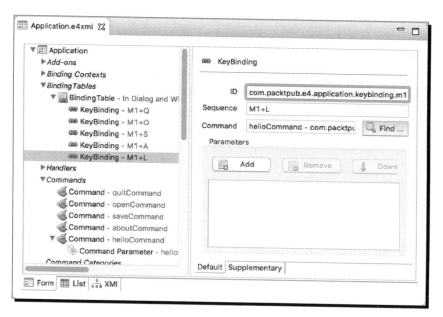

4. Run the application, and press **M1+L** (*Cmd + L* on macOS, *Ctrl + L* on Windows/ Linux). The `Hello` command will be run.

What just happened?

A **Direct Menu Item** is a way of hooking up a **Menu Item** directly to an executable method in a very simple way, without needing to have a separate command and handler defined. For application-wide operations, such as quitting the application, using a **Direct Menu Item** may be appropriate.

However, if the command needs to be handled in different contexts, then it is more appropriate to define a handler which can be replaced in different scopes.

Unlike a **Handled Menu Item**, the **Direct Menu Item** cannot have command parameters associated with it. Nor can a **Direct Menu Item** have a keybinding assigned.

To associate a keybinding with a command, an associated context must be selected. This is typically the **In Dialogs and Windows** context, although other contexts can be selected as well (such as **In Dialogs** and **In Windows**). These are stored in the **Binding Table** node in the `Application.e4xmi` file.

The sequence can be a single character, or it can be a sequence of characters. Combinations of characters are represented with a + joining them. The meta characters (M1, M2, M3, M4, and so on) are defined in the `org.eclipse.ui.bindings` extension point:

- M1 is the *Cmd* key on macOS and the *Ctrl* key on Windows
- M2 is the *Shift* key on all platforms
- M3 is the *Alt* key on all platforms
- M4 is the *Cmd* key on macOS

When the binding is invoked, it will execute the command specified in the list. As a command, it can have associated parameters like the **Handled Menu Items**.

Use the M1 key definition instead of `Ctrl` for normal keyboard shortcuts, since this will provide the correct behavior on different operating systems.

Time for action – creating a pop-up menu and a view menu

Pop-up and view menus are defined declaratively in the `Application.e4xmi` file. These are specific to a part, so the option is defined underneath the part declaration.

1. Open the `Application.e4xmi` file.
2. Navigate to the **Application | Windows and Dialogs | Trimmed Window | Controls | Perspective Stack | Perspective | Controls | PartSashContainer | Part Stack | Part (Hello) | Menus** node.

3. Right-click on the **Menus** node and choose **Add child | Popup Menu**. Set the **ID** to `com.packtpub.e4.application.popupmenu.hello`, which will be used in code later.

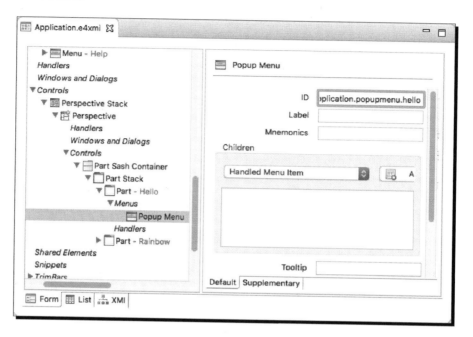

4. Right-click on the **Popup Menu** and choose **Add child | Handled Menu Item**. This is exactly the same as for other menus; fill in the details as follows:

1. **Label:** `Hello`

2. **Command:** `helloCommand - com.packtpub.e4.application.command.hello`

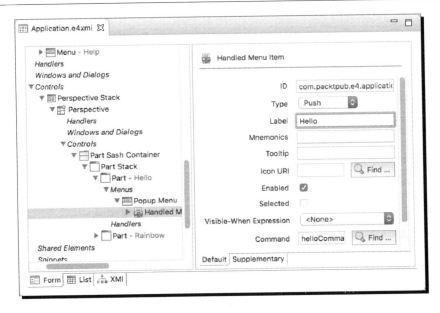

5. Right-click on the **Menus** node again, and choose **Add child | View Menu**. Give the menu a label `View Menu` and right-click to choose **Add child | Handled Menu Item**. Use the same label and command as for the pop-up menu.

6. Run the application. On the top-right, there will be a triangular drop-down which should contain the view menu. However, the pop-up menu won't be triggered, because the SWT component has to be bound to the pop-up menu through its ID in code.

7. Add a line to the `Hello` class's `create` method that registers the context menu with the ID specified. To do this, a new parameter `EMenuService menu` needs to be passed, from which `registerContextMenu` can be called. Since this returns a `boolean` value indicating success, log an error if the registration does not work:

```
public void create(Composite parent, EMenuService menu) {
  if (!menu.registerContextMenu(parent,
    "com.packtpub.e4.application.popupmenu.hello")) {
    logService.log(LogService.LOG_ERROR,
      "Failed to register pop-up menu");
  }
  . . .
```

8. Run the application, and right-click on the hello label or elsewhere in the `Hello` part. The pop-up menu should be shown, and the `Hello` command can be run.

What just happened?

The pop-up menu can be associated with a part, but it doesn't get shown by default. Instead, it has to be registered with a SWT widget. The popup can be for the entire part's component, or it can be just for specific components in the part.

The EMenuService is the interface to the E4 menus. It gets injected into the creation of the widget and provides the detector to listen to the mouse and keyboard events that trigger the popup menu.

Adding a **View Menu** is exactly the same as a **Popup Menu**, except that no additional code is required to make it happen.

Creating custom injectable classes

The injection framework in E4 allows custom injectable classes and services. As well as registering OSGi services, POJOs can be defined and instantiated on demand.

The rules for allowing a type to be instantiated automatically are:

* It must be a non-abstract class
* It must have a non-private default constructor
* It must be annotated with @Creatable

Time for action – creating a simple service

POJOs can be instantiated and made available in the E4 context, such that they can be injected into other classes or created on demand. This allows an application to be built in a flexible manner without tight coupling between services.

1. Create a class StringService in the com.packtpub.e4.application package with a @Creatable annotation, and a process method that takes a string and returns an uppercase version:

```
import org.eclipse.e4.core.di.annotations.Creatable;
@Creatable
public class StringService {
  public String process(String string) {
    return string.toUpperCase();
  }
}
```

2. Add an injectable instance of `StringService` to the `Rainbow` class:

    ```
    @Inject
    private StringService stringService;
    ```

3. Use the injected `stringService` to `process` the color choice before posting the event to the event broker:

    ```
    public void selectionChanged(SelectionChangedEvent event) {
      IStructuredSelection sel = (IStructuredSelection)
       event.getSelection();
      Object colour = sel.getFirstElement();
      broker.post("rainbow/color",
        stringService.process(color.toString()));
    }
    ```

4. Run the application. Go to the **Rainbow** part and select a color; switch back to the **Hello** part, and the selected color (for example, **Red**) should be shown, but in upper case, such as **RED**.

What just happened?

By marking a POJO with `@Creatable`, when the dependency injection in E4 needs to satisfy a type, it knows that it can create an instance of the class to satisfy the injection demand. It will invoke the default constructor and assign the result to the injected field.

Note that the resulting instance is not stored in the context; as a result, if additional instances are required (either in a separate field in the same part, or in an alternative part), the dependency injection will create new instances for each injection.

Generally, the use of injectable POJOs in this way should be restricted to stateless services. If the service needs state that should be shared by multiple callers, register an OSGi service instead, or use a singleton service injected in the context.

Time for action – injecting subtypes

Although creating a POJO can be an efficient way of creating simple classes, it can be limiting to have a concrete class definition scattered through the class definitions. It is a better design to use either an abstract class or an interface as the service type.

1. Create a new interface in the `com.packtpub.e4.application` package, called `IStringService`. Define the `process` method as abstract:

```
public interface IStringService {
  public abstract String process(String string);
}
```

2. Modify the existing `StringService` so that it implements the `IStringService` interface:

```
public class StringService implements IStringService {
  ...
}
```

3. Modify the reference in the `Rainbow` class to refer to the `IStringService` interface instead of the `StringService` class:

```
@Inject
private IStringService stringService;
```

4. Run the application, switch to the **Rainbow** tab, and a dependency injection fault will be shown in the host Eclipse instance's **Console view**:

```
org.eclipse.e4.core.di.InjectionException:
  Unable to process "Rainbow.stringService":
    no actual value was found for the argument "IStringService".
```

5. Although the runtime knows that the `StringService` is a `@Creatable` instance, it doesn't look for subtypes of an interface by default. To inject an alternative type, modify the `Activator` and add a binding as follows:

```
public class Activator implements BundleActivator {
  public void start(BundleContext bundleContext) throws
  Exception {
    Activator.context = bundleContext;
    InjectorFactory.getDefault().
    addBinding(IStringService.class).
      implementedBy(StringService.class);
  }
}
```

6. Run the application and the part should be created correctly.

What just happened?

Using an interface for the service type is best practice, since it further decouples the use of the service with its implementation. In order for the dependency injection framework to provide an instance of an abstract type (whether an interface or abstract class, or even a concrete class without a `@Creatable` annotation), a binding needs to be created for the injector.

The binding just created tells the `InjectorFactory` to create an instance of `StringService` when an `IStringService` is required.

Have a go hero – using the tools bridge

Although Eclipse 3.x parts can run in an Eclipse 4 IDE, to take advantage of the E4 model, the code has to be implemented as a POJO such that it can be registered with a model. To fit an E4 POJO into an Eclipse 3.x IDE, the E4 bridge has to be used. Install the **Eclipse E4 Tools Bridge for 3.x** from the E4 update site, which provides the compatibility views.

Now create a class called `HelloView` which extends `DIViewPart<Hello>` and passes the instance of the `Hello` class to the super-class' constructor. Register the `HelloView` in the `plugin.xml` as would be the case with Eclipse 3.x views, and the part is now visible either as a standalone part in Eclipse 4 or as a wrapped view in Eclipse 3.x.

Pop quiz – understanding E4

Q1. What is the application model and what is it used for?

Q2. What is the difference between a part and a view?

Q3. Are extension points still used in Eclipse 4?

Q4. What is the Eclipse 4 context?

Q5. What annotations are used by Eclipse 4, and what is their purpose?

Q6. How can messages be sent and received on the event bus?

Q7. How is the selection accessed in Eclipse 4?

Summary

Eclipse 4 is a new way of building Eclipse applications, and provides a number of features that make creating parts (views/editors), as well as obtaining service references and communication between parts much easier. If you are building Eclipse-based RCP applications, then there is no reason not to jump on the Eclipse 4 framework to take advantage of its features. If you are building plug-ins that will run on both Eclipse 3.x and Eclipse 4, then you have to consider backward compatibility requirements before you can make the switch. One way of supporting both is to use the workbench compatibility plug-in (which is what Eclipse 4.x uses if you download the SDK or one of the EPP packages) and continue to use the Eclipse 3.x APIs. However, this means the code cannot take advantage of the Eclipse 4.x mechanisms. Another approach is to write Eclipse 4-based plug-ins, and then wrap them in a reverse compatibility layer. Such a layer is provided in the **Eclipse E4 Tools Bridge for 3.x** feature, which is available from the E4 tools update site. This provides classes `DIViewPart`, `DISaveableViewPart` and `DIEditorPart`, which can be used to provide an adapter for an E4 part in an Eclipse 3.x view extension point.

In the next chapter, we'll look at approaches to migrate applications towards Eclipse 4 technologies, as well as some of the considerations that need to take place before migrating.

8
Migrating to Eclipse 4.x

In the last chapter, we looked at the way Eclipse 4 RCP applications are built. We'll now look at how to migrate an existing solution based on Eclipse 3.x APIs to Eclipse 4.x, and the pros and cons of migrating to the new infrastructure.

In this chapter, we shall:

- Migrate an existing Eclipse 3.x view to an Eclipse 4.x view using the e4view extension
- Replace deprecated Action classes with generic classes
- Create code to show a toolbar, view menu, and pop-up menu
- Create an e4xmi fragment to migrate to Eclipse 4.x models
- Define commands, handlers, toolbars, view menus, and pop-up menus in the model
- Do forward selection between Eclipse 3.x views and Eclipse 4.x parts

Why Eclipse 4.x?

The first question that needs to be asked when migrating an application from the Eclipse 3.x APIs is "Why migrate to Eclipse 4.x at all?" If the goal is to provide plug-ins for an Eclipse IDE, then there may be little benefit from migrating existing plug-ins to the new APIs. Under the covers, Eclipse provides a **compatibility layer** that implements the Eclipse 3.x APIs, which will continue to work for some time; this allows plug-ins developed and tested against previous versions of Eclipse to work as before.

There are significant benefits from a rich client platform perspective; there really is little need to build Eclipse 3.x-based RCP applications any more. Since RCP applications tend to be self-contained units (and often do not support the same extensibility that the IDE does), it should be easy to move over to using it. This can be done piece by piece as the views or other functionality is migrated. The reasons for migrating to the Eclipse 4.x model for plug-ins for an Eclipse 3.x IDE are much more limited, and there are some compatibility issues with regard to selection and pop-up menus that need to be addressed. These will be uncovered in this chapter.

Time for action – creating a migration component

In order to demonstrate how to migrate a plug-in to Eclipse 4.x technology, a simple example needs to be created. For this purpose, the Eclipse plug-in example library will be used, although the exact sample used by this book can also be checked out from the book's GitHub repository at `https://github.com/alblue/com.packtpub.e4/`

1. Create a new plug-in project by navigating to the **File | New | Project...** menu and choosing the **Plug-in Project** option. Use `com.packtpub.e4.migration` as the name of the project, click on **Next**, and then accept the defaults by clicking on **Finish**.

2. Open the `META-INF/MANIFEST.MF` file and go to the **Overview** tab. Click on the **Extensions** link on the right-hand side, under the **Extension/Extension Point Content** group:

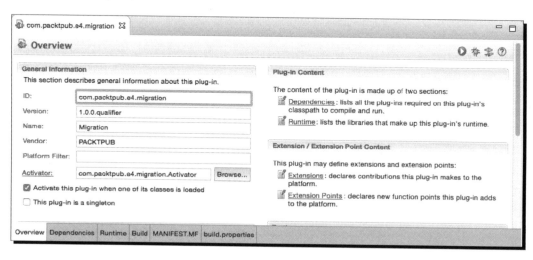

3. If a dialog **Extension pages hidden** is displayed, click on the **Yes** button to ensure that the **Extensions** tab is shown:

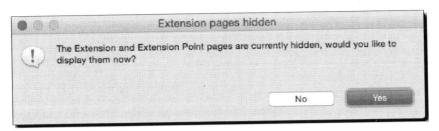

4. Go to the **Extensions** tab and click on the **Add...** button. Type `views` in the filter and uncheck the **Show only extension points from the required plug-ins** option to show the list. Select **Sample View** and click on **Next**:

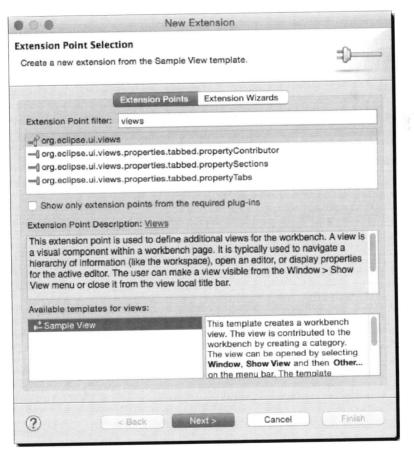

5. Click on the **Finish** button and accept the defaults to create the plug-in.

 An error may temporarily be seen with a message **Plug-ins declaring extensions or extension points must set the 'singleton' directive to 'true'**. If this is not fixed automatically by the wizard, go to the **Overview** page and ensure that the **This plug-in is a singleton** checkbox is selected.

6. Right-click on the project and choose **Run As | Eclipse Application** to launch the IDE. Navigate to the **Window | Show View | Other...** menu in the launched Eclipse instance and choose **Sample Category | Sample View**. A simple view should be shown:

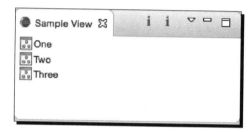

What just happened?

In order to migrate an existing application, a sample plug-in needs to be used. The version of the extension point in Eclipse's built-in wizards currently uses the Eclipse 3.x APIs (these samples were taken from Eclipse Neon; the exact code used can be seen from the book's GitHub repository).

A sample view was created using the `view` extension point, showing a table viewer populated with sample data. The table viewer has a number of actions (which are an Eclipse 2.x technology), along with a view menu, a toolbar, and a context-sensitive pop-up menu. Subsequent sections will show how to refactor each of these in turn into their Eclipse 4.x equivalents.

Time for action – updating to e4view

The `e4view` extension point allows a view to be loaded into an Eclipse 4.x application without the need of a specific superclass. This allows existing Eclipse 3.x views to be upgraded to an Eclipse 4.x view as follows.

1. Open the `SampleView` class and remove the `extends ViewPart` superclass definition. This will introduce some errors in the code, which will be fixed shortly.

2. Add a `@PostConstruct` annotation to the `createPartControl` method. Use *Cmd + Shift + O* on macOS or *Ctrl + Shift + O* on other platforms to automatically add the `import javax.annotation.PostConstruct` statement.

3. Add a `@Focus` annotation to the `setFocus` method. This time, the automatic import won't work, but a quick fix will suggest adding the dependency. Alternatively open the `MANIFEST.MF` file, go to the **Dependencies** tab, and add `org.eclipse.e4.ui.di` bundle as a dependency. Now switch back to the `SampleView` class, perform the organize imports with the previous keystroke, and `import org.eclipse.e4.ui.di.Focus` should be added automatically.

4. Open the `plugin.xml` file and change the `view` element to `e4view` for the `SampleView` entry:

   ```
   <e4view class="com.packtpub.e4.migration.views.SampleView" .../>
   ```

5. The final step (for this section) is to comment out the sections that refer to the `getView` and `getViewSite` method calls, to fix any remaining compile errors.

6. Launch the target Eclipse instance and open the **Sample View**. It should show the list but without any of the local menus:

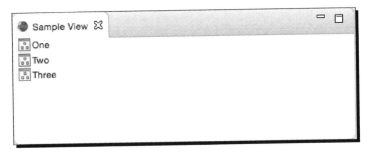

What just happened?

At the moment, the view is not quite as functional as it was before; the view actions are not connected and the code uses the deprecated JFace `Action` class instead of commands and handlers. This will be upgraded in the next section.

The view was migrated from extending `ViewPart` to one with no superclass, and the relevant Eclipse 4.x annotations of `@PostConstruct` and `@Focus` were added, as described in *Chapter 2, Creating Views with SWT*. Since the superclass provided the `getSite` and `getViewSite` methods, references to those calls had to be commented out.

Time for action – upgrading the actions

The JFace `Action` class is used in pop-up menus using the Eclipse 2.x model, but in Eclipse 3.x and Eclipse 4.x, the separation between handlers (code that does the work) and commands (logical operations such as copy that may be processed by different handlers) allows for a more flexible system, as described in *Chapter 4, Interacting with the User*. The first step is to replace the actions with handlers.

1. Open the `SampleView` class and go to the `makeActions` method, which creates anonymous inner subclasses of `Action` with an associated `run` method. To convert these, they will need to be `static` inner classes, so highlight the first `new Action` expression and navigate to the **Refactor | Convert Anonymous Class to Nested...** menu.

2. In the **Convert Anonymous Class to Nested** dialog that appears, ensure that **public** and **static** are selected, and give it the name `HandlerOne`:

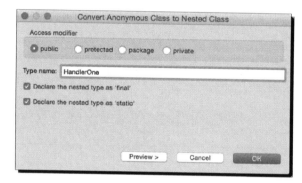

3. Do the same steps for the other two actions, calling them `HandlerTwo` and `DoubleClick`.

4. To fix the compile-time errors introduced by making the inner classes `static`, change the `showMessage` method to `public` and `static` and replace the first parameter with `null`:

```
public static void showMessage(String message) {
   MessageDialog.openInformation(
   // viewer.getControl().getShell(),
   null,
   "Sample View",
   message);
}
```

5. The `DoubleClick` handler will also need to comment out references to the non-static `viewer`; the selection can be passed in as an argument instead, as follows:

```
public static final class DoubleClick {
  public void run(
    @Named("selection") IStructuredSelection selection) {
    SampleView.showMessage("Double-click detected on "
      + selection.getFirstElement());
  }
}
```

6. The `hookDoubleClickAction` method will need to pass the current selection to the `DoubleClick` class, which can be accessed from the `DoubleClickEvent` parameter. Modify it as follows:

```
private void hookDoubleClickAction() {
  viewer.addDoubleClickListener(new IDoubleClickListener() {
    public void doubleClick(DoubleClickEvent event) {
      new DoubleClick().run(
        (IStructuredSelection) event.getSelection());
    }
  });
}
```

 At this point, the class should be free of compile-time errors; fix any remaining issues before moving forward.

7. Although the classes could be kept as an inner class, Eclipse 4.x bugs prevent inner classes from being used as handlers. To resolve this, extract the `HandlerOne`, `HandlerTwo`, and `DoubleClick` classes to their own files by using the **Refactor | Move Type to New File...** menu. If the `showMessage` method has not been updated, the refactoring will suggest changing it to `public`.

8. The next step is to remove the `Action` superclass and annotate the run method with the `@Execute` annotation from the `org.eclipse.e4.core.di.annotations` bundle. To do this, open the `META-INF/MANIFEST.MF` file, go to the **Dependencies** tab, and add the `org.eclipse.e4.core.di.annotations` bundle. Then the run method of the `HandlerOne, HandlerTwo,` and `DoubleClick` classes should be annotated with `@Execute`:

```
public class HandlerOne {
  @Execute
  public void run() {
    showMessage("Action 1 executed");
  }
}
```

9. Since Eclipse 4.x doesn't require that the handlers be instantiated in the class, delete the `contributeToActionBars`, `fillContextMenu`, `fillLocalPullDown`, `fillLocalToolBar`, `hookContextMenu`, and `makeActions` methods and the `action1`, `action2`, and `doubleClickAction` fields.

10. The code is now a lot cleaner, but it doesn't have the functionality from before; it is necessary to register the handlers with the menus. This will be done in the next step.

What just happened?

Since Eclipse 4.x handles the creation of menus and wires elements to handlers, the custom code that builds up menus isn't required. By recursively removing references to `Action`, the handler code can be reduced to a minimum.

Of course if the application is run now, there will be no menus or interactivity. These will be added in the next step.

Time for action – creating toolbars

The first step is to add the toolbar icons, which are the informational icons in the top right. In the original implementation, these were direct `Action` elements inserted into a `ToolBar`, which is part of the Eclipse 3.x interface. To achieve this with Eclipse 4.x, models using `MDirectToolItem` will be created and added to an `MToolBar`.

1. Create a `private` method `createToolBar` in the `SampleView` class. Add a call to the bottom of the `createPartControl` method to ensure that it is called at view creation time.

2. Inside the `createToolBar` method, create an instance of an `MDirectToolItem` object using the `MMenuFactory.INSTANCE.createDirectToolItem()` expression. It may be necessary to follow the quick-fix to add `org.eclipse.e4.ui.model.workbench` to allow the automatic import to find the class. Assign it to a local variable `one`.

3. Add a tooltip `Action 1 tooltip` by calling `one.setTooltip()`.

4. To show the informational icon, a `platform` URI must be created. This uses the fully qualified plug-in name and the path within that bundle. In Eclipse 3.x, this was handled automatically by the `ISharedImages` reference and associated `ImageDescriptor`; in Eclipse 4.x, a URI must be used instead. Add a method called `one.setIconURI` with the URI `platform:/plugin/org.eclipse.ui/icons/full/obj16/info_tsk.png` as the argument.

Normally the icon would be stored locally in the current bundle rather than cross-referencing an icon from a different environment. Relying on a specific path in a different bundle is fragile; for example, this icon used to be called `info_tsk.gif` in older versions of Eclipse.

5. The direct handled item needs to be associated with a `bundleclass` URI, which has the plug-in name and class name of the handler itself. This will then be called when the user clicks on the toolbar item. Add a call to `one.setContributionURI` with the URI `bundleclass://com.packtpub.e4.migration/com.packtpub.e4.migration.views.HandlerOne` as the argument.

 Verify that the call to set the handler is `setContributionURI`, as opposed to `setContributorURI`. If the wrong method is used, the action may display but won't have any effect when clicked.

6. The `createToolBar` method should look like:

```
private void createToolBar() {
  MDirectToolItem one =
  MMenuFactory.INSTANCE.createDirectToolItem();
  one.setTooltip("Action 1 tooltip");
  one.setIconURI("platform:/plugin/org.eclipse.ui/"
  + "icons/full/obj16/info_tsk.png");
  one.setContributionURI
  ("bundleclass://com.packtpub.e4.migration/"
    + "com.packtpub.e4.migration.views.HandlerOne");
}
```

7. The next step is to create an `MToolBar` to hold the newly created items. This uses the `MMenuFactory` as before, this time calling `createToolBar()`. Add in the tool item by calling `add` on the `children` of the `MToolBar`. It will look like:

```
MToolBar toolBar = MMenuFactory.INSTANCE.createToolBar();
List<MToolBarElement> children = toolBar.getChildren();
children.add(one);
```

8. Next the toolbar needs to be added to the part. This requires obtaining the part itself, which is represented as an `MPart` in the Eclipse 4.x model. Since this won't be instantiated by the code, it needs to be injected into the instance. Add a new injected field of type `MPart` called `part`:

```
@Inject
private MPart part;
```

9. Finally, at the end of the `createToolBar` method, set the `toolBar` on the `part` as follows:

```
part.setToolbar(toolBar);
```

10. Run the Eclipse application and navigate to the **Window | Show View | Sample Category | Sample View** menu. An informational icon **i** should be shown on the right-hand side, which when clicked on brings up the **Action 1 executed** dialog:

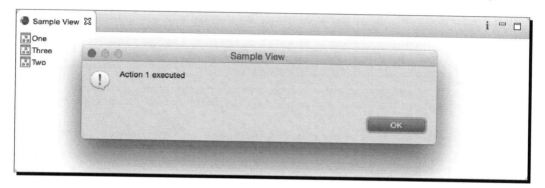

11. Repeat the same steps to add `Action 2` with `HandlerTwo` to the view.

What just happened?

A toolbar was programmatically created to add the action replicating the original Eclipse 3.x view. Although instances of model parts can be created by factories such as `MMenuFactory`, acquiring a reference to the current part requires injection of the `MPart` with an `@Inject` annotation. It's also possible to get injections of other model elements, such as `MWindow` and `MApplication`.

With a reference to the current part, the `MToolBar` can be set using the `setToolbar` method.

> Note that the method is capitalized `setToolbar` although the class is capitalized `MToolBar`.

It's possible to set a number of different fields in the direct handled item, such as whether it is enabled or visible. Changing this when the action is shown will result in it interactively updating in the user interface.

Finally, although the user interface can be created programmatically like this, it's almost certainly easier to build these using the fragment model editor. This approach will be shown later in this chapter.

Have a go hero – optimising the handler lookup

The contribution URI string can be a fragile reference to the handler. It's better to have a compile-time reference to a class instead. This can be achieved by acquiring the class, then using `FrameworkUtil` from the `org.osgi.framework` package to look up the containing bundle, and then use the symbolic name to create the `bundleclass` URI.

Add the following method and replace the constant argument to `setContributionURI` with a call to `getURI`:

```
private String getURI(Class<?> clazz) {
  Bundle bundle = FrameworkUtil.getBundle(clazz);
  if (bundle != null) {
    return "bundleclass://" + bundle.getSymbolicName() + "/" +
    clazz.getName();
  } else {
    return null;
  }
}
...
  one.setContributionURI(getURI(HandlerOne.class));
```

This will allow the class to still be used if it is renamed or moved to a different package or bundle.

Time for action – adding the view menu

The next step is to add the view menu, which is the drop-down menu shown by the triangle in the top-right of the original view. Adding this takes the same pattern as before, but the drop-down menu requires an additional tag to be shown as a view menu.

1. Add a method `createViewMenu` in the `SampleView` class. Add a call to the `createPartControl` method so that it is called when the view is created.

2. In the `createViewMenu` method, create an instance of `MMenu` using `MMenuFactory.INSTANCE.createMenu()`.

3. Add the `menu` to the `part` using `part.getMenus().add(menu)`.

4. To configure the `menu` as a view menu, add a tag `ViewMenu` using `menu.getTags().add("ViewMenu")`.

5. As with toolbar items, a menu item can either be handled or direct. A direct menu item is associated directly with a handler implementation class. Create a direct menu item with `MMenuFactory.INSTANCE.createDirectMenuItem()` and store it in a local field `one`. Set the tooltip and label appropriately, and use the same icon as the previous step.

6. Associate the menu item with the handler class, with the `setContributionURI` method as before. Either use a hard-coded string, `"bundleclass://com.packtpub.e4.migration/com.packtpub.e4.migration.views.HandlerOne"`, or use the `getURI` method as shown in the previous hero section.

7. Add the menu item using `menu.getChildren().add(one)`.

8. The method should now look like:

```
private void createViewMenu() {
  MMenu menu = MMenuFactory.INSTANCE.createMenu();
  part.getMenus().add(menu);
  menu.getTags().add("ViewMenu");
  List<MMenuElement> children = menu.getChildren();

  MDirectMenuItem one =
  MMenuFactory.INSTANCE.createDirectMenuItem();
  one.setLabel("Action 1");
  one.setTooltip("Action 1 tooltip");
  one.setIconURI("platform:/plugin/org.eclipse.ui/"
   + "icons/full/obj16/info_tsk.png");
  one.setContributionURI(getURI(HandlerOne.class));
  children.add(one);
}
```

9. When the application is run, clicking on the triangular menu icon on the top right will present the action, which can then be selected:

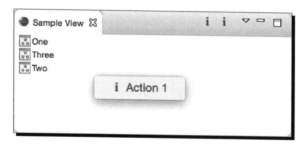

10. To replicate the original Eclipse 3.x view, a separator needs to be added. This is created with a call to `createMenuSeparator` from the `MMenuFactory`:

```
children.add(MMenuFactory.INSTANCE.createMenuSeparator());
```

11. Now add a direct menu item for `HandlerTwo` as well, using the same pattern as mentioned before.

12. Clicking on the menu should now show both actions, as before.

What just happened?

Adding a view menu item is very similar to adding a toolbar menu item. Each element has a model object (which begins with M), so MMenu stands for M(odel) Menu. These are then added using standard collections and added to the part as before.

The tags are a way of appending additional information to the model. These are sometimes used to disambiguate between different types of elements; in this case, it allows the menu to be shown as a view menu when the ViewMenu tag is added (without this tag, the menu won't be shown in the UI).

> The Eclipse 4.x compatibility layer also adds a menu:menuContribution tag to allow contributions to be added.

A direct menu item works in the same way as a direct toolbar item; the contribution URI (stored as a bundleclass URI) dictates which class will be invoked when the item is chosen from the menu.

Separators provide a horizontal line and can be used to separate items in a menu. When added at the end of a menu, there is no visible effect; but if they are added between menu items, the separator is shown.

Time for action – adding the pop-up

A **pop-up menu** is very similar to creating a toolbar or view menu; however, there are a few extra steps required to hook it up to the viewer and to ensure that the right pop-up menu is connected to the right part. As with the view menu, a tag is required; but instead of being a generic hard-coded value, the pop-up tag requires a tight binding with the pop-up menu.

1. Create a method called createPopupMenu in the SampleView class. It will need to take an SWT Control parameter, which will be the one that is used to trigger the menu.

2. Ensure that the createPopupMenu is called from the end of the createPartControl method, passing in the control from the viewer as the argument:

    ```
    createPopupMenu(viewer.getControl());
    ```

3. First, create a pop-up menu with a MMenuFactory.INSTANCE.createPopupMenu() call. Assign it to a local variable menu, so that it can be referred to throughout the method.

4. Set the elementId of the menu to be that of the part, using menu.setElementId(part.getElementId()).

5. Set a `tag` on the `menu` which is the concatenation of `popup:` and the part's `elementId`, using `menu.getTags().add("popup:" + part.getElementId())`.

6. Add `org.eclipse.e4.ui.services` to the list of dependent bundles in the `MANIFEST.MF` to allow the `EMenuService` class to be used.

7. Add an injected field `menuService` of type `EMenuService` to the `SampleView` class:

```
@Inject
private EMenuService menuService;
```

8. Add the `menu` to the `part` and get the `children` of the `menu` as before.

9. To ensure that the menu is shown when the control is clicked, use the `menuService` to register the context menu, using the part's `elementId`. The code should look like:

```
private void createPopupMenu(Control control) {
  MMenu menu = MMenuFactory.INSTANCE.createPopupMenu();
  menu.setElementId(part.getElementId());
  menu.getTags().add("popup:" + part.getElementId());
  part.getMenus().add(menu);
  menuService.registerContextMenu(control,part.getElementId());
  List<MMenuElement> children = menu.getChildren();
}
```

10. Creating a menu item is the same as before; the `MMenuFactory` is used to create an `MDirectMenuItem` instance, which is configured and then added to the `children` list. The code will look like this:

```
MDirectMenuItem one =
MMenuFactory.INSTANCE.createDirectMenuItem();
one.setLabel("Action 1");
one.setTooltip("Action 1 tooltip");
one.setContributionURI(getURI(HandlerOne.class));
one.setIconURI("platform:/plugin/org.eclipse.ui/"
 + "icons/full/obj16/info_tsk.png");
children.add(one);
```

11. Run the code and verify that right-clicking on the tree viewer shows the context-sensitive menu.

12. Add `Action 2` with the `HandlerTwo` implementation in the same way.

What just happened?

A pop-up menu was created using the factory methods in the MMenuFactory instance, and the menu items populated in a very similar way to the toolbar and view menus. To get the pop-up to show however requires a certain amount of steps to be taken in order to work as expected:

- The menu's elementId must be the same as the part's elementId
- The menu must have a tag that starts with popup: followed by the part's elementId
- The menuService must be used to register the control with the part's elementId

If any of these steps are missed or different values are used, then the control will not work as expected.

The value of the part's elementId could be hard-coded, but it is more efficient to use the getElementId method—and should the part's identity change in the future, then the menus will automatically continue to work.

Migrating to Eclipse 4.x patterns

Although the previous section demonstrated how to translate code from an Eclipse 3.x-based example into an Eclipse 4.x example, it's not the canonical way that Eclipse 4.x views or applications are written. Instead, the preferred approach is to generate a model fragment, loaded from a fragment.e4xmi file. This not only reduces the code but also dramatically simplifies the internationalization of messages.

Time for action – creating a model fragment

Eclipse 4.x applications use a **model fragment** to define the UI. It is necessary to create a model fragment to define the part descriptors, handlers, and commands to simplify the code shown previously. To start with, the e4view extension will be replaced by a **part descriptor** in the fragment.

1. Comment (or delete) the e4view extension from the plugin.xml to prevent it from being loaded.

2. Select the project, navigate to the **File | New...** menu, and choose **New Model Fragment** from the dialog.

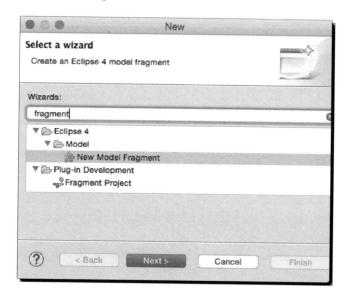

3. In the newly opened `fragment.e4xmi` file, click on **Model Fragments** and click on **Add** to add a new fragment.

4. Enter `org.eclipse.e4.legacy.ide.application` as the **Extended Element ID** and `descriptors` as the **Feature Name**.

5. Select **PartDescriptor** from the drop-down menu and click on **Add** to add a new **Part Descriptor** with the following fields:

1. **ID**: `com.packtpub.e4.migration.views.SampleView`

2. **Label**: `Sample View`

3. **Icon URI**: `platform:/plugin/com.packtpub.e4.migration/icons/sample.gif` (the **Find ...** button will allow the plug-in's contents to be browsed through a graphical user interface and the file selected instead of typing it in)

4. **Class URI**: `bundleclass://com.packtpub.e4.migration/com.packtpub.e4.migration.views.SampleView` (the **Find ...** button will allow the plug-in's classes to be browsed through a graphical user interface instead of typing it in)

5. The **ToolBar** checkbox should be selected

6. The **Closeable** checkbox should be selected

7. **Category**: `Sample Category`

6. The part descriptor should now look like:

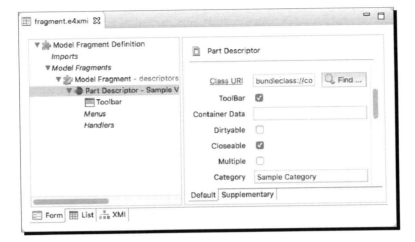

7. Switch to the **Supplementary** tab of the part descriptor, and add a tag by typing in `View` and clicking on the **Add** button:

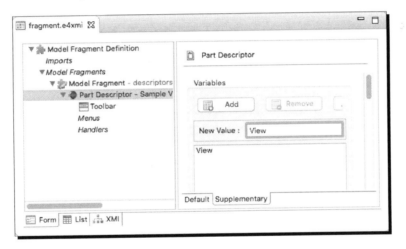

8. Now run the Eclipse instance and navigate to the **Window** | **Show View** | **Other** | **Sample Category** | **Sample View** menu. The **Sample View** should be displayed.

What just happened?

The Eclipse 3.x way of defining views was through a `view` extension point. To facilitate migration towards Eclipse 4.x APIs, an `e4view` extension was created. This allows a view to participate in the dependency injection provided by the Eclipse 4.x platform but in a simple way.

However, it is more appropriate to declare views with an Eclipse 4.x **fragment** and a **part descriptor**. The part descriptor represents the logical view (similar to an object class) whilst the part represents the actual instance shown in a window (similar to an object instance).

Parts in Eclipse 4.x are more flexible than views; they can have properties such as whether they are closable or not, or whether there can be multiple copies of them at one time. These options can be configured in the fragment rather than code.

To ensure that the view is presented in the **Show View** menu, a **tag** with the value `View` must be added in the **Supplementary** part of the fragment editor. If this is omitted or a different case is used, then the view will not show up and it will not be displayed in the **Show View** menu.

Time for action – migrating the commands and handlers

Menu items are typically decoupled from the code that is executed to promote flexibility and re-use. In both Eclipse 3.x and Eclipse 4.x, **commands** are used to represent logical operations whilst **handlers** are used to execute the code. In order to create menus, the handlers and commands must be defined in the fragment.

1. Open the `fragment.e4xmi` file and go to the **Model Fragments** element in the tree. Click on **Add** to add a new **Model Fragment**, and then use `org.eclipse.e4.legacy.ide.application` as the **Extended Element ID** and `commands` as the **Feature Name**.

2. Select **Command** from the drop-down menu and click on **Add** to add new commands. Create a command with the **ID** `com.packtpub.e4.migration.command.one` and a **Name** of `Action 1`; then do the same with `com.packtpub.e4.migration.command.two` and `com.packtpub.e4.migration.command.double`. It should now look like:

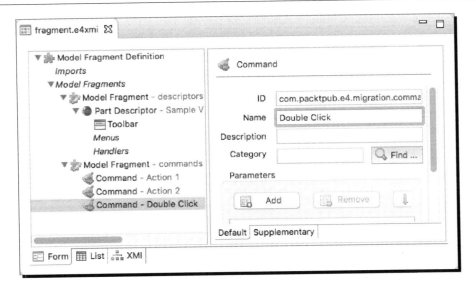

3. Click on **Model Fragments** and then **Add** to create a new **Model Fragment**, this time using a **Feature Name** of handlers. Ensure that the **Extended Element ID** is org.eclipse.e4.legacy.ide.application as before.

4. Add a **Handler** with an **ID** of com.packtpub.e4.migration.handler.one, associate it with the **Command** created previously. For the **Class URI**, select the class HandlerOne. Repeat the same for the HandlerTwo and DoubleClick classes. It should now look like this:

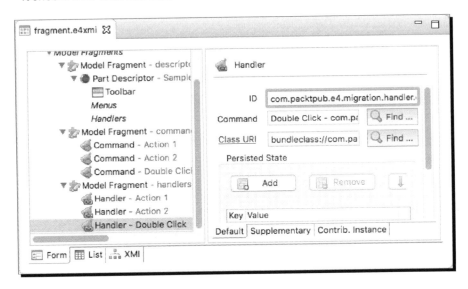

5. The commands and handlers are used when hooking up the code to menus or toolbars. To migrate away from the hard-coded way of representing the tools, delete (or comment) the `createToolbar` method in the `SampleView` class.

6. To add the commands to the toolbar with the fragment, go to the **Part Descriptor** for the **Sample View** in the **Model Fragment** list, and select the **Toolbar** icon. Choose **Handled Tool Item** from the drop-down list and click on **Add** to add an item.

7. In the **Handled Tool Item** form, fill out the fields as follows:

1. **ID:** `com.packtpub.e4.migration.handledtoolitem.action1`

2. **Label:** `Action 1`

3. **Tooltip:** `Action 1 tooltip`

4. Use `platform:/plugin/org.eclipse.ui/icons/full/obj16/info_tsk.png` in the **Icon URI** field, or click on **Find ...** to search for the file from the target platform, choosing the `org.eclipse.ui` version of the icon:

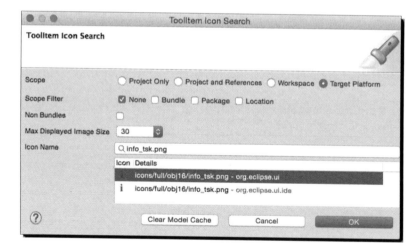

5. Ensure that the **Enabled** checkbox is selected

6. Click on the **Find ...** button next to the **Command** field to choose **Action 1** from the list

8. The **Handled Tool Item** should now look like this:

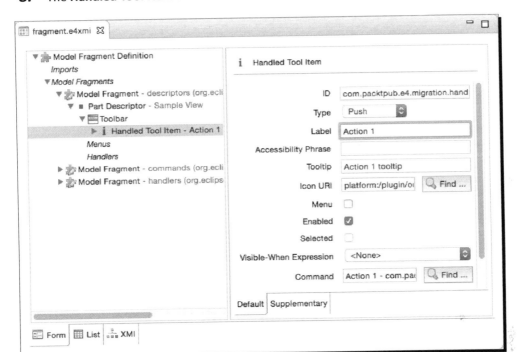

9. Run the application, and open the **Sample View** by navigating to **Window |
Show View | Other | Sample View**. On the right-hand side, there should be an
informational icon; when clicked on, it shows the **Action 1** dialog as before.

10. Repeat the same for the **Action 2** handler. Re-run the application and there should
be a second icon shown in the toolbar.

What just happened?

Instead of creating the toolbar programmatically, it was replaced with entries in the fragment
file. To allow the command to be re-used in other places, it was created with a separate
command and handler, which were also represented in the fragment.

This allowed the `createToolBar` method to be removed, since it serves no further
purpose. This allows around 20 lines of boilerplate code to be removed from the application.
A common feature of Eclipse 4.x applications is the reduced code in laying out and hooking
up the user interface and menus.

Time for action – creating the view menu

The view menu is the dropdown shown with a triangular icon, and is currently created in the
`SampleView` class in the `createView` method. This can be recreated in the fragment editor
by adding a **view menu** to the part descriptor.

1. Open the `fragment.e4xmi` file and navigate to the **Sample View** part descriptor.
    Under that, there is a **Menus** element and a dropdown choice box. Select **View
    Menu** from the list and click on the **Add** button to add a **View Menu**.

2. In the newly created **View Menu**, there is a drop-down choice box. Choose **Handled
    Menu Item** and click on **Add**.

3. Add the following to the **Handled Menu Item**:

    1. **Label:** `Action 1`

    2. **Tooltip:** `Action 1 tooltip`

    3. **Icon URI:** `platform:/plugin/org.eclipse.ui/icons/full/obj16/`
        `info_tsk.png` or use the **Find ...** button as before

    4. Ensure that the **Enabled** checkbox is selected

    5. Click on the **Find ...** button next to the **Command** field and choose the
        Action 1 command from the list

4. The **Handled Menu Item** should look like this:

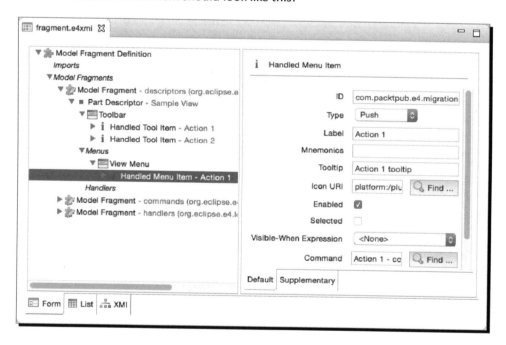

5. Comment out the `createViewMenu` from the `SampleView` class, and run the application. The view menu should still be shown with a single `Action 1`.

6. To replicate the original view, click on the **View Menu** element and use the drop-down to select a **Separator**; then repeat the above steps to add **Action 2** as an element. Now when the application is run, the view menu will be identical to the original implementation. It will look like:

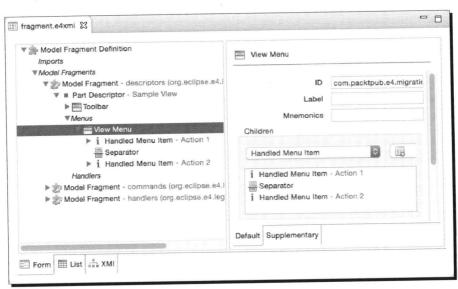

What just happened?

The view menu used to be created with the `createViewMenu` method. Instead of doing this programmatically, it can be created in the fragment, in a very similar way to the toolbar.

A tag `ViewMenu` is automatically added to the **View Menu** in the **Supplementary** tab, which allows the view to be shown. This takes the same effect as setting the tag manually from the code before.

Time for action – defining the pop-up view in the fragment

The pop-up menu can be created in an almost identical way to the view menu. As before, it needs to be registered with the menu service but the code can be dramatically simplified by representing it in the `fragment.e4xmi` file.

1. Go to the `fragment.e4xmi` file, and go to the **Menus** element beneath the **Sample View** part descriptor. Add a child **Popup Menu** to the **Menus** element, either with the context-sensitive menu and by choosing **Add child | Popup Menu**, or by selecting **Popup Menu** from the dropdown and clicking on the **Add** button.

2. In the newly created **Popup Menu**, set the **ID** to `com.packtpub.e4.migration.views.SampleView.popup`.

3. Select **Handled Menu Item** from the dropdown and click on **Add**.

4. Add the `Action 1` similar to before by setting these:

    1. **Label:** `Action 1`

    2. **Tooltip:** `Action 1 tooltip`

    3. **Icon URI:** `platform:/plugin/org.eclipse.ui/icons/full/obj16/info_tsk.png` or use the **Find ...** button as before

    4. Ensure that the **Enabled** checkbox is selected

    5. Click on the **Find ...** button next to the **Command** field and choose the **Action 1** command from the list

5. Repeat the same for the `Action 2` command.

6. Replace the `createPopupMenu` call from the `createPartControl` method with a call to register the pop-up menu with the viewer's control:

```
// createPopupMenu(viewer.getControl());
menuService.registerContextMenu(
  viewer.getControl(), part.getElementId() + ".popup");
```

7. Run the application, and right-click on the elements in the tree. The pop-up menu should be seen as before.

What just happened?

The pop-up menu is created in the same way as the view menu, but with a different top-level type. Creating a pop-up menu is easier in the model fragment, since there are fewer steps in hooking it up. However, it is still necessary to ensure that the SWT control is registered with the listeners to show the pop-up menu.

Unlike Eclipse 3.x menus, which are typically bound by the instance, Eclipse 4.x menus are tied by the identifiers stored in the element's ID. The identifier used in the `registerContextMenu` must be the same as the ID of the pop-up menu in the fragment. This can either be a well-known hard-coded string, or it can be dynamically created from the part's ID. In this case, the part's ID was appended with `.popup` to disambiguate it from the part itself.

Have a go hero – invoking the handler from the hookDoubleClick action

Currently the `hookDoubleClick` action instantiates and runs the handler directly. This can be changed to look up the command dynamically and then execute that instead.

To look up a command, inject an instance of `ICommandService` and then use `getCommand` with the ID of the command (`com.packtpub.e4.migration.command.double` in this case). It can be invoked with `command.executeWithChecks(new ExecutionEvent())`.

Selection is not transferred between Eclipse 3.x and Eclipse 4.x services. To ensure that the `ISelection` is injected appropriately, inject the `ESelectionService` into the part. Either the selection can be set just prior to the command being executed, or a selection listener can be added to the viewer that forwards the selection on to the Eclipse 4.x selection service:

```
@Inject
ESelectionService selectionService;

viewer.addSelectionChangedListener(new ISelectionChangedListener() {
  @Override
  public void selectionChanged(SelectionChangedEvent event) {
    selectionService.setSelection(event.getSelection());
  }
});
```

Pop quiz

Q1. What is the Eclipse 4.x replacement for `Action` instances?

Q2. How is a selection obtained from a `DoubleClickEvent`?

Q3. What tag needs to be added to allow a view menu to be shown?

Q4. How are classes connected to a handler?

Q5. What is the difference between a `platform:` URI and a `bundleclass:` URI?

Q6. What is the difference between a part and a part descriptor?

Q7. How is a pop-up menu connected to the viewer?

Q8. How can a selection be forwarded from an Eclipse 3.x view to an Eclipse 4.x part?

Summary

Eclipse 3.x applications will continue to work in the foreseeable future but the API is frozen and will not receive any updates. Being able to incrementally update an application by migrating views allows developers to take advantage of injection and UI management through fragments.

It's possible to migrate code by directly replacing the user interface building blocks with explicit calls to code services, as shown in the first half of this chapter. However, this will result in a large amount of code being written, which may be counter-productive. Instead, a more Eclipse 4.x-based approach is to create a model fragment file and define the parts, commands, handlers, toolbars, view menus, and pop-up menus in the fragment.

The next chapter will look at styling Eclipse 4.x applications.

9
Styling Eclipse 4 Applications

One of the biggest changes with the Eclipse 4 model is the separation of content from presentation. This allows the style of an Eclipse application to be configured separately from how the user interface is built and designed. This chapter shows how to style an Eclipse 4 application using styles and themes, similar to the way CSS is used to style HTML.

In this chapter, we shall:

◆ Style the UI with CSS

◆ Use the CSS Spy to debug stylesheet rules

◆ Create custom CSS styles and use them in code

◆ Use the dark style in a standalone application

◆ Create multiple themes and switch between them

Styling Eclipse with CSS

Eclipse 4 provides a model of the user interface (represented by classes such as `MApplication`, `MPart`, and `MWindow`) and allows a separate renderer to be able to display the content. This allows for different rendering engines to present the user interface, such as HTML (with RAP) or JavaFX (with e(fx)clipse). To separate content from presentation, the style can be applied in an external stylesheet, based on CSS.

Time for action – styling the UI with CSS

Eclipse 4 user interfaces are styled with CSS. Although this is loosely based on the CSS syntax used by browsers, the stylesheet is interpreted by the Eclipse 4 runtime. CSS stylesheets are composed of selectors and style rules: a selector can be one of a widget name (for example, `Button`), a model class name (for example, `.MPartStack`), or an identifier (for example, `#PerspectiveSwitcher`).

1. The default Eclipse 4 application with sample content (generated by the wizard in *Chapter 7, Creating an E4 Application*, will have an empty CSS file called `css/default.css`. Open this file, and add the following rule:

```
Shell {
   background-color: blue;
}
```

 The **File | New | Plug-in Project** menu can be used to create a new plug-in project, and the **Would you like to create a rich client application?** combined with the **This plug-in will make contributions to the UI** will allow the creation of an Eclipse 4 application for testing purposes if required. If this is chosen, ensure that the **Create sample content** option is selected so that the sample parts and menus are generated.

2. Run the application (by opening the `.product` file and clicking on the green play icon at the top right, if it's not available as a previous launch), and the background of the window (`Shell`) will be shown in blue.

3. Basic CSS color names and hex values can be used to represent color. Modify the `default.css` file as follows:

```
Shell {
   background-color: #00FF00;
}
```

4. Run the application, and the background color will be shown in green.

 Colors can be represented in RGB form using a 6-digit hex value, starting with the # character. The first two numbers represent 256 values for red, the second two green, and the last two blue. White is #FFFFFF and black is #000000. The hex values may be in upper or lower case.

5. It's possible to support vertical gradients in colors by specifying more than one color. Modify the `default.css` as follows:

```
Shell {
   background-color: yellow blue;
}
```

6. Run the application, and the background will be a gradient from yellow to blue.

7. The colors split at the 50% mark by default, but it is possible to specify where the break occurs as a percentage. Using 25% makes the switch to blue happen at the top quarter of the screen—conversely, using 75% makes the switch to blue happen at the bottom quarter of the screen. Modify the `default.css` as follows:

```
Shell {
   background-color: yellow blue 25%;
}
```

8. Run the application, and the background will be a gradient from yellow to blue but with the split near the top.

9. If more than two colors are specified, then multiple gradient points are specified. This can be used to create a rainbow-style effect. Modify the `default.css` as follows:

```
Shell {
    background-color: red orange yellow green blue indigo violet
                         15%    30%    45%   60%  75%    90%;

}
```

10. Run the application, and the background will be a rainbow style:

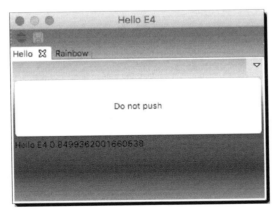

11. As well as using Java class names as selectors, IDs and CSS classes can also be used. For example, to target the **Hello** part, its ID can be used. The default one will be `com.packtpub.e4.application.part.0` if it is not explicitly specified at creation.

12. Go to the **Part** in the application viewer to see the ID. To translate it to CSS, use the `#` selector and replace `.` with `-` in the name. To place the rainbow only on the **Hello** part, use this rule instead:

```
#com-packtpub-e4-application-part-hello {
   background-color: red orange yellow green blue indigo violet
                     15%    30%     45%    60%   75%     90%;
}
```

13. Run the application, and the rainbow part should now be targeted to just the **Hello** part.

14. Another way of coloring each part is to use the pseudo class `.MPart`, which allows a rule to be targeted to all parts in the UI:

```
.MPart {
   background-color: red orange yellow green blue indigo violet
                     15%    30%     45%    60%   75%     90%;
}
```

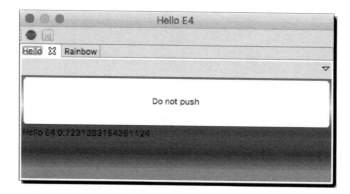

What just happened?

The `default.css` file created with the application wizard was modified to explore how to style properties declaratively. Although loosely based on the CSS specification, some differences are apparent. Style selectors can be:

♦ Widget (SWT) unqualified class names, such as `Button`, `Label`, and `Shell`

♦ CSS class names such as `.MPart`, `.MPartStack`, and `.MTrimmedWindow`

♦ CSS IDs such as `#IDEWindow`, `#org-eclipse-jdt-ui-MembersViewMStack`, and `#left`

There is also a "pseudo selector" that can be used to apply to certain subsets of the classes:

- `Shell:active`: Used for applying styles to the active `Shell`
- `Button:checked`: Used if a `Button` is checked
- `:selected`: Used if a tab folder/item is selected

In addition, CSS selectors can be combined. For example, to have the same rules applied to `.MPart` and an `.MPartStack`, use `.MPart,.MPartStack` as a selector. The comma represents "either."

Dependencies can be combined: `.MPart Label` will apply to `Label` elements that are contained anywhere inside an `.MPart`.

To restrict it to direct descendants, use `Shell > Label`. This will apply only to those `Label` elements that are immediately inside a `Shell`, but not `Label` elements that exist in a separate `Container` within the `Shell`.

Have a go hero – experiment with other CSS properties

A number of other CSS properties are available for customizing the look and feel of individual elements within the user interface. These can be targeted to generic components or specific elements (such as `CTabFolder` for tab-related properties).

The set of properties available for customization includes the following:

- `alignment` used for `Button` elements (for example, `up`) or `Label` (for example, `left`/`right`/`center`)
- `border-visible` is `true` if the border should be shown for `CTabFolder`
- `background-image`: an image referenced as a URL—`url('platform:/plugin/com.packtpub.e4.application/icons/icon.gif')`
- `color` as with `background-color`; names or hex values
- `font` can specify font name (for example, `Courier New`) and size (for example, `128px`)
- `font-family` the font name (for example, `Courier New`)
- `font-size` the font size (for example, `128px`)
- `font-adjust` the font size adjustment (the CSS3 name is `font-size-adjust`, so this may change)
- `font-stretch` the font stretch size
- `font-style` can be `italic` or `bold`
- `font-variant` the font variant (`normal`, `small-caps`, `inherit`)

- `font-weight` the font weight (normal, bold, bolder, lighter, inherit)—use `font-style` instead
- `margin` pixel space around the content (-top, -bottom, -left, -right)
- `maximized` if the widget is maximized or not
- `minimized` if the widget is minimized or not
- `padding` pixel space between elements (-top, -bottom, -left, -right)
- `text-align` can be left, right, center
- `text-transform` can be capitalize, uppercase, lowercase

There are some Eclipse-specific properties as well:

- `eclipse-perspective-keyline-color` the color of perspective lines
- `swt-background-mode` sets the background of the composite to be none, default, or force, corresponding to the Java call `Composite.setBackgroundMode(INHERIT_NONE/DEFAULT/FORCE)`. This ensures that the backgrounds of the children either override or inherit their parent's background.
- `swt-corner-radius` size in px for corner radius
- `swt-hot-background-color` the background color for hot components (with the `SWT.HOT` style set)
- `swt-hot-border-color` the border color for hot components (with the `SWT.HOT` style set)
- `swt-inner-keyline-color` the color of the inside line of the tabs, drawn by the CTabRenderer (see `swt-tab-renderer`)
- `swt-keyline-color` the keyline color
- `swt-maximize-visible` is true or false if the maximize icon is shown
- `swt-maximized` is true or false if the view is maximized (used as a selector)
- `swt-minimize-visible` is true or false if the minimize icon is shown
- `swt-minimized` is true or false if the view is minimized (used as a selector)
- `swt-mru-visible` is true (for "Indigo-like" tab behavior) or false (default)
- `swt-outer-keyline-color` the color of the outside line of the tabs, drawn by the CTabRenderer (see `swt-tab-renderer`)
- `swt-selected-tabs-background` the background color of selected tabs
- `swt-selected-tab-fill` the fill color of the selected tab

- `swt-selection-background-color` the color of the current selection
- `swt-selection-border-color` the border color of the current selection
- `swt-selection-foreground-color` the color of the current selection
- `swt-show-close` is `true` or `false` if the close icon is shown
- `swt-shadow-visible` is `true` or `false` if the shadow is visible
- `swt-shadow-color` the color of shadows, if visible
- `swt-simple` is `true` (for "new style" tabs) or `false` (for "old style" tabs, default)
- `swt-single` is `true` (to only show a single tab) or `false` (show multiple tabs, default)
- `swt-tab-outline` is `true` or `false` if the tab should have an outline:
- `swt-tab-renderer` is `null` for classic style, or a class URL such as: `url('bundleclass://org.eclipse.e4.ui.workbench.renderers.swt/ org.eclipse.e4.ui.workbench.renderers.swt.CTabRendering')`.
- `swt-tab-height` height of the tabs in `px`
- `swt-tab-position` is the position of the tabs and can be `top` or `bottom`
- `swt-text-align` can be `left`, `right`, `up`, `down`, `center`, `lead`, or `trail`
- `swt-tree-arrows-color` is the color that tree arrows are shown as (Windows only)
- `swt-tree-arrows-mode` is the mode that tree arrows are shown as; either `square` or `triangle` (Windows only)
- `swt-unselected-close-visible` is `true` or `false` if the close icon is shown on unselected tabs
- `swt-unselected-tabs-color` the color of unselected tabs
- `swt-unselected-image-visible` is `true` or `false` if the image is shown on unselected tabs

The reference to the `default.css` file is specified in the `plugin.xml`; the product property `applicationCSS` points to the top-level CSS file. It can also be overridden with command-line arguments `-applicationCSS` and `-applicationCSSResources`, both of which use a URL to identify the location of the main CSS file and its associated resources.

Time for action – using custom CSS classes

Very often when building a user interface, there will be a need to repeat styles across different components in the application. Instead of using the generic class type, or having to encode multiple styles on a part-by-part basis, CSS classes can be used to define a standard style and applied to individual widgets.

A label will be added to the sample part and associated with a CSS style, and that will be stored in the default CSS file.

1. Open the `Hello` class and go to the `create` method that creates the part's UI.

2. At the end of the method, add a new `Label`, which will be used to demonstrate the styling:

   ```
   Label label = new Label(parent, SWT.NONE);
   label.setText("Danger Will Robinson!");
   ```

3. Associate the label with a custom CSS class using the `setData` method on the SWT widget along with the `org.eclipse.e4.ui.css.id` key and the name of the CSS class:

   ```
   label.setData("org.eclipse.e4.ui.css.id",
     "DireWarningMessage");
   ```

4. Finally add the class to the `default.css` file so that it can be rendered appropriately:

   ```
   #DireWarningMessage {
     color: red;
     background-color: yellow;
   }
   ```

5. Run the application and the warning message should be shown at the bottom of the part in the style chosen:

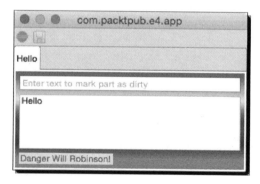

What just happened?

Any SWT widget can have an arbitrary amount of data stored with it using the `setData` method, which can be queried by any other code using the corresponding `getData` method. This is used by the rendering engine that configures how widgets should be rendered in the user interface.

The `org.eclipse.e4.ui.css.id` key is used to identify the CSS class name that should be used when styling the widget through the Eclipse 4 platform, and by using a common key, the application can have the same and consistent style applied to a number of different components.

 This key is defined in the `CSSSWTConstants` class in the `org.eclipse.e4.ui.css.swt` bundle if a compile time reference is desired.

Note that unlike HTML elements, a widget can only have a single CSS class, so it is not possible to have multiple classes associated with an element.

Using the Eclipse spies

Eclipse has several spies, which can be used to introspect the state of the running workbench. Some are available by default, such as the Plug-in Spy and the Menu Spy, but the ones relating to styling have to be separately installed from a snapshot build site at `http://download.eclipse.org/e4/snapshots/org.eclipse.e4.tools/latest/`

Time for action – using the CSS Spy

To provide interactive debugging, Eclipse 4 has the **CSS Spy**, a dialog that can provide information about the user interface widget under the mouse. This can be invoked from the **Quick Access** search box, by typing `css spy`, or by pressing the *Shift + Alt + F5* keys.

1. Move the cursor to the **Quick Access** search box by pressing *Cmd + 3* (on macOS) or *Ctrl + 3* (on other platforms), or by clicking in the search box with the mouse.

2. Enter `spy` in the quick access bar, and a list of Eclipse 4 spies will be shown, including the `CSS Spy`:

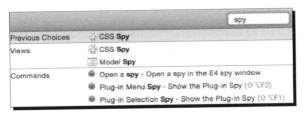

3. Select the **CSS Spy** from the list, and the spy view will be shown. The user interface is represented as a tree structure, and by selecting individual elements of the user interface, a red highlight box will show where the selected element is located on screen:

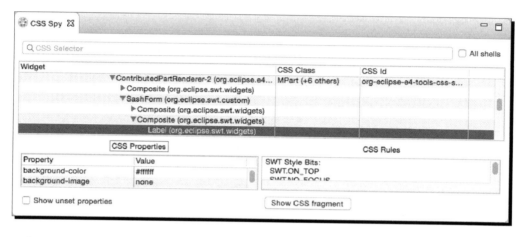

4. It is also possible to open the spy in its own window by pressing the *Alt + Shift + F5* keys:

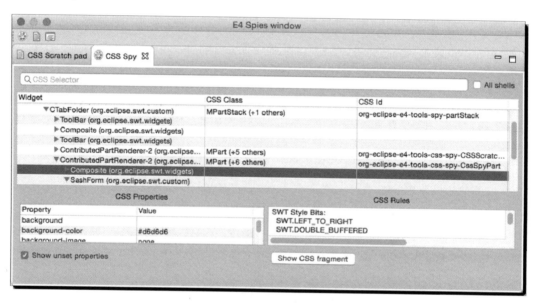

 If the CSS spy is not shown in a floating window, reset the perspective with **Window | Perspective | Reset Perspective...** and then press *Alt + Shift + F5* again.

5. The **E4 Spies Window** also has a **CSS Scratch Pad**, which can be selected by clicking on the notepad-like icon in the **E4 Spies Window** menu bar; alternatively it may be opened by pressing *Alt + Shift + F6*. It can be used to interactively test effects in both the spy window itself and also the main Eclipse window:

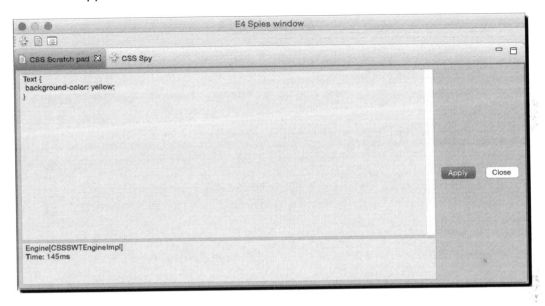

What just happened?

The CSS Spy provides a way to interactively inspect the running Eclipse instance in order to try out new styles and themes. By using the CSS Spy, either as a separate window or as a view within an existing Eclipse window, it is possible to create new CSS rules and verify what the effects will be through experimentation.

The *Alt + Shift + F5* key press will open the **CSS Spy**, and the *Alt + Shift + F6* key press will open the **E4 Spies Window**.

 Pressing *Alt + Shift + F3* will open the **Model Spy**, which allows the part to be introspected and non-style changes to be made, such as the title of the window or its position on screen. The *Alt + Shift + F4* keystroke is not used because on Windows platforms this conflicts with closing the window.

Time for action – integrating the spy into a product

Sometimes it is useful or necessary to be able to debug what an application looks like from the inside. Although the CSS Spy works in the Eclipse instance, it doesn't have any effect on the launched Eclipse 4 application. In order to use the spy in a runtime application, a number of bundles need to be added.

1. Open the `.product` file and switch to the **Contents** tab, which lists the plug-ins required by the product.

2. Click on **Add...** and select both the `org.eclipse.e4.tools.css.spy` plug-in to the product.

3. Click on the run button at the top of the product to launch with the new bundles.

 If the product doesn't launch successfully, manually add the required plug-ins to the launch configuration, or delete the launch configuration and then re-launch the product so that the correct plug-ins are installed.

4. Press *Alt* + *Shift* + *F5* to open the CSS Spy, and select the danger label in the application:

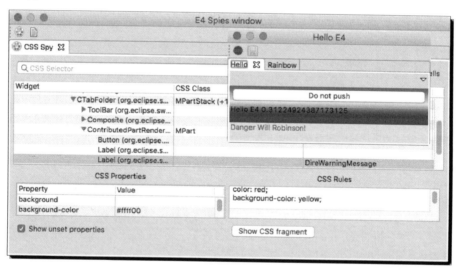

5. The bottom of the CSS Spy shows the current CSS properties and rules. The **Show CSS fragment** button can be used to open a window with CSS source that can be used to paste into a CSS file. In addition, the properties on the bottom left not only show what the current values of the properties are, but can also be used to change the existing values to experiment with the style of the application. Double-click on the value of the **background-color** property and enter a different value, such as `orange` or `#ff00ff`.

What just happened?

By adding the CSS Spy and the E4 Spies package to the application, the keyboard shortcuts and handlers to open the window were automatically added to the application. Now when the application is run, the developer can introspect the style of the application and observe effects to verify that the CSS styles are being applied correctly, such as the `DireWarningMessage` CSS class used here.

The CSS Spy can also be used to translate the current style of the user interface into a stylesheet, which can be used to update or fix rules elsewhere, and interactively changing values through the CSS properties can provide a way to debug content dynamically.

 It is expected that end-user applications will not ship with the E4 Spies bundled with the application. If they are added for testing purposes, they should be removed from the application that is published to reduce the size of the application and to limit the likelihood of accidentally opening the spies window.

Styling a custom widget

Widgets that have been created by the user can be styled using CSS with property handlers. As an example, the `ClockWidget` (created in *Chapter 2, Creating Views with SWT*) will be added to the E4 application and then upgraded to support custom styling.

Time for action – adding the clock

To add the clock to the Eclipse 4 application, a new part will be added which has a `ClockWidget` as its only content.

1. To use the `ClockWidget` in a different plug-in, the package needs to be exported. Open the `MANIFEST.MF` from the `com.packtpub.e4.clock.ui` project, and on the **Runtime** tab, click on **Add** to add the `com.packtpub.e4.clock.ui` package to the list of **Exported Packages**.

2. Create a new class called `ClockPart` in the `com.packtpub.e4.application.parts` package.

3. Add a `create` method with a `@PostConstruct` annotation that takes a `Composite parent` argument.

4. In the body of the `create` method, instantiate a new `ClockWidget` instance with arguments `parent`, `SWT.NONE`, and `new RGB(255,0,0)`. This will require that the `com.packtpub.e4.clock.ui` package is imported into the `com.packtpub.e4.application` plug-in. A quick-fix should offer this automatically, but it can be added by opening the `MANIFEST.MF`, going to the **Dependencies** tab, and adding the `com.packtpub.e4.clock.ui` package to the list of **Imported Packages**. At this point, the code should look like:

```
public class ClockPart {
  @PostConstruct
  public void create(Composite parent) {
    new ClockWidget(parent, SWT.NONE, new RGB(255, 0, 0));
  }
}
```

5. To add the part to the application, open the `Application.e4xmi` file in the model editor, and navigate inside to **Application | Windows and Dialogs | Trimmed Window | Controls | Perspective Stack | Perspective | Controls | Part Sash Container | Part Stack**.

6. Right-click on the **Part Stack** node and choose **Add Child | Part**.

7. Click on the newly created **Part** and add `Clock` as the label, and click on **Find** next to the **Class URI** field to select the newly created `ClockPart` class. It should fill the field with a URI reference `bundleclass://com.packtpub.e4.application/com.packtpub.e4.application.parts.ClockPart`.

8. Add the `com.packtpub.e4.clock.ui` plug-in to the product, and update the launch configuration (or delete it so that it is re-created automatically).

9. Run the application and a **Clock** tab should be seen, with the clock widget shown.

What just happened?

Adding a part was covered previously in *Chapter 2, Drawing a Custom View*, and now the Eclipse 4 application has a **Clock** part with the `ClockWidget`. It takes up the entire space of the application window and will be used to test setting the color of the second hand:

Time for action – using a CSS property

At present the color of the hand is set in the constructor of the `ClockWidget`, and cannot be changed after creation. It would be better if the style of the widget could be controlled externally using the CSS that is used to style the application. This is handled with an `ICSSPropertyHandler` subclass from the `org.eclipse.e4.ui.css.swt` plug-in.

1. Open the `plugin.xml` file from the `com.packtpub.e4.clock.ui` plug-in and switch to the **Dependencies** tab. Add the `org.eclipse.e4.ui.css.swt` and `org.eclipse.e4.ui.css.core` plug-ins to the list. To ensure that the bundle will work if these are missing, mark them both as **Optional** dependencies.

2. Create a new package `com.packtpub.e4.ui.internal.css` to store the classes necessary for CSS cooperation.

3. Create a new class `CSSPropertyClockHandler`, which extends `AsbtractCSSPropertySWTHandler`. The IDE will offer to auto-create the missing methods `applyCSSProperty` and `retrieveCSSProperty`, so create these as they will be used next.

4. In the `applyCSSProperty` method, set up an `if` block to verify that the `control` is an instance of `ClockWidget`, and exit the method if not. This will ensure that the only kinds of classes that are customized by this method are `ClockWidget` instances.

5. Cast the `control` argument to a `ClockWidget` and store it in a local variable `clock`.

6. Add a `switch` block that uses the `propertyName` to determine if it is `clock-hand-color`.

 Although an `if` statement would work in this case, if subsequent property names are added later, a switch will allow others to be seamlessly integrated in.

7. If the `propertyName` is `clock-hand-color`, use the `engine` to get hold of a `color` from the `value` argument with:

```
Color handColor = (Color)engine.convert(
  value, Color.class, control.getDisplay());
```

8. To set the hand color on the `ClockWidget`, the `ClockWidget` class needs to be updated. Open the `ClockWidget` class and add a new field, `private Color handColor`, along with `setHandColor` and `getHandColor` getter methods. Modify the `drawClock` method to use the `handColor` if available, and fall back to the `color` created in the constructor if not. The changes will look like:

```
public class ClockWidget extends Canvas {
  private final Color color;
  private Color handColor;
```

```
      public Color getHandColor() {
        if (handColor == null) {
          return color;
        } else {
          return handColor;
        }
      }
      public void setHandColor(Color color) {
        handColor = color;
      }
      private void drawClock(PaintEvent e) {
        ...
        if (handColor == null) {
          e.gc.setBackground(color);
        } else {
          e.gc.setBackground(handColor);
        }
      ...
```

9. Now the `ClockWidget` supports setting the `handColor`; the `CSSPropertyClockHandler` can be updated to set the color appropriately in the `applyCSSProperty` method:

```
protected void applyCSSProperty(Control control, String property,
CSSValue value, String pseudo, CSSEngine engine) throws Exception
{
  if (control instanceof ClockWidget) {
    ClockWidget clock = (ClockWidget) control;
    switch (property) {
      case "clock-hand-color":
        Color handColor = (Color)engine.convert(value,
        Color.class, control.getDisplay());
        clock.setHandColor(handColor);
        break;
      }
    }
  }
}
```

10. The `retrieveCSSProperty` method can be implemented similarly:

```
protected String retrieveCSSProperty(Control control, String
property, String pseudo, CSSEngine engine) throws Exception {
  if (control instanceof ClockWidget) {
    ClockWidget clock = (ClockWidget) control;
    switch (property) {
      case "clock-hand-color":
```

```
      return engine.convert(clock.getHandColor(),
      Color.class, null);
    }
  }
  return null;
}
```

11. To allow the `CSSPropertyHandler` to style a `ClockWidget`, an `org.eclipse.`
`e4.ui.css.core.propertyHandler` extension needs to be added to the
`plugin.xml`. Open this file, switch to the **Extensions** tab, and click on the
Add button. In the **New Extension** dialog, add the **org.eclipse.e4.ui.css.core.**
propertyHandler extension and click on **Finish**.

 If the extension doesn't show up in the list, unselect the **Show only**
extension points from the required plug-ins checkbox and it should show
up. Adding it will prompt the IDE to add the plug-in to the requirements
when this happens.

12. Right-click on the `org.eclipse.e4.ui.css.core.propertyHandler` extension
and select **New | handler**, if one is not automatically created by the IDE. Right-click
on the **handler** and select **New | property-name** if one is not automatically created
by the IDE. Enter `clock-hand-color` as the **name**.

13. Select the handler again, click on the **Browse** button by the **handler** field, and then
select the `CSSPropertyClockHandler` class.

 To provide a bridge between the SWT widgets and the Eclipse 4 application,
a shadow-dom like facade provides a representation of UI elements
without a particular windowing library. This is achieved with a subclass of a
`ControlElement` and an `IElementProvider` subclass.

14. Create a new class `ClockElement` in the `com.packtpub.e4.ui.internal.css`
package, which subclasses `ControlElement`, which passes the arguments to the
super constructor:

```
public class ClockElement extends ControlElement {
  public ClockElement(ClockWidget widget, CSSEngine engine) {
    super(widget, engine);
  }
}
```

15. To connect the `ClockElement` to the `ClockWidget`, an `IElementProvider` needs to be created. Create a class called `ClockElementProvider` that implements the `IElementProvider` interface, and implement the `getElement` method that returns a binding between the `ClockWidget` and the `ClockElement`:

```
public class ClockElementProvider implements IElementProvider {
  public Element getElement(Object element, CSSEngine engine) {
    if (element instanceof ClockWidget) {
      return new ClockElement((ClockWidget) element, engine);
    }
    return null;
  }
}
```

 The `Element` comes from the `org.w3c.dom` package; there are several classes called `Element` in the Java libraries, so verify that the right one is used.

16. Now that the `ClockElementProvider` class has been created, open the `plugin.xml` file and in the **Extensions** tab click on the **handler** underneath the **propertyHandler** node. Click on **Browse** next to the **adapter** field, and choose the `ClockElementProvider` to join them together.

17. To define the provider properly, an `elementProvider` needs to be created. Click on the **Add** button in the **Extensions** tab, choose the `org.eclipse.e4.ui.css.core.elementProvider` extension, and click on **Finish**. Right-click on the **elementProvider** node and choose **New | provider**. In the provider, click on the **Browse** button next to the **class** and choose the `ClockElementProvider`. Expand the **provider** node and the **widget** child should be present. Click on the **Browse** button next to the **class** field and choose `ClockWidget`.

18. The resulting `plugin.xml` should look like:

```
<extension point="org.eclipse.e4.ui.css.core.propertyHandler">
  <handler composite="false"
   adapter="com.packtpub.e4.clock.ui.internal.css.ClockElement"
   handler="com.packtpub.e4.clock.ui.internal.css
   .CSSPropertyClockHandler">
    <property-name name="clock-hand-color"/>
  </handler>
</extension>
<extension point="org.eclipse.e4.ui.css.core.elementProvider">
  <provider class="com.packtpub.e4.clock.ui.internal.css
  .ClockElementProvider">
    <widget class="com.packtpub.e4.clock.ui.ClockWidget"/>
  </provider>
</extension>
```

19. Now modify the `css/default.css` stylesheet in the `com.packtpub.`
`e4.application`, and add a rule to style the `ClockWidget`:

```
ClockWidget {
    background-color: white;
    clock-hand-color: blue;
}
```

20. Run the application and verify that the color is set appropriately. Modify the CSS and
re-run the application. Does the color of the hand change?

What just happened?

Eclipse 4 uses a shadow-dom like model for representing the user interface. The `Widget`
hierarchy used by SWT has a parallel `Element` hierarchy that is used to represent the key
aspects of the widget in use. This allows other rendering engines, such as JavaFX to display
an Eclipse 4 user interface by simply modifying the presentation layer.

To bind this `Element` hierarchy to the `Widget`, the `elementProvider` extension is used.
This defines a relationship between the SWT `Widget` (in this case, `ClockWidget`) and a
corresponding `Element` object (in this case, `ClockElement`). The `elementProvider`
typically wraps the underlying `(Clock)Widget` with a `(Clock)Element`, in the
`getElement` method. The `ClockElement` needs to subclass `ControlElement` in
order to inherit the standard SWT properties; if it does not, then properties such as
`background-color` will not be applied.

Once this relationship has been defined, it is possible to associate an
`ICSSPropertyHandler` with one or more property names to elements. A single property
handler may provide support for multiple `property-name` definitions, or even support
multiple classes. Each name must be added in the `property-name` element of the
`propertyHandler` extension. For SWT widgets, the `AbstractCSSPropertySWTHandler`
class is typically used as the parent class.

In order to convert CSS color names into SWT `Color` objects, the `CSSEngine` that is
passed in as an argument can be used to dynamically cast objects into a target type with the
`convert` method. For conversion from a `String` into an SWT `Widget`, the third parameter
must be the SWT `Display` (typically from the control that was passed in); but for conversion
the other way (from a `Color` to a `String`), the third parameter is not required.

Themes

Although a standalone product may have a default custom stylesheet, it is sometimes an
advantage to allow the end user to customize the look and feel of the product, or to allow
different styles of user interface to suit the user. This is the purpose of **themes**, which are
available both in the Eclipse IDE and also in generated Eclipse 4 applications.

Time for action – going to the dark side

Eclipse 4 added several new themes for Eclipse, one of which was an updated dark theme. This can be added to an Eclipse 4 application through the use of the `org.eclipse.ui.themes` plug-in.

1. Edit the `.product` file and ensure that the `org.eclipse.ui.themes` is added as a required bundle of the product on the **Contents** tab. This will ensure that if the product is exported then it contains the required plug-in.

2. Update the launch configuration, by going to the **Run | Run...** menu and selecting the Eclipse 4 application. On the **plug-ins** tab, type `org.eclipse.ui.themes` into the search box, where type filter text is shown. Ensure that the checkbox next to the plug-in is checked.

3. Edit the `css/default.css` file and add the following to the top:

    ```
    @import url("platform:/plugin/org.eclipse.ui.themes/css/e4-dark.css");
    ```

4. Run the Eclipse 4 application and the application should be shown in the dark theme:

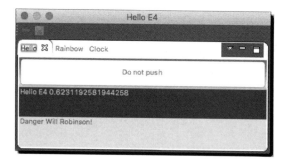

What just happened?

The standard Eclipse themes are delivered inside the `org.eclipse.ui.themes` plug-in. These take the form of CSS files and optional images that work together to provide a consistent experience.

The `platform:/plugin/...` URL is a way of referring to content in another plug-in. This is only valid if the named plug-in part of the launched application. By default, Eclipse products run with **plug-ins selected below only** set as the available dependencies, which is created initially from the dependencies of the product file.

When the application style is loaded, the `@import` URL is evaluated and the dark theme style is loaded from the `org.eclipse.ui.themes` plug-in.

Time for action – adding themes

Eclipse 4 ships with a **theme manager** which can be used to swap between themes (in essence, separate CSS files). The theme manager is available for inclusion in Eclipse 4-based applications by adding the `org.eclipse.e4.ui.css.swt` plug-in as a dependency to the application, and by adding one or more `org.eclipse.e4.ui.css.swt.theme` extension points.

1. Add the `org.eclipse.e4.ui.css.swt.theme` plug-in to the **Dependencies** tab of the `plugin.xml` file of the `com.packtpub.e4.application` project.

2. Go to the **plugin.xml** tab of the `plugin.xml` file (or edit the file as text) and add the following content to add blue and green themes:

```
<extension point="org.eclipse.e4.ui.css.swt.theme">
  <theme label="Blue Theme"
     id="com.packtpub.e4.ui.css.theme.blue"
     basestylesheeturi="css/blue.css"/>
  <theme label="Green Theme"
     id="com.packtpub.e4.ui.css.theme.green"
     basestylesheeturi="css/green.css"/>
</extension>
```

3. Create a text file with the name `blue.css` in the `css` folder of the project with the following content:

```
.MPart {
  background-color: blue;
}
```

4. Create another text file `green.css` in the `css` folder, substituting the background color for `green` instead of `blue`.

 Ensure that the `css` folder is present in the `build.properties` file if it isn't added already, so that all the stylesheets are available in the running application.

5. In the `plugin.xml` file, comment or remove the `applicationCSS` property from the product extension and replace it with a property `cssTheme` with the ID of the initial theme:

```
<property name="cssTheme"
 value="com.packtpub.e4.ui.css.theme.blue"/>
<!--
 property name="applicationCSS"
```

```
value="platform:/plugin/com.packtpub.e4
.application/css/default.css"
-->
```

6. The extensions tab will look like this:

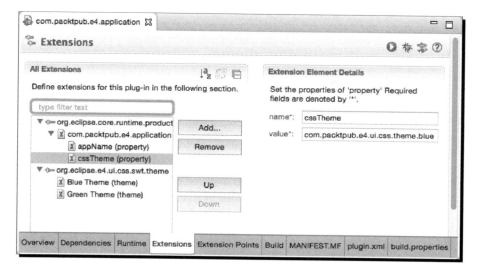

7. Run the application and the default theme should be displayed. Test that it works by changing the `cssTheme` to point to the green theme (`com.packtpub.e4.ui.css.theme.green`) instead.

What just happened?

Two different CSS files were added to the product, and defined as themes, each with their own label and ID. Each theme can have its own definitions, and the themes can use `@import` (describe in earlier sections of this chapter) to include the content of another style file.

Instead of passing a CSS to the product when it launches, the theme identifier can be used. This permits the style to be refactored or the CSS file to be renamed at a later stage without affecting any existing products. In addition, it is possible to use the themes to dynamically switch the style of the runtime, as is shown in the next section.

Time for action – switching between themes

The themes can be switched at runtime by interacting with the IThemeEngine, which can be acquired from the Eclipse 4 runtime service through injection. This provides a list of all installed themes, which can be used to populate the list viewer, and to allow the style to be changed.

1. Create a class called ThemePart in the com.packtpub.e4.application.parts package. Add an injected field IThemeEngine, and a create method annotated with @PostConstruct that takes a Composite parameter:

```
public class ThemePart {
  @Inject
  private IThemeEngine themeEngine;
  @PostConstruct
  public void create(Composite parent) {
  }
}
```

2. In the create method, add a ListViewer that is associated with an ArrayContentProvider:

```
ListViewer lv = new ListViewer(parent, SWT.NONE);
lv.setContentProvider(new ArrayContentProvider());
```

3. Add a selection listener to the list viewer so that when an item is selected, the element is compared with the list of themes; if one is found, set it through the theme engine:

```
lv.addSelectionChangedListener(e -> {
  ISelection sel = e.getSelection();
  if (sel instanceof IStructuredSelection && !sel.isEmpty()) {
    Object selectedElement =
      ((IStructuredSelection) sel).getFirstElement();
    for (ITheme theme : themeEngine.getThemes()) {
      if (selectedElement.equals(theme.getLabel())) {
        themeEngine.setTheme(theme, false);
      }
    }
  }
});
```

4. Finally, set the list viewer's input to a list of theme engines:

```
lv.setInput(themeEngine.getThemes().stream() //
  .map(ITheme::getLabel).collect(Collectors.toList()));
```

5. Now that the part is complete, it can be added to the `Application.e4xmi`. Add a new **Part** under the **Application | Windows and Dialogs | Trimmed Window | Controls | Perspective Stack | Perspective | Controls | Part Sash Container | Part Stack** entry in the model.

6. Run the application, and the viewer should show a list of available themes. Clicking on the themes should switch the user interface style:

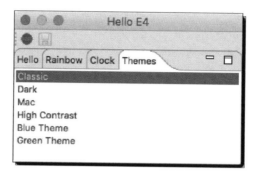

What just happened?

The theme engine is responsible for configuring the user interface when the theme changes, and will dynamically reconfigure the components as they are created. One of the benefits of having themes is that the user can switch between them, or even add new themes after the application has been launched and have them dynamically displayed in the list. Each theme is associated with an `id`, and it is this identifier (or the `ITheme` object) that is used to set the theme on the user interface.

The example shows building a list of themes by label and then searching for them when the theme changes. For a small set of themes this isn't a problem; but a better approach would be to add the `ITheme` objects into the viewer (or a dynamically populated menu) and then have them rendered as the label. That way, when the theme manager's `setTheme` method is called, the object can be used directly.

A `LabelProvider` could be used to translate the `ITheme` into a more suitable textual representation suitable for a viewer, which would allow the viewer to store the theme objects directly.

Have a go hero

Instead of having a set of themes displayed in the main user interface, it would be better if this was presented as a menu item. This can be achieved using a `DynamicMenuContribution` type in the user interface, and to use the `@AboutToShow` annotation to populate the available menu items, one per available theme. The same handler can be used to perform the style change, provided that the theme identifier is passed as part of the handler invocation.

Pop quiz – styling Eclipse 4

Q1. How can Eclipse 4 parts be styled?

Q2. What is an Eclipse 4 theme?

Q3. How are elements referenced in CSS files?

Q4. What CSS would be necessary to change all labels to italics?

Q5. How can the CSS Spy be opened?

Q6. How can the theme be changed at runtime?

Summary

Eclipse 4 can be styled by using a style language very similar to CSS, and the style can be created separately from the underlying UI content. These styles can be integrated into themes and allow the user to dynamically switch between them.

In the next chapter, we'll look at how to create features and update sites, which allows the plug-ins written so far to be served and installed into other Eclipse applications.

10
Creating Features, Update Sites, Applications, and Products

Features, Update Sites, Applications and Products – putting it together

Eclipse is much more than just an application; its plug-in architecture allows additional functionality to be installed. Plug-ins can be grouped into features, and both can be hosted on an update site. These allow functionality to be installed into an existing application, but it's also possible to build your own applications and products.

In this chapter, we shall:

- Create a feature that combines plug-ins
- Generate an update site containing features and plug-ins
- Categorize the update site
- Create an application
- Create and export a product
- Use a target platform to compile against a specific version of Eclipse

Grouping plug-ins with features

Although functionality is provided in Eclipse through the use of plug-ins, typically individual plug-ins aren't installed separately. Historically, the Eclipse platform only dealt with features, a means of grouping a number of plug-ins together. Although the P2 update system is capable of installing plug-ins separately, almost all functionality used in Eclipse runtimes is installed through features.

Time for action – creating a feature

A feature project is used in Eclipse to create, test, and export features. Features are used to group many plug-ins together into a coherent unit. For example, the JDT feature consists of 25 separate plug-ins. Features are also used in the construction of update sites, which are covered later in this chapter.

1. Create a feature project by going to **File | New | Project...** and then selecting **Feature Project**.

2. Name the project `com.packtpub.e4.feature`, which will also be used as the default name for the Feature ID. As with plug-ins, they are named in reverse domain name format, though typically they end with `feature` to distinguish them from the plug-in that they represent. The version number defaults to `1.0.0.qualifier`. The feature name is used for the text name shown to the user when it's installed, and will default to the last segment of the project name:

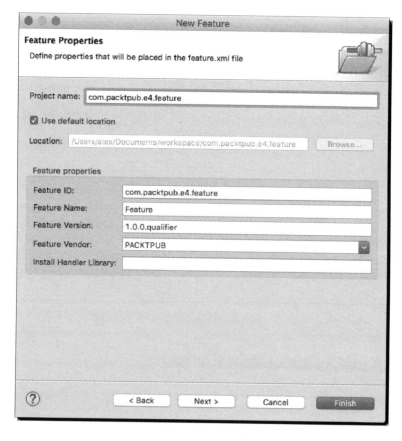

3. Click on **Next** and it will prompt to choose plug-ins. Choose `com.packtpub.e4.clock.ui` from the list:

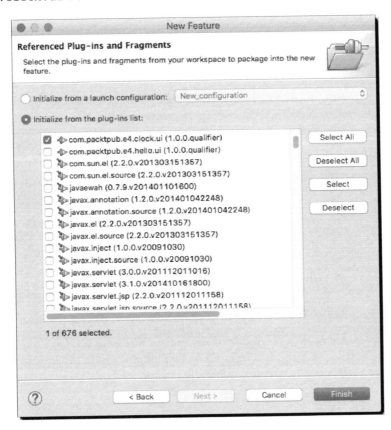

4. Click on **Finish** to create the feature project.

5. Double-click on the `feature.xml` file to open it in an editor, go to the **Included Plug-ins** tab, and verify that the clock plug-in has been added as part of the feature.

6. Add more information, such as feature descriptions, copyright notices, and license agreements via the **Information** tab.

What just happened?

A feature project called `com.packtpub.e4.feature` was created with a `feature.xml` file. The information specified in the dialog can be seen in this file and changed later if necessary:

```
<feature id="com.packtpub.e4.feature"
   label="Feature"
   version="1.0.0.qualifier"
```

```
    provider-name="PACKTPUB">
     <plugin id="com.packtpub.e4.clock.ui"
       download-size="0"
       install-size="0"
       version="0.0.0"
       unpack="false"/>
  </feature>
```

The `feature id` must be globally unique, as this is the identifier Eclipse and P2 will use for installation. The feature version follows the same format as plug-in versions, `major.minor.micro.qualifier`, where:

- Increments of `major` versions indicate backward-incompatible changes
- Increments of `minor` versions indicate new functionality with backward compatibility
- Increments of `micro` versions indicate no new functionality other than bug fixes

The qualifier can be any textual value. The special keyword `qualifier` is used by Eclipse to substitute the build number, which if not specified is formed from the date and timestamp.

The plug-in listed here is the one chosen from the wizard. It will default to `0.0.0`, but when the feature is published, it will choose the highest version available and then replace the version string for the plug-in.

There may also be other elements in the `feature.xml` file, such as `license`, `description`, and `copyright`. These are optional, but if present, they will be displayed in the update dialog when installing.

Time for action – exporting a feature

Once a feature has been created and has one or more plug-ins added, they can be exported from the workbench. An exported feature can be installed into other Eclipse instances, as the next section will demonstrate. Note that exporting a feature also builds and exports all the associated plug-ins.

1. To export a plug-in, go to **File | Export | Deployable features**. This will give a dialog with the option to select any features in the workspace.

2. Choose the **com.packtpub.e4.feature** and give a suitable directory location:

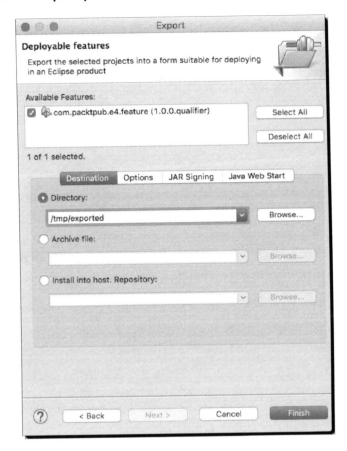

3. Click on **Finish** and the feature and all of its plug-ins will be exported.

4. Open the destination location in a file explorer and see the files created:

    ❑ `artifacts.jar`

    ❑ `content.jar`

    ❑ `features/com.packtpub.e4.feature_1.0.0.201605260958.jar`

    ❑ `plugins/com.packtpub.e4.clock.ui_1.0.0.201605260958.jar`

What just happened?

The **File | Export | Deployable features** action performed a number of steps under the covers. First, it compiled the referenced plug-ins into their own JARs. It then zipped up the contents of the feature project, and finally moved them both into the directory under the `features` and `plugins` subdirectories.

When a feature is exported, the associated plug-ins are built, and so problems in exporting are often caused by problems in compiling the plug-ins.

To debug problems with plug-in compilation, check the `build.properties` file. This is used to control the ant-based build that PDE uses under the covers. Sometimes PDE will flag warnings or errors in this file, especially if the source or compilation folders are moved or renamed after creating a project.

A `build.properties` file looks like:

```
source.. = src/
output.. = bin/
bin.includes = plugin.xml,\
               META-INF/,\
               .,\
               icons/
```

If there are any problems, verify that these correspond to paths in the plug-in's directory.

The `source..` is actually a reference to the current directory. If there are multiple JARs being created, then this will read `source.a.jar` and `source.another.jar`. The source directive is used if plug-ins have source exported; classes and other compiled output come from the `output` property. If the output directory is renamed (for example, `target/classes`) then ensure that the `output..` property is updated in the `build.properties` file.

If there are non-Java assets that need to be exported, they must be explicitly listed in this file. If a directory (such as `icons/`) is included, then this path will be re-created in the plug-in's Jar structure when it is created. Individual assets underneath the `icons/` folder do not need to be explicitly listed.

Time for action – installing a feature

Now that the feature has been exported, it can be installed into Eclipse. Either the current Eclipse instance can be used for this, or a new instance of Eclipse can be created by running the `eclipse` executable with a different workspace. (On macOS, double-clicking on the `Eclipse.app` will show the current Eclipse instance again. To run a second instance on macOS, open up the application in the terminal and run `eclipse` from the home of the application folder.)

1. To install the feature into Eclipse, go to **Help | Install New Software....**

2. In the dialog that is prompted, type the directory's URL in the **work with** field. If the feature was exported on Linux into `/tmp/exported`, then enter `file:///tmp/exported` into the **work with** field. If the feature was exported on Windows into `c:\temp\exported`, then enter `file:///c:/temp/exported` into the **work with** field. Note that on Windows, the directory slashes are reversed in the URL.

3. After the URL has been entered, press the *Enter* key. The message may say **no categorized items**. If so, uncheck the **Group items by category** checkbox and the feature should appear:

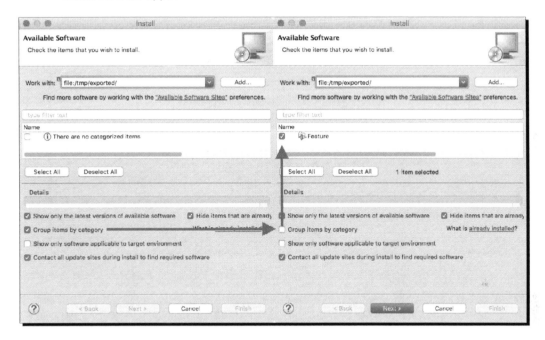

4. Click on the checkbox next to the feature and hit **Finish** to install the feature and associated plug-in in the Eclipse workspace.

5. Restart Eclipse to complete the install.

6. Verify that the various **Clock** views are available by going to **Window | Show View | Other | Timekeeping**.

What just happened?

The feature exported from the earlier step was imported from the same location. Unless the feature is categorized, it won't show up on the list of things to install. Unchecking the **Group items by category** checkbox shows all features, not just categorized ones.

The **Feature** name shown here is derived from the default value in the `feature.xml` file; it can be replaced with a more appropriate value if desired.

If the Eclipse instance isn't showing changes (for example, because the feature or plug-in has been modified), go to the **Preferences**, find **Install/Update | Available Software Sites**, and click on the exported repository. The **reload** button on the right-hand side will be enabled, and clicking on that will refresh from disk the contents of the repository:

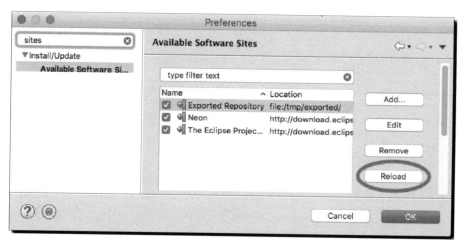

Once the repository is reloaded, go back into the **Help | Install New Software** and the update should be seen. If it is not, verify that the version ends with `.qualifier` on the end of the features' and plug-ins' version number. Without a monotonically increasing version number, Eclipse gets confused and cannot detect that the plug-in or feature has been changed, and so refuses to re-install it. Check also that the exported version of the plug-in and feature ends with a more recent date; or remove the contents of the exported folder, export, and then reload.

Time for action – categorizing the update site

The **Group items by category** mechanism allows a small subset of features to be shown in the list, grouped by category. Eclipse is a highly modular application, and a regular install is likely to include over 400 features and over 600 plug-ins. A one-dimensional list of all of the features will take up a significant amount of UI space and not provide the best user experience; and in any case, many of the features are subsets of the core functionality (Mylyn alone can install over 150 features, depending on what combinations are selected in the install).

This categorization works by providing a `category.xml` file (also known as `site.xml`), which defines a category and a collection of features within that category. When the **Group items by category** checkbox is selected, only the groups and features defined in the `category.xml` file are shown, and the rest of the features and plug-ins are hidden. These are usually done via a separate **Update Site Project**.

1. Create a new project called `com.packtpub.e4.update` as an **Update Site Project**. This will create a new project with a `site.xml` file (if it is renamed from `site.xml` to `category.xml`, it will fail; so don't do that).

2. Double-click on the `site.xml` file and it will open an editor.

3. Click on the **New Category** button and enter the following:

    1. **ID**: `com.packtpub.e4.category`

    2. **Name**: `PacktPub Example E4 Category`

    3. **Description**: `Contains features for the PacktPub E4 book by Alex Blewitt`

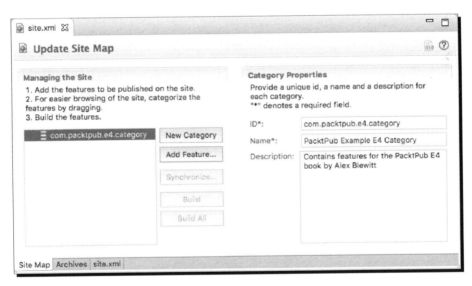

4. Ensure that the `com.packtpub.e4.category` is selected, and click on the **Add Feature** button.

5. Select the `com.packtpub.e4.feature` from the pop-up menu, and this will add it to the highlighted category:

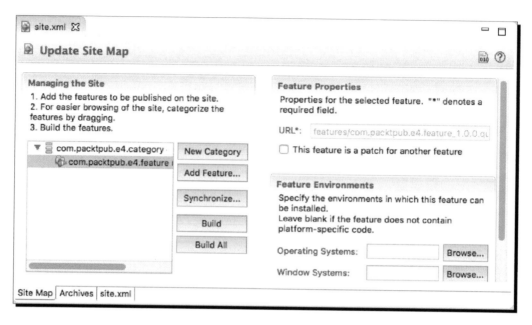

6. Click on the **Build All** button, and an update site will be materialized into the project folder:

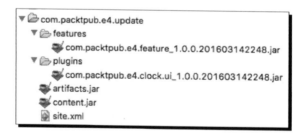

7. Finally, verify that the categories are set up correctly by going into **Help | Install New Software** and placing the path to the workspace in use.

8. Ensure that the **Group items by category** checkbox is selected, and the category containing the feature should be seen:

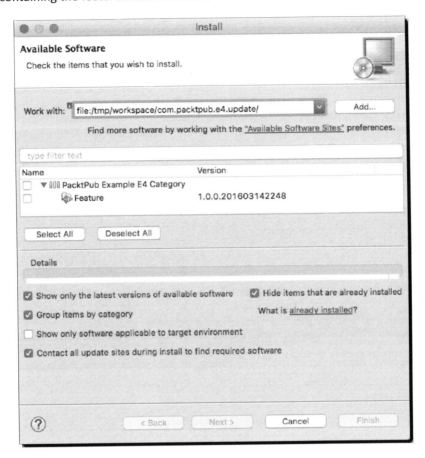

What just happened?

The `site.xml` file is not required by modern Eclipse runtimes, but the `artifacts.jar` and `content.jar` contain XML files required by P2 to perform installation. These contain a list of all the features and plug-ins, and what constraints are required for their installation (such as the packages a bundle exports or imports).

P2 generates a categorization from either a `site.xml` or `category.xml` file. These are essentially the same, but the update site has a nicer UI for editing and generating the content required:

```
<site>
  <feature id="com.packtpub.e4.feature" version="1.0.0.qualifier"
    url="features/com.packtpub.e4.feature_1.0.0.qualifier.jar">
```

```
       <category name="com.packtpub.e4.category"/>
   </feature>
   <category-def name="com.packtpub.e4.category"
    label="PacktPub E4 Example Category">
     <description>
       Contains features for the PacktPub E4 book by Alex Blewitt
     </description>
   </category-def>
 </site>
```

This file contains a list of features (which themselves contain plug-ins) and can be used to generate an update site, which is a `features` and `plugins` directory along with the top-level content. If the `artifacts.jar` or `content.jar` is missing (and there is no `site.xml` file), Eclipse will be unable to install content from the repository.

When the update site is built, it will replace the `.qualifier` with a build identifier, which is derived from the year/month/day/time. It is possible to override this with a different value if desired.

The `artifacts.jar` and `content.jar` files are ZIP files that contain a single `xml` file. This `xml` file is put in a `jar` solely for compression; it can be served (though less efficiently) as `artifacts.xml` or `content.xml` as well. Recent versions of Eclipse also support the xml file being compressed with `xz`, which provides better compression than either the xml file or the JAR file; these aren't generated with the build tools but can be compressed manually using the standalone command-line utility `xz`:

```
xz -ez9 artifacts.xml
xz -ez9 content.xml
```

This update site can be transferred to the host onto a remote server to allow installation into other Eclipse instances. Eclipse supports HTTP as well as FTP by default, although it can be extended to allow other protocols.

Generally only top-level features should be exposed in the update site. These may include other features or plug-ins, but only the top-level features are shown in the update site and in the installed list in Eclipse through the **Help | About | Installation Details** dialog.

Time for action – depending on other features

If a feature needs functionality provided by another feature, it can be declared via the `feature.xml` file of the feature itself. For example, installing the E4 feature may depend on some runtime components provided by JGit, so installing the JGit feature will mean that everything required is present.

To add JGit as a dependency to the E4 feature.

1. Edit the `feature.xml` file and go to the **Dependencies** tab:

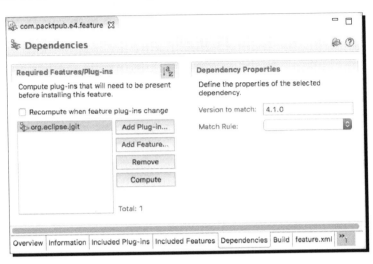

2. Click on **Add Feature** and select `org.eclipse.jgit` from the list. It will fill in a version range using the exact version specified in the plug-in; invariably it is better to substitute that with a lower-bound version number since that will allow the feature to be installed with a dependency that is slightly lower. This will result in a `feature.xml` that looks like:

```
<feature id="com.packtpub.e4.feature" label="Feature"
  version="1.0.0.qualifier" provider-name="PACKTPUB">
  <requires>
    <import feature="org.eclipse.jgit" version="4.0.0"
    match="greaterOrEqual"/>
  </requires>
  <plugin id="com.packtpub.e4.clock.ui"
    download-size="0"
    install-size="0"
    version="0.0.0"
    unpack="false"/>
<feature/>
```

3. Run the **Build All** again. The `features/` directory will contain just the `com.packtpub.e4.feature`, and the `plugins/` directory will contain just the `com.packtpub.e4.clock.ui` plug-in.

4. Install the feature again (or navigate to **Help | Check for Updates** if the directory has already been added). This time, as well as installing the example feature, it should prompt to install JGit, which it will get from the standard Eclipse update sites, provided that JGit is not already installed.

What just happened?

By adding a dependency on another feature, when it is installed into a running Eclipse platform, it requires that the other feature be present. Suppose the **Consult all update sites** checkbox is ticked; then if the feature is not installed and cannot be found from the current update site, other update sites will be consulted to acquire the missing feature.

Note that the JGit feature will not be present in the exported site. This is generally desirable since it is unnecessary to duplicate features that are available elsewhere. However, if this is desired then remove the dependency from the **Dependency** tab and add it to the **Included features** tab. This will result in the `requires` dependency being changed to an `includes` dependency in the `feature.xml` file.

Time for action – branding features

Features generally don't show up in the **About** dialog of Eclipse, as there is only space for a handful of features to show there. Only top-level features which have branding information associated with them are shown in the dialog.

1. Go to **Help | About** (or **Eclipse | About Eclipse** on macOS) and there will be a number of icons present, consisting of the top-level branded features that have been installed. These features have an associated branding plug-in, which contains a file called `about.ini` that supplies the information:

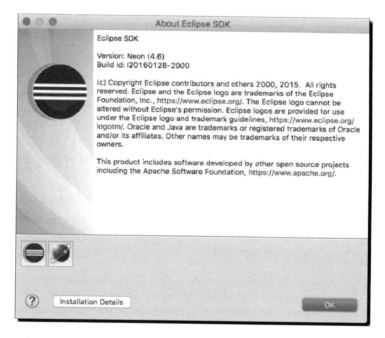

2. First, set up an association between the feature and its branding plug-in, by re-using the `com.packtpub.e4.clock.ui` plug-in from before. Open the `feature.xml` file, go to the **Overview** tab, and add the name of the branding plug-in as `com.packtpub.e4.clock.ui`:

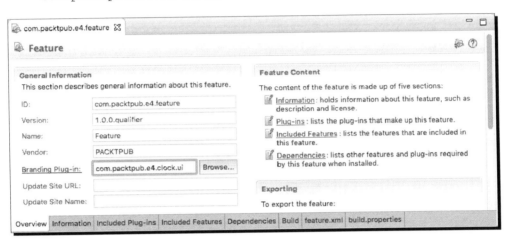

3. Now, create a file in the `com.packtpub.e4.clock.ui` plug-in called `about.ini` with the following content:

```
featureImage=icons/sample.gif
aboutText=\
Clock UI plug-in\n\
\n\
Example of how to use plug-ins to modularise applications\n
```

4. Build the update site, and install the plug-in into Eclipse. After restarting, go to the **Help | About** menu. Unfortunately, the about text won't be present. That's because despite the `about.ini` file being part of the plug-in, Eclipse doesn't bundle it into the plug-in's JAR. There is another change which is required in the `build.properties` file in the `com.packtpub.e4.clock.ui` plug-in to include the `about.ini` file explicitly:

```
bin.includes = plugin.xml,\
  META-INF/,\
  .,\
  icons/,\
  about.ini,\
  ...
```

Export the update site, and the plug-in JAR now has the `about.ini` included.

5. Reload the update site from the **Window | Preferences | Install/Update | Available Update Sites** window and do a **reload** on the exported repository.

6. Run **Help | Check for Updates** to pick up the changes, and restart Eclipse.

7. Go into the **About** screen to show the generic icon used by the feature:

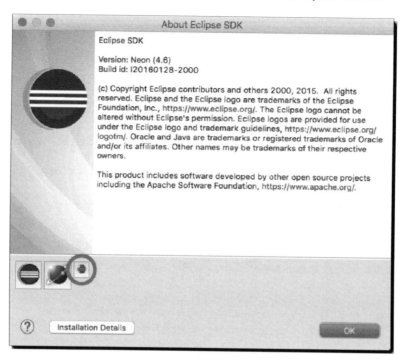

What just happened?

A feature is associated with a branding plug-in, which contains a section of text and an icon. This feature branding consists of an `about.ini` file, which is included in the associated branding plug-in, and optionally a 32 x 32 icon.

The icon generated by the same wizard is 16 x 16, so it shows up as a quarter of the size of other icons in this list. A feature icon should be of 32 x 32 size, as otherwise an inconsistent size will be seen. Supplying a 32 x 32 feature icon is left as an exercise for the reader.

Have a go hero – publishing the content remotely

Since update sites can be served on websites, upload the update content to a remote web server and install it from there. Alternatively use a web server such as Apache or those built into the operating system to serve the content via a local web server.

Building applications and products

An Eclipse runtime consists of groups of features, which are themselves groups of plug-ins. The application that they all live within is referred to as the **product**. A product has top-level branding, dictates what the name of the application is, and co-ordinates what platforms the code will run on, including ensuring that any necessary operating-system-specific functionality is present. In the previous chapter, a product based on Eclipse 4 was created; but products work in the same way for both Eclipse 3.x and Eclipse 4.x.

Time for action – creating a headless application

A product hands the runtime off to an application, which can be thought of as a custom Eclipse `Runnable` class. This is the main entry point to the application, which is responsible for setting up and tearing down the content of the application.

1. Create a new plug-in, called `com.packtpub.e4.headless.application`. Ensure that the **This plug-in will make contributions to the UI** is unselected and **Would you like to create a rich client application** is set to **No**:

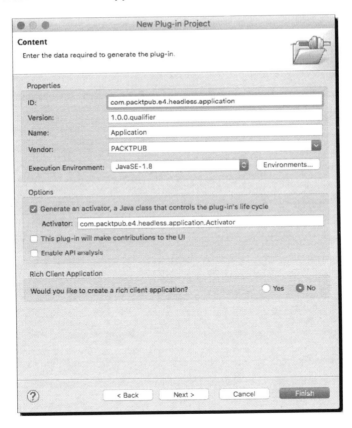

2. Click on **Finish** and the project will be created.

3. Open the project, select **Plug-in Tools | Open Manifest**, and go to the **Extensions** tab. This is where Eclipse keeps its list of extensions to the system, and where an application is defined.

4. Click on **Add** and then type `applications` into the box. Ensure that the **Show only extension points from the required plug-ins** is unchecked. Choose the `org.eclipse.core.runtime.applications` extension point and click on **Finish**:

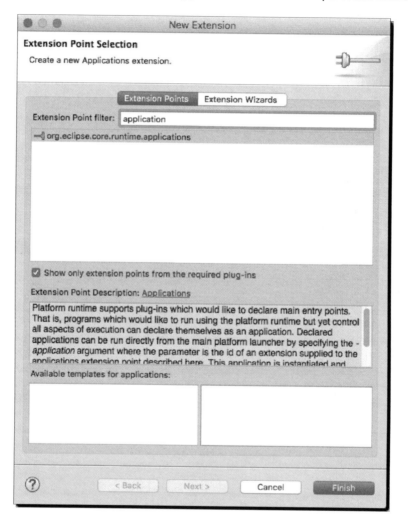

5. The editor will switch to a tree-based view. Right-click on `(application)` and choose **New | run** to create a new application reference:

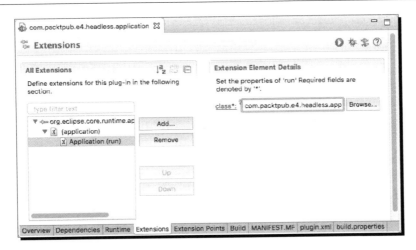

6. Use `com.packtpub.e4.headless.application.Application` as the class name and click on the underlined **class*:** link on the left to open a new class wizard, which pre-fills the class name and supplies the `IApplication` interface:

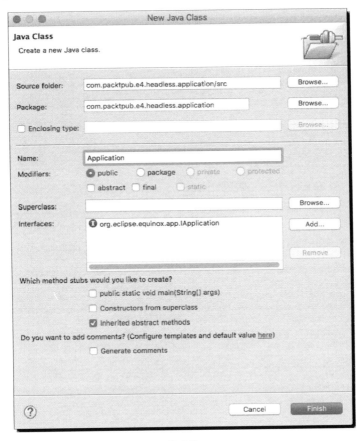

7. Implement the class as follows:

```
public class Application implements IApplication {
  public Object start(IApplicationContext c) throws Exception {
    System.out.println("Headless Application");
    return null;
  }
  public void stop() {
  }
}
```

8. Run the application, by going to the **Extensions** tab of the manifest and clicking on the run button at the top right, or via the **Launch an Eclipse application** hyperlink. **Headless Application** will be displayed in the **Console** view.

What just happened?

Creating an application requires an extension point and a class that implements the IApplication interface. Using the wizard, an application was created and the start method implemented with a simple display message.

When run is clicked, Eclipse will create a new launch configuration which points to an application:

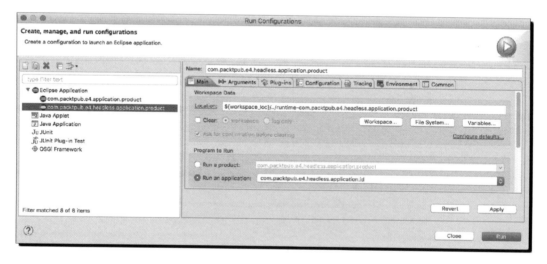

This references the automatically generated ID of the application from the `plugin.xml`. When Eclipse starts the runtime, it will bring up the runtime environment and then hand runtime control over to the application instance. At the end of the start method's execution, the application will terminate.

Time for action – creating a product

An Eclipse product is a branding and a reference to an application. The product also has control over what features or plug-ins will be available, and whether those plug-ins will be started or not (and if so, in what order).

Chapter 7, Understanding the Eclipse 4 Model and RCP Applications, created a product to bootstrap the E4 application (provided by the `org.eclipse.e4.ui.workbench.swt.E4Application` class), but this section will create a product that binds to the headless application created previously to demonstrate how the linkage works.

1. Use **File | New | Other | Plug-in Development | Product Configuration** to bring up the product wizard.

2. Select the `com.packtpub.e4.headless.application` project and put `headless` as the file name.

3. Leave the **Create a configuration file with the basic settings** selected.

4. Click on **Finish** and it will open up the `headless.product` file in an editor.

5. Fill in the details as follows:

  1. **ID:** `com.packtpub.e4.headless.application.product`

  2. **Version:** `1.0.0`

  3. **Name:** `Headless Product`

6. Click on **New** on the right of the product definition section, which will bring up a dialog to create a product. Fill in the dialog as follows:

  1. **Defining plug-in:** `com.packtpub.e4.headless.application`

  2. **Product ID:** `product`

  3. **Application:** `com.packtpub.e4.headless.application.id`

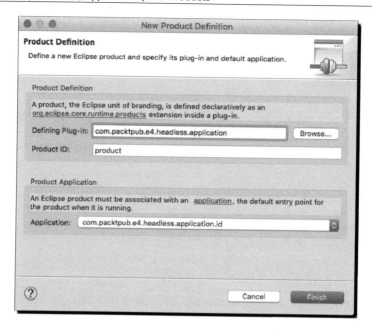

7. Click on the run icon at the top-right of the product to launch the product:

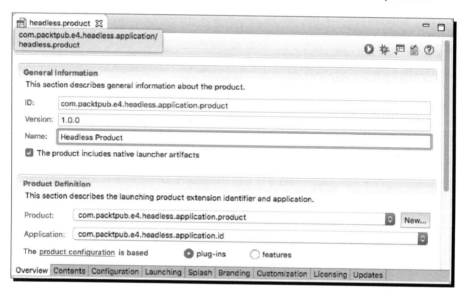

8. There will be an error reported, **java.lang.ClassNotFoundException: org.eclipse.core.runtime.adaptor.EclipseStarter**, because the runtime can't find the required plug-ins. Switch to the **Contents** tab, and add the following bundles:

1. `com.packtpub.e4.headless.application`

2. `org.eclipse.core.runtime`

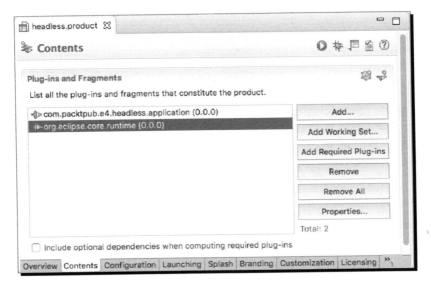

9. Click on **Add Required Plug-ins** and the rest of the dependencies will be added:

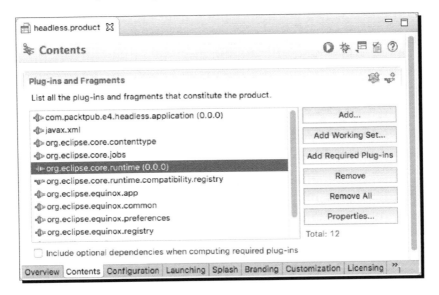

10. Run the product and the same **Headless Application** should be displayed as before.

11. Export the product, either via **File | Export | Plug-in Development | Eclipse Product**, or via the **Export** button at the top of the product editor, to a local directory.

12. From the directory where the product was exported, run `eclipse` to see the message being printed. On Windows, run `eclipsec.exe` to see the output. On macOS, run `Eclipse.app/Contents/MacOS/eclipse`.

What just happened?

Using and running a product may not seem that different from running an application, but the key difference between the two is that an application is a start point and one that can be installed into an existing Eclipse runtime, whereas a product is a standalone system that can be run independently.

A product defines the look and feel of the application's launch icons, specifies what will be bundled, and how it is launched. The product then hands over control to an application, which executes the runtime code.

The editor is a GUI for the product file, which is an XML file that looks like:

```xml
<?xml version="1.0" encoding="UTF-8"?>
<?pde version="3.5"?>
<product name="Headless Product"
    uid="com.packtpub.e4.headless.application.product"
    id="com.packtpub.e4.headless.application.product"
    application="com.packtpub.e4.headless.application.id"
    version="1.0.0"
    useFeatures="false" includeLaunchers="true">
<configIni use="default"/>
<launcherArgs>
    <vmArgsMac>-XstartOnFirstThread
        -Dorg.eclipse.swt.internal.carbon.smallFonts</vmArgsMac>
</launcherArgs>
<launcher>
    <solaris/>
    <win useIco="false">
        <bmp/>
    </win>
</launcher>
<vm/>
<plugins>
    <plugin id="com.packtpub.e4.headless.application"/>
    <plugin id="javax.xml"/>
    <plugin id="org.eclipse.core.contenttype"/>
```

```
            <plugin id="org.eclipse.core.jobs"/>
            <plugin id="org.eclipse.core.runtime"/>
            <plugin id="org.eclipse.equinox.app"/>
            <plugin id="org.eclipse.equinox.common"/>
            <plugin id="org.eclipse.equinox.preferences"/>
            <plugin id="org.eclipse.equinox.registry"/>
            <plugin id="org.eclipse.osgi"/>
      </plugins>
   </product>
```

Have a go hero – creating a product based on features

The product created previously specified an exact set of plug-ins that is needed to run the code. Many Eclipse applications are based on features, and products can also be defined by features.

Move the plug-in dependencies from the product to a feature, and then have the product depend on the feature instead. That way, when the feature is updated, it can be done externally to the product definition.

Target platforms

When building a feature set, it is sometimes necessary to test against different versions of the platform. To support this, PDE allows **target definitions** to be created, which are curated sets of features that PDE will build against. In any one workspace, Eclipse PDE allows for a single **target platform** to be active at any time, which defaults to the current Eclipse installation.

Time for action – creating a target definition

A target definition is a set of features and plug-ins that will be used to build plug-in and feature projects against. The target definition is an XML file that is typically persisted in a project or top-level container that can be shared in a source code repository for other developers to use.

1. Create a new project by navigating to the **File | New | Project...** menu and selecting **General | Project** with the name `com.packtpub.e4.target.mars`.

2. Create a new **Target Definition** by navigating to the **File | New | Other...** menu and searching for `target`:

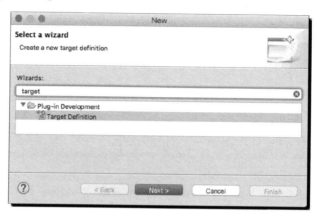

3. After clicking on **Next** choose the `com.packtpub.e4.target.mars` project to store the target definition, and call it `com.packtpub.e4.target.mars`. This will allow anyone building the project to use that target platform to build the project. Select the **Base RCP (Binary Only)** template:

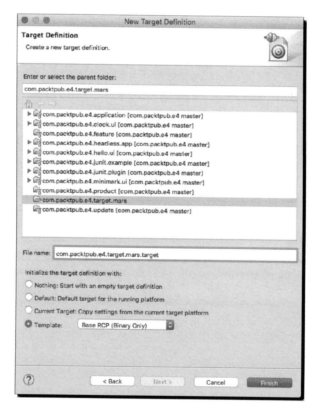

4. Open the newly created `com.packtpub.e4.target.mars.target` file and the target definition editor will be shown:

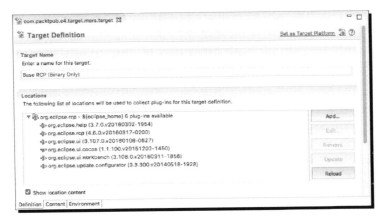

5. Clicking on **Set as Target Platform** will result in many compile errors, because the Base RCP feature doesn't contain E4 features such as `javax.inject`.

6. Change the **Target Name** to `Eclipse Mars` and click on **Add** to add new content.

7. Choose **Features** from the dialog, and then select **${eclipse_home}** from the dropdown and choose **org.eclipse.e4.rcp**, **org.eclipse.rcp** and **org.eclipse.platform** from the feature list, followed by clicking on **Finish**:

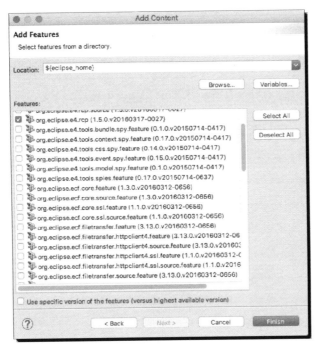

8. Save the edited target file, and click on **Set as Target Platform** again to refresh the content. Eclipse should re-build the files and have fewer errors than before.

What just happened?

A target platform was created, consisting of the basic RCP features and plug-ins, using both E4 and Eclipse 3.x functionality. The content is based on the running platform, which means that when run in different versions of Eclipse, different versions will be used.

> Some of the code created in the earlier chapters uses Eclipse 3.x technology; for example, bundles that depend on `org.eclipse.ui` have activators and handlers used by the older platform, and often miss out dependencies on `org.eclipse.jface` or `org.eclipse.core.runtime`. By removing the `org.eclipse.rcp` dependency from the target platform, it becomes possible to see where these dependencies are and to remove or upgrade them.

Time for action – switching to a specific version

The target platform created in the previous section is based on the Eclipse instance. It is much better to create a target platform for a specific version of Eclipse so that dependencies and testing can be performed against a specific version.

1. Open the `com.packtpub.e4.target.mars.target` target definition file and remove the **org.eclipse.e4.rcp**, **org.eclipse.platform** and **org.eclipse.rcp** features, which correspond to the features in the current Eclipse instance.

2. Click on **Add** and choose **Software Site**. In the **Work with** field, enter the update site for Eclipse Mars `http://download.eclipse.org/releases/mars/` and then choose the **Eclipse e4 Rich Client Platform** (`org.eclipse.e4.rcp`), **Eclipse Platform** (`org.eclipse.platform`), and **Eclipse RCP** (`org.eclipse.rcp`) features from this list:

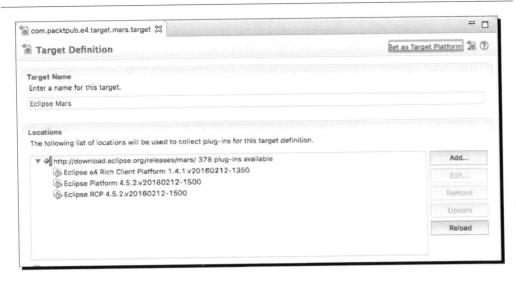

3. After the update dialog has finished downloading the requirements, click on **Set as Target Platform** again to rebuild the projects with the Mars-specific version of Eclipse.

What just happened?

Instead of depending on the current version of Eclipse, target platforms can be used to point to a remote update site that provides a specific version of Eclipse. Although the same feature names are used, the versions of those features will correspond to those present in the named version of Eclipse.

This enables additional platforms to be created; for example, it is possible to create a target platform for Eclipse Neon or for future releases. Testing between different versions of Eclipse is then a case of switching between different target versions and running the tests appropriately, instead of having to have multiple versions of Eclipse downloaded.

 Although it is not necessary to have a target platform in its own project, when Tycho is used to build the application in *Chapter 12, Automated Builds with Tycho*, having the targets in their own projects allows them to be used in separate builds.

Have a go hero – configuring target platforms for other releases

Create new projects, `com.packtpub.e4.target.neon` and `com.packtpub.e4.target.luna`, along with the corresponding `.target` files, that correspond to the download releases `http://download.eclipse.org/releases/neon/` and `http://download.eclipse.org/releases/luna/` respectively. Switch the target platform to each of these and rebuild the workspace. Does it build as expected?

 Building (and testing) against different versions of the platform will allow platform-specific dependencies to be identified and then fixed. Eclipse applications and plug-ins are often backward compatible with the past two released versions, and being able to test against older versions is the way to identify when dependencies creep in.

It is also possible to use explicit version numbers when defining the feature set of a target platform. This will ensure that a specific version of Eclipse is used, even if newer update sites are available on the remote site.

Pop quiz – understanding features, applications, and products

Q1. What is the keyword used in the version number that gets replaced by the timestamp?

Q2. What files get generated in an update site build?

Q3. What is the name of the file that allows an update site to be categorized?

Q4. What is the difference between feature requires and includes?

Q5. What is the difference between an application and a product?

Q6. What is an application's entry point?

Q7. What is a target definition and why is it used?

Summary

In this chapter, we covered how to create features and update sites, which allows plug-ins to be exported and installed into different Eclipse instances. The contents of the update site can be published to a web server and registered with the Eclipse marketplace to gain wide visibility. We also covered how to create applications and products that can be used to export top-level applications, and to define how target platforms can be used to compile against different versions of Eclipse.

In the next chapter, we will look at how to write automated tests for Eclipse plug-ins.

11

Automated Testing of Plug-ins

JUnit and SWTBot – automated testing of plug-ins

JUnit is the testing framework of choice for Eclipse applications, and can be used to run either pure Java tests or plug-in tests. If user interfaces need to be exercised, then SWTBot provides a facade onto the underlying Eclipse application, and can be used to drive menus, dialogs, and views.

In this chapter, we will:

- ◆ Create a JUnit test running as pure Java code

- ◆ Create a JUnit test running as a plug-in

- ◆ Write a UI test using SWTBot

- ◆ Interrogate views and work with dialogs

- ◆ Wait for a condition to occur before continuing

Using JUnit for automated testing

One of the original automated unit testing frameworks, JUnit has been in use at Eclipse for over a decade. Part of Eclipse's quality can be attributed to the set of automated unit tests that exercise both the UI and the non-UI (headless) components.

JUnit works by creating a test case with one or more tests—which usually correspond to a class and methods respectively. Conventionally, test classes end with `Test` but this is not a requirement. Multiple test cases can be aggregated into test suites, although implicitly a project becomes its own test suite.

Time for action – adding dependencies to the target platform

The target platform created in *Chapter 10, Target Platforms*, contained the necessary dependencies to build the plug-ins, but not to test them. To use the test cases in this platform, they need to be added. If the target platform isn't being used, just install SWTBot from the main update site; SWTBot has been part of the default Eclipse repository since Eclipse Mars.

1. Open the `com.packtpub.e4.target.mars.target` platform definition.

2. On the **Definition** tab, click on the Mars repository, and then click on **Edit**. This will allow other features to be added.

3. Search for SWTBot and add **SWTBot for Eclipse Testing**, **SWTBot for SWT Testing**, and **SWTBot IDE Features**. Click on **Finish** to update the target platform:

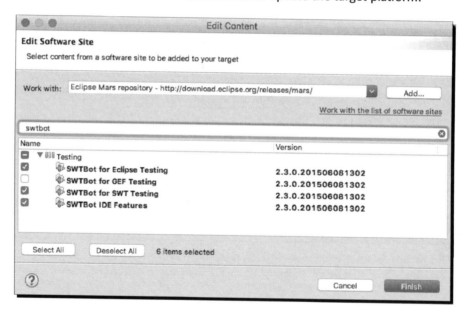

What just happened?

In order to use JUnit and SWTBot, they need to be added to the target platform. JUnit is part of the standard Eclipse installations, but if a target platform is being used, it won't necessarily be made available.

The SWTBot features can be added to the target platform, which will then transitively include the JUnit libraries as well.

For more information on target platforms, see *Chapter 10, Target Platforms*.

Time for action – writing a simple JUnit 4 test case

This part explains how to write and run a simple JUnit 4 test case in Eclipse.

1. Create a new Java project called `com.packtpub.e4.junit.example`.

2. Create a class called `MathUtil` in `com.packtpub.e4.junit.example`.

3. Create a `public static` method called `isOdd` that takes an `int` and returns a `boolean` if it is an odd number (using `value % 2 == 1`).

4. Create a new class called `MathUtilTest` in a package `com.packtpub.e4.junit.example`.

5. Create a method called `testOdd` with an annotation `@Test`, which is the way JUnit 4 signifies that this method is a test case.

6. Click on the quick-fix to **Add JUnit 4 library to the build path**, or edit the build path manually to point to Eclipse's `plugins/org.junit_4.*.jar`.

7. Implement the `testOdd` method as follows:

   ```
   assertTrue(MathUtil.isOdd(3));
   assertFalse(MathUtil.isOdd(4));
   ```

8. Add an `import static` of `org.junit.Assert.*` to fix the compiler errors.

9. Right-click on the project and choose **Run As | JUnit Test**, and the JUnit test view should be shown with a green test result:

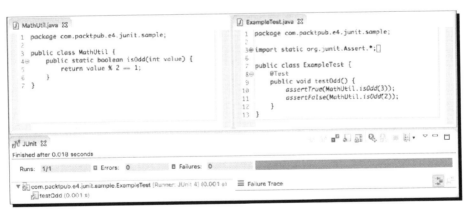

10. Verify that the test works by modifying the `isOdd` method to return `false` and re-running—a red test failure should be seen instead.

What just happened?

The example project demonstrated how JUnit tests are written and executed in Eclipse. The example works for both OSGi and non-OSGi projects, provided that JUnit can be resolved and executed accordingly.

Remember to annotate the test methods with @Test, as otherwise they won't be able to run. It can sometimes be helpful to write a method that knowingly fails first and then run the tests, just to confirm that it's actually being run. There's nothing more useless than a green test bar with tests that are never run but would fail if they do.

It is also possible to re-run tests from the JUnit view; the green run button allows all tests to be re-run, whilst the one with a red cross allows just the tests that have failed to be re-executed (shown as disabled in the previous example). It's also possible to re-run just a single test by right-clicking on the method in the JUnit view and selecting **Run**.

Time for action – writing a plug-in test

Although Java projects and Java plug-in projects both use Java and JUnit to execute, plug-ins typically need to have access provided by the runtime platform, which is only available if running in an OSGi or Eclipse environment.

1. Create a new plug-in project called com.packtpub.e4.junit.plugin.
2. Create a new JUnit test called PlatformTest in the com.packtpub.e4.junit.plugin package.
3. Create a method, testPlatform, which ensures that the Platform is running:

```
@Test
public void testPlatform() {
   assertTrue(Platform.isRunning());
}
```

4. Click on the quick-fix to add org.junit to the required bundles.
    1. Alternatively, open up the project's manifest by right-clicking on it and choosing **Plug-in Tools | Open Manifest**.
    2. Go to the **Dependencies** tab, click on **Add**, and select org.junit from the dialog.
    3. Ensure that org.eclipse.core.runtime is also added as a dependency.
5. Run the test by right-clicking on the project, choosing **Run As | JUnit Test** and seeing the error message fail with an assertion error.

6. Run the test as a plug-in, by right-clicking on the project, choosing **Run As | JUnit Plug-in Test**, and seeing the test pass:

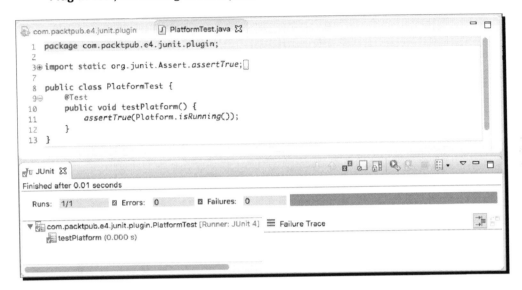

What just happened?

Although the test code is exactly the same, the way in which the tests are run is slightly different. In the first instance, it uses the standard JUnit test runner, which executes the code in a standalone JVM. Since this doesn't have the full Eclipse runtime inside, the test fails.

The plug-in test is launched in a different way; a new Eclipse instance is created, the plug-in is exported and installed into the runtime, the various OSGi services that are needed to power Eclipse are brought up, and then the test runner executes the plug-in in place.

As a result, running a plug-in test can add latency to the test process, because the platform has to be booted first. Sometimes quick tests are run as standalone Java tests, whilst integration tests run in the context of a full plug-in environment.

Code that is dependent on OSGi and the Eclipse Platform services needs to be run as plug-in tests.

Using SWTBot for user interface testing

SWTBot is an automated testing framework that allows the Eclipse user interface and SWT applications to be tested in place. Although writing tests and exercising the models behind an application can be essential, sometimes it is necessary to test the interaction of the user interface itself.

Time for action – writing an SWTBot test

The first step is to install SWTBot from the Eclipse update site. These examples were tested with `http://download.eclipse.org/technology/swtbot/releases/latest/` version 2.3.0, but check out the book's errata for up-to-date information.

1. Go to **Help | Install New Software** and enter the SWTBot update site.

2. Select everything except the GEF feature:

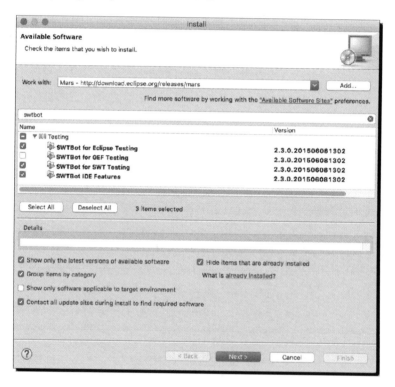

3. Click on **Next** to install.

4. Restart Eclipse when prompted.

5. Add the following bundle dependencies to the plug-in manifest for the `com.packtpub.e4.junit.plugin` **project**:

1. `org.eclipse.swtbot.junit4_x`

2. `org.eclipse.swtbot.forms.finder`

3. `org.eclipse.swtbot.eclipse.finder`

4. `org.eclipse.ui`

6. Create a class called `UITest` in the `com.packtpub.e4.junit.plugin` package.

7. Add a class annotation `@RunWith(SWTBotJunit4ClassRunner.class)`.

8. Create a method called `testUI` and with an annotation `@Test`.

9. Inside the `testUI` method, create an instance of `SWTWorkbenchBot`.

10. Iterate through the bot's `shells` and assert that the one that is visible has a title containing **Eclipse**. The code looks like:

```
package com.packtpub.e4.junit.plugin;
import static org.junit.Assert.assertTrue;
import org.eclipse.swtbot.eclipse.finder.SWTWorkbenchBot;
import org.eclipse.swtbot.swt.finder.junit.
SWTBotJunit4ClassRunner;
import org.eclipse.swtbot.swt.finder.widgets.SWTBotShell;
import org.junit.Test;
import org.junit.runner.RunWith;
@RunWith(SWTBotJunit4ClassRunner.class)
public class UITest {
  @Test
  public void testUI() {
    SWTWorkbenchBot bot = new SWTWorkbenchBot();
    SWTBotShell[] shells = bot.shells();
    boolean found = false;
    for (int i = 0; i < shells.length && !found; i++) {
      if (shells[i].isVisible()) {
        if (shells[i].getText().contains("Eclipse")) {
          found = true;
        }
      }
    }
    assertTrue(found);
  }
}
```

11. Run the test by right-clicking on the project and selecting **Run As | SWTBot Test**.

12. Verify that the JUnit tests have passed:

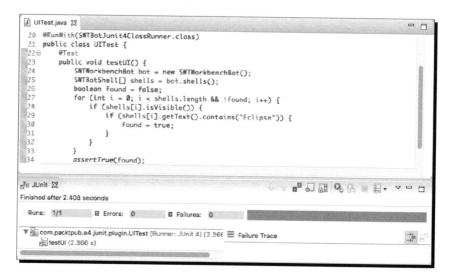

What just happened?

SWTBot is a UI testing mechanism that allows the state of the user interface to be driven programmatically. In this test, a new `SWTWorkbenchBot` was created to interact with the Eclipse workbench (for pure SWT applications, the `SWTBot` class exists).

The bot iterates through the available shells once the workspace has been opened. Although more than one shell is returned in the list, not all of them will be visible. The shell's title can be obtained through the `getText` method, which returns `Java - Eclipse SDK` if the Eclipse SDK package opens on the Java perspective by default—but this value may differ depending on what perspective and which Eclipse package is being used.

The application run is similar to an Eclipse product launch; combinations of plug-ins, start-up properties, and product or application choices can be made via the **Run** or **Debug** configurations menu. As with ordinary JUnit tests, the launch can be invoked in **Debug** mode and the breakpoints set.

Time for action – working with menus

Note that SWTBot works on a non-UI thread by default to avoid deadlock with modal dialogs and other user interface actions. If the tests need to interact with specific SWT widgets, it is necessary to invoke a `Runnable` via the UI thread.

To make this easier, the SWTBot framework has several helper methods that can provide a facade of the workspace, including the ability to click on buttons and show menus.

1. Create a new test method in the `UITest` class called `createProject` with a `@Test` annotation.

2. Create a new `SWTWorkbenchBot` instance.

3. Use the `menu` method of the `bot` to navigate the **File | Project...** menus, and perform a `click`.

4. Use the `shell` method of the `bot` to get the newly opened `shell` with a title of `New Project`. Activate the shell to ensure that it has focus.

5. Use the `tree` method of the `bot` to find a tree in the shell, and `expandNode` the `General` node, and finally `select` the `Project`.

6. Invoke the `Next >` button with a `click`. Note the space between the `Next` and the `>` symbol.

7. Find the `Text` object with the label titled `Project name:` and set its text to `SWTBot Test Project`.

8. Click on the `Finish` button.

9. The code will look like:

```
@Test
public void createProject() {
    SWTWorkbenchBot bot = new SWTWorkbenchBot();
    bot.menu("File").menu("Project...").click();
    SWTBotShell shell = bot.shell("New Project");
    shell.activate();
    bot.tree().expandNode("General").select("Project");
    bot.button("Next >").click();
    bot.textWithLabel("Project name:").
        setText("SWTBot Test Project");
    bot.button("Finish").click();
}
```

10. Run the test as a SWTBot Test, and verify that the `createProject` method does not throw an exception.

What just happened?

After creating the workspace bot, the **File | Project...** menu is selected. Since this opens up a new dialog, a handle needs to be acquired to point to the newly created shell.

To do this, a new `SWTBotShell` is created, which is a handle to a displayed shell. The title is used as a key to find a given shell. If one is not currently visible, it polls (every 500 ms by default) until one is found; or the default timeout period (5 s) ends when a `WidgetNotFoundException` is thrown.

The `activate` method waits until the dialog has focus. To navigate through a dialog, options such as `tree` and `textWithLabel` methods allow specific elements to be pulled out from the UI, with exceptions being raised if these are not found. If there is only one element of the particular type, then simple accessors such as `tree` may be sufficient, but if not, there are `xxxWithLabel` and `xxxWithId` accessors that can find a specific element in a particular section.

To set an ID on an SWT object such that it can be found with the `withId`, call `widget.setData(SWTBotPreferences.DEFAULT_KEY, "theWidgetId")`.

When objects are accessed, they aren't the underlying SWT widgets directly. Instead, they are wrappers, much like how the `SWTWorkspaceBot` is a wrapper for the workspace. Although the code is calling `setText` on what looks like a label, in fact the code is running on a non-UI thread. Instead, it posts a runnable to the UI thread with an instruction to set the text; but all of this is done by SWTBot under the covers.

One thing that's immediately obvious from this is that when using labels, the tests are highly specific to the localization of the product. The tests will fail if the application is run in a different language, for example. They are also implicitly tied to the structure of the application; if the UI changes significantly, then it may be necessary to re-write or update the tests.

Have a go hero – using resources

Automated testing exercises code paths, but it is often necessary to verify that not only has the user interface reacted in the right way, but also the side effects have happened correctly.

In this case, to find out if a project has been created, use the `ResourcesPlugin` (from the `org.eclipse.core.resources` bundle) to get the workspace, from which the root will provide a means of accessing an `IProject` object. Use the `exists` method of the project to determine that the project has been successfully created.

Amend the `createProject` method to verify that at the start of the method, the project does not exist, and does exist at the end of the method.

Note that the `getProject` method of the `IWorkspaceRoot` will return a non-null value regardless of whether the project exists or not.

Working with SWTBot

There are some techniques that help when writing SWTBot tests, such as organizing the test code and hiding the welcome screen at start up, which otherwise might distort the test run.

Time for action – hiding the welcome screen

When Eclipse starts, it typically displays a welcome page. Since this often gets in the way of automated user testing, it is useful to close it at startup.

1. In the `createProject` method, within a `try` block, obtain a view with the title `Welcome`.

2. Invoke the `close` method.

3. The code will change to look like this:

```
SWTWorkbenchBot bot = new SWTWorkbenchBot();
try {
  bot.viewByTitle("Welcome").close();
} catch (WidgetNotFoundException e) {
  // ignore
}
```

4. Run the test, and the welcome screen should be closed before the test is run.

What just happened?

Upon startup, the IDE will show a welcome screen. This is shown in a view with a **Welcome** title.

Using the `viewByTitle` accessor, the (SWTBot wrapper) view can be accessed. If the view doesn't exist, then an exception will be thrown; so for safety, check and catch any `WidgetNotFoundException`, since not finding the welcome screen is not a failure.

Having found the welcome page, invoking the `close` method will close the view.

Time for action – avoiding SWTBot runtime errors

Once more test methods are added, the runtime may start throwing spurious errors. This is because the order of the tests may cause changes, and ones that run previously may modify the state of the workbench. This can be mitigated by moving common setup and tear-down routines into a single place.

1. Create a `static` method `beforeClass`.

2. Add the annotation `@BeforeClass` from the `org.junit` package.

3. Move references to creating a `SWTWorkbenchBot` to the `static` method, and save the value in a `static` field.

4. The code looks like:

```
private static SWTWorkbenchBot bot;
@BeforeClass
public static void beforeClass() {
  bot = new SWTWorkbenchBot();
  try {
    bot.viewByTitle("Welcome").close();
  } catch (WidgetNotFoundException e) {
    // ignore
  }
}
```

5. Run the tests and ensure that they pass appropriately.

What just happened?

The JUnit annotation `@BeforeClass` allows a single `static` method to be executed prior to any of the tests running in the class. This is used to create an instance of the `SWTWorkbenchBot`, which is then used by all other tests in the class. This is also an opportune location to close the **Welcome** view, if it is shown, so that all other tests can assume that the window has been cleaned up as appropriate.

Do not call the `bot.resetWorkbench()` as otherwise subsequent tests will fail in the test cases.

Working with views

As with menus and dialogs, views that have been created can be interrogated with SWTBot as well.

Time for action: showing views

To show other views, the same mechanism is done in the UI tests as a user would do, by navigating the **Window | Show View | Other...** menu.

1. Create a new method, `testTimeZoneView`, with an `@Test` annotation.

2. From the bot, open the **Window | Show View | Other...** dialog.

3. Get the shell with the title `Show View` and activate it.

4. Expand the `Timekeeping` node and select the `Time Zone View` node (the view created in *Chapter 2, Creating Views with SWT*).

5. Click on the **OK** button to have the view shown.

6. Use the `bot.viewByTitle()` method to acquire a reference to the view.

7. Assert that the view is not `null`.

8. The code looks like:

```
@Test
public void testTimeZoneView() {
    bot.menu("Window").menu("Show View").menu("Other...").click();
    SWTBotShell shell = bot.shell("Show View");
    shell.activate();
    bot.tree().expandNode("Timekeeping").select("Time Zone View");
    bot.button("OK").click();
    SWTBotView timeZoneView = bot.viewByTitle("Time Zone View");
    assertNotNull(timeZoneView);
}
```

9. Run the tests and ensure that they pass.

What just happened?

Using the built-in Eclipse mechanism to switch views, the bot navigated the **Window | Show View | Other... | Timekeeping | Time Zone View** menu hierarchy to bring the view to the screen.

Once shown, the `viewByTitle` method of the `bot` can be used to get a reference to the widget, and verify that it is not `null`.

Being able to select a view programmatically is such a common occurrence that it can help to have a utility method be able to open a view on demand.

Time for action – interrogating views

Having been able to acquire a reference to the view, the next step is to deal with specific user interface components. For standard controls such as `Button` and `Text`, the `bot` provides standard methods to acquire. To get hold of other components, the widget hierarchy will have to be interrogated directly.

1. In the `testTimeZoneView` method, get the `Widget` from the returned `SWTBotView`.

2. Create a `Matcher` using the `WidgetMatcherFactory` to find `widgetsOfType(CTabItem.class)`.

3. Use the `bot.widgets` method to search for a list of `CTabItem` instances in the view's widget.

4. Ensure that the number of elements returned is equal to the number of time zone regions.

5. The code looks like:

```
SWTBotView timeZoneView = bot.viewByTitle("Time Zone View");
assertNotNull(timeZoneView);
Widget widget = timeZoneView.getWidget();
org.hamcrest.Matcher<CTabItem> matcher =
  WidgetMatcherFactory.widgetOfType(CTabItem.class);
final java.util.List<? extends CTabItem> ctabs =
  bot.widgets(matcher, widget);
Set<String> regions = ZoneId.getAvailableZoneIds() // get zones
  .stream().filter(s -> s.contains("/")) // with / in them
  .map(s -> s.split("/")[0]) // get first part
  .collect(Collectors.toSet()); // and convert to a set
assertEquals(regions.size(), ctabs.size());
```

6. Run the tests and ensure that they pass.

What just happened?

Although it is possible to write code to walk the user interface tree directly, the widgets have to be interrogated on the UI thread and so care has to be taken to find the children.

SWTBot provides a generic `Matcher` mechanism, which is a predicate that can return `true` if a certain condition occurs. The `Matcher` provided by `widgetOfType` matches items which have a certain class type; similarly many other matchers can be instantiated with the `withXxx` calls, such as `withLabel` and `withId`. The `Matcher` instances can be combined with `allOf` and `anyOf` methods providing and/or logic respectively.

The `widgets` method walks through the tree recursively to find all widgets that match the particular specification. A single-argument version finds all elements from the active shell; the two-argument version allows a specific parent to be searched, which in this case is the `TimeZoneView` itself.

Finally, the size of the list is compared with the number of time zone groups, which is dynamically calculated from the running platform.

Interacting with the UI

Care needs to be taken which thread the user interface is interrogated from. This section will show how to obtain values and wait for asynchronous results to be delivered by the workbench.

Time for action – getting values from the UI

If the test tries to access a property from the returned widget, there will be an exception thrown. For example, `ctabs.get(0).getText()` will result in an **Invalid thread access** SWT error.

To perform testing on widgets, the code has to run in the UI thread. Either the `Display.getDefault().syncExec()` or the equivalent `Synchronizer` class can be used, but SWTBot has a `UIThreadRunnable` that can launch code and a general interface called `StringResult`, which is like a `Runnable` that can return a `String` value through `syncExec`.

1. At the end of the `testTimeZone` method of the `UITest` class, create a new `StringResult` and pass it to `UIThreadRunnable.syncExec()`.

2. In the `run` method, get the first `CTabItem` and return its text value.

3. After the `Runnable` method has run, assert that the value is `Africa`.

4. The code looks like:

```
String tabText = UIThreadRunnable.syncExec(new StringResult() {
  @Override
  public String run() {
    return ctabs.get(0).getText();
  }
});
assertEquals("Africa", tabText);
```

5. Run the tests and ensure they all pass.

What just happened?

To interact with widgets, code must be run on the UI thread. To run code on the UI thread in SWT, it needs to be wrapped into a `Runnable`, which needs to be posted to the display (or `Synchronizer`) and executed there.

Using a `syncExec` method call means that the result is guaranteed to be available for testing. If an `asyncExec` method call is used, then the result may not be available by the time the following assert operation runs.

To pass a value back from the UI thread to a non-UI thread, the result has to be stored in a variable. This has to be either a field on the class or a value in a final array. The `StringResult` of the SWTBot package effectively wraps this up in the `UIThreadRunnable`, in which an `ArrayList` is created to hold the single element.

Java 8 makes this significantly easier in that it allows lambda methods to be executed. For example, the execution can be replaced with the much shorter version as a lambda:

```
String tabText = UIThreadRunnable.syncExec(() ->
  ctabs.get(0).getText());
```

Time for action – waiting for a condition

Typically an action may require some result to happen in the user interface before testing can continue. Since the SWTBot can run much faster than a human can, waiting for the result of an action may be necessary. To demonstrate this, create a Java project with a single source file and then use the conditions to wait until the class file is compiled.

1. Create a new method in the `UITest` class called `createJavaProject`.

2. Use the `bot` to create a new Java project by copying the `createProject` method as a template.

3. Add the `org.eclipse.core.resources` as a dependency to the plug-in.

4. Add a method `getProject`, which takes a `projectName` and returns an `IProject` from `ResourcesPlugin.getWorkspace().getRoot().getProject()`.

5. At the end of the `createJavaProject` method, use the `getProject` method with the test project to get the folder `src`.

6. If the folder does not exist, `create` it.

7. Get the file from `src` called `Test.java`.

8. Create it with the contents from `class Test{}` bytes as a `ByteArrayInputStream`.

9. Look for a dialog with the title `Open Associated Perspective?` and if it exists, click on the `Yes` button.

10. Use the `bot.waitUntil` method to pass in a new anonymous subclass of `DefaultCondition`.

11. In the `test` method of the condition, return if the project's folder `bin` has a file called `Test.class`.

12. In the `getFailureMessage` of the condition, return a suitable message.

13. The code looks like:

```
@Test
public void createJavaProject() throws Exception {
  String projectName = "SWTBot Java Project";
  bot.menu("File").menu("Project...").click();
  SWTBotShell shell = bot.shell("New Project");
  shell.activate();
  bot.tree().expandNode("Java").select("Java Project");
  bot.button("Next >").click();
  bot.textWithLabel("Project name:").setText(projectName);
  bot.button("Finish").click();
  final IProject project = getProject(projectName);
  assertTrue(project.exists());
  final IFolder src = project.getFolder("src");
  final IFolder bin = project.getFolder("bin");
  if (!src.exists()) {
    src.create(true, true, null);
  }
  IFile test = src.getFile("Test.java");
  test.create(new ByteArrayInputStream(
    "class Test{}".getBytes()), true, null);
  try {
    SWTBotShell dialog =
     bot.shell("Open Associated Perspective?");
    bot.button("Yes").click();
  } catch (WidgetNotFoundException e) {
    // ignore
  }
  bot.waitUntil(new DefaultCondition() {
    @Override
    public boolean test() throws Exception {
      return bin.getFile("Test.class").exists();
    }
    public String getFailureMessage() {
      return "File bin/Test.class was not created";
    }
  });
  assertTrue(bin.getFile("Test.class").exists());
}
```

14. Run the test and verify that it passes OK.

15. Comment out the `waitUntil` call and verify that the test fails.

What just happened?

When the `Test.java` file is created in the project, an event is fired which runs the Java compiler. This in turn results in the creation of both the `bin` folder as well as the `Test.class` file that is being tested. However both of these operations occur on different threads, and so whilst the test is running, if it needs to act on the generated file it must wait until that file exists.

Although this example could have been implemented outside of SWTBot, it provides a simple way to block the execution until a particular condition occurs. This can be useful if the user interface is running some kind of long-running action and the code needs to wait until a certain dialog message is shown, or something that can be determined programmatically (such as the file's existence in this case).

Other types of conditionals and tests are possible; as well as the bot's `waitUntil` method, there is also a `waitWhile` method which has the opposite behavior.

Note that when the wait condition is commented out, the test fails, because the test execution thread will hit the assertion before the Java compiler has been able to run.

One advantage of using the wait code in SWTBot is that if the condition doesn't occur within a given timeout, then an exception is generated and the test will fail. Since the same wait condition is used elsewhere in SWTBot, the delay is configurable and can be changed externally.

Have a go hero – driving the new class wizard

Instead of using the creation of a source file as a text file, use SWTBot to execute the **File | New Class** wizard. Pass in the name of the project, the package, and the class, and both the source and the class file should be created in the background. This is how integration tests that show the application working from a user's perspective can be implemented, instead of having a set of tests that just shows the underlying libraries working as expected.

Pop quiz – understanding swtbot

Q1. What is the name of the JUnit test runner that is required for SWTBot?

Q2. How are views shown with SWTBot?

Q3. How do you get the text value of a field in a dialog?

Q4. What is a `Matcher` and when would it be used?

Q5. How can values from the UI trivially be returned to the user without having to worry about thread interaction?

Q6. When some asynchronous events are happening in the background, how can the test wait until a particular condition occurs without blocking the test?

Summary

Being able to test code automatically is a key part of creating quality software. Whether the tests exercise the underlying models or the user interface—or ideally a combination of both—more tests help highlight problems that occur when changes to the underlying framework happen, or when dependencies change and introduce unwanted side-effects.

The next chapter will show how to integrate everything with an automated build.

12
Automated Builds with Tycho

Tycho – automated builds based on Maven

The final part of the puzzle is how to build plug-ins automatically. Most plug-ins are now built with Tycho, a Maven plugin infrastructure for building Eclipse plug-ins.

In this chapter, we shall:

- ◆ Automate a plug-in build
- ◆ Automate a feature build
- ◆ Create an update site
- ◆ Execute UI and non-UI tests
- ◆ Sign the plug-ins
- ◆ Learn how to publish the update site

Using Maven to build Eclipse plug-ins with Tycho

Maven is an automated build tool that builds using a file called `pom.xml`, which declaratively specifies how and what to build. Maven projects have a **group**, an **artifact**, and a **version** that identify them in repositories such as the Central Repository, and a **packaging type** that tells Maven what it is trying to build. The default is `jar` since the widest use for Maven is for building Java archives; for Tycho, we need to use Eclipse-specific types.

Maven Tycho is a set of plug-ins that allow the building of Eclipse plug-ins. Tycho requires at least Maven 3 to work; the instructions in this chapter have been tested with Maven 3.3.9 and Tycho 0.25.0. Check out the book's errata page for up-to-date information.

Time for action – installing Maven

This step will install and use Maven to build a simple Java project to ensure that the tool is configured appropriately. The first time it runs, it will cache many Jars from Central into a folder `${user.home}/.m2/repository`; for subsequent runs, it will be much faster.

1. Go to `http://maven.apache.org/` and download the latest Maven `zip` (Windows) or Maven `tgz` (for macOS/Linux).

2. Unzip/untar the install into a convenient directory, referred to in these instructions as `MAVEN_HOME`.

3. Either add `MAVEN_HOME/bin` to the `PATH` or specify the full path to the Maven executable; run `mvn -version`, and a version message should be printed out. Maven requires a JDK (not just a JRE), which should be installed by following the instructions from the Java site.

4. Run `mvn archetype:generate -DarchetypeGroupId=org.apache.maven.archetypes -DarchetypeArtifactId=maven-archetype-quickstart -DarchetypeVersion=1.1` (all on one line) to create a new Maven project.

 Maven can also be run with Eclipse; if the m2e Eclipse tools are installed, **File | New | Project... | Maven | Maven Project** will show a wizard that allows an archetype to be chosen and the details entered graphically:

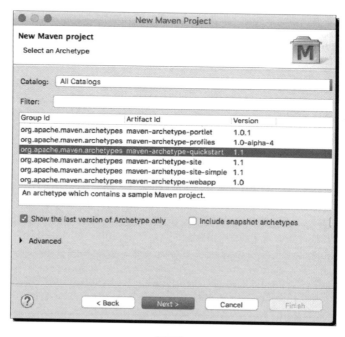

5. When prompted for the `groupId`, enter `com.packtpub.e4`.

6. When prompted for the `artifactId`, enter `com.packtpub.e4.tycho`.

7. When prompted for the version and package, press *Enter* to take the defaults of `1.0-SNAPSHOT` and `com.packtpub.e4` respectively.

8. Finally, press *Enter* to create the project:

```
Define value for property 'groupId':    com.packtpub.e4
Define value for property 'artifactId': com.packtpub.e4.tycho
Define value for property 'version':     1.0-SNAPSHOT
Define value for property 'package':    com.packtpub.e4
Confirm properties configuration:
groupId: com.packtpub.e4
artifactId: com.packtpub.e4.tycho
version: 1.0-SNAPSHOT
package: com.packtpub.e4
 Y: : Y
```

9. Change into the `com.packtpub.e4.tycho` directory created and run `mvn package` to run the tests and create the package:

```
[INFO] Scanning for projects...
[INFO]
[INFO] Building com.packtpub.e4.tycho 1.0-SNAPSHOT
[INFO]


 T E S T S


Running com.packtpub.e4.AppTest
Tests run: 1, Failures: 0, Errors: 0, Skipped: 0, Time elapsed:
0.009 sec


Results :


Tests run: 1, Failures: 0, Errors: 0, Skipped: 0

[INFO] Building jar: com.packtpub.e4.tycho-1.0-SNAPSHOT.jar
[INFO]
[INFO] BUILD SUCCESS
[INFO]
[INFO] Total time: 1.977s
[INFO] Final Memory: 15M/136M
```

What just happened?

The Maven launcher knows how to connect to the Central repository and download additional plug-ins. When it initially launches, it will download a set of plug-ins, which in turn have dependencies on other Jars that will be resolved automatically prior to the project building.

Fortunately, these are cached in the local Maven repository (which defaults to `${user.home}/.m2/repository`), so this is done only once. The repository can be cleaned or removed; the next time Maven runs, it will download any required plug-ins again.

When `mvn archetype:generate` is executed, a sample Java project is created. This creates a `pom.xml` file with the `groupId`, `artifactId` and `version` given and sets it up for a Java project.

When `mvn package` is executed, the operation depends on the packaging type of the project. This will default to `jar` if not specified, and the default `package` operation for `jar` is to run the `compile`, then run `test`, and finally create the Jar file of the package.

The Maven `quickstart` archetype is a useful way of creating a `pom.xml` file with known good values, and a way of verifying connectivity to the outside before moving ahead with the Eclipse-specific Tycho builds. If there's a problem with these steps, check out the troubleshooting guides at `http://maven.apache.org/users/` for assistance.

Time for action – building with Tycho

Now that Maven is installed, it's time to build a plug-in with Tycho. Tycho is a set of plug-ins for Maven 3 that emulates the PDE build system used by Eclipse. The Eclipse platform has moved to building with Tycho and Maven 3.

1. Change into the `com.packtpub.e4.clock.ui` project created in *Chapter 2, Creating Views with SWT*.

> The project can also be downloaded from the site's GitHub repository at `https://github.com/alblue/com.packtpub.e4/`

2. Create a file called `pom.xml` at the root of the project, with the following empty contents:

```
<?xml version="1.0" encoding="UTF-8"?>
<project xmlns="http://maven.apache.org/POM/4.0.0"
  xmlns:xsi="http://www.w3.org/2001/XMLSchema-instance"
  xsi:schemaLocation="http://maven.apache.org/POM/4.0.0
                   http://maven.apache.org/xsd/maven-4.0.0.xsd">
```

```
<modelVersion>4.0.0</modelVersion>
</project>
```

This can be copied from the `pom.xml` file generated in the previous section, since every `pom.xml` has this same signature.

3. Give the project a unique `groupId`, `artifactId`, and `version` by placing the following after the `modelVersion` tag:

```
<groupId>com.packtpub.e4</groupId>
<artifactId>com.packtpub.e4.clock.ui</artifactId>
<version>1.0.0-SNAPSHOT</version>
```

> The `version` has to match the one in the `plugin.xml`, with `.qualifier` replaced with `-SNAPSHOT`, and the `artifactId` has to be the name of the fully qualified plug-in name (the `Bundle-SymbolicName` in the `MANIFEST.MF` file).

4. Define the packaging type to be `eclipse-plugin`:

```
<packaging>eclipse-plugin</packaging>
```

5. If the build is now run with `mvn package`, an error message will be displayed: **Unknown packaging: eclipse-plugin**. To fix this, add Tycho as a build plugin:

```
<build>
  <plugins>
    <plugin>
      <groupId>org.eclipse.tycho</groupId>
      <artifactId>tycho-maven-plugin</artifactId>
      <version>0.25.0</version>
      <extensions>true</extensions>
    </plugin>
  </plugins>
</build>
```

6. Run the build again. This time, it will complain of an unsatisfiable build error:

```
[ERROR] Internal error: java.lang.RuntimeException:
 "No solution found because the problem is unsatisfiable.":
  ["Unable to satisfy dependency from
    com.packtpub.e4.clock.ui 1.0.0.qualifier to bundle
    org.eclipse.ui 0.0.0."] -> [Help 1]
```

7. Add the Neon (or Mars, Luna, and so on) release repository:

```
<repositories>
  <repository>
    <id>neon</id>
    <layout>p2</layout>
    <url>http://download.eclipse.org/releases/neon/</url>
  </repository>
  <!-- repository>
    <id>mars</id>
    <layout>p2</layout>
    <url>http://download.eclipse.org/releases/mars/</url>
  </repository -->
  <!-- repository>
    <id>luna</id>
    <layout>p2</layout>
    <url>http://download.eclipse.org/releases/luna/</url>
  </repository -->
</repositories>
```

8. Now run `mvn clean package` to build the plug-in.

What just happened?

All Maven projects have a `pom.xml` file that controls their build process, and Eclipse plug-ins are no different. The header for a `pom.xml` file doesn't change, and so generally this is copied from an existing one (or autogenerated by tools) rather than typed in by hand.

Each Maven `pom.xml` file needs to have a unique `groupId`, `artifactId`, and `version`. For `eclipse-plugin` projects, the name of the `artifactId` must be the same as the `Bundle-SymbolicName` in the `MANIFEST.MF`; otherwise an error is thrown:

```
[ERROR] Failed to execute goal
 org.eclipse.tycho:tycho-packaging-plugin:0.25.0:validate-id
  (default-validate-id) on project com.packtpub.e4.clock.uix:
 The Maven artifactId (currently: "com.packtpub.e4.clock.uix")
 must be the same as the bundle symbolic name
 (currently: "com.packtpub.e4.clock.ui") -> [Help 1]
```

The same is true for the `version` in the `pom.xml` file, which must match the version in the `MANIFEST.MF` file. Without this, the build will fail with a different error:

```
[ERROR] Failed to execute goal

 org.eclipse.tycho:tycho-packaging-plugin:0.25.0:validate-version

  (default-validate-version) on project com.packtpub.e4.clock.ui:
 Unqualified OSGi version 1.0.0.qualifier must match unqualified Maven
 version 1.0.1-SNAPSHOT for SNAPSHOT builds -> [Help 1]
```

Tycho knows how to build Eclipse plug-ins, by setting the packaging type to `eclipse-plugin`. However, in order for Maven to know about the `eclipse-plugin` type, Tycho has to be defined as a Maven plugin for the build. Importantly, it needs to be defined as an extension with `<extensions>true</extensions>`:

```
<plugin>
  <groupId>org.eclipse.tycho</groupId>
  <artifactId>tycho-maven-plugin</artifactId>
  <version>0.25.0</version>
  <extensions>true</extensions>
</plugin>
```

Although it's possible to hard-code the version of the Tycho plug-in like this, it's conventional to replace it with a property instead. This will be shown in the next section when parent projects are covered.

Finally, an Eclipse repository was added to the `pom.xml` file so that the build could resolve any additional plug-ins and features. This needs to be defined as a `p2` repository type to distinguish it from the `default` type, which stores Maven artifacts.

Note that it is best practice to *not* put repositories in `pom.xml` files in general. Instead, these can be extracted to a `settings.xml` file or to a target platform definition. This allows the same project to be built against different versions of Eclipse in future without changing the source, or to run against a closer mirror of the same. A settings file can be passed to Maven with `mvn -s /path/to/settings.xml`, which allows the plug-in's dependencies to be varied over time without mutating the `pom.xml` file.

Building features and update sites with Tycho

The process for building features and update sites is similar to that of plug-ins, but with different packaging types. However, it's common for features and plug-ins to be built in the same Maven build, which requires a little re-organization of the projects. These are typically organized into a **parent** project and then several **child** projects.

Time for action – creating a parent project

It's common for the parent and child projects to be located outside the workspace; for historical reasons, Eclipse doesn't deal well with nested projects in the workspace. It's also common for the parent project to host all of the Tycho configuration information, which makes setting up the child projects a lot easier.

1. Create a **General** project by navigating to the **File | New | Project | General | Project** menu.

2. Unselect **Use default location**.

3. Put in a location that is outside the Eclipse workspace.

4. Name the project `com.packtpub.e4.parent`.

5. Click on **Finish**.

6. Create a new file `pom.xml` in the root of the project.

7. Copy the content of the `com.packtpub.e4.clock.ui` plug-in's `pom.xml` file to the parent, but change the `artifactId` to `com.packtpub.e4.parent` and the packaging to `pom`.

8. Create a `properties` element in the `pom.xml` file and inside a `tycho.version` element with the value `0.25.0`, as well as an `eclipse` element with the value `http://download.eclipse.org/releases/neon/`.

9. Modify the reference to `0.25.0` in the existing Tycho `plugin` and replace it with `${tycho.version}`.

10. Modify the reference to `http://download.eclipse.org/releases/neon/` in the existing repositories `url` and replace it with `${eclipse}`.

11. Move the `com.packtpub.e4.clock.ui` plug-in underneath the parent project.

12. Add a `modules` element to the `pom.xml` file and underneath a `module` element with the value `com.packtpub.e4.clock.ui`.

13. The parent `pom.xml` file should look like:

```xml
<?xml version="1.0" encoding="UTF-8"?>
<project xmlns="http://maven.apache.org/POM/4.0.0"
  xmlns:xsi="http://www.w3.org/2001/XMLSchema-instance"
  xsi:schemaLocation="http://maven.apache.org/POM/4.0.0
                      http://maven.apache.org/xsd/maven-4.0.0.xsd">
  <modelVersion>4.0.0</modelVersion>
  <groupId>com.packtpub.e4</groupId>
  <artifactId>com.packtpub.e4.parent</artifactId>
  <version>1.0.0-SNAPSHOT</version>
  <packaging>pom</packaging>
  <properties>
    <tycho.version>0.25.0</tycho.version>
    <eclipse>http://download.eclipse.org
    /releases/neon/</eclipse>
  </properties>
  <modules>
    <module>com.packtpub.e4.clock.ui</module>
  </modules>
  <build>
    <plugins>
      <plugin>
        <groupId>org.eclipse.tycho</groupId>
```

```
          <artifactId>tycho-maven-plugin</artifactId>
          <version>${tycho.version}</version>
          <extensions>true</extensions>
        </plugin>
      </plugins>
    </build>
    <repositories>
      <repository>
        <id>eclipse</id>
        <layout>p2</layout>
        <url>${eclipse}</url>
      </repository>
    </repositories>
  </project>
```

14. Modify the `com.packtpub.e4.clock.ui/pom.xml` file and add a `parent` element with a `groupId`, `artifactId`, and `version` that are the same as the parent. It is possible to remove the `version` and `groupId` from the child `pom.xml` file, as it will default to the parent's `groupId` and `version` if not specified:

```
<parent>
  <groupId>com.packtpub.e4</groupId>
  <artifactId>com.packtpub.e4.parent</artifactId>
  <version>1.0.0-SNAPSHOT</version>
</parent>
```

15. Remove the `plugins` and `repositories` elements from the `pom.xml` file in the `com.packtpub.e4.clock.ui` project.

16. Now change into the parent project and run `mvn clean package`. The parent will be built, and in turn build all the modules in the list:

```
[INFO] Reactor Summary:
[INFO]
[INFO] com.packtpub.e4.parent ............. SUCCESS [0.049s]
[INFO] com.packtpub.e4.clock.ui ........... SUCCESS [1.866s]
[INFO]
[INFO] BUILD SUCCESS
```

What just happened?

Each plug-in is its own Eclipse project, and therefore its own Maven project. To build a set of projects together, there needs to be a parent POM, which acts as an aggregator.

At build time, Maven calculates the order in which projects need to be built, and then arranges the build steps appropriately.

The other benefit provided by a parent `pom.xml` file is the ability to specify standard build plug-ins and configuration information. In this case, the parent specifies the link with Tycho and its versions. This simplifies the implementation of the other plug-ins and features that lie underneath the parent project.

Time for action – building a feature

Features can be built in the same way as plug-ins, although this time the packaging type is `eclipse-feature`.

1. Move the `com.packtpub.e4.feature` project underneath the `com.packtpub.e4.parent` project.

2. Add the line `<module>com.packtpub.e4.feature</module>` to the parent `pom.xml` file.

3. Copy the `pom.xml` file from the clock plug-in to the feature project.

4. Modify the packaging type to `<packaging>eclipse-feature</packaging>`.

5. Change the `artifactId` to `com.packtpub.e4.feature`.

6. The resulting `pom.xml` file will look like:

```
<?xml version="1.0" encoding="UTF-8"?>
<project xmlns="http://maven.apache.org/POM/4.0.0"
  xmlns:xsi="http://www.w3.org/2001/XMLSchema-instance"
  xsi:schemaLocation="http://maven.apache.org/POM/4.0.0
                      http://maven.apache.org/xsd/maven-4.0.0.xsd">
  <modelVersion>4.0.0</modelVersion>
  <parent>
    <groupId>com.packtpub.e4</groupId>
    <artifactId>com.packtpub.e4.parent</artifactId>
    <version>1.0.0-SNAPSHOT</version>
  </parent>
  <artifactId>com.packtpub.e4.feature</artifactId>
  <packaging>eclipse-feature</packaging>
</project>
```

7. Run `mvn clean package` from the parent and it should build both the plug-in and the feature:

```
[INFO] Reactor Summary:
[INFO]
[INFO] com.packtpub.e4.parent .................. SUCCESS [0.070s]
[INFO] com.packtpub.e4.clock.ui ............... SUCCESS [1.872s]
[INFO] com.packtpub.e4.feature ............... SUCCESS [0.080s]
[INFO]
[INFO] BUILD SUCCESS
```

What just happened?

By adding the feature into the list of modules, the feature is built at the same time as everything else. The version of the plug-in built in the earlier is used to compose the feature contents. If the plug-in wasn't listed as part of the Maven build modules and it couldn't be resolved from a remote repository, then the build would fail.

The child module will inherit both the `groupId` and `version` of the parent project, if specified. As a result the version can be commented out (or removed) from the child modules, which makes managing the versions easier.

At present, the feature and plug-in are built but cannot be easily installed into an existing Eclipse instance. The assumption is that the plug-ins and features can be tested using PDE directly in Eclipse, and that therefore there's no need to directly install a plug-in or feature from the result of a build.

It's necessary to define an additional module—an update site—which will allow the plug-in to be installed or hosted.

Time for action – building an update site

The update site created in *Chapter 10, Adding an Update Site*, is used to provide a standard hosting mechanism for Eclipse plug-ins and features. This can be built automatically with Tycho as well.

1. Move the `com.packtpub.e4.update` project underneath the `com.packtpub.e4.parent` project.

2. Add the line `<module>com.packtpub.e4.update</module>` to the parent `pom.xml` file.

3. Copy the `pom.xml` file from the clock plug-in to the update project.

4. Modify the packaging type to `<packaging>eclipse-repository</packaging>`.

5. Change the `artifactId` to `com.packtpub.e4.update`.

6. The resulting `pom.xml` file will look like:

```
<?xml version="1.0" encoding="UTF-8"?>
<project xmlns="http://maven.apache.org/POM/4.0.0"
  xmlns:xsi="http://www.w3.org/2001/XMLSchema-instance"
  xsi:schemaLocation="http://maven.apache.org/POM/4.0.0
                    http://maven.apache.org/xsd/maven-4.0.0.xsd">
  <modelVersion>4.0.0</modelVersion>
  <parent>
    <groupId>com.packtpub.e4</groupId>
    <artifactId>com.packtpub.e4.parent</artifactId>
    <version>1.0.0-SNAPSHOT</version>
  </parent>
  <artifactId>com.packtpub.e4.update</artifactId>
  <packaging>eclipse-repository</packaging>
</project>
```

7. Rename the `site.xml` file to `category.xml`.

8. Verify that the `category.xml` file does not contain a `url` attribute and the `version` attribute is `0.0.0`, as otherwise an **Unable to satisfy dependencies** error may be seen:

```
<feature id="com.packtpub.e4.feature" version="0.0.0">
```

9. Run `mvn package` from the parent project, and it should now build the update site as well:

```
[INFO] Reactor Summary:
[INFO]
[INFO] com.packtpub.e4.parent ................. SUCCESS [0.048s]
[INFO] com.packtpub.e4.clock.ui ............... SUCCESS [1.416s]
[INFO] com.packtpub.e4.feature ................ SUCCESS [0.074s]
[INFO] com.packtpub.e4.update ................. SUCCESS [2.727s]
[INFO]
[INFO] BUILD SUCCESS
```

10. In the host Eclipse, install the update site by going to the **Help | Install New Software** menu, typing `file:///path/to/com.packtpub.e4.parent/com.packtpub.e4.update/target/repository` into the **work with** field, and installing the feature shown there. If it is not shown, uncheck the **Group items by category** checkbox.

11. Restart the host Eclipse after installing the plug-ins, and show the **Time Zone View** by navigating to **Window | Show View | Other... | Timekeeping | Time Zone View**.

What just happened?

Creating an update site is no different from creating a plug-in or feature project. There is a `pom.xml` file that defines the name of the update site itself, and it uses or detects the file called `category.xml` to generate the update site.

The `category.xml` file is functionally equivalent to the `site.xml` file created previously, and is a name change introduced by P2 long ago. However, the update site project still generates it using the old name, so it is necessary to rename it from `site.xml` to `category.xml` in order to be built with Tycho.

As with the Eclipse update project, when the update site is built, the versions of the features and plug-ins in the `category.xml` are replaced with the versions of the features and plug-ins just built.

Time for action – building a product

Building a product (a branded Eclipse application, or one that is launched from `eclipse -application` from the command line) can also be built with Tycho using the `eclipse-repository` packaging type. To do this, the app project needs to be built with Tycho and made available in the feature, and a new project for the product needs to be created.

1. Move the `com.packtpub.e4.application` project under the `com.packtpub.e4.parent` project.

2. Add the line `<module>com.packtpub.e4.application</module>` to the parent `pom.xml` file.

3. Copy the `pom.xml` file from the clock plug-in to the application project.

4. Change the `artifactId` to `com.packtpub.e4.application`.

5. The resulting `pom.xml` file will look like:

```
<?xml version="1.0" encoding="UTF-8"?>
<project xmlns="http://maven.apache.org/POM/4.0.0"
  xmlns:xsi="http://www.w3.org/2001/XMLSchema-instance"
  xsi:schemaLocation="http://maven.apache.org/POM/4.0.0
  http://maven.apache.org/xsd/maven-4.0.0.xsd">
  <modelVersion>4.0.0</modelVersion>
  <parent>
    <groupId>com.packtpub.e4</groupId>
    <artifactId>com.packtpub.e4.parent</artifactId>
    <version>1.0.0-SNAPSHOT</version>
```

```
    </parent>
    <artifactId>com.packtpub.e4.application</artifactId>
    <packaging>eclipse-plugin</packaging>
</project>
```

6. Modify the `com.packtpub.e4.feature/feature.xml` file to add the reference to the application plug-in:

```
<feature>
    ...
    <plugin
      id="com.packtpub.e4.application"
      download-size="0"
      install-size="0"
      version="0.0.0"
      unpack="false"/>
</feature>
```

7. Run `mvn clean package` from the parent, and the build should complete with the application plug-in. However, the product will not be materialized. Create an additional **General** project, called `com.packtpub.e4.product`. Move the `com.packtpub.e4.application.product` file from the `com.pactkpub.e4.application` project into the `com.packtpub.e4.product` project.

8. Copy the `com.packtpub.e4.application/pom.xml` file into the `com.packtpub.e4.product` project, and modify the `artifactId` to be `com.packtpub.e4.product`. Change the packaging type to `eclipse-repository`.

9. Add the product by adding the module to the parent `pom.xml` file with `<module>com.packtpub.e4.product</module>`.

10. Run `mvn clean package` from the parent, and it will complain with an error:

```
[ERROR] Failed to execute goal
   org.eclipse.tycho:tycho-p2-publisher-
   plugin:0.25.0:publish-products
   (default-publish-products) on project
   com.packtpub.e4.application:
   The product file com.packtpub.e4.application.product does
   not contain the mandatory attribute 'uid' -> [Help 1]
```

11. Edit the `com.packtpub.e4.product/com.packtpub.e4.application.product` and add a `uid` as a copy of the `id` attribute.

12. Switch to a feature-based build (if not already done so) and depend on the `org.eclipse.rcp` and `com.packtpub.e4.feature` features, removing the `plugins` element:

```
<product name="com.packtpub.e4.application"
 uid="com.packtpub.e4.application.product"
 id="com.packtpub.e4.application.product"
 application="org.eclipse.e4.ui.workbench.swt.E4Application"
 version="1.0.0.qualifier"
 useFeatures="true"
 includeLaunchers="true">
  <features>
    <feature id="com.packtpub.e4.feature" version="0.0.0"/>
    <feature id="org.eclipse.rcp" version="0.0.0"/>
  </features>
  <!--plugins>...</plugins -->
  ...
</product>
```

13. Run `mvn package` from the parent again, and the build should succeed. The `com.packtpub.e4.product/target/repository` now contains the product for the target platform that you're running on.

14. To build for more than one platform, add the following to either the product's `pom.xml` file or the parent `pom.xml` file:

```
<plugin>
  <groupId>org.eclipse.tycho</groupId>
  <artifactId>target-platform-configuration</artifactId>
  <version>${tycho.version}</version>
  <configuration>
    <environments>
      <environment>
        <os>win32</os>
        <ws>win32</ws>
        <arch>x86_64</arch> <!--arch>x86</arch-->
      </environment>
      <environment>
        <os>linux</os>
        <ws>gtk</ws>
        <arch>x86_64</arch> <!--arch>x86</arch-->
      </environment>
      <environment>
        <os>macosx</os>
        <ws>cocoa</ws>
        <arch>x86_64</arch>
```

```
      </environment>
    </environments>
  </configuration>
</plugin>
```

15. Now run the build and a product per OS should be built. The example builds for Windows, Linux, and macOS on a 64-bit architecture; to build for the 32-bit versions, duplicate the environment block and use `<arch>x86</arch>` instead.

> Note that Eclipse Neon on macOS only ships as a 64-bit build.

16. To materialize the products, and not just provide a P2 repository for them, add the `materialize-products` goal to the `com.packtpub.e4.application/pom.xml` file, as follows:

```
<build>
  <plugins>
    <plugin>
      <groupId>org.eclipse.tycho</groupId>
      <artifactId>tycho-p2-director-plugin</artifactId>
      <version>${tycho.version}</version>
      <configuration>
        <formats>
          <win32>zip</win32>
          <linux>tar.gz</linux>
          <macosx>tar.gz</macosx>
        </formats>
      </configuration>
      <executions>
        <execution>
          <id>materialize-products</id>
          <goals>
            <goal>materialize-products</goal>
          </goals>
        </execution>
        <execution>
          <id>archive-products</id>
          <goals>
            <goal>archive-products</goal>
          </goals>
        </execution>
      </executions>
```

```
      </plugin>
    </plugins>
  </build>
```

17. Run the build from the parent with `mvn clean package` and the build will create
`com.packtpub.e4.application/target/products/os/ws/arch`, as well as
creating archives (ZIP files) of them.

18. When running the product generated, an error may be seen (or can be seen running
`eclipse -consoleLog`):

`java.lang.IllegalStateException: Unable to acquire`

`  application service.`

`Ensure that the org.eclipse.core.runtime bundle is`

`  resolved and started (see config.ini).`

19. This is an Eclipse product error; in essence, Eclipse products need to have a number
of plug-ins started at boot time in order to run `eclipse -application`. Add this
to the `com.packtpub.e4.application.product` file:

```
<configurations>
  <plugin id="org.eclipse.core.runtime"
    autoStart="true" startLevel="4"/>
  <plugin id="org.eclipse.equinox.common"
    autoStart="true" startLevel="2"/>
  <plugin id="org.eclipse.equinox.ds"
    autoStart="true" startLevel="2"/>
  <plugin id="org.eclipse.equinox.simpleconfigurator"
    autoStart="true" startLevel="1"/>
</configurations>
```

20. Run `mvn clean package` and try running the product again. This time it
should succeed.

What just happened?

Eclipse applications are built and made available as a P2 repository or as archived
downloads. The P2 repository allows the product to be updated using the standard update
mechanisms; this is how updates from 4.6.0 to 4.6.1 to 4.6.2 occur. The archives are used to
provide direct download links, as are found at `http://download.eclipse.org` for the
standard packages.

For RCP-based applications, it is easier to build on the RCP feature, which provides the
necessary platform-specific fragments for SWT and filesystems. Although building a product
based on plug-ins is possible, almost all RCP and SDK applications are built upon either the
RCP feature or the IDE feature respectively.

For Eclipse to launch successfully, a number of plug-ins need to be started when the application starts. This is controlled with the `config.ini` file, which in turn is read by the `simpleconfigurator`, so this needs to be started at the launch of the runtime. In addition, the E4 platform requires **Declarative Services (DS)** to be installed and started, as well as the runtime bundle.

By decomposing the projects into a feature and then having the same feature used for both the SWTBot and product definitions, it becomes the de-facto place for adding new content. Then these are automatically visible in the product, the automated tests, and the update site.

Time for action – using the target platform

Although building against a remote repository works as expected, it may have dependencies on plug-ins or features that aren't represented in the target platform created in *Chapter 10, Using a Target Platform*. To compile against a target platform, a new Maven module needs to be created.

1. Move the `com.packtpub.e4.target.mars` project underneath the `com.packtpub.e4.parent` project.

2. Add the line `<module>com.packtpub.e4.target.mars</module>` to the parent `pom.xml` file.

3. Comment out the `repositories` tags in the parent `pom.xml` file.

4. In the `configuration` element of the `target-plugin-configuration` entry, add the co-ordinates of the `com.packtpub.e4.target.mars` project:

```
<plugin>
  <groupId>org.eclipse.tycho</groupId>
  <artifactId>tycho-platform-configuration</artifactId>
  <version>${tycho.version}</version>
  <configuration>
    <target>
      <artifact>
        <groupId>com.packtpub.e4</groupId>
        <artifactId>com.packtpub.e4.target.mars</artifactId>
        <version>${project.version}</version>
      </artifact>
    </target>
    <environments>
      ...
    </environments>
  </configuration>
</plugin>
```

5. Copy the `pom.xml` file from the `com.packtpub.e4.clock.ui` plug-in to the `com.packtpub.e4.target.mars` project.

6. Modify the packaging type to `<packaging>eclipse-target-definition</packaging>`.

7. Run the build from the parent project by running `mvn clean package`. An error will be seen with a missing dependency:

```
[ERROR] Cannot resolve project dependencies:

[ERROR]   Software being installed: com.packtpub.e4.feature.
feature.group 1.0.0-SNAPSHOT

[ERROR]   Missing requirement: com.packtpub.e4.feature.feature.
group 1.0.0-SNAPSHOT requires 'org.eclipse.jgit.feature.group
4.0.0' but it could not be found
```

8. The failure occurs because the target platform doesn't define a dependency on JGit, but the feature requires it. As a result it cannot build unless the dependency is added to the target platform as well. Add the following lines to the `com.packtpub.e4.target.mars.target` definition, or edit the definition in the target platform editor to add the EGit feature:

```
<unit id="org.eclipse.egit.feature.group"
version="4.1.1.201511131810-r"/>
```

9. Run the build again, and the build fails with a different dependency requirement:

```
[ERROR] Cannot resolve project dependencies:

[ERROR]   Software being installed: com.packtpub.e4.application.
product 1.0.0-SNAPSHOT

[ERROR]   Missing requirement: com.packtpub.e4.application.product
1.0.0-SNAPSHOT requires 'org.eclipse.equinox.executable.feature.
group 0.0.0' but it could not be found
```

10. This can be resolved by adding (for example) the Equinox SDK to the target definition file:

```
<unit id="org.eclipse.equinox.sdk.feature.group"
version="3.11.2.v20160202-2102"/>
```

11. The target definition file now looks like:

```
<?xml version="1.0" encoding="UTF-8" standalone="no"?>
<?pde version="3.8"?>
  <target name="Eclipse Mars" sequenceNumber="7">
  <locations>
    <location includeAllPlatforms="false"
     includeConfigurePhase="true" includeMode="planner"
     includeSource="true" type="InstallableUnit">
      <unit id="org.eclipse.e4.rcp.feature.group"
```

```
            version="1.4.1.v20160212-1350"/>
          <unit id="org.eclipse.platform.feature.group"
           version="4.5.2.v20160212-1500"/>
          <unit id="org.eclipse.rcp.feature.group"
           version="4.5.2.v20160212-1500"/>
          <unit id="org.eclipse.swtbot.feature.group"
           version="2.3.0.201506081302"/>
          <unit id="org.eclipse.swtbot.eclipse.feature.group"
           version="2.3.0.201506081302"/>
          <unit id="org.eclipse.swtbot.ide.feature.group"
           version="2.3.0.201506081302"/>
          <unit id="org.eclipse.egit.feature.group"
           version="4.1.1.201511131810-r"/>
          <unit id="org.eclipse.equinox.sdk.feature.group"
           version="3.11.2.v20160202-2102"/>
          <repository
          location="http://download.eclipse.org/releases/mars/"/>
        </location>
      </locations>
    </target>
```

12. When the build is run again using `mvn clean package`, it builds the applications successfully:

```
[INFO] Reactor Summary:
[INFO]
[INFO] com.packtpub.e4.parent ................ SUCCESS [  0.056 s]
[INFO] com.packtpub.e4.clock.ui .............. SUCCESS [  1.528 s]
[INFO] com.packtpub.e4.application ........... SUCCESS [  0.262 s]
[INFO] com.packtpub.e4.feature ............... SUCCESS [  0.057 s]
[INFO] com.packtpub.e4.update ................ SUCCESS [  1.432 s]
[INFO] com.packtpub.e4.product ............... SUCCESS [ 15.573 s]
[INFO] com.packtpub.e4.target.mars ........... SUCCESS [  0.002 s]
[INFO]
[INFO] BUILD SUCCESS
```

What just happened?

Instead of building against whatever content is available in the upstream repository, the Tycho build now uses the target definition file created earlier. The target definition is referenced as an external artifact in the Tycho build process (in this case, `com.packtpub.e4.target.mars`) and is included in the project. However, this doesn't necessarily have to be the case; it would be possible to re-use a previously published artifact for referencing the downloads. The advantage of including it in the current project means that if additional dependencies are required, then they can be added in here.

The target platform needed to have additions in order to build with Tycho. In this case, it exposed the fact that there were missing Equinox components (which are present in every Eclipse release) that are required for installing the product. Although these aren't used by code directly (so they don't need to be added to the classpath, for example), they are required in order to run correctly. In order to use these, they must be present in the target platform, and so the Equinox and EGit features needed to be added.

 Note that if the dependency for EGit wasn't declared in the `com.packtpub.e4.feature`, then it wouldn't need to be added here.

Have a go hero – depending on Maven components

Sometimes it is necessary to depend on components which have been built by ordinary Maven jobs. Although it's not possible to mix and match Tycho and ordinary Maven reactor builds in the same build, it is possible to allow Tycho to resolve Maven components as part of the target platform.

Since ordinary Maven dependencies are represented by the `<dependencies>` tag, it is possible to define additional dependencies that can be consumed or used by Tycho builds. Normally Tycho won't use this information, but to allow Tycho to resolve those and make them available as OSGi bundles for the purposes of the Eclipse build, modify the configuration for the target-platform-configuration and add the line `<pomDependencies>consider</pomDependencies>` to the `<configuration>` element.

 Note that only OSGi bundles are added to the dependencies list; others are silently ignored.

Testing and releasing

The final step of an Eclipse build is to ensure that any automated tests are run, and any versions that need to be bumped for the release stage are done prior to the code being published.

Time for action – running automated tests

Although a plug-in's code-based tests (those under `src/test/java`) will be run automatically as part of a Maven build, very often it is necessary to test them in a running Eclipse application. The previous chapter covered creating automated UI tests; now they will be run as part of the automated build.

1. Move the `com.packtpub.e4.junit.plugin` project underneath the `com.packtpub.e4.parent` project.

2. Add the line `<module>com.packtpub.e4.junit.plugin</module>` to the parent `pom.xml` file.

3. Copy the `pom.xml` file from the `com.packtpub.e4.clock.ui` plug-in to the `com.packtpub.e4.junit.plugin` project.

4. Modify the packaging type to `<packaging>eclipse-test-plugin</packaging>`.

5. Change the `artifactId` to `com.packtpub.e4.junit.plugin`

6. To run the Tycho tests, add the following as a build plugin:

```
<build>
  <sourceDirectory>src</sourceDirectory>
  <plugins>
    <plugin>
      <groupId>org.eclipse.tycho</groupId>
      <artifactId>tycho-surefire-plugin</artifactId>
      <version>${tycho.version}</version>
      <configuration>
        <useUIHarness>true</useUIHarness>
        <useUIThread>false</useUIThread>
        <product>org.eclipse.sdk.ide</product>
        <application>org.eclipse.ui.ide.workbench</application>
      </configuration>
    </plugin>
  </plugins>
</build>
```

7. Now running `mvn integration-test` should run the tests. If run on OS X, a line must be added to the configuration for the JVM:

```
<configuration>
  <useUIHarness>true</useUIHarness>
  <useUIThread>false</useUIThread>
  <argLine>-XstartOnFirstThread</argLine>

  ...
</configuration>
```

8. In order for the tests to make the JDT available, it needs to be added to the target platform. Add the **Java Development Tools** to the target platform, or add the following line to the `com.packtpub.e4.target.mars.target` file:

```
<unit id="org.eclipse.jdt.feature.group" version="3.11.2
.v20160212-1500"/>
```

9. Although the tests run, they do not pass, because the SWTBot environment is giving the bare minimum dependencies required for the JUnit plug-in. In this case, it doesn't even include the clock plug-in developed earlier.

To fix this, a dependency needs to be added to the `pom.xml` file so that the test runtime can instantiate the correct workspace, including both the clock plug-in and the Eclipse SDK—since the tests rely on the workbench for the **Open View** command and the JDT for the Java project. This is achieved by defining a `target-platform-configuration` plugin and specifying either Eclipse features or specific bundles by their ID:

```
<plugin>
  <groupId>org.eclipse.tycho</groupId>
  <artifactId>target-platform-configuration</artifactId>
  <version>${tycho.version}</version>
  <configuration>
    <dependency-resolution>
      <extraRequirements>
        <requirement>
          <type>p2-installable-unit</type>
          <id>com.packtpub.e4.clock.ui</id>
          <versionRange>0.0.0</versionRange>
        </requirement>
        <requirement>
          <type>eclipse-feature</type>
          <id>org.eclipse.platform</id>
          <versionRange>0.0.0</versionRange>
        </requirement>
        <requirement>
```

```
        <type>eclipse-feature</type>
        <id>org.eclipse.jdt</id>
        <versionRange>0.0.0</versionRange>
      </requirement>
    </extraRequirements>
  </dependency-resolution>
</configuration>
</plugin>
```

10. If a test failure with the `testUI` method occurs (because the word **Eclipse** isn't seen in the title) change the implementation to:

```
if (shells[i].isVisible()) {
  String text = shells[i].getText();
  if (text.contains("Eclipse")
    || text.contains("Resource")
    || text.contains("Java")) {
    found = true;
  }
}
}
```

11. Finally, run `mvn integration-test` and the tests should run and pass.

What just happened?

The `tycho-surefire-plugin` allows SWTBot applications to be launched, the tests executed, and then a return value indicating whether or not they were successful to be passed back to the Maven build process.

Although it may seem that specifying the product or application will also bring in the necessary dependencies, that isn't the case. When the SWTBot test is run, it seems to pay no attention to the application or product when considering dependencies. As a result, these have to be added manually to the `pom.xml` file so that SWTBot sets up the right environment for the tests to run in.

The SWTBot tests written previously also had an implicit dependency on the SDK, from asserting the title of the workbench window to expecting the **Show View** menu to be present. These are examples of loosely coupled dependencies; they aren't code-related, but to run, they do require the environment to be pre-seeded with the necessary plug-ins and features.

Normally, if applications or features are being developed, then these can be used to add the required dependencies instead of individual plug-ins. In the example, the `com.packtpub. e4.clock.ui` plug-in was added explicitly and the `org.eclipse.platform` and `org.eclipse.jdt` features were added as well.

Note that the naming convention for P2 feature installable units is to add the suffix `.feature.group` to the end of the name; so the `com.packtpub.e4.clock.ui` plug-in dependency could be replaced with `com.packtpub.e4.feature.feature.group` as a dependency instead (since the feature contains the plug-in).

Using features for dependencies makes them easier to maintain, as the test project can depend only on the feature, and the feature can depend on the necessary plug-ins. If a dependency needs to be added, it has to be added only to the feature and it will apply to the update site, runtime, and test projects.

Finally, it is possible to determine whether or not a build is running on a macOS operating system dynamically, and use a value for the `-XstartOnFirstThread` argument. This can be achieved by setting a property using profiles that are automatically selected based on the operating system:

```
<profiles>
  <profile>
    <id>OSX</id>
    <activation>
      <os><family>mac</family></os>
    </activation>
    <properties>
      <swtbot.args>-Xmx1024m -XstartOnFirstThread</swtbot.args>
    </properties>
  </profile>
  <profile>
    <id>NotOSX</id>
    <activation>
      <os><family>!mac</family></os>
    </activation>
    <properties>
      <swtbot.args>-Xmx1024m</swtbot.args>
    </properties>
  </profile>
</profiles>
```

The `OSX` profile is automatically enabled for the `mac` family builds, and the `NotOSX` profile is automatically enabled for any non `mac` family builds (with the negation character `!` at the start of the family name).

Time for action – changing the version numbers

When a new version of the project is released, the plug-in and feature numbers need to be updated. This can be done manually, by modifying the `pom.xml` and `MANIFEST.MF` version numbers, or by running the `tycho-versions-plugin:set-version` tool.

1. From the parent directory, run (all on one line):

```
mvn org.eclipse.tycho:tycho-versions-plugin:set-version
  -DnewVersion=1.2.3-SNAPSHOT
```

2. The output should say **SUCCESS** for the parent and **SKIPPED** for the others:

```
[INFO] Reactor Summary:
[INFO]
[INFO] com.packtpub.e4.parent ................. SUCCESS [5.569s]
[INFO] com.packtpub.e4.clock.ui ............... SKIPPED
[INFO] com.packtpub.e4.junit.plugin ........... SKIPPED
[INFO] com.packtpub.e4.feature ................ SKIPPED
[INFO] com.packtpub.e4.update ................. SKIPPED
```

3. Now run a build to verify that the versions were updated correctly:

```
[INFO] Building com.packtpub.e4.parent 1.2.3-SNAPSHOT
[INFO] Building com.packtpub.e4.clock.ui 1.2.3-SNAPSHOT
[INFO] Building com.packtpub.e4.junit.plugin 1.2.3-SNAPSHOT
[INFO] Building com.packtpub.e4.feature 1.2.3-SNAPSHOT
[INFO] Building com.packtpub.e4.update 1.2.3-SNAPSHOT
[INFO] Reactor Summary:
[INFO]
[INFO] com.packtpub.e4.parent ................. SUCCESS [0.001s]
[INFO] com.packtpub.e4.clock.ui ............... SUCCESS [0.561s]
[INFO] com.packtpub.e4.junit.plugin ........... SUCCESS [0.176s]
[INFO] com.packtpub.e4.feature ................ SUCCESS [0.071s]
[INFO] com.packtpub.e4.update ................. SUCCESS [2.764s]
```

4. Finally, once the development is complete, build with a release version:

```
mvn org.eclipse.tycho:tycho-versions-plugin:set-version
  -DnewVersion=1.2.3.RELEASE
```

What just happened?

The Tycho `set-versions` plugin is very similar to the Maven `version:set` plugin; however, Tycho makes changes for both the `META-INF/MANIFEST.MF` file (needed by Eclipse) and the `pom.xml` file (needed by Maven).

Development version numbers in Maven end in `-SNAPSHOT` to indicate that they are a mutable release, and there's special handling in Maven builds to get the latest snapshot build. For Eclipse builds, the equivalent special name is `.qualifier`, which is appended onto the end of the plug-in and feature builds.

For simple projects, where there is a single plug-in and feature, it can often make sense to have the two versions kept in sync. Sometimes, when there are two highly related plug-ins in the same feature (for example, JDT and JDT UI), then it can also make sense in keeping them in sync. For larger projects where a single build may have multiple modules, it can make sense to have different version numbers on a plug-in by plug-in basis.

The version numbers in OSGi and therefore Eclipse plug-ins follow semantic versioning, in which the version number component consists of a major version, a minor version, and a micro version, as well as an optional qualifier. The major, minor and micro versions default to 0 if not present, while the qualifier defaults to the empty string. Typically, the qualifier is used to encode either a build timestamp or a build revision identifier (such as that produced by `git describe` on modern version control systems). The major/minor/micro are sorted numerically, but the qualifier is sorted alphabetically.

Unfortunately, OSGi version numbers and Maven version numbers differ in agreement on what the highest value is. For Maven, the empty qualifier is the highest (that is, `1.2.3.build < 1.2.3`), whereas for OSGi it is the other way around (`1.2.3.build > 1.2.3`). As a result, organizations such as SpringSource have created a de-facto policy of using a qualifier of `RELEASE` to indicate the release build, since `1.2.3.build < 1.2.3.RELEASE`. They also use `M1`, `M2`, `M3` for milestone releases and `RC1`, `RC2` for release candidates, since all of these are less than `RELEASE`. As a result, the progression for Eclipse build qualifiers tends to follow `-SNAPSHOT`, `M1`, `M2`, `RC1`, `RC2`, `RELEASE`.

Have a go hero – enabling builds for other plug-ins

Apply the same `pom.xml` builds to allow the other plug-ins built in the other chapters as part of the automated build. This includes the headless application (the product can be moved into the same product) and the Minimark editor. The standalone JUnit test will need to be built as a `jar` instead of an `eclipse-plugin`, and examples are available at the Maven homepage or the book's GitHub repository.

Signing update sites

When installing the content into a repository, Eclipse will report whether the plug-ins are signed or not. Digital signatures ensure that the contents of the plug-ins have not changed, and the identity of the signer can be verified.

Time for action – creating a self-signed certificate

To sign content, a private key and public key must be used. The private key is used for signing the content, and the public key is used for verifying that the content has not been modified. A key-pair can be created using the Java `keytool` utility on the command line.

1. Run `keytool` to see a list of options, and to verify that it is on the path.

2. Create a new key-pair by running (all on one line):

   ```
   keytool -genkey
    -alias packtpub
    -keypass SayK3ys
    -keystore /path/to/keystore
    -storepass BarC0der
    -dname "cn=packtpub,ou=pub,o=packt"
   ```

3. Verify that the key was generated correctly:

   ```
   keytool -list -keystore /path/to/keystore -storepass BarC0der
   ```

4. Create a JAR file for testing purposes, for example by zipping the contents of the directory:

   ```
   jar cf test.jar .
   ```

5. Sign the JAR to verify that it works, by running (all on one line):

   ```
   jarsigner
    -keypass SayK3ys
    -storepass BarC0der
    -keystore /path/to/keystore
    test.jar
    packtpub
   ```

6. Verify the Jar signature by running:

   ```
   jarsigner -verify test.jar
   ```

What just happened?

The Java `keytool` program manages keys and certificates for the use of Java programs wanting to sign content. Each entry in the keystore has an **alias** (to allow for ease of reference if there are many) and an associated key password and store password.

The **keystore** is created at the location given, protected with a store password `BarC0der`. To use any of the keys in the keystore, the store needs to be unlocked with this password first.

To use the private key, we need to give the key password, which is `SayK3ys`. Typically the key passwords will be different from the store password; if multiple keys are present, it is good practice to have a different password for each one.

The distinguished name (`dname`) is an LDAP identifier for the owner of the key. This is represented as a series of `name=value` comma-separated pairs. At a minimum, they need a common name (`cn`) and then some kind of organizational identifier. In this case, the organizational unit (`ou`) is `pub` and the organization (`o`) is `packt`.

Another common way of representing ownership is to use the domain components (`dc`), so an alternative is to use something like `cn=e4,dc=packtpub,dc=com` where each element in the `packtpub.com` domain is split into its own `dc` element in the distinguished name. Note that the order of elements is significant.

The `jarsigner` tool is used to sign a JAR and needs access to the store, the store's password, and the key's password. The alias can be supplied, in which case it will use that one—but if it is left out, then it will use any matching key in the chain (which assumes that the passwords are unique for the keys, as is best practice).

Finally the `jarsigner` can also be used to check whether a signature is correct or not using the `-verify` argument.

Time for action – signing the plug-ins

Integrating signatures into a Tycho build is a matter of adding a plug-in to the build script. In addition, Java properties need to be passed in to provide access to the arguments required by the `jarsigner` tool.

1. Add the plug-in to the parent `pom.xml` file:

```
<plugin>
  <groupId>org.apache.maven.plugins</groupId>
  <artifactId>maven-jarsigner-plugin</artifactId>
  <version>1.4</version>
  <executions>
    <execution>
      <id>sign</id>
```

```
        <goals>
          <goal>sign</goal>
        </goals>
      </execution>
    </executions>
    <configuration>
      <verbose>true</verbose>
      <!-- alias>packtpub</alias -->
      <keystore>${project.parent.basedir}/keystore</keystore>
      <!-- storepass>...</storepass -->
      <!-- keypass>...</keypass -->
    </configuration>
  </plugin>
```

2. Run `mvn package` and an error is shown:

```
[ERROR] Failed to execute goal
 org.apache.maven.plugins:maven-jarsigner-plugin:1.4:sign (sign)
 on project com.packtpub.e4.parent:
 The parameters 'alias' for goal
 org.apache.maven.plugins:maven-jarsigner-plugin:1.4:sign
 are missing or invalid -> [Help 1]
```

3. Pass in the arguments required by `jarsigner`, which can be supplied inside the `pom.xml` file or as Java system properties with a `jarsigner` prefix as follows (all on one line):

```
mvn package
 -Djarsigner.alias=packtpub
 -Djarsigner.keypass=SayK3ys
 -Djarsigner.storepass=BarC0der
```

4. If it is successful, the output should show:

```
[INFO] --- maven-jarsigner-plugin:1.4:sign (sign) @
  com.packtpub.e4.clock.ui ---
[INFO] 1 archive(s) processed
[INFO] --- maven-jarsigner-plugin:1.4:sign (sign) @
  com.packtpub.e4.feature ---
[INFO] 1 archive(s) processed
[INFO] --- maven-jarsigner-plugin:1.4:sign (sign) @
  com.packtpub.e4.update ---
[INFO] 1 archive(s) processed
```

5. To run the sign step conditionally, a profile can be used. Move the jarsigner plugin from the `build` to a separate top-level element `profiles` in the `pom.xml` file:

```
<profiles>
  <profile>
    <id>sign</id>
    <build>
      <plugins>
        <plugin>
          <groupId>org.apache.maven.plugins</groupId>
          <artifactId>maven-jarsigner-plugin</artifactId>
          . . .
        </plugin>
      </plugins>
    </build>
  </profile>
</profiles>
```

6. Now run the build with `mvn package`, and verify that it runs without signing.

7. Run the build with signing enabled by running `mvn package -Psign` to enable the `sign` profile; it should ask for the alias, as before.

8. To automatically enable the sign profile whenever the `jarsigner.alias` property is provided, add the following to the profile:

```
<profile>
  <id>sign</id>
  <activation>
    <property>
      <name>jarsigner.alias</name>
    </property>
  </activation>
  <build>
    . . .
  </build>
</profile>
```

9. Now run the build as `mvn package -Djarstore.alias=packtpub ...` to verify that signing runs without needing to specify the `-Psign` argument.

What just happened?

By adding the `maven-jarsigner-plugin` to the build, Maven signed any Jar that was built (including the `content.jar` and `artifacts.jar`, which don't really need to be signed). This is a standard pattern for building any signed Java content in Maven and isn't Tycho or Eclipse specific.

The parameters to `jarsigner` are specified as system properties. The `-D` flag for Maven, like Java, is used to specify a system property on the command line. The `maven-jarsigner-plugin` reads its properties with a prefix of `jarsigner`, so the alias is passed as `jarsigner.alias` and the keystore as `jarsigner.keystore`. Other parameters are documented on the `maven-jarsigner-plugin` page at `https://maven.apache.org/plugins/maven-jarsigner-plugin/sign-mojo.html`.

Note that the location of the store needs to be specified as a full path, since the plug-in will run with different directories (specifically the `target` directory of the build). Attempting to use a relative path will fail. Generally the location of the keystore and the passwords won't be part of the source code repository at all, but configured at build time with the build agent.

Time for action – serving an update site

Now that the update site has been developed, tested and automatically built, the final stage is to upload the contents of the update site (under `com.packtpub.e4.update/target/repository`) and make it available on a website or FTP server so that others can install it. If Python 2.7+ is installed, run a simple web server as follows.

1. Change to the directory `com.packtpub.e4.update/target/repository`.

2. Run the Python `SimpleHTTPServer` module (for Python 2) or the `http.server` module (for Python 3):

```
python -m SimpleHTTPServer 8080
Serving HTTP on 0.0.0.0 port 8080 ...
```

```
python3 -m http.server 8080
Serving HTTP on 0.0.0.0 port 8080 ...
```

3. Verify the update site by adding `http://localhost:8080/` as a remote update site in Eclipse.

If you don't have Python installed, then some operating systems have a means to serve web-based content already, or another web server can be used. macOS has web sharing where files in `~/Sites` are served from, Linux systems typically have Apache configured to allow per-user web sharing in `~/public_html`, and Microsoft Windows has IIS with files served from the default `c:\intepub\wwwroot`. See the operating system's documentation for details.

What just happened?

An update site is simply an HTTP server that serves the contents of the `content.jar` and `artifacts.jar` files, along with their `plugins` and `features` directories.

If Python 2.7 or above is installed, a module called `SimpleHTTPServer` exists which can be run from the `update/target/repository` directory to allow the update site to be installed from `http://localhost:8080/`. For Python 3 the module is called `http.server`. Uploading the contents of the repository to a remote website is left as an exercise for the reader.

Finally, once published to a publicly visible website, it's possible to register the location of the update site at the Eclipse marketplace at `http://marketplace.eclipse.org`, so that other Eclipse users can find the update site from the Marketplace client.

Pop quiz – understanding automated builds and update sites

Q1. What is a **GroupId, ArtifactId and Version (GAV)**?

Q2. What are the six types of packaging needed to build and test plug-ins, features, products and update sites?

Q3. How can the version numbers of plug-ins and features be updated in Maven?

Q4. Why and how are Jars signed?

Q5. How can a simple HTTP server be run in Python?

Q6. Where are Eclipse features typically registered for others to find?

Summary

This chapter concludes the creation of Eclipse plug-ins and features. Since the final step is building and making it available to others, the steps in this chapter focused on how to automate the builds with Tycho and then take the published update site and make it available for others.

The final chapter will introduce the Eclipse development process, and how to contribute patches to Eclipse.

13
Contributing to Eclipse

Making Eclipse better – one commit at a time

Now that you know how to write plug-ins and do development and testing inside Eclipse, you can fix issues and create new features for the Eclipse platform. This chapter shows how to work with Eclipse's source, create bugs with the Eclipse bug tracking system, and submit changes into Gerrit at Eclipse.

In this chapter, we shall:

- Import the source of plug-ins through the plug-in view
- Check out projects from Git
- Raise bugs in the Eclipse bug-tracking system
- Submit changes to Gerrit

Open source contributions

Eclipse is an open source code base, and has been written by thousands of individuals across the years. The Eclipse Foundation are the stewards of the code, but the foundation staff themselves are few in number and generally do not write the code for Eclipse itself; rather, they look after the ancillary services (bug tracker, git and Gerrit source code repositories, news groups, wiki, and website) and the EclipseCon and DevoxxUS conferences around the world (`http://eclipsecon.org, http://devoxx.us`). There are commercial companies who build their products on Eclipse and contribute to the underlying platform, but there are many open-source volunteers who contribute their time and effort to improve Eclipse. This chapter will show you how you can make a contribution to Eclipse by checking out a repository, raising a bug, and filing a patch.

Importing the source

Eclipse ships with source code for the provided plug-ins with the **Eclipse SDK** and the **Eclipse IDE for Committers** packages. The source is also available for installation from the Eclipse update site; the features generally have **Source** or **Developer Resources** in the name. Once the sources are installed into the running Eclipse application, plug-ins can be debugged and modified.

Time for action – installing the sources

In order to be able to see the source for a particular plug-in, it needs to be installed. This is achieved using the same installation dialog that has been covered previously in this book.

1. Go to **Help | Install New Software** and choose the repository that is associated with the release of Eclipse that is being used:

   ❑ http://download.eclipse.org/releases/neon/

   ❑ http://download.eclipse.org/releases/mars/

2. Ensure that the **Group items by category** checkbox is deselected. This will show all plug-ins, not just the main ones. Typically the source plug-ins are not shown in the main listing. In addition, deselecting this checkbox will result in a faster search in the next step.

3. Optionally deselect the **Hide items that are already installed** checkbox. This will ensure that the plug-ins show up even if they are already installed.

4. Search for source in the search box. This will result in a set of plug-ins being shown:

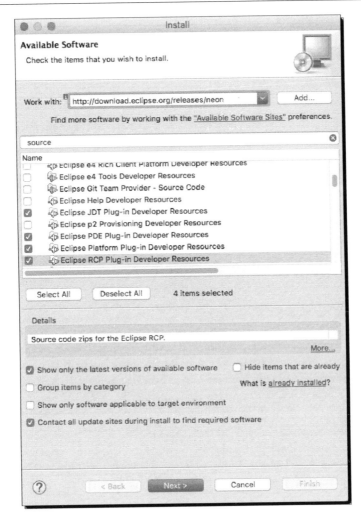

5. Select the following plug-ins and then click on **Finish**. If all the plug-ins are already installed, then the **Finish** button may be disabled:

      ❑   **Eclipse JDT Plug-in Developer Resources**

      ❑   **Eclipse PDE Plug-in Developer Resources**

      ❑   **Eclipse Platform Plug-in Developer Resources**

      ❑   **Eclipse RCP Plug-in Developer Resources**

What just happened?

When the developer resources are installed into Eclipse, a set of `source` plug-ins are installed. For example, for the `org.eclipse.core.runtime` plug-in, there will be a corresponding `org.eclipse.core.runtime.source` plug-in that contains the individual source files. These can be seen in the `plugins/` directory inside the Eclipse install.

The developer resources are included in the **IDE for Eclipse Committers** package and the **Eclipse SDK**, but typically not included in other packages.

Time for action – debugging the platform

To debug the platform, make sure that at least one plug-in project is open and that it depends on the plug-ins that need to be debugged. This allows the editor to be opened for any of the classes for debugging.

1. Ensure that a plug-in that uses the Eclipse UI is open in the workspace, such as `com.packtpub.e4.hello.ui` or `com.packtpub.e4.clock.ui`. This will ensure that the platform classes are available.

2. Use the **Navigate | Open Type** menu or press *Ctrl + Shift + T (Cmd + Shift + T* on macOS) to open the **Open Type** search dialog. Type in `Shell` and select the **Shell** from the `org.eclipse.swt.widgets` package. Double-click or click on **OK** to open the file.

> If the source code isn't shown, verify that the **Eclipse Platform Plug-in Developer Resources** plug-in has been installed and that there is an open plug-in project that depends on `org.eclipse.ui` or `org.eclipse.swt`. If the **Open Type** menu isn't shown, switch to the **Java** perspective or the **Java Browsing** perspective to enable it, or open a Java source file.

3. Go to the `setText` method and put a breakpoint in at the start of the method.

4. Go to the **Debug | Debug Configurations** menu, and underneath the **Eclipse Application**, click on the new icon to create a new launch configuration. Ensure that the **org.eclipse.sdk.ide** product is selected in the **Program to Run** section:

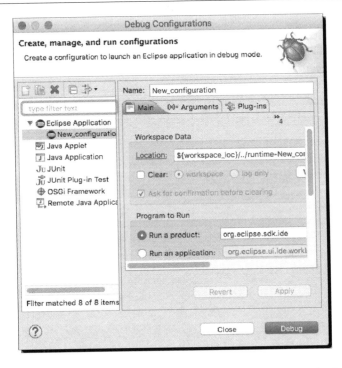

5. Click on **Debug** to launch the Eclipse instance. It should stop at the breakpoint shortly afterwards, for the workspace chooser dialog with a title like **Eclipse** or **Eclipse SDK** or for the main platform with **Eclipse Platform**.

What just happened?

Being able to understand Eclipse bugs and start to fix them requires being able to debug through the platform. This requires being able to see the source code and know how to be able to step through the code as it's executing.

When a class file is loaded in the debugger, or a file is opened through direct (or indirect) navigation, Eclipse tries to find the source code associated with the plug-in and show that instead. Each Jar on the project's classpath can have an associated **Java Source Attachment** or a **Javadoc Location** with it.

When PDE loads a project, the entries under the **Plug-in Dependencies** tab will show the dependencies for the project, and if the corresponding `source` plug-in is also installed and available in the workspace, then it will be wired up to both the **Java Source Attachment** and the **Javadoc Location** as well. As a result, when the class file is loaded, the source attachment will be searched for the corresponding file and will be shown automatically.

The title being set triggers the breakpoint in the `Shell` class (which is SWT's equivalent of a window). This call will be triggered from a number of different call paths; one way of understanding how Eclipse works is to put a breakpoint in a known location and see where it is being called.

Time for action – modifying the platform

Once the location of interest has been found, it is necessary to modify the code to attempt a fix. For example, if the developer wanted to ensure that the window's title was all in upper case, it would be necessary to inject a `title.toUpperCase()` call. However, since the `.class` file is read-only, it is necessary to import the plug-in's source into the workspace to change the implementation.

1. Using the **Window | Show View | Other...** menu or the **Quick Access** box, open the **Plug-ins** view from the **Plug-in Development** category. This will show a list of all plug-ins installed into the system.

2. Type `org.eclipse.swt` to scroll down the list, and select both the `org.eclipse.swt` bundle and the `org.eclipse.swt.*` fragment that corresponds to the platform. For example, on macOS this will start with `org.eclipse.swt.cocoa`, while on Windows it will start with `org.eclipse.swt.win32`; and on Linux, `org.eclipse.swt.gtk`:

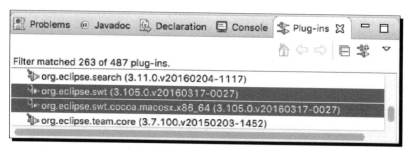

3. Right-click on the selected items and choose **Import As | Source Project** to load the source code projects into the workspace. After a brief period of compilation, the projects should be ready to use.

4. Close the existing files and then use **Open Type** to re-open the `Shell` from the `org.eclipse.swt.widgets` package. Instead of showing `Shell.class` in the editor title, it should now say `Shell.java` and should be mutable.

5. Go to the `setText` method and add a re-assignment of the `string` to convert it to upper case:

```
public void setText(String string) {
  checkWidget();
  if (string == null) error (SWT.ERROR_NULL_ARGUMENT);
  if (window == null) return;
  string = string.toUpperCase();
  super.setText(string);
```

6. Run the launch configuration again and the window titles should be displayed in capital letters.

What just happened?

Debugging and introspecting variables can be done without source code, but in order to make changes, it is necessary to import the source code. Eclipse provides an easy way to import source code associated with the plug-in using the **Plug-ins** view and using **Import As | Source Project**.

When importing as a source project, a project is set up and the source code imported in and compiled. This will give the ability for the compiler to pick up any problems with code changes for the projects that are in the workspace.

 It is not possible to use this import technique for plug-ins that have no associated source plug-in.

If the only changes required are to modify the `plugin.xml` (for example, adding another extension), then the project can be imported as a **Binary Project** or **Binary Project with Linked Content**. Both of these options are faster, since the previously compiled code is used instead of recompiling with source. The only difference is whether the Jar file is copied into the project or a project link (like a symlink) is used to refer to the Jar from the platform's `plugins` directory. In neither case can the existing source files be modified.

Once the source code is available, it can be changed and debugged just like any other plug-in project. In addition, the version of the source code is guaranteed to be the same as the version of the installed plug-in.

Checking out from Git

Although local changes can be made for testing purposes, in order to get a change uploaded, it is necessary to check out the project from Eclipse's servers at the canonical `git.eclipse.org` repository. This requires a Git plug-in (using EGit) and optionally a command-line Git tool as well.

Time for action – checking out from EGit and Git

Eclipse's version control system of choice (and indeed, of many sane people's choice) is Git, the canonical distributed version control system for open-source projects. The EGit implementation in Eclipse is bundled by default for almost all of the standard packages, although it doesn't exist in the SDK package. The `git` command-line client is available for most operating systems and can be downloaded from `http://git-scm.com`.

1. It may be necessary to install the Eclipse Git team provider, but most packages of Eclipse come with EGit built in. If not, it can be installed using the **Help | Install New Software...** menu; select the main Eclipse repository for the release (Neon, Mars, and so on) and search for `git`. Install the **Eclipse Git Team Provider** from the **Collaboration** group:

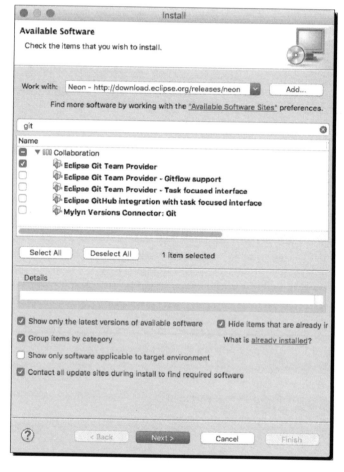

2. Restart Eclipse to complete the installation process.

3. Since the `org.eclipse.swt` projects were imported from a source snapshot in the previous section, they need to be deleted before they can be cloned. Right-click on the `org.eclipse.swt` projects and choose **Delete**, including selecting the **Delete project contents on disk** option.

4. To check out the SWT project from the Eclipse Git servers, navigate to **File | Import... | Projects from Git** and click on **Next**. Choose the **Clone URI** and then enter `http://git.eclipse.org/gitroot/platform/eclipse.platform.swt. git` in the **URI** details at the top:

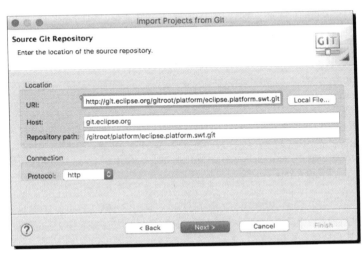

5. Clicking on **Next** will then show what branches to check out; typically this will include **master**, which is the head of the development branch. Select only the master branch and then click on **Next**:

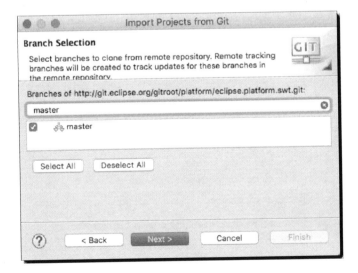

6. After the project has been cloned, the wizard will prompt to search for projects. Select the `org.eclipse.swt` project but not the others. When the wizard completes, the project will be in the workspace. There will be some compile errors at this point, which will be fixed in the next section.

What just happened?

The Git support in Eclipse provides a way of cloning repositories to the local disk, and then checking out the projects once the clone is complete. Repositories at Eclipse are available to check out from `http://git.eclipse.org/gitroot/` although the GitWeb browser is available at `http://git.eclipse.org/c/`. There is a Gerrit-based review system that hosts the repositories and reviews at `http://git.eclipse.org/r/` as well, which will be covered in a later section in this chapter. There are clones of many Eclipse repositories at GitHub under the `https://github.com/eclipse/` organization as well, although not all repositories are mirrored.

Projects at Eclipse are organized in two levels. The top level is generally a high-level partitioning; examples include `platform`, `mylyn`, `egit`, `jdt`, and `pde`. The Git repositories are a second level down and often include either the prefix of the project or the prefix excluding the `org` component.

Plug-ins developed in the same feature are typically co-hosted in the same repository. Each project organizes the layout in a different way, but will often have the name of the plug-in at the top level of the project, or underneath a `bundles` directory.

When a repository is cloned to the local disk, a copy of the project and all its history are made available. EGit will default to `~/git` as the storage location for Git repositories; this can be changed in the **Preferences | Team | Git** preferences pane in the **Default repository folder** entry. Each repository can have one actively checked-out branch at a time; this is typically **master** for ongoing development, but there are branches for the release streams.

Finally, the import wizard searches for the `.project` entries in order to import them into the workspace.

The **Plug-ins** view also allows projects to be imported from the repository by choosing **Import As | Project from a Repository**. If the Manifest contains an `Eclipse-SourceReferences` header containing a standard `scm:` Maven repository URL, then the project will automatically be imported from that location.

Time for action – configuring the SWT project

There are a couple of extra steps that are specifically required in order to work with SWT. The first is setting up the main SWT project for the specific operating system, and the second is obtaining the pre-compiled native libraries that are required in order to communicate with the operating system.

1. Firstly, the project's platform-specific `.classpath` needs to be copied (or symlinked) so that the project compiles. Since SWT has a number of platform-specific elements, they need to be referred to in the classpath. In the root of the `org.eclipse.swt` project, there are three files: `.classpath_cocoa` (for macOS), `.classpath_gtk` (for Linux), and `.classpath_win32` (for Windows). Copy or symlink the appropriate one to `.classpath` in order to compile the project.

 On Windows, Explorer may not be able to display or rename files that start with a dot character. Use either the command prompt and `rename` or `copy` commands, or use Eclipse's **Navigator** view (which will show the dot files) to rename or copy the entries appropriately.

2. Once the `.classpath` file has been copied, select the `org.eclipse.swt` project, use the **File | Refresh** menu to refresh the project, and clean the project with the **Project | Clean...** menu to perform the rebuild. At this point the project should be compile-error free.

3. Running an Eclipse application at this point is likely to fail with an error message like:

   `java.lang.UnsatisfiedLinkError: Could not load SWT library.`

   `Reasons:`

   `   no swt-cocoa-4616 in java.library.path`

   `   no swt-cocoa in java.library.path`

 There is a tight one-to-one binding between the Java SWT project and the associated native library. Each time a new API is added, the version number (shown here as `4616`) is bumped. The first two digits are notionally the Eclipse release (4.6 is the version for Neon) and this is the 16th revision so far. When the Java code is executed, it triggers the load of the native library; and if the versions do not match, then SWT will not be able to operate correctly.

4. Although it is possible to compile the native SWT libraries directly, it is non-trivial to do so. There are `build.sh` and `build.bat` scripts that are used to compile the native libraries, but it is easier to obtain pre-built binaries for the specific operating system. These are stored in another repository at Eclipse, and can be checked out using the same means shown before (or through the command line with `git`) using the URI `http://git.eclipse.org/gitroot/platform/eclipse.platform.swt.binaries.git`. Import the appropriate platform-specific fragment into the workspace, such as `org.eclipse.swt.cocoa.macosx.x86_64`. This will contain a fragment that contains the native libraries, and will bind itself to the `org.eclipse.swt` bundle.

5. Now that the project and native libraries are available, running a newly launched Eclipse application should work without further errors. If there are problems, verify that the version numbers stored in the `Library.java` file (concatenation of the `MAJOR_VERSION` and `MINOR_VERSION`) are the same as the version of the native libraries.

6. Finally, make the change to the `setText` method in the `Shell` class to perform the capitalization, and test the change. There should be a change marker > in the hierarchical view showing that a change has been made to a file under version control.

What just happened?

The SWT project is unique in the Eclipse ecosystem, in that it is a mixture of both Java code and native components. As a result, it needs slightly more set up than a traditional Eclipse project to get working. There are different subfolders used for each operating system, and the choice of `.classpath` sets that up correctly. Then additionally there are native bindings for the libraries, which need to be present at run-time that merge the two together.

The `org.eclipse.swt` project contains all of the code necessary to build SWT for a specific platform. The project's contents are split over several subdirectories, partitioned into different units based approximately on the subpackages of the `org.eclipse.swt` bundle. Each of these subfolders has a `common` folder, along with specific windowing folders. The `common` folder typically has Java source files that are platform independent, while the window-specific folders have a `library` (for native code) and corresponding Java source files.

The **Eclipse PI** folder (short for **Platform Interface**) has the libraries used for interacting with the operating system. Unlike AWT, each of the SWT widgets are implemented individually for each supported operating system. These provide interactions with base components such as `NSWindow` (for macOS), `WNDCLASS` (for Windows), or `GtkWidgetClass` (for Linux). For each natively available windowing widget, there is a corresponding Java class that provides the API for that widget. This makes building application-specific code easy to debug, since the majority of it is in Java, which allows the Java debuggers to be used.

These natively wrapped components are then used in multiple independent versions of the `Shell` class. The `Shell` class used by macOS is implemented in terms of `NSWindow` and `objc_msgSend`, while the `Shell` class used by Windows and Linux are implemented in their own ways.

 As a result, a widget like `Shell` will exist in different locations; under the `Eclipse SWT` folder, there are three `Shell.java` files, under the `cocoa`, `win32` and `gtk` directories. New features implemented in SWT have to be implemented in triplicate.

Finally, many of the binaries use Java primitive data types (such as `int` and `long`) to represent native memory pointers, for use in passing backwards and forwards to the native library. On 32-bit platforms an `int` will be used, and on 64-bit platforms a `long` will be used. Because Java doesn't have a word size, and using a 64-bit value on all platforms is overkill and requires additional casting, there is a convention to use a special syntax to represent pointers and native sizes in SWT:

```
long /*int*/
long[] /*int[]*/
double /*float*/
double[] /*float[]*/
```

These special comments indicate that the value is supposed to be architecture dependent, a `64 /* 32 */` bit type or arrays of them. The `replace64` target in the `buildFragment.xml` ant build file performs this re-writing when building for a 32-bit platform automatically.

Contributing to Eclipse

Creating a bug fix and offering it to a project is a great way to make contributions to Eclipse. This section will show how to get involved and get to the stage where it's possible to file bugs and fixes against an upstream Eclipse project.

Creating bugs on Bugzilla

As an open source project, everything starts with a bug. Eclipse uses **Bugzilla**, an open source bug tracking tool initially created by Mozilla to manage bugs for their web browser.

Time for action – creating an account at Eclipse

All Eclipse foundation systems use the same account information, including name and e-mail address. In order to participate in the Eclipse foundation systems, an account is required.

1. Go to the `https://dev.eclipse.org/site_login/` page to create an **account**. This contains the **terms of use** (visible at `http://www.eclipse.org/legal/termsofuse.php`) and the **privacy policy** (visible at `http://www.eclipse.org/legal/privacy.php`).

2. There are additional options which may be relevant, such as signing up for the Eclipse newsletter and an explicit checkbox to say that you have read the terms and privacy policy. This sign-up page may change from time to time.

3. Click on the **Create Account** button and a new user account will be created with the given name and e-mail address. There may be an additional e-mail confirmation step to verify that the e-mail address step is correct.

4. Once the account is created, log in to the site at `https://dev.eclipse.org/site_login/` to verify that the password is correctly set up. It should be possible to visit the Eclipse wiki at `http://wiki.eclipse.org` and the forums at `https://www.eclipse.org/forums/`, or IRC channels listed at `https://wiki.eclipse.org/IRC`.

5. In order to be able to push changes, it is necessary to electronically sign the **Eclipse Contributor License Agreement**. More information can be found at the CLA page for your account at `https://dev.eclipse.org/site_login/myaccount.php#open_tab_cla`.

6. Finally, ensure that the account is valid for logging in to `https://bugs.eclipse.org`.

What just happened?

An account is required in order to use any of the Eclipse foundation systems. Having created this account, it is now possible to log in to any of them using the same credentials. These also involve the acceptance of the terms of use and the privacy policies; violations of these may result in the account being suspended.

There are a number of tools that the Eclipse foundation manages; Bugzilla is one of the key ones. All changes that are added to Eclipse need to be associated with a bug, and being able to use the interface effectively is a key part of being an effective Eclipse contributor or committer.

Time for action – creating a bug

Reporting bugs in Eclipse is a simple way of getting involved. These steps will use the example of the title case of SWT as an example, although this is not likely to be accepted as a real bug!

1. Open a web browser and go to `https://bugs.eclipse.org` in order to create a bug. It may be necessary to log into the account if the option is not set. It may be beneficial to uncheck the **Restrict this login session to this IP address**, as otherwise if the computer's IP address changes, then it will be necessary to log in again.

2. Once logged in, a **File a Bug** button will be displayed; alternatively the **new** link at the top of the page will allow a bug to be created.

3. The Eclipse bug wizard will show the steps necessary to create a bug. The form will guess the operating system and hardware type based on the browser information, but for non-OS-specific bugs such as documentation, these should be set to **All**.

4. The bugs are categorized into different areas; **Technology** contains general plug-ins that are language agnostic, such as **EGit** and **Tycho**. **Mylyn** has its own top level, while other languages and tools are under the **Tools** category. Finally, items relating to the **Platform**, **PDE**, or **JDT** are under the **Eclipse** category.

5. Each product may have a number of components, such as whether it's relating to a behavior in the UI or documentation. This is generally used as an indicator to route the request to the right team, but it can be moved later.

6. Finally, check that the version and severity are appropriately set for the bug. Enter a short summary and a description, and click on **Submit Bug** to enter the details.

What just happened?

Creating a bug involves going to `https://bugs.eclipse.org` and filling in the details.

A good bug description has a number of things:

◆ The **summary** should be concise, and summarize the problem in 60 characters or less. It should also uniquely identify the problem for later retrieval.

◆ The **description** should describe the problem in sufficient detail that those reading the bug can understand the problem and be able to replicate it. Providing more information, such as the version of the operating system or the windowing system, may be necessary if there's a chance that the bug is specific.

◆ Any **attachments** to the bug can be added when it is created, or can be added later. An attachment has a file name and a brief description; the file type will be automatically detected in most cases, but may be necessary to add if it's not clear. An attachment can be deleted or superseded later by a new attachment.

◆ The **importance** and **target milestone** are used by the project owners to schedule bugs and record when they are to be fixed. These generally shouldn't be changed by reporters.

 There is more information on how to write a good bug at the wiki page `https://wiki.eclipse.org/Bug_Reporting_FAQ`.

Have a go hero

It is possible to configure Mylyn with Bugzilla to be able to report a bug in Eclipse. If Mylyn is not installed (it comes by default with most Eclipse packages, but not the Eclipse SDK), then it is possible to report a bug using the IDE itself. Install the **Mylyn Task Connector for Bugzilla** from the update site (if it is not already installed in the platform), and after restarting, open the **Task Repositories** view. The **Add Task Repository** button on the right-hand side allows a Bugzilla repository to be connected, which allows entering `https://bugs.eclipse.org/bugs` as the remote URL endpoint. From here, **Tasks** can be created (which are bugs in the remote tracker) and **Queries** (which are lists of bugs).

Submitting fixes

It is possible to submit fixes for bugs through a couple of tools. The old way is to create a patch and attach it to Bugzilla, but this has largely been superseded by the use of Gerrit to perform reviews.

Time for action – setting up a Gerrit profile

Gerrit is a distributed version control system review tool that can be used to upload patches for review and ultimate merging with the repository. It provides a Git interface and acts as a remote Git server, so using it with existing tools or command lines is trivial.

1. Navigate to the Gerrit user interface at `https://git.eclipse.org/r/` and ensure that the profile is correctly set up. The name and e-mail address will be taken from the information provided when creating the Eclipse account.

 A password is required in order to push changes to Gerrit. This can be done either through a Gerrit-specific randomly generated HTTP password, or through an uploaded SSH key. Note that while the e-mail address and login details used to access Gerrit are the same as for Bugzilla, for pushing changes through Git a different password is used.

2. An HTTP password can be generated by going to `https://git.eclipse.org/r/#/settings/http-password` and clicking on the **Generate Password** button. This shows the user name and the password to use for the HTTPS URLs, which will be of the form `https://git.eclipse.org/r/platform/eclipse.platform.swt.git`. This is the same as the one used to clone the repository initially, except replacing the `gitroot` for `r` in the URL.

3. To use SSH, a private/public key is required. This can be generated by command-line tools, or through Eclipse itself. Navigate to the **Preferences** menu, and then under the **General | Network Connections | SSH2** panel there is a **Key Management** tab which can be used to generate an **SSH keypair**. Clicking on the **Generate RSA Key...** or **Generate DSA Key...** buttons will result in a new public/private key being generated. The window shows the **public** part of the keypair (which can be pasted into Gerrit at `https://git.eclipse.org/r/#/settings/ssh-keys`). The private part is not shown, but the **Save Private Key...** allows the private key to be saved to a file, by default, `~/.ssh/id_rsa` or `~/.ssh/id_dsa`—but using a host-specific name such as `~/.ssh/id_rsa-gerrit` may be sensible. The private key can then be selected on the command line, or through an entry in the `~/.ssh/config` file:

```
Host git.eclipse.org
IdentityFile ~/.ssh/id_rsa-gerrit
User myusername
```

4. Verify that running `ssh` into Gerrit works as expected, using port `29418`:

```
$ ssh -p 29418 git.eclipse.org

    ****    Welcome to Gerrit Code Review    ****

    Hi My Name, you have successfully connected over SSH.

    Unfortunately, interactive shells are disabled.
    To clone a hosted Git repository, use:

    git clone ssh://myusername@git.eclipse.org:29418/REPO_NAME.git

Connection to git.eclipse.org closed.
```

On Windows, the command-line tool `plink` can be used to perform ssh connections. This is part of the `putty` package which is available from `http://www.chiark.greenend.org.uk/~sgtatham/putty/download.html`. In order to use this from Eclipse or command line, set an environment variable `GIT_SSH` to point to the full path of the `plink` executable.

What just happened?

Setting up a Gerrit account is necessary in order to be able to push changes to the review system. The majority of development with Eclipse is done with Gerrit and being able to trigger builds and run tests automatically is a key advantage.

Gerrit can be authenticated using a randomly generated HTTP password, or through an SSH interface running on port `29418`. These are separate from the Eclipse account information used to log into Bugzilla and other tools.

Using an SSH connection is generally easier on Linux and macOS servers, because the information can be stored securely in the keychain or through a key agent. It may be easier to use HTTP as a communication protocol on Windows, or when behind a firewall.

It's possible to test the connection to Gerrit using the command line and see if the **Welcome** message is displayed. This is worth doing to verify that it has been set up correctly before trying to push code.

Time for action – committing and pushing a patch

To submit patches to Gerrit, the change must first be committed locally, and the remote repository pointed to Gerrit. Then the change can be pushed and the builds triggered.

1. When committing for the first time, Git will ask for a user name and an e-mail address. That's because changes in Git are associated with a name and e-mail address and nothing else. In Eclipse, triggering a commit will bring up a dialog asking for these details; alternatively they can be specified in the **Preferences** | **Team** | **Git** | **Configuration** panel under the `user.name` and `user.email` values. Alternatively the git command line can be used to set them, using:

```
$ git config --global user.name "My Name"
$ git config --global user.email "my.email@example.com"
```

2. The change can be committed in Eclipse by right-clicking on the project (or folder) and choosing **Team | Commit**. This will show a dialog or view of information where the details can be entered. The general Eclipse practice is to put the bug on the first line, along with a short subject, and then more detailed information underneath. Gerrit also requires a `Change-Id` line in the commit, which can be automatically added by clicking on the Gerrit icon on the top right of the commit dialog; a `Signed-off-by` line is generated by clicking on the pen icon next to the Gerrit icon:

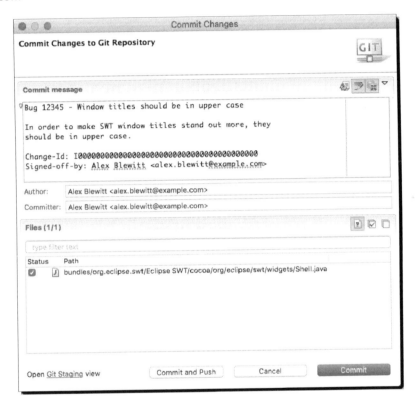

3. Once the change has been committed, it can be pushed to the remote server using `ssh://git.eclipse.org:29418/platform/eclipse.platform.swt.git` with a push `refspec` of `HEAD:refs/for/master`. This can be performed on the command line as follows:

```
$ git push ssh://git.eclipse.org:29418/platform/eclipse.platform.
swt.git HEAD:refs/for/master
```

4. To save time, these defaults can be configured for the project directly:

```
$ git remote set-url --push origin ssh://git.eclipse.org:29418/
platform/eclipse.platform.swt.git
$ git config remote.origin.push HEAD:refs/for/master
```

5. It is also possible to set this with Eclipse's **Git Repositories** view from repositories that have been cloned in Eclipse. Expanding the repository shows the remotes, including what the repository pushes to or pulls from:

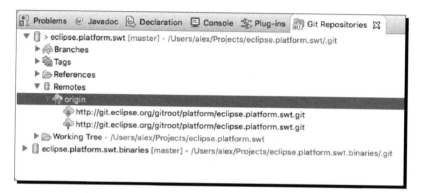

6. Right-clicking on the origin provides a menu which can be used to **Configure Push...**, but an easier way is to choose **Gerrit Configuration...**, which shows a dialog that can be used to select ssh or http, and have the configuration generated automatically:

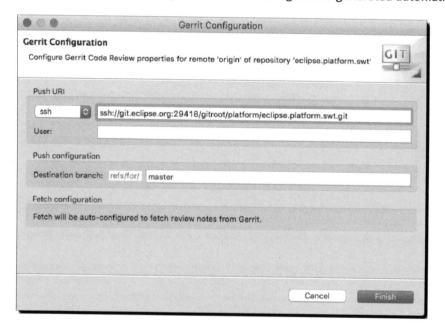

7. It is now possible to push the changes to trigger a Gerrit patch by running `git push` from the command line, or by right-clicking on the project and choosing **Team | Repository | Push to Upstream**.

 If the push is rejected, check that you have signed the Eclipse Contributor License Agreement at `https://dev.eclipse.org/site_login/ myaccount.php#open_tab_cla` (sometimes there is a delay between signing this and Gerrit recognizing the new information), In addition, verify that your committer e-mail address is the same one associated with your profile, and that the `Signed-off-by` field is present in the commit. You may need to `git commit --amend` or `git commit --amend --reset-author` in order to fix these problems.

What just happened?

When committing patches for Eclipse, there are several things that need to be followed. The git commit message must be sensible; typically the first line will contain the bug identifier and a short description, followed by a blank line, and then multiple paragraphs of text. The footer must include a `Signed-off-by`, and most projects also require a Gerrit `Change-Id` at the bottom.

Eclipse can be used to generate these automatically, but if working on the command line, these can be set by installing a commit message hook. This will add the `Change-Id` based on the content of the message, and the `Signed-off-by` can be added by supplying a `-s` argument to `git commit`. To install the hook, the remote Gerrit instance can supply a template via HTTP or SSH, which can then be used to place it in the right location, `.git/ hooks/commit-msg`:

```
$ scp -P 29418 git.eclipse.org:/hooks/commit-msg .git/hooks/
$ curl -o .git/hooks/commit-msg http://git.eclipse.org/r/tools/hooks/
commit-msg
```

It's possible to fetch review commentary by adding a fetch refspec for `refs/notes/*`, which can then be shown with `git log --notes=review` or `git show --notes=review`:

```
$ git config --add remote.origin.fetch +refs/notes/*:refs/notes/*
$ git fetch
$ git log --notes=review
$ git show --notes=review
```

Setting the project up for Gerrit access involves changing the remote push URL and ensuring that the changes go through the review. This can also be done by manually editing the `.git/config` file instead:

```
[remote "origin"]
  url =
  http://git.eclipse.org/gitroot/platform/eclipse.platform.swt.git
  fetch = +refs/heads/*:refs/remotes/origin/*
  fetch = +refs/notes/*:refs/notes/*
  pushurl =
  ssh://git.eclipse.org:29418/gitroot/platform/
  eclipse.platform.swt.git
  push = HEAD:refs/for/master
[branch "master"]
  remote = origin
  merge = refs/heads/master
[gerrit]
  createchangeid = true
```

Have a go hero

Gerrit reviews and review comments can also be seen with Mylyn, by installing the **Mylyn Reviews Connector for Gerrit** and using the **Task Repositories** view to create a task repository for the Eclipse Gerrit server. Create the repository using the URL `https://git.eclipse.org/r/` and verify the connectivity using the **Validate Settings** button.

Queries are possible using the Gerrit textual syntax for displaying information. This is described in Gerrit's help page on the search terms at `https://git.eclipse.org/r/Documentation/user-search.html`. These include `is:open` (for showing all open changes) and `owner:self` (for the authenticated users' changes). It's also possible to find all the open changes for a particular project; for example, to see all open changes against the SWT project, a filter `project:platform/eclipse.platform.swt is:open` can be used.

Summary

The first step in getting involved with the Eclipse projects is understanding how they work. The Eclipse plug-ins all come with source code and the IDE is self-sufficient for debugging and developing plug-in code. It's possible to view this source code for debugging purposes or to import the source code for modification processes, without needing to talk to remote Eclipse sites.

However, being able to fix bugs and provide patches upstream helps improve Eclipse for everyone; and once the fix has been identified, using Bugzilla to create a bug and Gerrit to receive the patch is the next logical step.

This chapter has shown how to follow all of these steps to be able to contribute to Eclipse. The rest is up to you.

A

Using OSGi Services to Dynamically Wire Applications

This appendix will present **OSGi services** as a means of communicating and connecting applications. Unlike the Eclipse extension point mechanism, OSGi services can have multiple versions available at runtime and can work in other OSGi environments, such as Felix or other commercial OSGi runtimes.

Services overview

In an Eclipse or OSGi runtime, each individual bundle is its own separate module, which has explicit dependencies on library code via `Import-Package`, `Require-Bundle`, or `Require-Capability`. These express static relationships and provide a way of configuring the bundle's classpath.

However, this presents a problem. If services are independent, how can they use contributions provided by other bundles? In Eclipse's case, the Extension Registry provides a means for code to look up providers. In a standalone OSGi environment, OSGi services provide a similar mechanism.

A **service** is an instance of a class that implements a **service interface**. When a service is created, it is *registered* with the services framework under one (or more) interfaces, along with a set of properties. Consumers can then *get* the service by asking the framework for implementers of that specific interface.

Services can also be registered under an abstract class, but this is not recommended. Providing a service interface exposed as an abstract class can lead to unnecessary coupling of client to implementation.

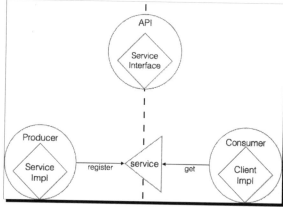

This separation allows the consumer and producer to depend on a common API bundle, but otherwise be completely disconnected from one another. This allows both the consumer and producer to be mocked out or exchanged with different implementations in the future.

Registering a service programmatically

To register a service, an instance of the implementation class needs to be created and registered with the framework. Interactions with the framework are performed with a `BundleContext`—typically provided in the `BundleActivator.start` method and stored for later use, or resolved dynamically from `FrameworkUtil.getBundle().getBundleContext()`.

Creating an activator

A bundle's activator is a class that is instantiated and coupled to the lifetime of the bundle. When a bundle is started, if a manifest entry `Bundle-Activator` exists, then the corresponding class is instantiated. As long as it implements the `BundleActivator` interface, the `start` method will be called. This method is passed an instance of `BundleContext`, which is the bundle's connection back to the hosting OSGi framework.

Although creating an activator may seem a simple way of registering a service, it is better to use declarative services, which are covered later in this appendix.

Create a new plug-in project `com.packtpub.e4.timezones`, to host a service for supplying `ZoneId` instances. Create a class called `com.packtpub.e4.timezones.internal.TimeZonesActivator` that implements the `org.osgi.framework.BundleActivator` interface.

Add the `Bundle-Activator` and `Import-Package` to the `META-INF/MANIFEST.MF` file as follows:

```
Import-Package: org.osgi.framework
Bundle-Activator:
   com.packtpub.e4.timezones.internal.TimeZonesActivator
```

Now when the bundle is started, the framework will automatically invoke the `start` method of the `TimeZonesActivator`, and correspondingly the `stop` method when the bundle is stopped. Test this by inserting a pair of `println` calls:

```
public class TimeZonesActivator implements BundleActivator {
  public void start(BundleContext context) throws Exception {
    System.out.println("Bundle started");
  }
  public void stop(BundleContext context) throws Exception {
    System.out.println("Bundle stopped");
  }
}
```

Now run it as an **OSGi framework** by going to **Run | Run Configurations... | OSGi Framework**. Ensure that all the workspace and target bundles are deselected with the **Deselect all** button. Add the `com.packtpub.e4.timezones` bundle, the Equinox console `org.eclipse.equinox.console` and the gogo shell `org.apache.felix.gogo.shell`. Ensure that the **Include optional dependencies** checkbox is not selected and click on **Add Required Bundles**, to build a list of the required steps.

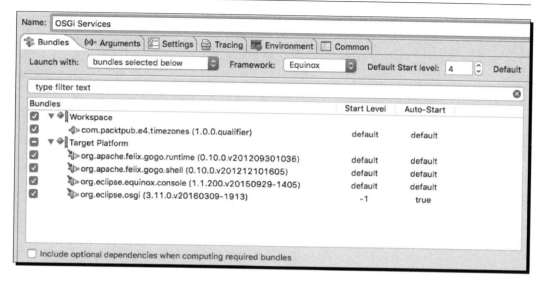

The required bundles are:

- `com.packtpub.e4.timezones`

- `org.apache.felix.gogo.runtime`

- `org.apache.felix.gogo.shell`

- `org.eclipse.equinox.console`

- `org.eclipse.osgi`

On the console, when the bundle is started (which happens automatically if the **Default Auto-Start** is set to `true`), the **Bundle started** message should be seen.

> If the bundle does not start, `ss` in the console will print a list of bundles and `start 2` will start bundle with the id 2. Afterwards, `stop 2` can be used to stop bundle 2. Bundles can be stopped/started dynamically in an OSGi framework.

Registering a service

Once the `TimeZonesActivator` is created, a `BundleContext` will be available for interaction with the framework. This can be persisted for subsequent use in an instance field, but can also be used directly to register a service.

The `BundleContext` provides a method called `registerService`, which takes an interface, an instance, and an optional `Dictionary` of key/value pairs. This can be used to register instances of the timezone provider with the runtime.

A `TimeZonesService` interface needs to be provided, along with an implementation. Create an interface called `TimeZonesService` in the `com.packtpub.e4.timezones` package as follows:

```
package com.packtpub.e4.timezones;
import java.time.ZoneId;
import java.util.Map;
import java.util.Set;

public interface TimeZonesService {
  public Map<String, Set<ZoneId>> getTimeZones();
}
```

Create an implementation in the `TimeZonesProvider` class, using the code developed in the *Creating an Empty TimeZone View* section of *Chapter 2, Creating Views with SWT*, in the `com.packtpub.e4.timezones.internal` package as follows:

```
public class TimeZonesProvider implements TimeZonesService {
  public Map<String, Set<ZoneId>> getTimeZones() {
    Supplier<Set<ZoneId>> sortedZones =
      () -> new TreeSet<>(new TimeZoneComparator());
    return ZoneId.getAvailableZoneIds().stream() // stream
      .filter(s -> s.contains("/")) // with / in them
      .map(ZoneId::of) // convert to ZoneId
      .collect(Collectors.groupingBy( // and group by
      z -> z.getId().split("/")[0], // first part
      TreeMap::new, Collectors.toCollection(sortedZones)));
  }
}
```

The `TimeZonesComparator` allows time zones to be compared by their ID:

```
public class TimeZonesComparator implements Comparator<ZoneId> {
  @Override
  public int compare(ZoneId o1, ZoneId o2) {
    return o1.getID().compareTo(o2.getID());
  }
}
```

Now that the provider is available, it can be registered as a service in the `TimeZonesActivator` method `start` as follows:

```
public void start(BundleContext context) throws Exception {
  context.registerService(TimeZonesService.class,
    new TimeZonesProvider(), null);
}
```

Now start the framework again. In the console that is launched, look for the result corresponding to the `timezones` bundle:

```
osgi> bundles | grep timezones
com.packtpub.e4.timezones_1.0.0.qualifier [5]
  {com.packtpub.e4.timezones.TimeZonesService}={service.id=42}
```

This shows that the bundle 5 has started a service, using the interface `com.packtpub.e4.timezones.TimeZonesService`, and with service ID 42.

It is also possible to query the runtime framework for services of a known interface type directly using the `services` command and an LDAP style filter:

```
osgi> services
  "(objectClass=com.packtpub.e4.timezones.TimeZonesService)"

{com.packtpub.e4.timezones.TimeZonesService}={service.id=42}
  "Registered by bundle:"
    com.packtpub.e4.timezones_1.0.0.qualifier [5]
  "No bundles using service."
```

The results displayed represent the service instantiated by the timezones bundle. It can be introspected using the `service` command by passing the `service.id`:

```
osgi> service 42
TimeZones [Africa=[Africa/Abidjan, Africa/Accra, Africa/...
```

Priority of services

Services have an implicit order, based on the order in which they were instantiated. Each time a service is registered, a global `service.id` is incremented.

It is possible to define an explicit **service ranking** with an integer property. This is used to ensure relative priority between equivalent services, regardless of the order in which they are registered. For services with equal `service.ranking` values, the `service.id` values are compared.

 OSGi R6 provides an additional property, `service.bundleid`, which is used to denote the `id` of the bundle that provides the service. This is not used to order services and is for informational purposes only.

To pass a priority into the service registration, create a helper method called `priority` that takes an `int` and returns a `Hashtable` with the key `service.ranking` using that value. This can be used to pass a priority into the service registration methods:

```
public class TimeZonesActivator implements BundleActivator {
  public void start(BundleContext context) throws Exception {
    context.registerService(TimeZonesService.class,
      new TimeZonesProvider(), priority(1));
  }
  private Dictionary<String, Object> priority(int priority) {
    Hashtable<String, Object> dict = new Hashtable<>();
    dict.put("service.ranking", Integer.valueOf(priority));
    return dict;
  }
}
```

Now when the framework starts, the services are displayed in priority ordering:

```
osgi> services | grep timezones
{com.packtpub.e4.timezones.TimeZonesService}=
 {service.ranking=1, service.id=42, service.bundleid=5,
  service.scope=singleton}
"Registered by bundle:"
 com.packtpub.e4.timezones_1.0.0.qualifier [5]
```

`Dictionary` was the original Java Map interface, and `Hashtable` the original HashMap implementation. They fell out of favor in Java 1.2 when `Map` and `HashMap` were introduced (mainly because they weren't synchronized by default), but OSGi was developed to run on early releases of Java (JSR 8 proposed adding OSGi as a standard for the Java platform back in 1999). Not only that, early low-powered Java mobile devices didn't support the full Java platform, instead exposing the original Java 1.1 data structures. Because of this history, many APIs in OSGi refer to only Java 1.1 data structures, so that low-powered devices can still run OSGi systems.

Using the services

The `BundleContext` can be used to acquire services as well as register them.

One way of obtaining an instance of `BundleContext` is to store it in the `TimeZonesActivator.start` method as a `static` variable. That way, classes elsewhere in the bundle will be able to acquire the context, along with an accessor method. A better way is to use `FrameworkUtil.getBundle(class).getBundleContext()` instead.

A `TimeZonesFactory` can be created to acquire the `TimeZoneService`. OSGi services are represented via a `ServiceReference` (which is a sharable object representing a handle to the service); this in turn can be used to acquire a service instance:

```
public class TimeZonesFactory {
  private static final Bundle bundle =
    FrameworkUtil.getBundle(TimeZonesService.class);
  private static final BundleContext context =
    bundle.getBundleContext();
  private static final ServiceReference<TimeZonesService> sr =
    context.getServiceReference(TimeZonesService.class);
}
```

The service instance is acquired with the `context.getService(ServiceReference)` call. The contract is that the caller 'borrows' the service, and when finished should return it with an `ungetService(ServiceReference)` call. This can be wrapped in a block taking a `Consumer<TimeZonesService>` (which makes it easy to use with lambdas):

```
public static void use(Consumer<TimeZonesService> consumer) {
  TimeZonesService service = context.getService(sr);
  try {
    consumer.accept(service);
  } finally {
    context.ungetService(sr);
  }
}
```

Technically the service is only supposed to be used between the `getService` and `ungetService` call as its lifetime may be invalid afterwards; instead of returning a service references, the common pattern is to pass in a unit of work that accepts the service and call the `ungetService` afterwards.

 Note that the preceding example requires better error handling, such as checking for `null` and responding appropriately to the caller. This is left as an exercise for the reader.

Lazy activation of bundles

By default bundles are not started when they are accessed for the first time. If the bundle needs its activator to be called prior to using any of the classes in the package, it needs to be marked as having an **activation policy** of **lazy**. This is done by adding the following entry to the `MANIFEST.MF` file:

```
Bundle-ActivationPolicy: lazy
```

The manifest editor can be used to add this configuration line, by selecting **Activate this plug-in when one of its classes is loaded**.

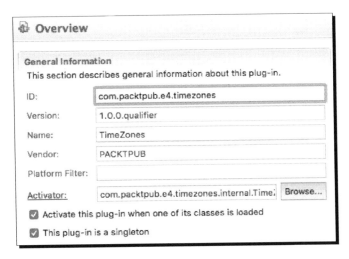

Comparison of services and extension points

Both mechanisms (using the extension registry and using the services) allow for a list of services to be contributed and used by the application. What are the differences between them and are there any advantages to one or the other?

Both the registry and services approaches can be used outside of an Eclipse runtime. They work the same way when used in other OSGi implementations (such as Felix) and can be used interchangeably. The registry approach can also be used outside of OSGi, although that is far less common.

The registry encodes its information in the `plugin.xml` file by default, which means that it is typically edited as part of a bundle's install (it is possible to create registry entries from alternative implementations if desired, but this rarely happens). The registry has a notification system that can listen to contributions being added and removed.

The services approach uses the OSGi framework to store and maintain a list of services. These don't have an explicit configuration file and in fact can be contributed by code (such as the `registerService` calls previously covered) or by declarative representations (which are covered in the next section).

The separation of how the service is created versus how the service is registered is a key difference between this and the registry approach. Like the registry, the OSGi services system is able to generate notifications when services come and go.

One key difference in an OSGi runtime is that bundles depending on the Eclipse registry must be declared as **singletons**; that is, they have to use the `;singleton:=true` directive on the `Bundle-SymbolicName`. This means there can only be one version of a bundle that exposes registry entries in a runtime, as opposed to multiple versions in the general services case.

While the registry does provide mechanisms to be able to instantiate extensions from factories, these typically involve simple configurations and/or properties that are hard-coded in the `plugin.xml` files themselves, which would not be appropriate for storing sensitive details such as passwords. On the other hand, a service can be instantiated from whatever external configuration information is necessary and then registered, such as a JDBC connection for a database.

Finally extensions in the registry are declarative by default and are activated on demand. This allows Eclipse to start up quickly as it does not need to build the full set of class loader objects or run code, and then bring up services on demand. Although the approach previously didn't use declarative services, it is possible to do this as covered in the next section.

Registering a service declaratively

Registering services imperatively in the `start` method of an `Activator` method is one way of installing services in an OSGi framework. However it requires that the bundle be started, which requires that either the bundle is started automatically or has classes (such as API classes) accessed by default. Both approaches will mean that additional code has to run to bring the system into the desired state.

An alternative is to use one of the declarative service approaches, which represent the service definition in an external file. These are processed using an **extender pattern**, which looks out for bundles with a given file or files and then instantiates the service from this definition. It combines the declarative nature of the extension registry with the flexibility of OSGi services.

There are two providers of declarative service support, which both achieve a similar result but use slightly different configuration files and approaches. They are **Declarative Services** and **Blueprint**. Since the most common use case for Eclipse plug-ins is to use Declarative Services, they will be covered here (Blueprint is covered in *Mastering Eclipse Plug-in Development* by the same author).

Declarative Services

Declarative Services, or simply **DS**, was the original declarative implementation for instantiating services in a declarative fashion in an OSGi runtime. Both Equinox and Felix have DS modules, and it is a required part of the Eclipse 4 runtime, so can be trivially expected to be present. In the OSGi specification, it is referred to as the **Services Component Runtime** (**SCR**), which is why the associated package names use `org.osgi.service.component.`

The DS bundle needs to be started before it can process bundles; as a result, it is typically started early on. It listens to bundles being installed and then looks for a specific header in the `META-INF/MANIFEST.MF`:

```
Service-Component: OSGI-INF/*.xml
```

If the DS bundle finds this header, it looks for files contained in the bundle itself matching the file pattern specified. This is a comma-separated list, and can use a single wildcard `*` character (which will match file names but not directories).

The **service document** is then loaded and parsed, and used to instantiate and register services with the OSGi runtime environment. The XML document uses namespaces to represent the component, using `http://www.osgi.org/xmlns/scr/v1.2.0`. Different versions of SCR use different endings; v1.0.0 is defined as the first version, with v1.1.0 the second. The current version (as of the writing of this book) uses the suffix v1.3.0.

Each service document defines a single service, which has an implementation class as well as an identifier. The service can be registered under one or more interfaces, as well as optional priorities.

This can be used to remove the custom code in the `TimeZonesActivator` created previously, by deleting the class and removing the `Bundle-Activator` from the manifest.

If the application is run now, the service won't be registered. To register these as OSGi services declaratively, create a file called `OSGI-INF/timezones.xml`:

```xml
<?xml version="1.0" encoding="UTF-8"?>
<scr:component xmlns:scr="http://www.osgi.org/xmlns/scr/v1.1.0"
 name="TimeZonesProvider">
 <implementation
  class="com.packtpub.e4.timezones.internal.TimeZonesProvider"/>
  <service>
   <provide
    interface="com.packtpub.e4.timezones.TimeZonesService"/>
  </service>
</scr:component>
```

> Don't forget to tell Eclipse to consider this part of the build by adding `OSGI-INF/` to the `build.properties` file in the `bin.includes` property.

As long as a declarative services provider is installed in the application and started, the service will be created on demand.

> Client bundles should be able to express a dependency on a Declarative Services provider by using the following requirement in the manifest:
>
> ```
> Require-Capability:
>   osgi.extender;osgi.extender="osgi.component"
> ```
>
> However, this is not yet implemented in Eclipse.
>
> The launch configuration can detect whether or not declarative services are installed with the **Validate Bundles** button, but at the moment the **Add Required Bundles** button does not resolve the problem. At present the `org.eclipse.equinox.ds` bundle must be resolved manually to fix this problem. It will also require `org.eclipse.equinox.util` and `org.eclipse.osgi.services` to be added to the launch configuration.

Properties and Declarative Services

Declarative Services can also be used to register properties with the service when it is registered. These properties can be sourced either from the services XML file or an external properties file.

To add the `service.ranking` property to the registered service, add the following into the services document:

```xml
<?xml version="1.0" encoding="UTF-8"?>
<scr:component xmlns:scr="http://www.osgi.org/xmlns/scr/v1.1.0"
  name="TimeZonesProvider">
  ...
  <property name="service.ranking" type="Integer" value="2"/>
</scr:component>
```

When the application is restarted, the `services` console command will show that the `service.ranking` property is associated with the `TimeZonesService`:

```
osgi> services | grep timezones
{com.packtpub.e4.timezones.TimeZonesService}=
  {service.ranking=2,
   component.name=TimeZonesProvider,
   component.id=0,
```

```
service.id=48,
service.bundleid=11,
service.scope=bundle}
```

 If the property isn't listed, add a -clean argument to the Eclipse runtime console; sometimes the files are cached and PDE doesn't always notice when files are changed.

The property types can be one of:

- String (default)
- Long
- Double
- Float
- Integer
- Byte
- Character
- Boolean
- Short

Additionally, arrays of elements can be specified by placing them in the body of the element instead of as an attribute:

```
<?xml version="1.0" encoding="UTF-8"?>
<scr:component xmlns:scr="http://www.osgi.org/xmlns/scr/v1.1.0"
  name="TimeZonesProvider">
  ...
  <property name="compass.point" type="String">
    NORTH
    EAST
    SOUTH
    WEST
  </property>
</scr:component>
```

Service references in Declarative Services

As well as hard-coded values, it is also possible to set up references to services in DS. The service implementation can have bind and unbind methods, which are called when a service becomes available or goes away.

These can be mandatory or optional; if the dependency is mandatory then the service is not presented until its dependencies are available. If they are optional, the service can come up and be assigned later. They can also be single-valued or multi-valued. These are encoded in the relationships **cardinality**:

- ◆ `0..1`: This service is optional, either zero or one instance needed
- ◆ `1..1`: This service is mandatory, exactly one instance needed (default)
- ◆ `0..n`: This service is optional, may have zero or more instances
- ◆ `1..n`: This service is mandatory, may have one or more instances

This can be used to inject a `LogService` (from the `org.osgi.service.log` package; it may be necessary to add this as an imported package to the bundle) into the component. Modify the `TimeZonesProvider` to accept an instance of the `LogService` by adding a `setLog` and `unsetLog` method:

```
private LogService logService;
public void setLog(LogService logService) {
  this.logService = logService;
}
public void unsetLog(LogService logService) {
  this.logService = null;
}
```

This can be used to report on how many time zones are loaded in the `getTimeZones` method of the `TimeZonesProvider` class:

```
if (logService != null) {
  logService.log(LogService.LOG_INFO,
    "Time zones loaded with " + timeZones.size());
}
```

To configure DS to provide a log service, the following must be added to the `timezones.xml` file:

```
<scr:component name="TimeZonesProvider"
 xmlns:scr="http://www.osgi.org/xmlns/scr/v1.1.0">
 ...
 <reference interface="org.osgi.service.log.LogService"
  cardinality="0..1" name="log"
  bind="setLog" unbind="unsetLog"/>
</scr:component>
```

This tells DS that the log service is optional (so it will bring the service up before a `LogService` is available), and that `setLog(log)` will be called when it is available. DS also provides an `unbind` method which can be used to remove the service if it goes away. The instance is provided for both the `setLog` and `unsetLog` method, which may look strange—but when setting multiple elements the methods are typically called `addThing` and `removeThing`, which may be more appropriate.

Multiple components and debugging Declarative Services

Although this seems to imply that an XML file can only contain one component, in fact an XML parent element can be defined with multiple `scr` namespaced children. Since all elements outside the `scr` namespace are ignored, it is possible to embed an XHTML document with an `scr` namespaced element inside, and still have it picked up by Declarative Services:

```
<xhtml>
  <h1>Example HTML file with SCR elements</h1>
  <h2>Component One</h2>
  <scr:component name="One" xmlns:scr="http://...">
    ...
  </scr:component>
  <h2>Component Two</h2>
  <scr:component name="Two" xmlns:scr="http://...">
    ...
  </scr:component>
</xhtml>
```

Note that many developers will use a one-to-one mapping between service components and corresponding XML files; it is rare to see a single XML file with multiple service components. It is recommended to only put one component per XML file for ease of maintenance.

When using DS inside Equinox, using `-Dequinox.ds.print=true` gives additional diagnostic information on the state of the declarative services, including highlighting what services are waiting. For Felix, specifying `-Dds.showtrace=true` can increase logging, as can `-Dds.loglevel=4`.

Dynamic Service annotations

Although XML allows for flexibility, it has fallen out of fashion in the Java community in favor of Java annotations. The 1.2 version of the OSGi DS specification provides annotations that can be used to mark the code such that a build time processor can create the service component XML files automatically.

Note that the standard OSGi annotations are not read at runtime by the service but only build-time tools such as `maven-scr-plugin`. As a result they should be optionally imported, since they aren't needed at runtime, or with `compile` scope if using a Maven-based build.

To use the annotations, add the following as an `Import-Package` for the bundle in the `MANIFEST.MF`:

```
Import-Package:
 org.osgi.service.component.annotations;
 version="1.2.0";
 resolution:=optional
```

The `@Component` annotation can now be added to the individual classes that should be represented as services. Add this to the `TimeZonesProvider`:

```
import org.osgi.service.component.annotations.Component;
@Component(name="TimeZonesProvider2",
  service={TimeZonesService.class},
  property={"service.ranking:Integer=1"})
public class TimeZonesProvider implements TimeZonesService {
  ...
}
```

Processing annotations at Maven build time

If using Maven Tycho to build bundles, it is possible to add a Maven plug-in to generate the service xml files from components. Maven Tycho is covered in more detail in *Chapter 12, Automated Builds with Tycho*.

To configure the `maven-scr-plugin` to a build, first add the following dependency to the `pom.xml` file:

```
<dependencies>
  <dependency>
    <groupId>org.apache.felix</groupId>
    <artifactId>org.apache.felix.scr.ds-annotations</artifactId>
    <version>1.2.8</version>
    <scope>compile</scope>
  </dependency>
</dependencies>
```

This both provides the `org.osgi.service.component.annotations` classes as well as the processing engine necessary to generate the components. Note that even if other dependencies are given (say, `osgi.enterprise` or `equinox.ds`) this isn't sufficient on its own to generate the `service.xml` files.

Next the plugin needs to be added to the `pom.xml` file:

```
<build>
  <plugins>
    <plugin>
      <groupId>org.apache.felix</groupId>
      <artifactId>maven-scr-plugin</artifactId>
      <version>1.22.0</version>
      <configuration>...</configuration>
      <executions>...</executions>
    </plugin>
  </plugins>
  <sourceDirectory>src</sourceDirectory>
</build>
```

The source directory needs to be specified to match the value of the source attribute of the `build.properties` file (which is used by `eclipse-plugin` instead of `sourceDirectory`), as otherwise the `maven-scr-plugin` cannot find the source files.

The plug-in needs to be configured specifically for `eclipse-plugin` projects. Firstly, the supported projects default to `jar` and `bundle` for the `maven-scr-plugin`, so it needs to be given additional configuration to permit processing `eclipse-plugin` projects.

Secondly the service files are written to `target/classes/` by default. Although this will work, it makes for more difficult debugging in Eclipse. Instead, the `maven-scr-plugin` can be configured to write it to the project root, which will place the service files under `OSGI-INF`. This permits the code to be tested in Eclipse as well as exported using the standard build tools:

```
<configuration>
  <supportedProjectTypes>
    <supportedProjectType>eclipse-plugin</supportedProjectType>
  </supportedProjectTypes>
  <outputDirectory>${basedir}</outputDirectory>
</configuration>
```

Finally, to hook it in with the standard build process, add the following to the build:

```
<executions>
  <execution>
    <id>generate-scr</id>
```

```
      <goals>
        <goal>scr</goal>
      </goals>
    </execution>
  </executions>
```

Now when the package is built, the service descriptor xml file will be automatically be regenerated based on the annotations. The file name is derived from the class name.

Dynamic services

The OSGi specification defines four different layers:

- **Security Layer**: In this layer, all actions are checked against a security permissions model
- **Module Layer**: In this layer, modules are specified as bundles that have dependencies
- **Life Cycle Layer**: This layer bundles coming and going and firing events
- **Service Layer**: In this layer, dynamic services that come and go

The Services layer allows bundles to communicate by defining an API that can cross bundle layers. However, the services layer also allows the services to come and go dynamically, instead of being fixed at runtime.

This mechanism allows services to be exported over a network, and since the network can come and go (as can the remote endpoint) the OSGi services layer can replicate that same functionality.

Responding to services dynamically coming and going may add a slight difficulty to the client code, but it will be more robust in case of failure. The following sections will present different ways of achieving dynamism in services.

Resolving services each time

The easiest way of working with dynamic services is to list the services each time they are needed. The example so far uses this technique to allow different services to be contributed.

This technique can work if the list of services is infrequently needed. However each time the lookup is performed, there is a cost to the acquisition, which may not be desirable.

Using a ServiceTracker

The OSGi framework provides a `ServiceTracker` class which can be used to simplify the acquisition of one or more services in a standard way. Provided in the `org.osgi.util.tracker` package, the `ServiceTracker` class has a constructor that takes a class and a `BundleContext` object, along with an optional filter specification.

 The `ServiceTracker` has an `open` method which must be called prior to use, as otherwise it will not return any services.

Add the package to the `timezones` bundle's manifest as an import:

```
Import-Package: org.osgi.util.tracker
```

Modify the `TimeZonesFactory` so that a `ServiceTracker` is acquired in a `static` initializer, and that `open` is called. This simplifies the `use` method to simply delegate to the service tracker:

```
public class TimeZonesFactory {
  private static final Bundle bundle =
    FrameworkUtil.getBundle(TimeZonesService.class);
  private static final BundleContext context =
    bundle.getBundleContext();
  private static final ServiceTracker<TimeZonesService,
    TimeZonesService> tracker =
    new ServiceTracker<>(context,TimeZonesService.class, null);
  static {
    tracker.open(); // Remember to call this!
  }
  public static void use(Consumer<TimeZonesService> consumer) {
    consumer.accept(tracker.getService());
  }
}
```

The `ServiceTracker` also has a `close` method, which should be called when services are no longer required to be tracked.

 Generally tying the service tracker's lifecycle to another lifecycle is more appropriate, as otherwise this can leak implementation.

Filtering services

The service tracker, as it is currently implemented, returns all compatible services that implement the interface (if `true` is passed to the `open` call, both compatible and incompatible services are returned; this should generally not be used).

It is also possible to use a filter to restrict the list of services that are returned. OSGi filters are specified using the LDAP filter syntax, which uses prefix notation and parentheses to group elements. Here is how to read it:

- A and B: `(&(A)(B))`
- A or B: `(|(A)(B))`
- Not A: `(!(A))`
- A equals B: `(A=B)`
- A contains B: `(A=*B*)`

These can be nested to form complex queries.

The `services` command in the Equinox console allows a filter to be evaluated. Each service is published into the registry, and the filter `objectClass=` allows services matching a particular interface to be found, as was done earlier in the chapter:

```
osgi> services "(objectClass=*.TimeZonesService)"
{com.packtpub.e4.timezones.TimeZonesService}={service.ranking=2,
  component.name=TimeZonesProvider, component.id=0, service.id=48}
```

It's possible to filter on other properties as well. For example, DS registers a `component.id` property with a service, so this can be used to create a filter for just DS registered components:

```
osgi> services "(&(objectClass=*.TimeZonesService)(component.id=*))"
{com.packtpub.e4.timezones.TimeZonesService}={service.ranking=2,
  component.name=TimeZonesProvider, component.id=0, service.id=48}
```

This looks for services ending in `TimeZonesService` and which have a value for the `component.id` property.

Filters can be included in the `ServiceTracker` to ensure that only desired services are picked up. For example, to include only services that aren't registered by DS, the following can be coded into the `ServiceTracker`:

```
Filter filter = context.createFilter(
  "(&(objectClass=*.TimeZonesService)(!(component.id=*)))");
st = new ServiceTracker<TimeZonesService, TimeZonesService>(
  context, filter, null);
st.open();
```

This may be useful to enable debugging; the filter could be overridden by a system property, for example. Note that the `createFilter` method throws a checked syntax exception if it is invalid, which must be handled in the code.

Obtaining a BundleContext without using an activator

Since the `ServiceTracker` needs the `BundleContext` to register a listener, it is conventional to set up a `BundleActivator` for the sole purpose of acquiring a `BundleContext`.

Since this incurs a performance penalty, using a different mechanism to acquire the context will speed the start-up process. Fortunately there is a class, `FrameworkUtil`, that can be used to acquire a `Bundle` for any given class, and from there, the `BundleContext`. This allows the implementation of the `TimeZonesActivator` to be removed:

```
BundleContext context = FrameworkUtil.
    getBundle(TimeZonesFactory.class).getBundleContext();
```

Using this mechanism adds no performance penalty and should be used in favor of a global static instance to the `BundleContext`. It also potentially allows the bundle's activator to be removed from the bundle.

 If the bundle is not started, it will not have a `BundleContext` and so the returned value here may be `null`. Code should defensively handle this case.

Dependent Services

It is fairly common that an OSGi service depends on other OSGi services. As such it can help if the services are set up and made available when the bundles are available. The Declarative Services approach can be used to register services on demand when the requirements are satisfied.

For DS, when the cardinality of the relationship is not optional (in other words, the relationship is `1..1` or `1..n`), then the service won't be started until the required dependent services are available. For example, a menu service may not be required until the graphical user interface service is present; and services that wish to contribute to the menu service won't be able to work until the menu service is present.

Delaying the creation of the services until they are needed will result in shorter start-up times of the application.

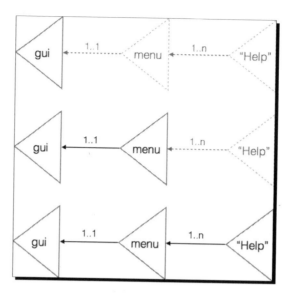

Dynamic service configuration

OSGi provides a standard configuration mechanism called **config admin**. This allows the location of configuration information to be decoupled from the code that requires the configuration. Configuration is passed through to services via a `Map` or `Hashtable`, and they can configure themselves appropriately.

As with other parts in OSGi, this can also be dynamically updated. When the configuration source changes; an event can flow through to the service or component to allow it to reconfigure itself.

Installing Felix FileInstall

Config admin itself is an OSGi service, and it may be supplied by different configuration agents. The de facto standard is Apache Felix's **FileInstall**, which can also be used to install bundles into an OSGi runtime.

FileInstall is available from the Apache Felix site at `http://felix.apache.org` as well as Maven Central. Search for `org.apache.felix.fileinstall` at `http://search.maven.org` and download the latest Jar. It can be imported into Eclipse as a plug-in project with **File | Import | Plug-in Development | Plug-ins and Fragments** to enable it to run in a test runtime.

The system property `felix.fileinstall.dir` must be specified to use FileInstall. It defaults to `./load` from the current working directory, but for the purpose of testing, this can be specified by adding a VM argument in the launch configuration that appends `-Dfelix.fileinstall.dir=/tmp/config` or some other location. This can be used to test modifications to configuration later.

 Make sure that FileInstall is configured to start when the runtime begins, so that it picks up configurations. This can be done by specifying the start level on the OSGi framework launch configuration page, or by using the console to verify that the bundle's state is **ACTIVE**.

Installing ConfigAdmin

To configure services, ConfigAdmin needs to be installed into the runtime as well. The two standard implementations of these are Felix ConfigAdmin and Equinox Config Admin. The latter does not come with Eclipse by default, and the Felix version is available from Maven Central and should be preferred. Search for `org.apache.felix.configadmin` at `http://search.maven.org`, download the latest Jar, and then import this as a plug-in project to Eclipse with **File | Import | Plug-in Development | Plug-ins and Fragments** so that it can be used as a bundle in the OSGi framework.

Configuring Declarative Services

A component created by Declarative Services can have configurations passed in a `Map`. A component can have an `activate` method, which is called after the component's dependencies have become available (along with a corresponding `deactivate` method). There is also a `modified` method, which can be used to respond to changes in configuration without stopping and restarting the component.

To configure the `TimeZonesProvider` with config admin, add a `configure` method that takes a `Map` of values. If it's non-`null` and there is a key `max`, then parse it as an `int` and use that as the `max` value. Use this to set a limit on the number of time zones returned in the `getTimeZones` method:

```
private long max = Long.MAX_VALUE;
public Map<String, Set<ZoneId>> getTimeZones() {
...
  .filter(s -> s.contains("/")) // with / in them
  .limit(max) // return this many only
  .map(ZoneId::of) // convert to ZoneId
...
}
```

```java
public void configure(Map<String, Object> properties) {
    max = Long.MAX_VALUE;
    if (properties != null) {
        String maxStr = (String) properties.get("max");
        if (maxStr != null) {
            max = Long.parseLong(maxStr);
        }
    }
}
```

To ensure that the method gets called, modify the service component document to add the `activate="configure"` and `modified="configure"` attributes:

```xml
<scr:component xmlns:scr="http://www.osgi.org/xmlns/scr/v1.1.0"
    modified="configure" activate="configure"
    name="TimeZonesProvider">
```

Finally, create a properties file with the contents `max=1` called `TimeZonesProvider.cfg`, and place it in the location of the `felix.fileinstall.dir`.

Now when the application is run, the configuration should be loaded and configure the `TimeZonesProvider`, such that when the time zones are requested, it shows a maximum of one value.

If nothing is seen, verify that the `felix.fileinstall.dir` is specified correctly using `props | grep felix` from the OSGi console. Also verify that the Felix `fileinstall` and `configadmin` bundles are started. Finally, verify that the methods in the component are `public void` and are defined correctly in the component config.

Service factories

A service factory can be used to create services on demand, rather than being provided up front. OSGi defines a number of different service factories that have different behaviors.

Ordinarily services published into the registry are shared between all bundles. OSGi R6 adds a `service.scope` property, and uses the `singleton` value to indicate that the same instance is shared between all bundles.

Service factories allow multiple instances to be created, and there are three different types:

- `ServiceFactory`, which creates a new instance per bundle (registered with `service.scope=bundle` in OSGi R6)

- `ManagedServiceFactory`, which uses config admin to create instances per configuration/pid (registered with `service.scope=bundle` in OSGi R6)

- `PrototypeServiceFactory`, which allows multiple instances per bundle (newly added in OSGi R6 registered with `service.scope=prototype`)

The `ServiceFactory` allows a per-client bundle instance to be created, to avoid bundles sharing state. When a client bundle requests a service, if the bundle has already requested the service then the same instance is returned; if not, a service is instantiated. When the client bundle goes away, so does the associated service instance.

A `ManagedServiceFactory` provides a means to instantiate multiple services instead of a single service per component. Multiple instances of a service can be created, each with their own configuration using `service.pid-somename.cfg`. Each bundle shares the instances of these services, but other client bundles will instantiate their own. Like `ServiceFactory`, if the service has been requested before, the same bundle will be returned.

The `PrototypeServiceFactory` was added in OSGi R6 (available since Eclipse Luna) as a means of providing a bundle with multiple instances of the same service. Instead of caching the previously delivered service per bundle, a new one is instantiated each time it is looked up. The client code can use `BundleContext.getServiceObjects(ref)` `.getService()` to acquire a service through the `PrototypeServiceFactory`. This allows stateful services to be created.

Creating the EchoService

As an example, consider an `EchoServer` that listens on a specific `ServerSocket` port. This can be run on zero or many ports at the same time. This code will be used by the next section, and simply creates a server running on a port and sets up a single thread to accept client connections and echo back what is typed. The code here is presented without explanation other than its purpose, and will be used to create multiple instances of this service in the next section.

When this is instantiated on a port (for example, when `new EchoServer(1234)` is called) it will be possible to `telnet` to the `localhost` on port `1234` and have content echoed back as it is typed. To close the connection, use *Ctrl +]* and then type `close`:

```
public class EchoServer implements Runnable {
  private ServerSocket socket;
  private boolean running = true;
  private Thread thread;
  public EchoServer(int port) throws IOException {
    this.socket = new ServerSocket(port);
    this.thread = new Thread(this);
    this.thread.setDaemon(true);
    this.thread.start();
  }
  public void run() {
    try {
      byte[] buffer = new byte[1024];
```

```
          while (running) {
            Socket client = null;
            try {
              client = socket.accept();
              InputStream in = client.getInputStream();
              OutputStream out = client.getOutputStream();
              int read;
              while (running && (read = in.read(buffer)) > 0) {
                out.write(buffer, 0, read);
                out.flush();
              }
            } catch (InterruptedIOException e) {
              running = false;
            } catch (Exception e) {
            } finally {
              safeClose(client);
            }
          }
        } finally {
          safeClose(socket);
        }
      }
      public void safeClose(Closeable closeable) {
        try {
          if (closeable != null) {
            closeable.close();
          }
        } catch (IOException e) {
        }
      }
      public void stop() {
        running = false;
        this.thread.interrupt();
      }
    }
```

Creating an EchoServiceFactory

Create an `EchoServiceFactory` that implements `ManagedServiceFactory`, and register it as a managed service factory in a component:

```
<?xml version="1.0" encoding="UTF-8"?>
<scr:component xmlns:scr="http://www.osgi.org/xmlns/scr/v1.1.0"
  name="EchoServiceFactory">
  <implementation
```

```
      class="com.packtpub.e4.timezones.internal.EchoServiceFactory"/>
    <service>
     <provide
       interface="org.osgi.service.cm.ManagedServiceFactory"/>
    </service>
    <property name="service.pid" type="String"
      value="com.packtpub.e4.timezones.internal.EchoServiceFactory"/>
  </scr:component>
```

The EchoServiceFactory is responsible for managing the children that it creates and, since they will be using threads, appropriately stopping them afterwards. The ManagedServiceFactory has three methods; getName, which returns the name of the service, and updated and deleted methods for reacting to configurations coming and going. To track them, create an instance variable in the EchoServiceFactory called echoServers which is a map of pid to EchoServer instances:

```
  public class EchoServiceFactory implements ManagedServiceFactory {
    private Map<String, EchoServer> echoServers =
     new TreeMap<String, EchoServer>();
    public String getName() {
      return "Echo service factory";
    }
    public void updated(String pid, Dictionary<String, ?> props)
     throws ConfigurationException {
    }
    public void deleted(String pid) {
    }
  }
```

The updated method will do two things; it will determine if a port is present in the properties, and if so, instantiate a new EchoServer on the given port. If not, it will deconfigure the service:

```
  public void updated(String pid, Dictionary<String, ?> properties)
   throws ConfigurationException {
    if (properties != null) {
      String portString = properties.get("port").toString();
      try {
        int port = Integer.parseInt(portString);
        System.out.println("Creating echo server on port " + port);
        echoServers.put(pid, new EchoServer(port));
      } catch (Exception e) {
        throw new ConfigurationException("port",
          "Cannot create a server on port " + portString, e);
      }
```

```
    } else if (echoServers.containsKey(pid)) {
      deleted(pid);
    }
  }
}
```

If an error occurs while creating the service (because the port number isn't specified, isn't a valid integer, or is already in use), an exception will be propagated back to the runtime engine, which will be appropriately logged.

The `deleted` method removes it if present, and stops it:

```
public void deleted(String pid) {
  System.out.println("Removing echo server with pid " + pid);
  EchoServer removed = echoServers.remove(pid);
  if (removed != null) {
    removed.stop();
  }
}
```

Configuring the EchoServices

Now that the service is implemented, how is it configured? Unlike singleton configurations, the `ManagedServiceFactory` expects the `pid` to be a prefix of the name, followed by a dash (-) and then a custom suffix.

Ensure that the `timezones` bundle is started, and that the `EchoServiceFactory` is registered and waiting for configurations to appear:

```
osgi> ss | grep timezones
13 ACTIVE com.packtpub.e4.timezones._1.0.0.qualifier
osgi> start 13
osgi> bundle 13 | grep service.pid
{org.osgi.service.cm.ManagedServiceFactory}={
service.pid=com.packtpub.e4.timezones.internal.EchoServiceFactory}
```

Now create a configuration file in the Felix install directory `com.packtpub.`
`e4.timezones.internal.EchoServiceFactory.cfg` with the content `port=1234`.
Nothing happens.

Now rename the file to something with an `-extension` on the end, such as `-1234`.
The suffix can be anything, but conventionally naming it for the type of instance being created (in this case, a service listening on port `1234`) makes it easier to keep track of the services. For example, create `com.packtpub.e4.timezones.internal.`
`EchoServiceFactory-1234.cfg` with contents `port=1234` in the configuration directory. When this happens, a service will be created:

```
Creating new echo server on port 1234
```

Telnetting to this port can see the output being returned:

```
$ telnet localhost 1234
Connected to localhost.
Escape character is '^]'.
hello
hello
world
world
^]
telnet> close
Connection closed by foreign host.
```

Creating a new service pid will start a new service; create a new file called `com.packtpub.` `e4.timezone.internal.EchoServiceFactory-4242.cfg` with the contents `port=4242`. A new service should be created:

```
Creating new echo server on port 4242
```

Test this by running `telnet localhost 4242`. Does this echo back content as well?

Finally, remove the service configuration for port `1234`. This can be done by either deleting the configuration file, or simply renaming it with a different extension:

```
Removing echo server
```

Verify that the service has stopped:

```
$ telnet localhost 1234
Trying 127.0.0.1...
telnet: unable to connect to remote host
```

> `FileInstall` only looks at `*.cfg` files, so renaming the file to `*.cfg.disabled` has the same effect as deleting it, while making it easy to restore it subsequently.

Summary

This appendix looked at OSGi services as an alternative means of providing dependent services in an Eclipse or OSGi application. By registering services either imperatively at bundle startup in an activator, or by using one of the declarative services representations, an operational system can evolve by connecting services together in a single runtime. Different approaches for configuration were shown, with either embedded values in the service component document, or derived from external properties or configuration with config admin.

B

Pop Quiz Answers

Chapter 1 – Creating Your First Plug-in

Eclipse workspaces and plug-ins

1. An Eclipse workspace is the location where all the projects are stored.

2. The naming convention for Eclipse plug-in projects is to use a reverse domain name prefix, such as `com.packtpub`. Additionally UI projects typically have a `.ui.` in their name.

3. The three key files in an Eclipse plug-in are `META-INF/MANIFEST.MF`, `plugin.xml`, and `build.properties`.

Launching Eclipse

1a. Quit the application with **File | Exit**.

1b. Use the stop button from the **Debug** or **Console** views.

2. Launch configurations are similar to pre-canned scripts which can start up an application, set its working directory and environment, and run a class.

3. Launch configurations are modified with the **Run | Run Configurations...** or **Debug | Debug Configurations...** menus.

Debugging

1. Use the **Debug | Debug configurations** or **Debug | Debug As...** menus.

2. Set step filters via the preferences menu to avoid certain package names.

3. Breakpoints can be: conditional, method entry/exit, enabled/disabled, or number of iterations.

4. Set a breakpoint and set it after a **hit count** of 256.

5. Use a conditional breakpoint and set `argument==null` as the condition.

6. Inspecting an object means opening it up in the viewer so that the values of the object can be interrogated and expanded.

7. The expression watches window allows arbitrary expressions to be set.

8. Multiple statements can be set in the breakpoint conditions provided that there is a return statement at the end.

Chapter 2 – Creating Views with SWT

Understanding views

1. In the Eclipse 3.x model, views must be subclasses of `ViewPart`. In the Eclipse 4.x model, parts do not need to have an explicit superclass.

2. In the Eclipse 3.x model, views are registered via an `org.eclipse.ui.views` extension point in the `plugin.xml`.

3. The two arguments that most SWT objects have are a `Composite` parent and an integer flags field.

4. When a widget is disposed, it will have its native resources released to the operating system. Any subsequent actions will throw an `SWTException` with a Widget is disposed message.

5. The Canvas has many drawing operations; to draw a circle, use `drawArc()`, and specify a full orbit.

6. To receive drawing events, a `PaintListener` must be created and associated with the control by using the `addPaintListener` method.

7. UI updates not on the UI thread will generate an `SWTException` with an `Invalid thread access` error.

8. To perform an update on a widget from a non-UI thread, use the `asyncExec` or `syncExec` methods from `Display` (3.x) or `UISynchronize` (4.x) to wrap a `Runnable` or lambda that will run on the UI thread.

9. `SWT.DEFAULT` is used to indicate default options in the flags parameter that is passed to the construction of an SWT widget.

10. Create a `RowData` object with the given size, and associate it with each widget.

Understanding resources

1. Resource leaks occur when an SWT `Resource` is acquired from the OS but then not returned to it via a `dispose` method prior to the object being garbage collected.

2. The different types of resources are `Color`, `Cursor`, `Font`, `GC`, `Image`, `Path`, `Pattern`, `Region`, `TextLayout`, and `Transform`.

3. Run the Eclipse instance in tracing mode, with `org.eclipse.ui/debug` and `org.eclipse.ui/trace/graphics` set, specified in a debug file, and launched with `-debug`.

4. Use the `Display.getDeviceData()` to get the `objects` arrays, and iterate through them.

5. The right way is to register a `DisposeListener` with the view, and the wrong way is to override the `dispose` method.

Understanding widgets

1. Using the `setFocus` method to set the focus on a particular widget.

2. Invoking `redraw` will allow the widget to redraw itself.

3. The `combo` can have a `SelectionListener` associated with it.

4. The `widgetDefaultSelected` is what is called when the default value is used, typically an empty value.

Using SWT

1. Use the `Tray` and `TrayItem` widgets.

2. The `NO_TRIM` means don't draw the edges of the window, or the close/maximize/minimize buttons.

3. Use `setAlpha` to control a widget's transparency, including shells.

4. `setRegion` with a path describing the shape.

5. A `Group` allows you to group things together with a standard item.

6. Most composites use a null layout manager by default; it's only shells and dialogs that have a non-default value.

7. Use a `ScrolledComposite`.

Chapter 3 – Creating JFace Viewers

Understanding JFace

1. `getImage()` is called to determine what image to show for an entry, while `getText()` is used to determine the text value of an entry.

2. The `hasChildren()` method is used to determine whether or not an element is shown with an expandable element, and `getChildren()` is used to calculate a list of children.

3. An `ImageRegistry` is used to share images between plug-ins or different views in plug-ins, with a means of clearing up the resources when the view is disposed.

4. Entries can be styled with an `IStyledLabelProvider`.

Understanding sorting and filters

1. Specifying a `ViewerComparator` can allow elements to be sorted in a different order other than the default one.

2. The `select()` method is used to filter elements, which is originally derived from the Smalltalk terminology.

3. Multiple filters can be combined by setting an array of filters, or by writing a filter to combine two or more filters together.

Understanding interaction

1. Add a `DoubleClickListener` to the view.

2. `Dialog` subclasses are used to create a `Dialog` with custom content.

Understanding tables

1. To show the headers, get the `Table` from the viewer, and use it to call the `setHeaderVisible(true)`.

2. `TableViewerColumn` instances are used to set properties on individual columns and to bind the label provider for the columns.

3. An `ArrayContentProvider` can be used to store items as an array.

4. The `TableViewerColumn` is a class in the JFace package which defines where the data comes from; the `TableColumn` is the underlying SWT widget that the width of the column.

Understanding selection

1. Viewers have the `getSelection` and `setSelection` methods to get and set the selection, using the `ISelection` interface (or more commonly the `IStructuredSelection` interface).

2. The `ISelectionChangedListener` interface is used to receive notifications for selection changes from a viewer.

3. E4 uses the `ESelectionService` to maintain the selected object in the workspace, which can be injected into a part.

4. Although the currently selected object can be injected as a field into a part, it is more common to use an optional method with a `@Named` argument of `IServiceConstants.ACTIVE_SELECTION`.

Chapter 4 – Interacting with the User

Understanding menus

1. A command can be associated with a handler to provide a menu item. Handlers are indirection mechanisms that allow the same menu (example **Copy**) to take on different commands based on which context they are in. It is also possible to have a default command id associated with a menu to avoid this indirection.

2. The M1 key is an alias for *Cmd* on macOS, and for *Ctrl* on other platforms. When defining standard commands like copy (M1+C) it has the expected behaviour on both platforms (*Cmd* + *C* for macOS and *Ctrl* + *C* for others).

3. Keystrokes are bound to commands via a binding, which lists the key(s) necessary to invoke and the associated command/handler.

4. A menu's locationURI is where it will contribute the entry to the UI. These are specified either as relative to an existing menu's contribution, or to its generic additions entry. It is also possible to specify custom ones which are associated with custom code.

5. A pop-up menu is created by adding a menu to the part descriptor, and then enabling contributions by registering with the EMenuService.

Understanding jobs

1. The syncExec() will block and wait for the job to complete before continuing code. The asyncExec() will continue to run after posting the job but before it completes.

2. The UISynchronize instance can be used to run jobs on UI and non-SWT UI threads.

3. The UIJob will always run on the UI thread of the runtime, and direct access of widgets will not run into a thread error. Care should be taken to minimize the amount of time spent in the UI thread so as not to block Eclipse. The Job will run on a non-UI thread, and so does not have access to acquire or modify UI-threaded objects.

4. The Status.OK_STATUS singleton is used to indicate success in general. Although it is possible to instantiate a Status object with an OK code, doing so only increases the garbage collection as the Status result is typically discarded after execution.

5. The CommandService can be injected using DI by using @Inject ICommandService into the E4 view.

6. An icon can be displayed by setting a property on the Job with the name IProgressConstants2.ICON_NAME.

7. SubMonitors are generally easier to use at the start of a method, to ensure that the monitor being passed in is correctly partitioned as appropriate for the task in hand. The SubProgressMonitor should generally not be used.

8. The cancellation should be checked as frequently as possible, so that as soon as the user clicks on **cancel**, the job is aborted.

Understanding errors

1. An informational dialog is shown with `MessageDialog.openInformation()` (and `.openWarning()` and `.openError()` as well). There is also a `MessageDialog.openConfirmation()`, which returns the value of a yes/no answer to the user.

2. The `StatusReporter` provides a means to report statuses such that they can be handled appropriately, but without a UI association.

3. Status reporting is asynchronous by default, although a `BLOCK` option exists to make it synchronous.

4. To combine the results of many things into one report, use a `MultiStatus` object.

Chapter 5 – Storing Preferences and Settings

Understanding preferences

1. The default style is `FLAT` but this can be overridden to provide `GRID`, which provides a better layout for preference pages.

2. There are many subclasses of `FieldEditor`, which include editors for `Boolean`, `Color`, `Combo`, `Font`, `List`, `RadioGroup`, `Scale`, `String`, `Integer`, `Directory`, and `File`.

3. To provide searching in a preference page, keywords must be registered via the `keyword` extension point.

4. The `@Preference` annotation, in conjunction with an `@Inject` annotation, allows a preference store to be injected or a single preference value.

5. If a method is annotated/marked with `@Inject` and the method parameter is marked with `@Parameter`, then the method will be called whenever the value changes.

Chapter 6 – Working with Resources

Understanding resources, builders, and markers

1. If an editor complains of a missing document provider, install an instance of `TextFileDocumentProvider` with the `setDocumentProvider()` method on the editor.

2. An `IResourceProxy` is used by a builder to provide a wrapper around an `IResource`, but which doesn't require the construction of an `IResource` image.

3. An `IPath` is a generic file component that is used to navigate files in folders and projects.

4. A nature is a flavor of a project that enables certain behaviors. It is installed with an update to the project descriptor for the given project.

5. Markers are generally created by a builder—though they can be created by any plug-in on a resource. There is a specific function on the resource that can be used to create a marker of a specific type.

Chapter 7 – Creating Eclipse 4 Applications

Understanding E4

1. The application model is stored in the `e4xmi` file, and provides a way of representing the entire state of the application's UI. It is also persisted on save and then reloaded at startup, so positions of parts and their visibility are persisted. The model is also accessible at runtime via the various M* classes such as `MApplication` and `MPart`, and can be queried and mutated at runtime.

2. Parts are a more generic form of views and editors. Unlike Eclipse 3.x, not everything needs to fit into a `View` or `Editor` category; they are all just parts that contain UI components underneath, and can be organized appropriately.

3. Although extension points aren't used for things like commands, keybindings or views, they are still used to define other extensions to Eclipse such as builders, marker types, and language parsers. The only thing that the Eclipse 4 model moves out of the extension points are the UI-related concepts. Even then, in the Eclipse 4 IDE the backward compatibility mode ensures that all the UI-related extension points are still rendered. For developing IDE plug-ins, the Eclipse 3.x APIs will likely be around for the next couple of Eclipse releases.

4. The Eclipse 4 contexts are essentially a series of `HashMap` objects that contain values (objects) associated with keys. Parts can dynamically obtain content from their context, which includes all the injectable services as well as dynamically changing content such as the current selection. A context is implicit in every part, and inherits up the containment chain, terminating with the OSGi runtime.

5. There are several annotations used by Eclipse 4, including `@Inject` (used to provide a general 'insert value here' instruction to Eclipse), `@Optional` (meaning it can be null), `@Named` (to pull out a specific named value from the context), `@PostConstruct` (called just after the object is created), `@PreDestroy` (called just before the object is destroyed), `@Preference` (to pull out a specific preference value or the preference store), `@EventTopic` and `@UIEventTopic` (for receiving events via the event admin service and on the UI thread respectively), `@Persist` and `@PersistState` (for saving data and view data), `@Execute` and `@CanExecute` (for showing what method to execute, and a Boolean conditional which has a Boolean return to indicate if it can run), `@Creatable` (to indicate that the object can be instantiated), and `@GroupUpdate` (to indicate that updates can be deferred).

6. Messages are sent via the `EventBroker`, which is accessible from the injection context. This can use `sendEvent` or `postEvent` to send data. On the receiving side, using the `@UIEventTopic` or `@EventTopic` annotations is the easiest way to receive values. As with preferences, if it's set up as a method parameter then the changes will be notified.

7. Selection can be accessed using the value from the context with a method injection or value injection using `@Named(IServiceConstants.ACTIVE_SELECTION)`.

Chapter 8 – Migrating to Eclipse 4.x

1. Actions are replaced with handler classes, and annotated with the `@Execute` annotation.

2. A `DoubleClickEvent` provides selection through the `getSelection` method.

3. A view menu will only be shown if the supplementary tab has a tag with `ViewMenu`.

4. Classes are connected to a handler by specifying a contributor URI with a `bundleclass:` URI.

5. A `platform:` URI allows references to resources in other plug-ins, such as graphics or property files; a `bundleclass:` URI allows a reference to a class in a plug-in. The class reference will be automatically converted to a Java `Class`.

6. A part represents a rendered part that is shown on the window; a part descriptor represents the definition of the part such that it can be instantiated on demand.

7. Once the pop-up menu has been created, it is necessary to use the `EMenuService` to register the control handler to the ID specified of the pop-up menu.

8. The selection can be obtained from the viewer using `getSelection`, but this will not trigger when it changes—to receive events when it does change, the viewer will need to have a selection listener added, which can then forward it to the Eclipse 4.x `ESelectionService`.

Chapter 9 – Styling Eclipse 4 Applications

Styling Eclipse 4

1. Eclipse 4 parts can be styled with CSS, and the underlying renderer applies the styles on the fly, including if the CSS styles change. This allows theme managers to apply different color combinations in Eclipse 4 in ways not possible in Eclipse 3.

2. An Eclipse 4 Theme is a pre-configured set of colors and styles that can be applied to a user environment, as well as dynamically switched at runtime.

3. Elements can be referenced by a CSS class name (such as `.MPart`), by an ID (with # as a prefix and substituting–for example `.` in identifier names), or by a Java class name directly.

4. To change all labels in Eclipse to italics, the CSS would look like:

```
Label { font-style: italic }
```

5. The CSS Spy is opened by pressing *Alt + Shift + F5*.

6. The `IThemeEngine` can be used to acquire a list of themes and change them dynamically in the application.

Chapter 10 – Creating Features, Update Sites, Applications, and Products

Understanding features, applications, and products

1. The keyword `qualifier` is replaced with a timestamp when plug-ins or features are built.

2. The files are `artifacts.jar` and `content.jar` as well as one file per feature/plug-in built.

3. The older `site.xml` can be used, or a `category.xml` file which is essentially equivalent.

4. If a feature requires another, then it must be present in the Eclipse instance in order to install. If a feature includes another, then a copy of that included feature is included in the update site when built.

5. An application is a standalone application that can be run in any Eclipse instance when it is installed. A product affects the Eclipse instance as a whole, replacing the launcher, icons, and default application launched.

6. An application is a class that implements `IApplication` and has a `start()` method. It is referenced in the `plugin.xml` file and can be invoked by ID with `-application` on the command line.

7. A target definition is used to define set of plug-ins to compile against, when set as a target platform.

Chapter 11 – Automated Testing of Plug-ins

Understanding swtbot

1. The unit runner that is required is `SWTBotJunit4ClassRunner`, which is set up with an annotation `@RunWith(SWTBotJunit4ClassRunner.class)`.

2. Views are set up by driving the menu to perform the equivalent of **Window | Show View | Other...** and driving the value of the dialog.

3. To get the text value of a dialog, use `textWithLabel` to find the text field next to the associated label, and then get or set the text from that.

4. A `Matcher` is used to encode a specific condition, such as a view or window with a particular title. It can be handed over to the SWTBot runner to execute in the UI thread and return a value when it is done.

5. To get values from the UI, use a `StringResult` (or other equivalent types) and pass that into the `syncExec` method of `UIThreadRunnable`. It will execute the code, return the value, and then pass that to the calling thread.

6. Use the bot's `waitUntil` or `waitWhile` methods, which block execution of the test until a certain condition occurs.

Chapter 12 – Automated Builds with Tycho

Understanding automated builds and update sites

1. The **GroupId**, **ArtifactId**, and **Version** make a set of co-ordinates known as a **GAV**, which Maven uses to identify dependencies and plugins. The group is a means of associating multiple artifacts together, and the artifact is the individual component name. In OSGi and Eclipse builds, the group is typically the first few segments of the bundle name, and the artifact is the bundle name. The version follows the same syntax as the bundle's version, except that `.qualifier` is replaced with `-SNAPSHOT`.

2. The six types are `pom` (used for the parent), `eclipse-plugin` (for plug-ins), `eclipse-test-plugin` (for running plug-in tests and UI tests), `eclipse-feature` (for features), `eclipse-repository` (for update sites and products), and `eclipse-target-definition` (for defining target platforms).

3. Version numbers can be updated with `mvn org.eclipse.tycho:tycho-versions-plugin:set-version -DnewVersion=version.number`. Note that although `mvn version:set` exists, it will not update the plug-in versions if chosen.

4. Jars are signed to ensure that the contents of the Jar have not been modified after creation. Eclipse looks at these Jars at runtime to ensure that they are not modified, and warns if they are unsigned or if the signatures are invalid. The standard JDK tool `jarsigner` is used to sign and verify Jars; the JDK tool `keytool` is used to manipulate keys.

5. A simple HTTP server can be launched with `python -m SimpleHTTPServer`. In Python 3, the command is `python3 -m http.server`.

6. Eclipse features are typically published in the Eclipse Marketplace at `http://marketplace.eclipse.org`. This includes both open-source and commercial plug-ins.

Index

A

activation policy, of lazy **388**
alias **351**
applications
  building **289**
  headless application, creating **289-292**
automated tests
  running **344-347**

B

Blueprint **390**
breakpoints
  types **21**
  working with **29, 30**
bug
  attachments **371**
  creating, on Eclipse **371, 372**
  description **371**
  importance **372**
  summary **371**
  target milestone **372**
  URL **372**
Bugzilla
  about **369**
  bugs, creating **369**
builds
  enabling, for other plug-ins **349**

C

cardinality **394**
clock widget
  updating **58**
clock widgets, and views
  creating **32, 33**
  custom view, drawing **35-37**
  hour and minute hands, drawing **47**
  layouts, using **44-46**
  reusable widget, creating **41-43**
  second hand, animating **39, 40**
  seconds hand, drawing **37, 38**
  UI thread, running on **40, 41**
code
  updating, in debugger **18**
command parameters
  passing **208-210**
commands
  about **103, 204, 238**
  binding, to keys **111-114**
  contributing, to pop-up menus **117-120**
  creating **106-111**
compatibility layer **221**
conditional breakpoints
  setting **22-24**
  using **22**
ConfigAdmin
  installing **403**

contexts
  about 114
  changing 114
CSS properties 251, 252
CSS Spy 255
custom injectable classes
  creating 216
  simple service, creating 216, 217
  subtypes, injecting 218
  tools bridge, using 219
custom widget
  clock, adding 259, 260
  CSS property, using 261-265
  styling 259
  themes 265

D

debugger
  code, updating in 18
Declarative Services (DS)
  about 340, 390-392
  annotations 395, 396
  annotations, processing at Maven
      build time 396-398
  configuring 403
  debugging 395
  multiple components 395
  properties 392, 393
  service references 393-395
Dependent Services 401
DevoxxUS
  URL 357
direct menu and keybindings
  creating 211-213
dynamic service configuration
  about 402
  ConfigAdmin, installing 403
  Declarative Services, configuring 403
  Felix FileInstall, installing 402
  service factories 404
dynamic services
  Life Cycle Layer 398
  Module Layer 398
  resolving 398
  Security Layer 398

Service Layer 398
ServiceTracker, using 399

E

E4 Spies Window 257
E4 tools
  installing 104-106
  reference 180
Eclipse
  about 1
  account, creating 370
  bug, creating 371, 372
  bugs, creating on Bugzilla 369
  contributing to 369
  environment, setting up 2-4
  fixes, submitting 372
  reference links 358
Eclipse 4 application
  about 247
  creating 180-186
  E4 tooling, installing 180, 181
  experiment, with CSS properties 251-253
  part, creating 186-190
  styling, with CSS 247
  UI, styling with CSS 248-251
  using, custom CSS classes 254, 255
Eclipse 4 (E4) model 34
Eclipse 4.x
  about 221, 222
  actions, upgrading 226-228
  e4view, updating to 224, 225
  handler lookup, optimizing 231
  migration component, creating 222-224
  popup, adding 233, 234
  toolbars, creating 228-230
  view menu, adding 231, 232
Eclipse 4.x patterns
  commands, migrating 238-241
  handler, invoking from double click action 245
  handlers, migrating 238-241
  migrating to 235
  model fragment, creating 235-237
  pop-up view, defining in fragment 243, 244
  view menu, creating 242, 243

Eclipse application
  launching, from within Eclipse 10-13
Eclipse plug-in
  building, with Tycho 326-328
  building with Tycho, Maven used 323
  URL 222
Eclipse-specific properties 252, 253
Eclipse spies
  CSS spy, using 255-257
  spy, integrating into product 258, 259
  using 255
EGit
  using 364-366
errors
  reporting 132
  showing 133-135
exceptional breakpoints
  using 24
exceptions
  catching 24-26
extender pattern 390

F

features
  branding 286-288
  content, publishing remotely 288
  creating 274-276
  depending, on other features 284-286
  exporting 276-278
  installing 278, 279
  plug-ins, grouping 273
  products, creating 297
  update site, categorizing 280-283
features and update sites
  building 332-334
  building, with Tycho 329
  Maven components, depending on 343
  parent project, creating 329-331
  product, building 335-339
  target platform, using 340-343
Felix FileInstall
  installing 402
FieldEditors Eclipse preferences
  implementing 137

filtering 85
fixes
  Gerrit profile, setting up 372-374
  patch, committing 374-378
  patch, pushing 374-378
  submitting 372

G

Gerrit profile
  setting up 372-374
Git
  EGit, checking out from 364-366
  checking out, from 363-366
  SWT project, configuring 367-369
git command-line client
  URL 364
GitWeb browser
  URL 366
graphics context (gc) 37

H

handlers
  about 103, 204, 238
  creating 106-111
headless application
  creating 289-292
HTTP password
  URL 373

I

interaction
  about 89
  double-click listener, adding 90-92
items
  filtering, in viewer 87, 88
  sorting, in viewer 85-87

J

Java
  URL 2
Java Virtual Machine Tools Interface (JVMTI) 18
JFace 71

jobs and report progress
about 121
cancellation, dealing with 124, 125
job properties, setting 129-131
null progress monitors, using 127, 128
operations, running in background 121, 122
reporting 123, 124
sub monitors, using 127, 128
sub-progress monitors, using 125-127
subtasks, using 125-127
taskbar, displaying 132
UIJob, using 123
JUnit, for automated testing
about 303
dependencies, adding to target platform 304
plug-in test, writing 306, 307
simple JUnit test case, writing 305, 306

K

KeyBinding 111
key files, Eclipse plug-in
build.properties file 10
META-INF/MANIFEST.MF file 9
plugin.xml file 9
keystore 351

M

ManagedServiceFactory 405
MANIFEST.MF 33, 34
markers
error markers 173-175
file detection, fixing 177
marker type, registering 175, 176
using 173
Maven
about 323
installing 324, 325
Maven projects
artifact 323
group 323
version 323
Maven Tycho 323
menu
about 103
wiring, to command with handler 204-207

menu items
about 204
disabling 115-117
enabling 115-117
method entry
breaking at 21
method exit
breaking at 21
model fragment
about 235
creating 235
Model Spy 257

N

natures
creating 169-172
enabling, for selected object type 173
using 169

O

open source contributions
about 357
checking out, from Git 363
platform, debugging 360-362
platform, modifying 362, 363
source, importing 358
sources, installing 358-360
OSGi services
about 381
dynamic service configuration 402
dynamic services 398
overview 381
registering declaratively 390
registering programmatically 382

P

packaging type 323
part descriptor 235
plug-in
creating 5-9
debugging 14-18
grouping, with features 273
modifying 13
**Plug-in Development Environment (PDE)
   feature 2**

plugin.xml file **34**
pop quiz answers **411-421**
pop-up menu
  about 233
  creating 213-216
preference changes
  responding to 141
preference pages
  about 142
  creating 142, 143
  error messages, creating 144, 145
  field editors, aligning with grid 146, 147
  field editors, using 149, 150
  placing 147, 148
  set of values, selecting from list 145, 146
  warning, creating 144, 145
preferences
  individual preferences, injecting 140
  injecting 139, 140
  searching for 151
products
  about 289
  building 289
  creating 293-296
  creating, based on features 297
PrototypeServiceFactory **405**

R

resources
  Color instance 48
  leak, finding 49-52
  leak, plugging 52, 53
  managing 47
reverse domain name format **9**

S

selection
  about 98
  adding, to table view 101
  changes, responding to 99-101
  propagating 98, 99
service **381**
service document **391**
service factories
  about 404
  EchoService, creating 405

EchoServiceFactory, creating 406, 407
EchoServices, configuring 408
ManagedServiceFactory 404
PrototypeServiceFactory 404
ServiceFactory 404
types 404
service interface **381**
service ranking **386**
service, registering programmatically
  activator, creating 382, 383
  lazy activation, of bundles 388
  priority, of services 386, 387
  service, registering 384-386
  services, versus extension points 389
  using 387
services and contexts
  events, dealing with 197-200
  logging, adding 191, 192
  selection, obtaining 194-196
  UI, interacting with 202, 203
  using 191
  values, calculating on demand 200, 201
  window, obtaining 193, 194
Services Component Runtime (SCR) **391**
ServiceTracker
  BundleContext, obtaining without
    using activator 401
  services, filtering 400
  using 399
singletons **390**
sorting **85**
SSH keypair
  about 373
  URL 373
Standard Widget Toolkit (SWT) **31**
step filters
  about 19
  debugging with 19
  setting up 19-21
SWTBot
  about 307
  runtime errors, avoiding 314
  welcome screen, hiding 313
  working with 313
SWTBot, for user interface testing
  about 307
  menus, working with 310-312

resources, using 312, 313
SWTBot test, writing 308-310
SWT widgets
  about 58
  effects 62, 63
  groups and tab folders 64-69
  items, adding to tray 58-60
  modal 62
  time zones, enhancing 70
  user, responding to 60, 61
  using 58

T

tabular data
  about 93
  time zones, viewing in tables 93-97
target definitions
  about 297
  creating 297-300
target platforms
  about 297
  configuring, for other releases 302
  specific version, switching to 300, 301
  target definition, creating 297-300
themes
  about 265
  adding 267, 268
  dark theme 266
  switching 269, 270
toolbars
  using 120
TreeViewers
  creating 72-77
  images, adding for regions 84
  images, using in JFace 77-81
  label providers, styling 82-84
Tycho
  Eclipse plug-ins, building with 326-328

U

UI
  condition, waiting for 318-320
  interacting with 317
  new class wizard, driving 320
  values, obtaining from 317, 318

UI thread 40
update sites
  plug-ins, signing 351-354
  self-signed certificate, creating 350, 351
  serving 354, 355
  signing 350
user interaction
  about 54, 55
  input, responding to 56, 57
user preference 137

V

value
  persisting 138, 139
variables
  inspecting 26-29
  watching 26-29
version numbers
  changing 348, 349
viewer
  items, filtering 87, 88
  items, sorting 85, 86
view menu
  about 242
  creating 213-216, 242, 243
  using 120
views
  creating 31-33
  displaying 315
  expanding 89
  filtering 89
  interrogating 316, 317
  working with 314

W

workspace
  builder, building 158-161
  builder upgrades 168
  deletion, handling 166-168
  editor, creating 154-156
  incremental builds, implementing 165
  markup parser, writing 157, 158
  resources, creating 164, 165
  resources, iterating through 161-163
  using 153

98868167R00251

Made in the USA
Lexington, KY
10 September 2018